Shaw Lachlan

The History of the Province of Moray

Shaw Lachlan

The History of the Province of Moray

ISBN/EAN: 9783337202613

Printed in Europe, USA, Canada, Australia, Japan

Cover: Foto ©ninafisch / pixelio.de

More available books at **www.hansebooks.com**

THE
HISTORY
OF THE
Province of MORAY.

ELGIN.

EDINBURGH:
Printed and Sold by William Auld.
Sold at London by John Donaldson, Corner of Arundel-Street
N.º 195 Strand.
M.DCC.LXXV.

THE HISTORY

OF THE

PROVINCE of MORAY:

Extending, from the Mouth of the River SPEY, to the Borders of LOCHABER in *Length*; and from the MORAY-FRITH, to the GRAMPIAN HILLS in *Breadth*: And,

Including, a part of the Shire of BANFF to the East; The whole Shires of MORAY and NAIRN; and the greatest part of the Shire of INVERNESS.——All which was Anciently called THE PROVINCE OF MORAY, before there was a Division into Counties.

———ANTIQUAM EXQUIRITE MATREM.

By the Reverend Mr LACHLAN SHAW, Minister of the Gospel at ELGIN.

EDINBURGH:
Printed and Sold by WILLIAM AULD.
Sold at LONDON, by JOHN DONALDSON, Corner of Arundel Street, Nº 195. Strand.
M,DCC,LXXV.

CONTENTS.

	Page
INTRODUCTION	1

PART I.

The Name of the Country of Moray	5
The Extent of the Country of Moray	6
The Situation of the Country of Moray	8
The Division of the Country	9

PART II.

The GEOGRAPHY of MORAY.

	page		page
The River Spey	10	FARQUHARSON of Invercauld	43
The Parish of Bellie	11	Badenach	44
Family of GORDON	12	Family of MACINTOSH	ib.
The Parish of Dundurcoss	15	Family of MACPHERSON	50
The Parish of Rothes	17	The Parish of Alvie	53
The Parish of Knockando	18	The Parish of Kingusie and Inch	54
Family of GRANT	ib.	The Parish of Laggan	56
The Parish of Boharm	23	The Parish of Speymouth	57
The Parish of Mortlich	24	The Parish of Urquhart	58
Family of DUFF	26	Family of INNES	59
The Parish of Aberlaure	29	The Parish of Lanbride	63
The Parish of Inveravon	30	The Parish and Royal Burrough of Elgin	64
The Parish of Kirkmichael	32	The Parish of Birnie	68
The Parish of Cromdale	34	The Parish of Dallas	ib.
The Parish of Abernethie	36	The Parish of Kenedar	69
The Parish of Duthel	38	The Family of GORDON of Gordonstoun	70
The Parish of Rothemurchus	39		
GRANT of Rothemurchus	40		
SHAW of Rothemurchus	41		

x   CONTENTS.

	page		page
Knights Baronets of Nova Scotia	72	The Parish of Aldern	108
The Parish of Duffus	73	The Town and Parish of Nairn	110
Morays of Duffus	74	The Parish of Calder	112
The Parish of St Andrews	77	The Family of Calder	113
The Parish of Spynie	78	The Parish of Croy	117
Leslie of Finrossie	79	The Family of Rose of Kilravock	118
The Dunbars	81	The Parish of Daviot	122
The Dunbars of Westfield	82	The Parish of Ardersier	124
The Parish of Alves	85	The Parish of Pettie	125
The Parish of Kinloss	87	The Town and Parish of Inverness	126
The Parish and Town of Forres	88	Forbes of Culloden	128
The Parish of Rafford	90	Robertson of Inshes	ib.
Family of Cummine	91	The Parish of Durris	130
The Parish of Edinkylie	92	The Parish of Boleskin	133
Family of Cummine of Rylucas	93	Family of Lovate	ib.
		The Parish of Kilmanivack	140
The Parish of Ardclach	95	Family of MacDonald of Glengary	141
The Parish of Moy	97		
The Parish of Dyke	98	The Parish of Urquhart	142
Earls of Moray	100	The Parish of Kirkhill	144
Family of Brodie	105	The Parish of Kiltarlatie	145

PART III.

The NATURAL HISTORY of MORAY.

	page		page
Air, Light, Cold, Heat	147-148	Materials for Building	155
The Rain, the Snow	149	Fuel	ib.
The Winds, the Mountains	ib.	Mines, Dyeing	156
The Hills and Valleys	150	Salt Water	ib.
The Plains, the Soil	151	Fresh Waters	157
The Corn	ib.	Animals	ib.
Flax and Hemp	152	Tame Beasts	ib.
Potatoes and Mustard	ib.	Wild Beasts	158
Garden Fruits	ib.	Viporous Animals, Fowls	160
Wild and Medicinal Herbs	153	Water Animals	161
Forrests, Woods	154	Rarities	162

PART IV.

The CIVIL and POLITICAL HISTORY of MORAY.

	page		page
The Inhabitants	166	Viscounts	181
Their Language	167	Lords	ib.
Way of Living, Manners	168	Counties	182
Genius	170	Inverness County	ib.
Agriculture, Improvements	172	Nairn County	184
		Moray County	185
Manufactures	173	Regalities	ib.
Trade and Commerce	174	Baronies	186
Commodities for Export	ib.	Jurisdictions Abolished	187
Civil Government	176	Courts of Judicature	188
Feudal Customs	ib.	Roll of Barons	190
Titles of Honour	177	Burroughs	191
Count or Earl	178	Inverness	ib.
Thanes	180	Elgin	193
Dukes	181	Nairn	196
Marquis	ib.	Forres	197
Earls	ib.	Burghs of Barony	199

PART V.

The MILITARY HISTORY of MORAY.

	page		page
Royal Forts	203	Ruthven Barrack	207
At Elgin	ib.	Fort-George at Arderfier	ib.
Forres	ib.		
Nairn	204	Fortalices	ib.
Inverness	ib.	At Duffus	ib.
Urquhart	205	Raite	208
Oliver's Fort	206	Abernethie	ib.
Fort-George at Inverness	ib.	Ruthven	ib.
		Lochindort	ib.
Fort Augustus	ib.		

xii CONTENTS.

	page		page
Battles, &c.	209	Glenlivat, anno 1594	221
At Forres	ib.	Aldern, anno 1645	224
Obelisk at Forres	ib.	Cromdale, anno 1690	225
Burgus	210	Invernefs, anno 1715	227
At Mortlich, anno 1010	211	Culloden, anno 1746	ib.
Spey, anno 1078	212	Military Roads	228
Spey, anno 1110	213	Military Cuftoms	229
Urquhart, anno 1160	ib.	Young Chiefs	230
Invernahavon, anno 1386	215	Officers	ib.
Perth, anno 1396	216	Enfigns	ib.
Drumnacoub, an. 1427	217	Bards	ib.
Elgin, anno 1452	ib.	Pypers	231
Clachnacharie, anno 1454	219	Fiery Crofs	ib.
Cean-Loch-Lochie, anno 1544	220	Cry to War	ib.
		Badge	ib.
		Bards	ib.
		Omens, &c.	232

PART VI.

The ECCLESIASTIC HISTORY of MORAY.

SECT. I. *The Heathen or Pagan Church.*

	page		page
DRUIDS	234	Sacrifices and Ceremonies	242
Whence fo called	235	Judges	243
Their Office	ib.	Their Meetings	ib.
Their Religion	ib.	The Vates	244
Priefts	236	The Bards	ib.
Their Worfhip	237	Female Druids	245
Stated Worfhip	ib.	Druid Temples	246
Circles	ib.	Druid Deities	247
Solemn Worfhip	238	Druid Cuftoms	248
Carns	239	In Hectic Fevers	ib.
March Solemnity	240	In Contagious Difeafes	ib.
May Solemnity	ib.	The Moon's Changes	249
Mid-Summer Solemnity	241	Cuftoms at Burials	ib.
Hallow-Eve Solemnity	ib.	Conflagration	ib.
		Druidifm whence derived	250

CONTENTS.

Sect. II. *The Primitive Church.*

	page		page
Christianity Planted in Scotland	251	Keledees	251
		Their Purity	252

Sect. III. *The Romish or Popish Church.*

	page		page
I. The Regular Clergy	254	The Cathedral of Elgin	
An Abbey	ib.	Described	277
Kinloss Abbey	255	The Chapter House	278
The Priories	257	Dimensions of the Cadral	279
Urquhart Priory	258	How Demolished	ib.
Pluscardine Priory	259	The College	280
Kingusie Priory	261	Canons	281
The Convents	ib.	Prebendaries	ib.
Black Friars	262	Erection of the College	ib.
Gray Friars	ib.	Transplanted	282
Gray Sisters	ib.	List of the Canons	ib.
Preceptory of Maison Dieu	263	The Precinct	283
St Nicholas' Hospital	ib.	The Burrough	ib.
Templar Knights	264	The Bishop's Palace	284
Johannite Knights	265	At Kenedar	ib.
II. The Secular Clergy	ib.	At Spynie	ib.
The Bishopric of Murtlac	ib.	The Palace of Spynie described	285
Its Erection, Diocess, Translation, Bishops	266	Revenues of the Bishopric of Moray	286
The Bishopric of Moray	268	Dignified Clergy	288
List of The Bishops of Moray	ib.	Dean	ib.
		Arch-Dean	ib.
Diocess	272	Chantor	ib.
The Cathedral Church	274	Chancellor	ib.
At Spynie	ib.	Treasurer	ib.
At Elgin	275	Chapter	ib.
The Cathedral at Elgin founded and built	276	Inferior Clergy	289
		Parsons	ib.
Burnt and rebuilt	ib.	Vicars	ib.

CONTENTS.

	page		page
Mensal Churches	289	Government of the Diocess	291
Common Churches	290	Chapter	ib.
Chapels of Ease	ib.	Synod	ib.
Free Chapels	ib.	Deanries	ib.
Domestic Chapels	ib.	Consistory	292
Private Chapels	ib.	Regality	ib.
Altarage	291	Arms of the See of Moray	ib.
Obit and *Dirge*	ib.		

SECT. IV. *The Protestant Church.*

	page		page
1st, The several Periods since the Reformation	293	VII Period, 1690—to the present time	303
I. Period, 1560—1572	ib.	Presbytery established	ib.
Super-Intendants	294	Remarks upon the several Changes of Church Government	304
Commissioners	ib.		
Assemblies	ib.		
Synods	ib.	Threnodia	314
Presbyteries	ib.	2d, The Protestant Bishops of Moray since the Reformation	317
Sessions	ib.		
II. Period, 1572—1592	295		
Tulchan Bishops	ib.	The Cathedral	319
Presbyteries Erected	296	Palace, Chapter, Jurisdiction	320
III. Period, 1592—1610	ib.		
Presbyterian Government Established	ib.	Revenues	321
Overturned	297	Feu duties of the Bishopric	322
IV Period, 1610—1638	298	3d, The Ministers of Parishes since the Reformation	324
Episcopacy re-established	ib.		
Condemned	299	Presbytery of Strathboggie	
V Period, 1638—1662	300	Mortlich Parish	ib.
Presbytery revived	ib.	Bellie Parish	325
Overturned	ib.	Presbytery of Aberlaure	
VI Period, 1662—1690	301	Dundurcos Parish	326
Prelacy restored	ib.	Rothes Parish	ib.
Ministers ejected	302	Knockando Parish	327
Conduct of Bishops	ib.	Boharm Parish	328
Prelacy a grievance	303	Aberlaure Parish	329
		Inveravon Parish	330

CONTENTS.

	page		Page
Presbytery of Abernethie		Presbytery of Nairn	
Kirkmichael Parish	331	Ardclach Parish	351
Cromdale Parish	ib.	Aldern Parish	352
Abernethie Parish	332	Nairn Parish	353
Duthel Parish	ib.	Ardersier Parish	ib.
Alvie Parish	333	Calder Parish	354
Kingusie and Insh	334	Croy & Dalcross Parish	355
Presbytery of Elgin		Presbytery of Inverness	
Dipple Parish	335	Moy & Dalarassie Parish	ib.
Essil Parish	ib.	Daviot and Dunlichtie	356
Speymouth Parish	336	Pettie and Brachlie	ib.
Urquhart Parish	337	Inverness Parish	357
Lanbribe Parish	338	Durris Parish	360
Birnie Parish	339	Kirkhill Parish	361
Elgin Parish	340	Kiltarlatie Parish	ib.
St. Andrews Parish	342	Presbytery of Abertarf,	
Kenedar Parish	ib.	Urquhart, and Glenmoriston	362
Ugston Parish	343		
Duffus Parish	344	Boleskin and Abertarf	363
New Speynie Parish	345	Laggan Parish	ib.
Alves Parish	346	Number of Inhabitants in Moray	364
Presbytery of Forres			
Kinloss Parish	347	4th The State of Religion in the Province from the Reformation	ib.
Rafford Parish	348		
Dallas Parish	ib.		
Forres Parish	249	State of Popery in Moray	379
Edinkylie Parish	ib.	Society for Propagating Christian Knowledge	380
Moy and Dyke Parish	350		

Contents of the APPENDIX.

No 1.	King Robert's Charter to Ranulph Earl of Moray	383
No 2.	St Nicolas's Hospital at Spey	386
No 3.	Collatio ad Capellam Sancti Nicolai	387
No 4.	Carta Super Ecclesia de Rothais	ib
No 5.	Collatio Ecclesiæ de Artendol	ib
No 6.	Concessio de Ecclesia de Inveravon	388
No 7.	Collatio de Ecclesia de Inveravon	ib
No 8.	Indenture, Robert Stuart and Isabel MacDuff	ib
No 9.	Donatio super Ecclesiam de Cromdale	389
No 10.	Charta de Fynlarg	ib
No 11.	Collatio Ecclesiæ de Inveralyen	390
No 12.	De Rotemorchus	ib
No 13.	Concessio super Ecclesiam de Rotemorchus	391
No 14.	Carta de Innes	ib
No 15.	Munimenta Domus Dei (Maison Dieu) juxta Elgyn	392
No 16.	Collatio de Daldeleyth	393
No 17.	Carta Dunecani Regis	ib
No 18.	Estimation of Geddes and Kilravock	394
No 19.	Carta de Urchanbeg	ib
No 20.	Homagium Domini de Loveth	395
No 21.	The Valued Rent of the Shire of Moray	396
No 22.	Concessio de Inverlochtie	399
No 23.	Charter to the Burrough of Invernefs	ib
No 24.	Charters to the Burrough of Elgin	401
No 25.	Charter to the Burrough of Forres	402
No 26.	A Papal Bull to Kinlofs	403
No 27.	Charter of Strathyla in Strathboggie to Kinlofs	406
No 28.	The Cathedral and Chanons at Spynie	407
No 29.	Concessio super Præbendis de Kingufy, &c.	408
No 30.	Procurationes Decanatuum	409
No 31.	Super Transmutatione Sedis	410
	Confirmatio	411

CONTENTS.

No 32. The Burning of the Cathedral — 412
No 33. Concessio de Ecclesia de Fermua, &c. — ib
No 34. Confirmatio de Ecclesia de Deveth — 413
No 35. Concessio de Ecclesia de Dalergusie — ib
No 36. Carta de Forrays et de Dyke — ib
No 37. Carta Ecclesiæ Cathedrali — 414
No 38. Donatio Regis Willielmi — ib
No 39. Concessio Logynanadel — ib
No 40. De situ Molendini de Auchterspynie — 415
No 41. Collatio Ecclesiæ de Kylealargy — ib
No 42. Collatio de Ross — ib
No 43. Collatio Annuitatis Ecclesiæ Cathedrali — 416
No 44. Concessio Advocationis de Duffus — ib
No 45. Tack of the Teinds of Ruthven in Strathboggie — ib
No 46. From the Book of Assignations anno 1570, in the Lawyers Library. — 417
No 47. Original Writs belonging to Campbell of Calder — 420
No 48. An Abstract of King Charles IId's Letter to the Presbytery of Edinburgh. — 421
No 49. Synod of Moray's Address to the Earl of Middleton, July 2. 1661 — 422
No 50. The Bishops Address to King James VII. November 3d, 1688 — 423
No 51. Erection of the Presbytery of Nairn — 424
No 52. Oath of Trust — 425
No 53. Charter to Sir Robert Gordon of Gordonstoun, of Lands in Nova Scotia; containing a Patent creating him a Knight Baronet of the Order of Nova Scotia; by King Charles I. anno 1626 — 426
Royal Warrant by King Charles I. to the Knights Baronets of Nova Scotia, anno 1629. — 452
INDEX — 454

[xviii]

LIST of the FAMILIES whose GENEALOGIES
are traced in this WORK.

THE Family of GORDON	12
GRANT	18
DUFF	26
GRANT of Rothemurchus	40
SHAW of Rothemurchus	41
FARQUHARSON of Invercauld	43
MACINTOSH	44
MACPHERSON	50
INNES	59
GORDON of Gordonstoun	70
MORAYS of Duffus	74
LESLIE of Finrossie	79
DUNBARS	81
DUNBARS of Westfield	83
CUMMINE	91
CUMMINE of Rylucas	93
EARLS of MORAY	100
BRODIE	105
CALDER	113
ROSE of Kilravock	118
FORBES of Culloden	128
ROBERTSON of Inches	ib.
LOVATE	133
MACDONALD of Glengary	141

THE
HISTORY
OF THE
PROVINCE of MORAY.

INTRODUCTION.

IN vain shall one expect to find a rational account of the ancient state of SCOTLAND or NORTH BRITAIN, unless he consult the Roman writers. GEOFFRY of Monmouth will have North Britain called *Albania*, from Albanactus son of Brutus, the grandson of Æneas the Trojan. And HECTOR BOECE calleth the same country *Scotia* from SCOTA, the daughter of one of the Pharaohs kings of Egypt. These, and the like, are fables, below the dignity of History, and fit only for venal bards.

In describing the antient state of the Southern provinces of this kingdom, the Roman writers are sure guides, that may be relied on. TACITUS's account of the expeditions of Julius Agricola,

INTRODUCTION.

Agricola, Herodian, Dion Caffius, Ammianus Marcellinus, Claudian, and others, throw much light upon our history, give an account of the actions of the Romans in Britain during 400 years, describe their colonies, forts, camps, prætentures, naval stations, and military ways; and give some account of the natives, with whom the Romans had any intercourse, and whom they call in the general, *Britanni, Britones*, and *Caledonii*; and more particularly, *Scoti, Picti, Atacold, Vecturiones, Decaledones, Vacomagi, Ladeni,* &c. But it was the misfortune of the Northern parts of Scotland, that the Romans (from Julius Cæsar's first descent into Britain, to about *A. D.* 426 that they abandoned the Island,) never, that I have found, penetrated into them, excepting once in the reign of the Emperor Septimus Severus, in the beginning of the third Century, of whom Xiphilinus writeth, that he marched into the northmost extremity of the Island. " Ingreffus eft in Cale-
" doniam, eamque dum pertransiret, habuit maxima negotia,
" quod sylvas cæderet, et loca alta perfoderet, quodque paludes
" obruerit aggere, et pontes in fluminibus faceret: Nec ab
" inceptis desiit, quousque ad extremam partem insulæ venit;
" ubi diversum, quam apud nos sit, cursum solis, itemque
" noctium et dierum, tam æstivorum quam hybernorum,
" magnitudinem diligentissime cognovit." In this expedition, Severus lost 50,000 of his army, without once fighting the Caledonians, being overcome by cold, hunger, and fatigue: And after him, no Roman marched so far into the North.

I have said, it was the misfortune of the Northern Countries, that the ROMANS were so little acquainted with them: for, where-ever they settled, they softened the rough temper, and civilized the rude manners of the natives. They introduced letters, arts, and sciences. They taught agriculture, and laid the foundations of cities and towns, navigation and commerce.

merce. Hence the many towns and villages, on both sides of the Frith of Forth, had their rise from the Roman colonies, forts, and naval stations: And the foundation of the culture and fertility of the Lothians, was laid by their industry: While the Western coast, from the Clyde Northward, into which the Romans never entered, (though better furnished by nature with bays, harbours, and creeks) remained long uncivilized, without towns, trade, or commerce.

It is true, Julius Agricola sent a fleet of ships to sail round the Island, of which TACITUS says, " Hanc oram novissimi maris " tunc primum Romana classis circumvecta, insulam esse Britan- " niam affirmavit, ac simul incognitas ad id tempus insulas, quas " *Orcades* vocant, invenit, domuitque; dispecta est et *Thyle*." * To this navigation, I question not, we owe the Geographical Tables of Ptolemy in the second century: Which Tables, as Gerard Mercator observeth, are pretty exact, if what he placeth towards the East is turned to the North. In their descents, the captains of these ships described the coasts, discovered the people inhabiting them, and gave them the names we have in Ptolemy's Tables: Not new Latin names, (the Romans seldom, if ever, gave such to any place or people they discovered or conquered) but the names the natives gave them in their own language, and to which these sailors, or perhaps Ptolemy, gave a new termination, and softened some British words, by the change of one or more letters. Such names are, *Vernicones*, or the inhabitants of the Merns; *Morini*, of Mar; *Tazali*, of Buchan; *Cantini*, of Ross; *Cante*, of Caithness; *Cornavii*, of Strathnaver; and *Æstuarium Vararis*, the Frith of Moray. All these are British words, with Latin inflexions: and let me add, that, as these navigators could only discover the coasts, so Ptolemy only describeth the coasts, and not the inland parts.

In

---

* TACIT. VITA AGRICOLÆ, Cap. 10. Sect. 5.

INTRODUCTION.

In the middle ages of our nation, we have mention, and little more than mention, of Moray and the inhabitants thereof. A manuscript, *De Situ Albaniæ*, (a trifling performance in the twelfth century) speaking of the ancient division of Albania into seven kingdoms, says, " Sexta divisio est Muref et Ros," *Excerpta ex veteri chronico Regum Scotorum* beareth, " Donev-
" aldus, filius Constantini, apud oppidum Fother occisus est a
" gentibus." " Malcolmus filius Domnail cum exercitu
" perexit in Moreb." *Nomina Regum Scotorum ex Registro Prioratus St Andreæ*, says, " Dovenal Mac Constantin mortuus est in
" Fores." " Malcolmus Mac Dovenald interfectus est in Ulurn
" (forte Aldern) a Moraviensibus." " Duff Mac Malcolm
" interfectus est in Fores, et absconditus sub ponte de Kinlos,
" et sol non apparuit quamdiu ibi latuit." *Innes's critical Essay, Vol. II. Appendix*. After the tenth century, we have so frequent accounts of Moray, that I shall not descend to particulars.

There are few countries in Scotland (except Moray) but Descriptions of them may be met with in print or in manuscript. Even in the Northern parts, Dr Niccolson, in his Scottish Historical Library, mentions Descriptions of Shetland, Orkney, Caithness, Sutherland, Buchan, Merns, and others. But I have not been so fortunate, as to have read or heard of a Description of the Country of Moray. This renders the task I have cut out for myself, the more difficult. I walk on untrodden ground, having no author, ancient or modern, to conduct me; and I must rest contented, with what materials my sphere of reading, and the testimony of credible persons, have furnished me.

PART

PART I.

THE NAME, EXTENT, SITUATION and DIVISION of MORAY.

The NAME of the Country of MORAY.

PTOLEMY, speaking of CALEDONIA (or rather of Sylva Caledonia) says, That it extended, "A Lelalonio Lacu usque ad Æstuarium Vararis." It is generally allowed, that, by the Æstuarium Vararis, is meant, The Frith of Moray; and hence some have conjectured, that Moray was anciently called, *Varar*. But it is of the Frith, not of the country, that Ptolemy speaketh, and Friths were denominated from the rivers that emptied into them. As *Æstuarium Tai, Bodotrie, Glotæ*, the Friths of Tay, Forth, Clyde. *Varar*, therefore, must be the name of a river that falleth into the Frith of Moray; and a river of that name there is, which enters into the very head of that Frith. It is now commonly called, the River of Beaulie, and the Highlanders call it, *Avon na Manach*, i. e. the Monk's River, because the Priory of Beaulie stood on the bank of it; But the true name of it is, *Farar*. It floweth out of Loch *Monar*, in the hills of Ross, and the valley through which it runneth is called *Strath-Farar*

Farar. Now the Romans did, and we do, often change the digamma F into V, as in Knife, Knives; Shelf, Shelves, &c. Agricola's fleet coasting along would search every frith and bay, into the head of it, to know if it communicated with the Western Sea, or not; and having come to the head of this Frith, and finding a river falling into it called by the natives *Farar*, they changed the F into V, and called it *Varar*; and from it, they named the Frith *Æstuarium Vararis;* but this gave no name at all to the country.

The only name by which I have found the country called, is *Moravia* or *Moray*. Hector Boece writes, that, in the first century, a colony from Moravia in Germany settled in this country, and gave it the name of the country from which they came. But he did not consider, that, at that time, the country called *Moravia* was called *Marcomania*, and the inhabitants, *Marcomani* and *Quadi (Tacit. de Mor. Germ.* cap. 42.) Others, finding the word *Mureff* in some ancient manuscripts, and *Rief* signifying *Bent*, will have it called *Mureff*, from the abundance of that grass growing on the sea shore. But, in my opinion, those have changed the V into F, and made it *Mureff*, instead of *Mureo* or *Murav*. The Highlanders call it *Murav* or *Morav*, from the celtic words *Mur* or *Mor* the Sea, and *Taobh* or *Tav* the Side; and in construction, *Mor'av, i. e.* the Sea-side. This, I think, is the true notation of the name, answering to the situation of the country, by the side of the sea.

The EXTENT of the Country of MORAY.

PTOLOMY doth not touch this point, nor doth any ancient writer that I know; I cannot be of opinion, that *Moravia* comprehended no more than the plain and champaign ground by the sea side; which is all that is strictly called MORAY in our day. But I include within the province or country, as it was before the division of it into counties or shires, all the plain country by the sea side, from the mouth of the river Spey, to the river of Farar or Beaulie, at the head of the Frith; and all the valleys, glens, and straths, situated betwixt the Grampian mountains South of Badenoch, and the Frith of Moray, and which discharge rivers into that Frith. And I incline to give the country this large extent, for the reasons following:

The plain country by the sea side, from Spey to Nefs, is always called MORAY, and I see no reason for extending it Eastward beyond the mouth of Spey: But that it extended Westward to the river of Beaulie, is probable from the notation of the word *Morav*; for so far the Frith extends, and the country taking its name from the Frith, it is reasonable to extend the one as far as the other. This is much strengthened by what we find in *Dalrymple's Collection*, p. 199; " That King Alex- " ander I. pursued the Moray-men that conspired against him, " from Innergoury over Spey into Murray-land, and at the " Stockford above Beaulie passed over to Rofs." This fixes the boundaries both to the East and West, viz. the rivers of Spey and Beaulie. The situation of the country of Rofs, northward from MORAY, confirms this. Its name, *Rofs*, signifieth a Peninsula, or a head, or point of land jutting out between rivers or friths; and it is the Frith of MORAY with that of Tain, that form this peninsula, or Rofs.

The bounds by the sea-side being thus fixed, MORAY extended towards S. S. W. to the head of Loch Lochie, on the borders of Lochaber. This one observation throweth abundant light on this assertion. Our historians agree, that the castle of Urquhart in MORAY held out bravely for King David Bruce

against

against Edward Baliol. This castle did not stand in Urquhart near Elgin; for there are no vestiges of a fort or castle there, nor any tradition that ever there was such a fort. But on the West bank of Lochness, there was a strong fort, the walls whereof do still remain. This sheweth, that Lochness, with the glens around it, was in the country of MORAY. And that the whole course of the River Spey, even to Lochaber, was in the province or country of MORAY, may be gathered from King Robert Bruce's charter of the *Comitatus Moraviensis* to Thomas Randulph Earl of MORAY; (Append. N° I.) To all which let me add, that the Highlanders always did, and as yet do, march and bound the countries by the hills and rivers.

According to this view of the country of Moray, it extends from East to West by the side of the Frith, i. e. from Spey-mouth to Beaulie 39 Scottish, or about 60 English miles: And the river *Farar*, from Loch-Monar to Beaulie, runneth 30 Scottish miles from S. W. to N. E. Thus the utmost extent, from N. E. to S. W. is 69 Scottish or 104 English miles. And, if we take the breadth from the Frith at Inverness, to the braes of Glenfeshie in Badenoch, it is about 38 Scottish, or 57 English miles.

The SITUATION of the Country of MORAY.

This Country lieth in the 57th degree of north latitude, and Spey-mouth is about 35 minutes East from Edinburgh. With respect to the neighbouring countries, the MORAY Frith and the river of Farar separate it from Ross to the North, and from Spey-mouth towards the S. E. the South, and S. W. It bordereth upon the Enzie, Strathdovurn, Strathdone, Braemar, Athole, Ranach, and Lochaber.

The Division of the Country.

The Division of this Country may be considered in a threefold view.

I. The Natural Division, which is twofold. First, Into Lowlands and Highlands. The Lowlands are those plains that are not intermixed with mountains and hills, but are situated near the Frith, and are in some places four, in some six miles broad. The Highlands are the straths and valleys on the sides of rivers, separated from the Lowlands by mountains and hills. This points to the Second natural division, which is made by the rivers that fall into the Frith. And here the strath or valley of Spey makes the first division; which runing from the Frith to the borders of Lochaber, is inclosed on both sides by a chain of hills, and is a barrier to the Low Country, covering it from one end to the other. In the Lowlands, the other rivers divide the country from East to West, into five unequal divisions. Thus, From Spey to Lossie, 6 miles. From Lossie to Ern or Findern, 9 miles. From Findern to Nairn, 7 miles. From Nairn to Ness, 12 miles. And from Ness to Farar, 5 miles. And all these rivers run almost parallel to one another, from S. W. to N. W.

II. The Civil or Political Division, into counties or shires, for the more easy distribution of justice to the people. A part of the county of Banff, the whole county of Elgin and Forres, the whole county of Nairn, and a part of the County of Inverness, lye within this province or Country.

III. The Ecclesiastic Division, into parishes, presbyteries, dioceses and commissariots. I here only mention the political and ecclesiastic divisions, of which I shall in the following parts treat at large.

PART II.

THE GEOGRAPHY OF MORAY.

IN viewing the Geographical face of this country, I shall follow the Natural Division of it above mentioned, passing from one parish forward to another; and in every parish, observing the situation of the church, the extent of the parish, the principal Baronies, Heritors, and Seats or Dwellings; and what else merits observation.

The Valley of the River Spey makes the first branch of the Natural Division; and therefore I shall first describe this Strath or Valley, after I have given some account of the River.

The River SPEY.

This River has its fountains on the borders of Lochaber. It floweth out of a small lake, about half a mile in length, called Loch-Spey, and running from S. W. to N. E. it watereth the countries of Badenoch, Strath-Spey, and Rothes, and then turning due north, it dischargeth its stream into

into the Moray Firth at Germach, after a courfe of about 60 Scottifh, or 90 Englifh miles. It feemeth to have its name from the Teutonick or Piftifh word, *Spe (Sputum)* becaufe the rapidity of it raifeth much foam or froath. Many leffer rivers from the Grampian Mountains fwell its ftreams fo much, that the manufcript *De Situ Albaniæ*, written in the twelfth Century, calleth it (in the Latin of thefe days) " Magnum et miferabile " flumen, quod vocatur *Spe*." The ftrath of this River is inclofed to the N. and W. by a ridge of hills, which beginning in the parifh of Urquhart near the fea, run above Elgin, Forres, Invernefs, and Loch-nefs, to Lochaber. And to the S. and E. a part of the Grampian mountains runneth along Strath-Spey and Badenoch, and feveral glens jutt into thefe mountains, which fhall be defcribed in their proper place. I proceed now to

The Parifh of BELLIE.

This parifh in Irifh is called, *Bealidh, i. e. Broom*. It is fituated on the eaft bank of the river Spey, at the mouth of it. The Church ftandeth near the bank of the River, two miles above the Frith. The great ornament of this Parifh, is the houfe of Gordon Caftle, the Seat of the Duke of GORDON. This houfe was founded by George Earl of Huntly, who died *A. D.* 1507. It is a large and grand pile: But confifting of feveral apartments built at different times, it cannot be very regular. The rooms of State are grand, well finifhed and furnifhed, with fine pictures: And the Library containeth a valuable collection of Books. The houfe is environed with parks and inclofures, and much planting, old and young. The gardens are fpacious, well laid out, and watered with a pond and *Jet d'eau*. But the houfe, by its low fituation betwixt the River

ver to the West and a high hill to the East, commandeth no view of the adjacent country. It was formerly called, *the Bog of Gight*, in Irish, *Bog na gaoith*, *i. e.* the Windy Bog. Closs by the Castle standeth the village of Fochaber, so called, in my opinion, from the Irish *Fo-bobir*, *i. e.* Below the Well, for above it in the face of the hill is a well or fountain, the waters whereof serve the town. The town is a burgh of barony, hath a weekly market, and in the centre of it there is a court house, with a steeple of modern architecture. It has a post-office, and at the west of it, is the passage over Spey, called the Boat of Bog, upon the post road. As little more of this parish than the town of Fochaber falleth within the province of Moray, I shall not dwell any longer on the description of it. In some parishes (as in this) I shall meet with families of eminence and distinction, of which I shall only give a succinct account, as a full historical or genealogical deduction would too much swell this Work.

The FAMILY of GORDON.

This is one of the most illustrious Families in the kingdom, for quality, antiquity, possessions, and people. There are, besides the DUKE, three Peers of this name, viz. The Earls of Aberdeen and Aboyne, and the Viscount of Kenmure, with a numerous and opulent gentry. I leave others to fetch the Gordons from Gordinia in Thessaly, or to derive them from Cæsar's Gorduni. I shall only observe, that Adam de Gordon (1) (so he is commonly called) ancestor of this family, for his services to Malcolm Kenmore, obtained from him the lands of Gordon in the Merse. The Chartulary of Kelso, and the Ragman's Roll, give some account of Richard (2) probably son of

the

the said Adam, (3) Thomas senior, (4) Thomas junior, (5) Alicia and her husband Adam Gordon, father of (6) Sir Adam Gordon, whose eminent services to King Robert Bruce were rewarded with a grant of the Lordship of Strathbogie forfeited by David de Strathbogie, Lord thereof. And though this Lord was, in King David Bruce's reign, restored to his own lands, yet, afterwards revolting to the English, he was again forfeited, and the grant of the Lordship was confirmed by Robert II. anno 1376, to the grandson of Sir Adam Gordon, viz. (7. 8.) John, son of Sir Alexander *(pen. D. Gord.)*. To this John, King David Bruce had given the forrest of the Enzie and Boyne. John was killed in the battle of Otterburn, anno 1388. And his Son, (9) Sir Adam, was killed in the battle of Hamildun, anno 1401, leaving no issue but a daughter and heiress called (10) Elizabeth. This Lady married Alexander Seaton, second son of Sir William Seaton of Winton, which occasioned the distinction of the Seaton Gordons, and the ancient Gordons; for she had two uncles, commonly called, Jock of Scurderg, and Tom of Ruthven, and who (says Straloch) bore the paternal arms, without any mark of illegitimacy; and of those the ancient Gordons are descended.

Elizabeth's son (11) Alexander, assumed the name of Gordon, and was created Earl of Huntley, anno 1449. He did the most significant service to King James II. by defeating the Earl of Crawford in the battle of Brechin, 18th May 1452, and thereby breaking the confederacy against that King. This was fully rewarded, by a grant of the Lordship of Brechin, the Hereditary Sheriffship of Aberdeen, and Crawford's precedency in Parliament. Yet, upon the King's reconciliation to Crawford, Huntley generously resigned Brechin in his favours, and got the Lordship of Badenoch, and the lands of Brae-Lochaber. His great estate was increased, by marrying the only child of Sir William.

William Kieth, and Grand-daughter of Sir Alexander Fraser Thane of Cowie, with whom he got the lands of Touch, Fraser, Aboyne, Glentanir, Glenmuik, and Clunie. And, by his second wife, Ægidia Hay heiress of Bog of Gight and a part of Enzie, he obtained these lands. In a confirmation of his lands by King James II. anno 1457, the onerous cause (says Burnet of Crimond) was, *For keeping the Crown on our Head:* But this charter is now lost. Dying anno 1479, his son (12) George, was Lord Chancellor, founded Gordon-Castle, erected the Priory of Kinglassie, and left three sons, viz. Alexander, Adam who married the heiress of Sutherland, and William of Gight. (13) Alexander, was made Hereditary Sheriff of the county, and Constable of the Castle of Inverness: And, by a Charter, 24th March 1505, got the Castle of Inverlochie in Lochaber, and the adjacent lands *(pub. Arch.)*. And dying 1523, was succeeded by his Grand-son, son of John, who died 1517. viz. (14) George, a man of unbounded ambition. He was Lord Chancellor, and the 13th February 1548, got a charter of the Earldom of Moray, the Lordships of Abernethie, Petty, Brachlie and Strathern; the castles of Tarnua, Abernethie and Hall hill, the fishing of Spey, Lossy and Findhorn. He had likewise the administration of the Earldoms of Marr and Orkney, the Lordship of Shetland and Bailiery of Strathdee. In the Queen Regent's tour to the North, he entertained her so sumptously, that (says Straloch) Monf. D'Osel advised her to humble him: And in 1554, he was divested of his said acquisitions, and rebelling against Queen Mary, lost his life in the battle of Corrichee, anno 1562. Brevity only allows me to mention his son (15) George, whose son (16) George, caused murder the Earl of Moray in Dunibrisle, anno 1592, fought the battle of Glenlivat 1594, was created Marquis 17th April 1599, and died 1636: His son (17) George was beheaded in 1649, whose

son

son (18) Lewis died 1653, and was father of (19) Duke George.

In 1650, the family of HUNTLEY was addebted to ARGYLE, a million of merks Scots; and the judicial rent of HUNTLEY's estate was 50,000 Merks, whereof 10,000 annually were allowed to the Marchioness Dowager and the Earl of Aboyne *(Vide Argyle's tryal)*. And Lord Lorn lived in Gordon Castle from 1653, to February 1st 1661. The family of Huntley was saved from being sunk under this debt by Argyle's forfeiture in 1661, when the King remitted the whole of it. George was created Duke of Gordon 1st November 1684. His son (20) Alexander. His son (21) Cosmo-George. And his son (22) Alexander, is now Duke. And thus the noble Family has flourished during two and twenty generations.

The Duke of Gordon beareth quarterly. 1. Az. 3 Boars heads couped Or, for Gordon. 2. Or, 3 Lions heads crased Gules, for Badenoch. 3. Or, 3 crescents within the Royal tressure Gules, for Seaton. And 4. Az. 3 Frases Arg. for Fraser of Cowie. Crest. A hart's head proper, attired with ten tynes, issuing out of a Marquiss's coronet Or. Supporters, two deer hounds argent, collared Gules, and on each collar three buckles Or. Motto, B Y D A N D.

The Parish of DUNDURCROSS.

This parish is next to Bellie up the river: So called from *Dun* a Hill, *Dur* Water, and *Cos* Foot, for there the river runneth at the foot of the hill. It is situated on both sides of the river. On the west side, the church standeth about half a mile from the south end of the parish; about $3\frac{1}{4}$ miles S. of Speymouth church, and one mile N. of Rothes. North from the church lie the lands of Gorbatie, the property of Sir Robert Gordon

Gordon of Gordonston: And below these on the river, are the lands of Orton, lately belonging to a branch of the family of Innes, and now to the Earl of Fife. Near to the church is a part of the Lordship of Rothes, and now the property of the Earl of Findlater.

On the east side of the River, the parish stretches about four miles in length, and in some parts more than a mile in breadth. In the north end is *Ordewhish* pertaining to the Duke of Gordon. South of which, on the river side, is *Cairntie*, lately purchased by Sir Ludovick Grant from Alexander Hay, whose ancestors had been for some generations heretors of it. And south and east of *Cairntie*, is the barony of *Mulben*, the freehold of Sir James Grant. This, it is said, was the first land that the Family of GRANT had on the River Spey, and which they obtained by marriage with the daughter and heir of Wiseman of *Mulben*, about 350 years ago. A brook that falleth into the river at the passage boat, called the Boat of bridge, was formerly called *Orkil*; and the lands on the banks of it were called Inverorkil, which lands Muriel de Polloc mortified, in the Thirteenth Century *ineunte*, for building an hospital there, of which hospital some vestiges still remain (Append. No II.): And at the mouth of this brook, there was a bridge of wood over the river, the pier of which, on the east side, is yet to be seen. It was called *Pons de Spe* (Append. Nº III.) And was the only bridge I have found upon that river till of late. In the south corner of the parish, on the river's bank, are the lands of *Aitkenwa*, for several generations the property of a branch of the family of Rothes, and now pertaining to the Earl of Findlater, as a part of the barony of Rothes. The whole of this parish is in the county of Elgin. Next to it is,

The

The Parish of ROTHES.

This parish in Irish is called, *Rauis.* q. *Raudh-uis*, i. e. *Red water*, from the red banks of the river and brooks. It extendeth on the river-side, in a beautiful plain, from N. N. E. to S. S. W. about two miles, and in the lower end, a defile, called the Glen of Rothes, stretcheth among the hills towards Elgin, 3 miles to the N. N. W. The church standeth upon the side of a brook, a quarter of a mile from the river, and half a mile from the north end of the parish. One mile S. of Dundurcross church: 3 miles N. of Aberlaure, and about 5 miles N. E. of Knockando. In the year 1238, Eva de Mortach (daughter of Muriel de Polloc, who was daughter of Petrus de Polloc) was Domina de Rothes (*Chart. Mor.*) In the end of King Alexander the IIId's reign, Norman Lesly of Lesly in the Garioch married the daughter and heiress (it is said) of Watson of Rothes, and from that time, the Barony continued to be the property of the family of Lesly, 'till in the beginning of this Century, Captain John Grant of Easter Elchies made a purchase of it. And his grandson, John Grant Baron of Exchequer, sold the Barony of Rothes, and the Baronies of Easter Elchies and Edinvillie, anno 1758, to James Earl of Findlater. The east side of the Glen of Rothes pertaineth in feu-holding to Robert Innes of Blackhills, and the west side is the feu property of Robert Cumming of Loggie. Near the church, stood the castle or Fortalice of Rothes, which carries the marks of an ancient building. It stood on a green mount, surrounded by a dry ditch or Fosse, and is now in ruins. The whole of this parish is in the county of Elgin or Moray. S. W. from Rothes is,

The Parish of KNOCKANDO.

The Parish of Knockando, in Irish, *Knoc-canach*, i. e. the *Merkat hill*, is bounded by the river to the S. and E. by the hills on the N. and W. And extends by the side of the river, about 6 miles in length, and generally one mile in breadth, and in some parts, two miles. The church standeth a quarter of a mile from the river, about two miles below the S. W. end of the parish, 2 miles N. of Inviravon, 5 miles S. W. of Rothes, and about 3 miles S. W. of Aberlaure. In the lower end of the parish, on the borders of Rothes, is a rocky hill called, *Craig Elachie*, i. e. The Ecchoing or Sounding Craig: And from it to another craig called Elachie, on the borders of Badenoch, stretcheth the country of Strath-spey, commonly said to be between the two craig Elachies, extending about 22 miles in length, but unequal in breadth: A country inferior to few, if to any, in the North of Scotland, for the conveniencies of life. Besides abundance of grain for the inhabitants, it is beautified and enriched with much wood and timber, watered by many rivulets, and well stored with cattle, great and small: And as the most confiderable inhabitants of it are Gentlemen of the name of GRANT, I shall, before I describe this parish, give a succinct account of this Family.

The FAMILY of GRANT.

From what country to fetch the GRANTS originally, I know not. Some make the names, *Suene, Allan,* &c. indications of a Norvegian extraction. Others make the sirname, *Grande,* of French original. These two may be compounded, by fetching them from Norway into Normanday in France, and thence into Britain with William the Norman Conqueror. But, if we allow them a Scottish origin, the name will bear us out. For, in the Irish, *Grant* signifies *Gray* or *Hoary*. And one

one tribe of the Grants is called *Keran*, or *Kiaran*, much the same with *Gray* or Grant. But, in this, I determine nothing.

Not to carry up their antiquity (as an inexact and unchronological Tree of the family doth) to Woden the Heathen, their descendants can be traced back 500 years, with strong presumptions of a much higher antiquity. (1) In an agreement betwixt the Bishop of Moray and Bisset of Lovat, anno 1258, Robertus de Grant vicecomes de Invernefs is witness *(Chart. Mor.)* (2.) Joannes de Grant was one of these Barons, with Radulphus his brother, whom King Edward I. sent prisoners from Berwick to London, anno 1296. They were not liberate till 30th July 1297, when they were obliged to engage to serve King Edward abroad " contra quoscunque inimicos d. d. Regis." *(Rym. Vol.* II. *p.* 776. (3.) Robertus de Grant is one of the Barons in Ragman's Roll, *(Prynne, Vol.* III. *p.* 657) about anno 1300 ; and the author of the Remarks on that Roll, calleth him the Ancestor of the Family of GRANT *(Nisb. Herald. Vol.* II. *Remarks on Ragman's Roll, p.* 35.) (4.) John de Grant was one of the Commanders in the battle of Halidon-hill, anno 1333 ; and anno 1359, the same gentleman, with Sir Robert Erskine and Norman Lesley, were ambassadors to the Court of France to renew the ancient league *(Abercr. Hist. Folio, Vol.* II. *p.* 124.). And (5.) Robert Grant Esq; was much in favour with King Robert II. and in 1385, was one of these Barons, among whom were distributed 50,000 crowns of gold, remitted from France to animate the Scots to invade England. *(Rym.)* Men of such distinction and eminence in those early ages, are an undeniable historical presumption, that the Name and Clan were, even in these days, numerous, powerful, and much respected. I cannot indeed instruct, that these five gentlemen were the successive Representatives of the Family, although I think it highly probable. But the following descents, from father to son, admit of no question ; viz. (6.) Maude or Matildis heiress married Andrew Steuart,

Steuart, son of Sir John Steuart sheriff of Bute, who was son of King Robert II. *(Geneal. Tree.)* And their son was (7.) Patrick, who married the daughter and heiress of Wiseman of Mulben; and by her was father of (8.) John Roy. This gentleman married Bigla Cumming heiress of Glenchernich. He had two sons, viz. Duncan his heir, and Duncan progenitor of the Clan Donachie or Family of Gartenbeg. (9.) Duncan, whom in 1479 I find designed Duncan Grant of *Freuchie (Cart. pen. Kilr.)* married Muriel, daughter of Malcolm Laird of M'Intosh, by whom he had John his heir, and Patrick ancestor of the family of Ballindalach. (10.) John, the *Bard-Roy*, or Red poet, married Elizabeth Ogilvie daughter of Findlater, by whom he had John his heir. He had likewise a natural son, called John More, ancestor of the family of Glenmoriston. (11.) John, by his Lady, a daughter it is said of Rothes, had three sons, viz. James, his heir, John of whom Corimonie is descended, and Patrick ancestor of Bonhard. (12.) James called *Shemuis nan Creach*, i. e. the Ravager, married a daughter of Lord Forbes, and dying anno 1553, was succeeded by his son (13.) John Baold, i. e. *Simple*, who, by his first wife, Margaret daughter of Steuart Earl of Athole, had Duncan his heir, and Patrick ancestor to Rothemurchus; and by his second wife, Isobel Barclay daughter of Towie, he had Archibald of Bellentom. (14.) Duncan died 1581 before his father, who died 1585, and his wife Margaret, daughter of the Laird of M'Intosh, left John his heir; Patrick, of whom is *Easter Elchies*; and Mr James, of whom are *Moyness* and *Larg*. (15.) John of Freuchie who died anno 1622, leaving by his wife, Lilias Moray daughter of Tullibardin (16.) Sir John, called, *Sir John sell the land*, who, by Mary Ogilvie daughter of Finlater, had eight sons, of whom James succeeded him: Colonels John and Patrick left no male issue; nor did Alexander, nor George governor of Dunbarton: Of the other three,

three, Mungo of Kincherdie was ancestor to Knockando and to Kincherdie: The 7th was Robert of Muckerach; and the 8th Thomas of Belmacaan. Sir John died anno 1637. (17.) James married Mary Steuart daughter of the Earl of Moray, and dying anno 1663, left two sons, Ludovick, and Patrick of Wester Elchies. I need not descend farther to mention (18) Ludovick who died in 1718, father of (19) Brigadier Alexander, who dying 1719, was succeeded by his brother (20.) Sir James. He dying 1747, was succeeded by his son (21.) Sir Ludovick, to whom, anno 1773, succeeded his son (22.) Sir James, now living.

I have dwelt thus much on the descents of the House of GRANT, that the branches of it might appear, and to avoid repetitions. Besides the branches abovenamed, there are other three that claim a higher antiquity: viz. The Clan ALAN, or family of ACHERNACK. The Clan CHIARAN, or family of DILLACHAPLE: And the Clan PHADRICK, or family of TULLOCHGORM. These contend, that they sprung from the House of GRANT, before they came from Stratherick into Strathspey. That the ancient residence of the Grants was in Stratherick, cannot reasonably be questioned. The names of their ancient or old seats in Stratherick (as Gartmore, Gartbeg, Dillachaple, &c.) are given to their new seats in Strathspey. But, at what precise time they came into Strathspey (surely not all at one time) I pretend not to determine. The Laird of GRANT was designed of Freuchie before 1479; and I think it probable that they began to come to Spey-side about, or before the year 1400.

The armorial bearing of Grant is, Gules, three antique crowns Or. Crest, a burning hill proper. Motto, STAND SURE. Supporters, two savages proper.

I now return to describe the Parish of Knockando. In the North East end, next to Rothes, is the barony of Easter Elchies, which has been the heritage of a branch of the House of Grant for above 150 years, and during six generations, but sold as above mentioned. It is accommodated with a good house, spacious inclosures, and much barren wood near the river. Next up the river, is the barony of Wester Elchies: About the year 1620, this was the heritage of Mr Lachlan Grant: Thereafter it came to Patrick, the first of this family, whose son, James, was father of Ludowick, who died 1757, father of James then a minor. Farther up the river is Bellintom, the patrimonial estate of (1.) Archibald of Bellintom, whose sons were, Archibald, John of Aruntullie and Alexander of Alachie, (2.) Archibald was father of (3.) Sir Francis of Cullen late Lord of Session, created a Baronet anno 1705, and whose sons are, (4.) Sir Archibald of Monimus, who in 1758 purchased from Sir Ludowick Grant the freehold of Bellintom and some superiorities, by which he is a Baron in the County of Moray: William of Prestongrange late Lord of Session and Justiciary, and Mr Francis. Next to Bellintom, up the river, is the barony of Knockando, with a good house of modern architecture on the bank of the river. The first of this family was Mungo of Kincherdie (p. 21.) whose eldest son James purchased Knockando from Ludowick Laird of Grant. James was father of Ludowick who died 1751, and of Alexander Grant of Grantfield; and Ludowick was father of James, whose son Ludowick is now living. And in the S. W. end of the parish is the barony of Kirdels, the freehold of James Grant of Ballendaloch: All these baronies within the shire of Moray, are richly accommodated with salmon fishing in the river, and woods on the banks of it.

I now return to the East side of the river, and over against Rothes, is,

BOHARM Parish.

The Parish of BOHARM, anciently and truly written, *Bocharn*; for over against the plains of Rothes, and on the east bank of the river, is a high hill called *Ben-eggin*, i. e. The Hill with clefts, and round a great part of the hill this parish windeth: Hence called *Bocharn*, i. e. a Bow or arch about the carn or hill. It is in length about four miles, and in few place above half a mile in breadth, lying on the east side of a brook that runneth into the water of Fiddich. The church standeth on the south side of the hill, two miles West of Botrisnie, two miles North East of Aberlaure, two miles and a half South East of Rothes, and about three miles North of Mortlich. This parish (all in the county of Banff,) was, in the reign of K. William the Lion, about anno 1210, the property of William Moray, son of William, and grandson of Freskyn Moray of Duffus. He is designed, Dominus de Petty, Brachlie, Bocharin, &c. *(Cart. Mor.)* and from his son Walter, descended Sir Andrew Moray Lord Bothwell. Willielmus filius Willielmi Freskin, had his castle and seat in Boharm, *(Appendix, N° V.)* probably at Galival, where some vestiges do still remain. At this time the freeholds are, *Arntullie*, the seat of Alexander Grant, of which he purchased the freehold from Sir Ludowick Grant, anno 1757. His father, Thomas of Achoinany and Arntullie, died 1758, and was son of Walter, son of John of Arntullie, second son of Archibald the first of Bellintom. It is pleasantly situated at the foot of Ben-eggin, on the bank of Spey, and capable of great improvement, by inclosing and planting. This gentleman is likewise proprietor of Galival and of Newton, which lately pertained to a gentleman of the name of Anderson. To the East of the church are the lands of *Achmadies*, the property

of

of Sir James Grant. And thence Northward is the barony of *Achluncart*, which, for several generations, pertained to a branch of the House of Innes, and by an heiress came to a son of Stewart of Tanachie. This parish is well accommodated with moss ground for fuel, and generally is a rich and fertile soil, very early in ripening about Arntullie, but cold and late on the South East side of the hill. South from Boharm, on the rivulets of Fiddich and Dulenan, lieth,

The Parish of MORTLICH.

This parish, in ancient writings is called *Morthlach*, probably from *Mor-lag*, i. e. a Great Hollow, for it is a deep hollow, surrounded with hills. Before I enter this parish, I shall a little describe the two rivulets that water it: *Fiddich*, q. *Fiodhidh*, i. e. Woody, because its sides are covered with wood, hath its rise in the hills south of Mortlich towards Srathdon, and running N. E. about 3 miles, turneth almost due West for a mile, and then, after a course of 3 miles due North, it falleth into Spey. The other rivulet *Dulenan*, (properly *Tuilan*, from Tuil, a flood, because of its impetuous current) takes its rise in the hills of Glenlivat, and running N. E. parallell to Fiddich (but seperated from it by a ridge of hills) 3 miles, it mixes with it 3 miles above Spey.

The parish is in length from N. to S. 4 miles, and as much in breadth from E. to W. besides some skirts that lye near to *Botrifnie*, *Glas* and *Cabrach*. It is all environed with hills, except a small opening to the North. The church standeth on Dulenan, a little above the confluence with Fiddich, 2 miles S. S. E. of Aberlaure, and about 3 miles S. of Boharm. The parish (all in the shire of Banff) consists of the Barony of Kininvie, the Lordship of Belvenie, and the Barony of Auchindune.

dune. The house of Kininvie stands upon the rivulet Fiddich on the East side, environed with natural wood. A branch of the family of Lesly of Balquhan has enjoyed this Barony about 250 years, and of this Branch the Earl of Leven is descended. Next up Fiddich-side and the West-side of Dullen, are the lands of Balvenie, which comprehend Bochram, Little Tullich, Parkbeg, Clunie-more, Clunie-beg, Pilvaich, Littoch, &c. Of the Commissioners sent to London, 19. August 1423, to relieve King James I. was James Douglas of Balvenie *(Rym. Fœd. vol.* x. *p.* 298.) and 1446 John son of James Earl of Douglas was created Lord Balvenie, who, being forfeited 1455, for joining in his brother's rebellion, King James II. granted Balvenie to his uterine brother John Steuart Earl of Athole. That family sold it to Aberneathie Lord Salton, who, about 1606, disponed it to Lord Ochiltree. From him it came to Sir Robert Innes of Invermarkie, and from Sir Robert's heirs to Sutherland of Kinminity. About anno 1666, Alexander Lord Salton reduced his father's disposition to Lord Ochiltree, and conveyed the lands in 1670 to Arthur Forbes brother to Blackton, from whom Alexander Duff of Braco adjudged them, and got possession about 1687, and they are now the property of the Earl of Fife. Upon an eminence on the West-bank of Fiddich, stood the castle of Balvenie, the ancient seat of the Lordship, commanding a pleasant view of the valley; and half a mile below it, in a moist, low, and unwholesome soil, there is built a fine house of modern architecture, one of the seats of the Earl of Fife, adorned with gardens and planting.

In the south of the parish, betwixt the rivulets of Fiddich and Dulen, is the Barony of Achindune. This was formerly a part of the Lordship of Deskford, and Achindune and forrest of Fiddich were a part of the Barony of Ogilvie, erected in 1527 *(Pen. Findl.).* Afterwards it was purchased by, and is now the property

property of the Family of Gordon. The castle stood on a mount above the water of Fiddich; and from it Glenfiddich stretches S. W. about three miles among the hills; where is fine pasture ground and a forrest of red deer. Upon the head of Dulen lieth Glenrinness, a fertile valley, 2 miles long. The south-side of it is a part of the Barony of Achindune, and the north-side a part of the Lordship of Balvenie. Along the north-side runneth Benrinnes, a high hill, and a land mark for sailors in sailing into the Moray Frith. Before I proceed to the next parish, I shall give some account of

The Family of DUFF.

The Family of M'Duff Earl of Fife, (descended, in my opinion, of King Duffus, who was murdered in Forres about anno 965) was ancient and eminent, and flourished untill the year 1385. The sirnames of *Weem*, *M'Intosh*, *Tosheach*, *Shaw*, *Spens*, *Fife*, *Duff*, &c. are branches of that great Family. I have before me a genealogical manuscript account lately written, deducing the Lord Braco from the family of Fife. It consists of three successive branches.

I. The Earls of *Athole* of the name *de Strathbolgie*, descended of the Earls of FIFE, thus: (1) David, son of Duncan, the 6th Earl. In a donation to the See of Moray, by Malcolm the 7th Earl, " David filius quondam Duncani Comitis de Fife, " frater meus, anno 1226, is witness. Collatio Malcolmi Com. " de Fyfe, Episc. Morav. Test. Duncano et Davide fratribus " meis. Conventio inter Andream Episc. Morav. et nobi- " lem virum Davidem de Strathbolgie filium quondam Dunca- " ni Comitis de Fyfe, anno 1232." *(Cart. Moray)* He was father of (2) John de Strathbolgie, who became Earl of Athole in right of his wife Ada, co-heiress of Henry Earl of Athole, and was father of (3) David, who married Isabel co-heiress of Lord

Chilam

Chilam, and died 1284. His son (4.) John, executed at London 1308. His son (5.) David, killed at Kilblain anno 1335, by his wife Joan, daughter of John the Red Cuming Lord Badenoch, had several sons, whereof the eldest (6.) David, was forfeited for abetting the English interest, and died in England anno 1375, without male issue. This deduction of the Earls of Athole is instructed from the Chartulary of Moray, and Sir Wm Dugdale.

II. Branch, deduces the *Duffs* of *Muldavid* and *Craighead* thus: (1.) John, second son of David the 5th Earl of Athole, quitted the name of de Strathbolgie and assumed that of Duff, and had the lands of Muldavid and Craighead, &c. His son was (2.) David, &c. The line was carried down by eleven generations, to John Duff writer in Aberdeen, who died in Holland anno 1717, without issue; and in him the direct line of Craghead became extinct. I confess all the descents are well instructed, except the first. But one will desiderate, How doth it appear, that John, called the first of Craghead, was the 2d son of David 5th Earl of Athole? Or was at all his son? That ever he bore the name of Strathbolgie? That he assumed the name Duff? And for what reasons he did so? For all, or any of those, there is no voucher. Be it as it may, I pass on to

III. Branch, The family of *Clunybeg* and *Braco*. The direct line of Craighead becoming extinct in John Duff anno 1717, his grandfather John, (who died about 1660) was twice married. By his first wife Isabel Allan, he had John father of the foresaid John the writer. And by his second wife, daughter of John Gordon of Carnborraw, he had (1.) Adam Duff of Clunybeg, who, by his wife daughter of Gordon of Birkenburn, had Alexander of Kiethmore, William ancestor of Drummuir and Crombie, John ancestor of Corsindie, Peter and Adam. Clunybeg died anno 1677. (2.) Alexander of Keithmore married Helen daughter of Alexander Grant of Ellachie, and had

had Alexander of Braco, William of Dipple, and Patrick of Craigston. (3.) Alexander of Braco married Margaret, daughter of Sir William Gordon of Lesmore Bart. and had (4) William, who, leaving no male issue, was succeeded by his uncle (5.) William of Dipple, heir male and of entail, who, by his wife daughter of Sir George Gordon of Edinglassie, has left a son (6.) William. This gentleman married Jean, eldest daughter of Sir James Grant of Grant, and hath a numerous issue. In 1735, he was created Baron Braco of Kilbryde in the County of Cavon in Ireland; and, by patent to him and his heirs male, dated 10th April 1759, he was created Viscount Mac Duff and Earl Fife of that kingdom.

William, second son of Clunybeg, was Father of Alexander, who married Katharine Duff eldest daughter and heiress of Adam Duff of Drummuir, and by her had Robert of Drummuir, John of Coulbin, and William of Muirton. Robert was father of Archibald, now of Drummuir. William had a second son, James father of William Duff of Crombie advocate. Of Clunybeg's 3d son, John, is descended Duff of Corsindae. And of Keithmore's son, Patrick of Craigtton, are descended Hatton, Remnay, Craigslon, &c.

The Armorial bearing of DUFF Earl FIFE, of the Kingdom of IRELAND, is quarterly, 1. and 4. Or, a Lyon rampant Gules, armed and langued Azure, for Fife; 2. and 3. Vert, a Fess danzette Ermine, betwixt a Hart's head cabossed in Chief, and two Escallops in Base, Or, for Duff of Braco. Crest, a demy Lyon Gules, holding in his dexter paw a broad sword erected in pale proper, hilted and pomelled. Or, Motto above the Crest, DEUS JUVAVIT. And below the Shield, VIRTUTE ET OPERA. Supporters, two Savages wreathed about the heads and middles with Laurel, holding branches of trees in their hands, all proper.

ABERLAURE Parish.

The parish of *Aberlaure* (all in the County of Banff,) is called also *Skir-drustan*. It extendeth on the bank of Spey, from the mouth of Fiddich, three miles to the South West, and on all other sides is environed with hills, and no where above a mile in breadth, except a small skirt in Glenrinnes. The church standeth on the bank of the river, where a brook, flowing from the hills towards Mortlich, falleth into it two miles North West of Mortlich, two miles near to the West of Boharm, and three miles and a half North East of Inveravon. At the confluence of Fiddich and Spey, there is a passage boat, and another at the church.

The parish is now the property of five heritors. In the lower end is Mudhouse, a feu pertaining to Mr Anderson. Next up the river is the heritage of Gordon of Aberlaure. Further up the river, and on the South East of the brook, is Alachie. This was the heritage of Alexander Grant, third son of Bellentom, by whose daughter it came in mortgage to Duff of Keithmore, and was lately redeemed by Sir Ludowick Grant, who in 1758 disponed it to James Grant of Caron. In the face of the hill South West from Alachie, is Edinvillie. This was the property of Gordon of Faskine, from whom it came to Grant of Easter Elchies, and now is the property of the Earl of Findlater. * [See this Work, parish of *Rothes*, page 17.] Below Edinvillie towards the side of the river, is the Barony of Kinermonie. This was a part of the Lordship of Balvenie, and was given by Innes of Balvenie to his second

---

* The lands of Mudhouse, Aberlour, Alachie and Edinvillie were a part of the Lordship of Balvenie; and the lands of Caron were Church lands, and now hold of the family of Gordon.

second son, whose heirs exchanged it for Ortown, and now it is the property of the Earl of Fife. In the West end of the parish is Carron, at the foot of the hill of that name. It continued above 200 years, the property of a branch of the family of Grant of Glenmoriston, and Colonel John Grant, the last of Carron, being killed before Carthagena anno 1741, without male issue, Charles Grant of Ringorum became the male heir. From him Captain Lewis Grant of Achterblair, a branch of the Clan Allan (and who married Colonel Grant's eldest daughter), purchased his right, and now Captain James Grant his son, enjoyeth it, and in 1767 was made Baron of Mulderie in the county of Moray. I now proceed up the river to

The Parish of INVERAVON.

Here I must trace the rivers of Avon and Livat that water this parish. The river Avon riseth out of a lake of that name, about two miles in length, situated in a deep valley, between two of the highest hills in the kingdom, viz. Carn-gorm and Cairngorm-beg; and running thro' Glenavon, and the parishes of Kirk-michael and Inveravon, it emptieth into Spey at Ballendalach, after a course of about twenty miles. About three miles above the mouth of Avon, Livat falleth into it, which rising in the hills towards Strathdon, watereth Glenlivat for seven or eight miles, and mixeth with Avon at Drummuir. Both these waters are very impetuous; and Avon is so clear and deceiving, that, where to the eye it appeareth but a foot deep, it is commonly more than three-feet. This parish is very extensive, running on the bank of Spey from N. E. to S. W. above 3 and a half miles, and then S. S. E. above 8 miles. The church standeth on the bank of Spey, a furlong East from the mouth of Avon, 3 and a half miles S. W. of Aberlaure, 2 miles S.

S. of Knockando, 6 miles N. E. of Cromdale, and as many N. of Kirkmichael. Malcolm Earl of Fife gave this church, and a Davach of land in Inveravon, to the Bishop of Moray, (Appendix, N° VII.) which sheweth that this was once a part of the estate of the Eals of Fife, and probably came to the Grants by the favour of Robert Steuart Duke of Albany, (uncle to Andrew Steuart who married the heiress of Grant) to whom Isabel M'Duff, the heiress, disponed that great estate (Appendix, N° VIII.). The whole lower end of the parish (except Coulchoich, pertaining to the Duke of Gordon) is the Barony of Ballindalach. This, for above 200 years, was a part of the estate of the old family of Ballindalach, of whom Advie, Dellay, Dalvey, Tommavulin, &c. have descended. But being evicted and brought to a sale, was purchased by the Laird of Grant in the beginning of this Century, and given by the Brigadier with his sister to Collonel William Grant, second son to Rothimurchus, whose son James (since the death of his nephew William, son of his elder brother Alexander, without issue) now possesseth it, and has a beautiful seat at the confluence of Spey and Avon.

Three miles above Ballindalach, upon the same side of Avon, beginneth Glenlivat, which runneth up S. E. on both sides of Livat 5 miles, and holdeth of the Duke of Gordon, either in property or in superiority. In the face of Benrinnes, on the North side of Livat, is Morinsh, for several generations the property of Nairn of Morinsh, but now a part of the estate of Ballindalach. On the West side of Avon, for 3 miles from the mouth of it, lieth the barony of Kilmachlie. This was a part of the estate of Alexander Steuart, 4th son of King Robert II. Earl of Buchan, and Lord Badenoch and Strathavon, who, having no legitimate issue, gave the lands of Strathavon to his bastard son Sir Andrew, whose son Sir Walter sold Strathavon

to

to the family of Gordon; or rather, it came to Thomas, baftard fon of Alexander Steuart Earl of Marr, who was baftard fon of the Earl of Buchan, and Thomas fold it to Alexander Earl of Huntley. But Kilmachlie continued with a fon of Sir Andrew and his defcendants, untill Ludovick Laird of Grant purchafed it, and now it is a part of the eftate of Ballindalach. On the point where Avon and Livat join, ftands the caftle of Drummin, which was the feat of the Barons of Strathavon, and is now the refidence of Charles Steuart of Drummin, a branch of Kilmachlie. Here there is an arch of a ftone-bridge over Livat. This parifh is accommodated with much wood, rich pafture-ground, and plentiful falmon fifhing. The barony of Ballindalach is in the county of Moray: The reft is in Banff-fhire. Further up the river Avon is

The Parifh of KIRKMICHAEL.

This parifh is in the fhire of Banff. This Glen and Strath was a part of the eftate of M'Duff Earl of Fife in the 13th century, and was, anno 1389 June 22. refigned by Ifabel M'Duff heirefs, in the hands of King Robert III. in perpetuam remanentiam, *(Appendix* No VIII. *And* Skene *de verb. fignif. Tit. Arage).* It came afterwards to Alexander Lord Badenoch and Earl of Buchan, who left iffue only three baftard fons, viz. Alexander Earl of Marr in right of his wife, Sir Andrew of Sandhaugh, and Walter of Kinchardin. Sir Walter of Strahavon (fon of Sir Andrew) fold Strathavon, except Kilmachlie and Drummin, to Alexander Earl of Huntley, who difponed it to his fon Alexander, and he excambed it for the barony of Clunie. Again, George Earl of Huntley, who died anno 1576, gave Strathavon to his fon Alexander, whofe fon Alexander Gordon of Dunkintie fold Strathavon to his coufin George Earl

Earl of Huntley. Since that time, all this parish (except the Davack of Delnaboe) holds of Huntley in property or superiority.

It is all environed with hills, except a small opening towards Inveravon, and extends in length, on both sides of the river, from N. E. to S. W. seven miles: and about the middle of the parish, the rivulet Conglas (which riseth in the hills towards the River Don) after a course of 7 or 8 miles, falleth into Avon, and here the breadth of the parish is 3 miles. The church standeth on the East bank of Avon, 2 miles above the lower end of the parish, 6 miles S. W. of Inveravon, 4 miles E. of Cromdale, and 5 miles E. N. E. of Abernethie.

On the west side of the river, at the foot of Cromdale hill, are from N. to S. the lands of Inveraurie, Inverlochie, and Forletter, the property of the Duke of Gordon. Above these, on the banks of the river, is Delnaboe, for some generations the heritage of a branch of the Clan Allan, but now the property of Sir James Grant of Grant. Above Delnaboe on both sides of the river, are Achnahyle, once a mortgage of James Grant brother to Easter Elchies; Dellavorar, for three generations the Wadset of a branch of the M'Gregors; and Gavelack. These, and some other possessions, are now wadsetted by William Gordon, grandson to Glenbuket. Above Gavelack, Glenavon runneth into the Grampian hills about 12 miles, and is a rich pasture for cattle, and a forrest for red deer. On the east side of the river, below the church, is Dell; above the church is Ruthven-Camdale, where, in 1754, a bridge of three arches was built over the river on the military-road. Next is Cromdale Bhrid, or Brigida's Camdale. And on Conglas Rivulet are several possessions, particularly Achriachan, which, for about 200 years, was the inheritance of a branch of the Farquharsons, but is now the property of the Duke of Gordon. I now return to the banks of Spey, to describe

The Parish of CROMDALE.

The parish of *Cromdale*, i. e. the Crooked plain, about which the Spey windeth. This is three parishes united into one, viz. *Alvie*, *Cromdale*, and *Inverallen*, stretching on the east-side of the river above 6 miles, and on the west side near to 12 miles in length, and in the centre, about 4 miles in breadth; flanked to the east by Cromdale-hill, and to the west by the hills of Brae-Moray. The church of Cromdale standeth on the S. E. bank of the river, 6 miles S. W. of Inveravon, 4 miles N. E. of Abernethie, and 6 miles E. N. E. of Duthel. The three parishes (except a few mortgages) are the property of the Laird of Grant.

In the lower end is the parish of Advie, consisting of the baronies of Advie on the east, and of Tulchen on the west-side of the river. These, anciently a part of the estate of the Earl of Fife, came to the family of Ballendalach in the 15th Century, and continued their property till they were sold to Brigadier Alexander Grant. Grant of Advie was a branch of the family of Ballendalach, and Grant of Delly of Advie. Next up the river on the east-side, is Dalvey, which for several generations pertained to a branch of the family of Ballendalach, and about anno 1680, Robert of Dalvey purchased Dunlugas in the county of Banff, and sold Dalvey to James Grant of Gartenbeg, who in 1688 was created a Baronet; and dying soon after the Revolution, and his brother Lewis dying about 1698, both without legitimate issue, the lands of Dalvey (by an agreement with the heir male) came to Patrick Grant of Inverladenan, the chief of the Clan Donachie, and now they are the property of the Laird of Grant. Farther up on that side of the river, is the barony of Cromdale. This (and I doubt not with it Advie and Dalvey) was a part of the estate of M'Duff Earl of Fife,

(Appendix,

(Appendix, No VIII.) which, 22. June 1389, Isabel M'Duff daughter and heir of Duncan Earl of Fife, resigned "ad perpetuam re-
"manentiam, in the hands of King Robert III. the baronies of
"Strathurd, Strathbraan, Deasir, Foyer, with the isle of Tay
"and Logyahrie, all in Perthshire: The barony of Coul and
"O'neil in Aberdeenshire: The baronies of Cromdale and Af-
"fyne (probably Advie) in Invernesshire: The lands of Strath-
"avie and Abrondolie in Banff-shire: The barony of Calder in
"Linlithgowshire; and Kilsyth in Stirlingshire *(Skene de Verb.*
"*signif. Tit. Arage).*" This was afterwards the property of Nairn Baron of Cromdale, from whom Ludovick Grant of Grant purchased it. In Cromdale is Dellachaple the seat of the Head of the Clan Chiaran, Lethindie the seat of the ancient barons, Burnside the residence of William Grant of the Clan Allan, &c. Near the church is the passage-boat.

Over against Cromdale, and on the west-side of the river, is Achinarraw, where the Clan Chiaran first seated. Next is Dunan, the first seat of the Clan Allan; and next thereto, is the barony of Freuchie (i. e. Heathery, so called from a hillock, covered with heath, near the house of Grant) or of Castle-Grant. This (as also Achinarraw, Dunan, and all the lands of Inveralan) was anciently a part of the estate of Cumming Lord Badenoch. Here is the principal seat of the family of Grant. The house is a grand building, environed with gardens, inclosures, and much planting. The apartments in the house are well finished, and there is a valuable private library. Two miles south, the church of Inveralan standeth on the west bank of the river. In the 13th Century, about 1230, this church, and probably lands about it, pertained to Walter Moray Baron of Petty and son of William, son of Freskyn of Duffus (Appendix, No XI.). And anno 1236, King Alexander II. excambed with Andrew Bishop of Moray, the three Davachs of Fynlarg (near the church of Inveralan) for the forreſt of Cawood, and Logynfythenach in Brae-Moray (Appendix, No. X.). In the upper end of the pariſh is Tullochgorum, the ſeat of the chief of the Clan Phadrick, for near to 400 years. N. W. from Tullochgorum is Clourie, a mortgage belonging to a Branch of the Houſe of Grant. And north from Clourie is Muckerach, the firſt poſſeſſion of the Grants of Rothemurchus, where they built a good houſe anno 1598, but now in ruins. I now go up the river to

ABERNETHIE Pariſh.

The pariſh of Abernethie, i. e. the Mouth of *Nethie*, or the Impetuous Waſhie River. To this the pariſh of Kinchardine is united, and both lie on the South Eaſt ſide of the River. It extendeth from the borders of Cromdale to Rothemurchus, ſeven miles in length, and from Spey to Glenlochie, five miles in breadth, environed, except on the river, with a chain of hills. The Barony of Kinchardine is the property of the Duke of Gordon, and all the reſt, except a few wadſets, the property of the Laird of Grant. Abernethie is in the county of Moray, and Kinchardin in the county of Inverneſs. The church ſtandeth two furlongs from Spey, and as far from Nethie, four miles South Weſt of Cromdale; four miles Eaſt of Duthel, and ſix miles North Eaſt of Rothemurchus. The water of Nethie riſeth in the hills near to Loch-avon, and watering the pariſh from South to North, after a courſe of near ſeven miles, diſchargeth into Spey.

The Barony of Abernethie was a part of the eſtate of Cumming Lord Badenoch, where he had a houſe or fort near the church. (See Military Hiſtory) Upon the forfeiture of Cumming, it became a part of the Earldom of Moray, and as yet giveth the title of Lord Abernethie to that Earl. On the death of

Earl

Earl John Randulf anno 1346, the Earldom reverted to the Crown: and Abernethie, as a part of it, was given to "Dc- "lecto filio noftro Joanni de Dunbar, et Mariotæ fponfæ "ejus, filiæ noftræ chariffimæ, 9° Mart. anno regni 2° 1373." *(Rotul. Rob. II.)* At what time the Lairds of Grant firft obtained any part of Abernethie, I cannot determine; But they were in poffeffion of the lower parts early in the 16th Century, and thereafter they purchafed the upper part in the 17th Century, from the Earl of Moray. Let it be obferved, that the Davacks of Gartenmore, Rymore and Tulloch in Abernethie, and the Davacks of Tullochgorum, Clourie and Cour in Inverallan, were a part of the Lordfhip of Badenoch; and about anno 1600, the family of Huntly excambed thefe lands with John of Freuchie, for lands in Strathavon and Glenlivat, referving to Huntly a fervitude upon the fir wood of Rymore, for repairing Gordon caftle, and the caftle of Blairfindie in Glenlivat, which fervitude is ftill in force.

In the Eaft end of the parifh is Conegefs, a mortgage pertaining to Mr William Grant late minifter of Abernethie; And a half mile above Conegefs, is a bridge of four arches over Spey built on the military road in 1754. A mile further up is Achernack, for about 300 years the refidence of the Head of the Clan Allan. About the year 1560, James Grant of Achernack had a family of eight fons, whereof Duncan was heir: a 2*d* Gregor founded the family of Gartinmore; a 3*d* James was anceftor of Achterblair, now Carron; a 4*th* John, was the firft of the Grants of Eafter Lethendie and Burnfide; a 5*th* Allan, was anceftor of Mulachard; a 6*th* Mungo of Conegefs; a 7*th* Robert of Nevie; and the 8*th* Andrew. Near to Achernack is a paffage boat. At the mouth of Nethie is Coulnakyle, a pleafant feat, where Sir James Grant has built a neat new houfe. A mile up on Nethie, is *Letoch*, the mortgage of a gentleman

tleman of the Clan Allan; and a mile further up is *Lurg*, the feat of Robert Grant of Lurg, the 5th defcent from Duncan heir of Grant, who died anno 1581. Beyond Nethie, on the river Spey, is *Gartinmore* a mortgage of John Grant. South from which is *Rymore*, and South Weft thence is *Tulloch*, which had been for fix generations the property of a branch of the family of Ballendalach, lately extinct. A fkirt of the parifh of Abernethie lieth in a narrow valley called *Glenbruin* and *Glenlochie*, near the river Avon.

The Barony of Kinchardin lieth on the river Spey, betwixt Gartenmore and Rothemurchus. The church is in the middle of it, a furlong from the river. I obferved above, that Walter Stewart of Kinchardin was the 3d fon of the Earl of Buchan. His defcendants for ten defcents continued in good repute, till about the year 1683, John Roy, the laft Baron (a filly ignorant man), was in a manner cheated out of his eftate, by his brother-in-law Alexander M'Intofh, called the fheriff Baine, who made him fell it to the Marquifs of Huntley for a very triffle; and the family is extinct. For the extenfive fir woods in Abernethie and Kinchardin, fee the Natural Hiftory. And I crofs the river Spey to

DUTHEL Parifh.

The parifh of Duthel lieth on the Weft fide of the river: but the parifh of Rothemurchus that is united to it, is on the Eaft fide. Duthel is divided into two parts, by a ridge of hills running from South to North. The South Eaft fide of thefe hills is called *Deafoil*, i. e. Southward; and the North Weft fide is called *Tuathail*, i. e. Northward; and hence is the name, *Duthel*. The rapid rivulet *Tuilenan*, watereth this North fide of the parifh. It rifeth in the hills betwixt Badenoch and Strathern, and running North Eaft thro'

Duthel, it turneth due East, and after a course of sixteen miles falleth into Spey. There are upon it two stone bridges, one a furlong above the mouth of it, and the other a mile above the church. The church standeth on the West side of Tuilenan, six miles West South-West of Cromdale, four miles West of Abernethie, and about seven miles North of Alvie. On Tuilenan, from North to South, lies Tullochgriban, Mullachard, Achterblair, Inverladenan, &c. the seats of Gentlemen of the name of Grant.

The Deasoil, or South-side of the hills, stretcheth on the bank of Spey, from Tullochgorum to the borders of Badenoch, 5 miles in length, and not one mile in breadth. In the East-end is Gartenbeg the ancient seat of the Clan Donachie, of whom Sir Ludovick Grant of Dalvey is now the representer. Lauchlan Grant, now of Gartenbeg, is of that family†. Next is Kincherdie, the seat of a Branch of the house of Grant. Farther up is Aviemore, which (with Linechuirn) was the residence of a Branch of the family of Glenmoriston, now extinct. And on the borders of Badenoch is the Western Craig Elachie, which word is a motto of the Grant's arms, and is the *Crie de guerre*, or War-cry of the Clan. This parish is in the Shire of Moray for the most part, and the whole of it is a part of the estate of Grant.

The Parish of ROTHEMURCHUS.

The Parish of Rothemurchus is in the Shire of Inverness. It lieth on the S. E. of the river, and, including Glenmore in Kinchardine,

---

† Upon the West bank of the river, where now the passage boat of Gartenmore crosseth, stood the house of Cumming of Glenchernich, as yet called Bigla's house, because Bigla heiress of Glenchernich married to the Laird of Grant, was the last of the Cummines that enjoyed that land. The house stood on a green moate, fenced by a dry ditch, the vestages of which are yet to be seen. A current tradition beareth, that at night a Salmon-net was cast out into the Pool below the wall of the house, and a small rope, tyed to the net and brought in at the window, had a bell hung at it, which rung when a Salmon came into and shook the net.

Kinchardine Parish, it maketh a Semicircle, whereof the river is the diameter, and high mountains the circumference. The church standeth on the river, a half mile below the South end of the Parish, 6 miles South from Duthel; 6 miles S. W. from Abernethie; one and a half mile S. E. from Alvie. Close by the church is the house of Downe, the seat of Patrick Grant of Rothemurchus, a Baron in the County.

The Family of GRANT of ROTHEMURCHUS.

The first of this family was (1) Patrick of Mukerach, son of John Grant and Margaret Steuart daughter of the Earl of Atholc. Upon the forfeiting of Shaw of Rothemurchus, Patrick got Rothemurchus and Balnespick, in exchange for Mukerach. He was succeeded by his eldest son (2) Duncan, who, having no issue, was succeeded by his brother (3) John, father of (4) James, who had three sons, viz. Patrick, Collonel William, and Mr John who died a batchelor. Collonel William purchased the lands of Ballendalach, and was father of Alexander, and of James now of Ballendalach. (5) Patrick had three sons, viz. Patrick of Tullochgrue, Captain John who died a batchelor, and (6) James the eldest son, father of (7) Patrick now of Rothemurchus,

Rothemurchus was by King Alexander II. anno 1226, granted to Andrew Bishop of Moray, for a forrest, in exchange for other lands, (*Appendix*, N° XII.). And Bishop Andrew mortified it to the Cathedral of Elgin, for furnishing lights and candles (*Appendix*, N° XIII.). The Shaws and the Cummings had warm and bloody combats about this possession and Duchus of Rothemurchus. The pincipal seat was a fort in a loch, called *Loch an clan*, the walls whereof do still remain. And this leads me to give some account of

The

The Family of SHAW of ROTHEMURCHUS.

It is the general tradition, that the SHAWS are descended of Macduff Earl of Fife. Sir George MacKenzie, in his *Alphabetical manuscript of Genealogies*, says, "That Sheach or Shaw, son of MacDuff, was progenitor of this name." Sir Robert Sibbald dedicates his *Modern History of Fife* "To the Earl of Wemyss, Lord Elcho, and to the Nobility and Gentry of the name of Wemyss, Shaw, Toshean, Duff, Douglas, Lesley and Abernethy, descended of the Clan MacDuff." Mr Nisbet, in his *Marks of Cadency*, writeth, "That the Shaws are said to be descended of a younger son of MacDuff Earl of Fife." The Bishop of Carlyle, in his *Scottish Historical Library*, says, "I have seen a treatise of the origin and continuance of the Thanes and Earls of Fife sirnamed MacDuff, of whom the families of MacIntosh, Wemyss, Shaw, and Duff are descended." Let me add, that Dr Abercrombie, in his *Martial Atchievements*, observeth, that King Malcolm Canmore rewarded those who had contributed to his Restoration, from the names of which, or lands given to them, many ancient families have their sirnames, and particularly Gordon, Seaton, Lesley, Calder, Shaw, Strachan, Mar, &c.

These hints are sufficient to show the antiquity of this name, and their descent from MacDuff.

I see no reason to doubt, that the Shaws in the South and in the North were originally the same. But at what time they settled in the North I cannot determine. The Lord Lyon's Records bear, that Farquhardson of Invercauld (descended of Shaw of Rothemurchus) carries the Lyon of MacDuff as paternal arms; and a canton dexter, charged with a hand holding a dagger, point downwards; in memory of Shaw of Rothemurchus assisting in cutting off the Cummines. Unvaried tradition likewise beareth, that Shaw Corfhiaclach, *i. e. Buck-toothed*, of Rothemurchus, was Captain of the XXX Clan Chattan, in the memorable

memorable conflict againſt XXX Clan Cays, on the Inch of Perth, anno 1396, and that the Shaws poſſeſſed Rothemurchus long before that time; and ſo I may call it probable, that they ſettled in the North in the beginning at leaſt of the 14th Century.

The Lands of Rothemurchus having been granted, by King Alexander II. to Andrew Biſhop of Moray, annno 1226, *(Appendix, Nº XII.)* were held off the Biſhops in Leaſe, by the Shaws during a hundred years without diſturbance: But, about the year 1350, Cummine of Strathdallas having a Leaſe of theſe Lands, and unwilling to yield to the Shaws, it came to be decided by the Sword; and (1) James Shaw, Chief of the Clan, was killed in the Conflict. James had married a Daughter of Baron Ferguſon in Athole, and his Son (2) Shaw, called *Corfiachlach*, as ſoon as he came of age, with a body of Men, attacked Cummine, and killed him, at a place called to this day *Lagna-Cuminach*. He purchaſed the Freehold of Rothemorchus and Balineſpic; and by a daughter of MacPherſon of Clunie, had ſeven Sons, James the eldeſt, and Farquhar Anceſtor of the Farquharſons, &c. Shaw commanded the XXX Clan Chattan on the Inch of Perth, anno 1396, and dying about 1405, his Grave-ſtone is ſeen in the Church-yard. (3) James brought a Company of his Name to the Battle of Hardlaw, anno 1411, where he was killed. His Son, by a Daughter of Inveretie, (4) Alexander Kiar, by a daughter of Stuart of Kinchardine, had four Sons, of whom Dalc, Tordarroch, and Delnafert, are deſcended; and (5) John, by a Niece of MacIntoſh, was Father of (6) Allan, who, by a Daughter of the Laird of MacIntoſh, had (7) John Father of (8) Allan, who, having barbarouſly murdered his Step-Father Dallas of Cantray, was juſtly forfeited, and the Laird of Grant purchaſed the forfeiture about anno 1595. The Arms of Shaw are: Or, a Lion Rampant, Gul. Armed and Langued Az; a Fir-tree growing out of a Mount Prop. in Baſe; and, in a Canton Arg, a Dexter-hand Coup'd graſping a dagger, Gul.

FAR-

FARQUHARSON of INVERCAULD.

FARQUHAR, second son of Shaw of Rothemurchus, was Forrester to the Earl of Mar, about anno 1440; and, by a daughter of Robison of Lude, was father of (2) Donald, who, by a daughter of Calvene, had (3) Farquhar Beg, who married a daughter of Chisholm of Strathglass, and had (4) Donald, who married Isabel only child of Stuart of Invercauld and Aberarder, and by her obtained these lands, anno 1520: His son (5) Finlay More (from whom they are called *Clan Fhinlay*) was killed in the battle of Pinky, bearing the Royal Standard 1547. By a daughter of Garden of Balchoric, he had seven sons, of whom several respectable Families are descended. His eldest son (6) William had no Issue, and was succeeded by his brother (7) Robert, who married a daughter of Inverchroskie, and had (8) John, who, by a daughter of Gartley, had a Son (9) Robert, who married Anne daughter of Erskine of Pittodrie, and had Robert and Alexander. (10) Robert had no Male Issue, and was succeded by his brother (11) Alexander, who married a daughter of MacIntosh of that Ilk, and had William and John. (12) William died unmarried, and was succeeded by his Brother (13) John, who died in 1756; by Margaret daughter of Lord James Moray of Doualliebrother to the Marquis of Athole, he had James, and Anne married to Æneas MacIntosh of that Ilk. (14) James married Emilia, daughter of Lord George Moray, son of John Duke of Athole, and by her has Issue.

Invercauld bears Quarterly. 1 and 4, Or, a Lion Rampant, Gul. Armed and Langued Az. 2 and 3 Arg; a Fir-tree growing out of a Mount in Base seeded Prop. And on a Chief Gul. the Banner of Scotland displayed: And in a Canton, a Dexter-hand Couped Fessways, holding a Dagger point downward. Crest, A Lyon issuant Gul. holding a Sword in his Dexter-paw, hilted and pomilled, Or. Supporters, Two Cats Saliant. Motto. FIDE ET FORTITUDINE.

Having

Having described the country of Strathspey, I go up the river Spey, and enter into

BADENACH,

So called from *Badan*, a Bush or Thicket, because it was anciently full of wood. I cannot trace the possessors of this country higher than to the Cummines Lords of Badenach, who, I doubt not, were Lords of it in the 12th or beginning of the 13th Century. Upon their being forfeited by King Robert Bruce, Badenach made a part of the Earldom of Moray, granted to Sir Thomas Randolph, anno 1313 (*Appendix*, N° I.). The Earldom reverting to the Crown on the death of John Randolph, anno 1346, without issue male, George Dunbar Earl of March had, at least, the title of Earl of Moray, in right of his mother Agnes Randolph sister and heir of Earl John Randolph. And when King Robert II. granted the Earldom of Moray to John Dunbar, he excepted Badenach, Lochaber, and the castle of Urquhart out of the grant. The said King Robert, anno regni 1mo 1372, granted the sixty Davachs of Badenach to his son Alexander and his heirs, which failing, to his brother David and his heirs (*Rot. Robert* II.). Lord Alexander died anno 1394, without lawful issue: David likewise left no son, and the Lordship of Badenach remained in the Crown, till it was given to the Earl of Huntley, after the battle of Brechin anno 1452, in whose family it continueth. And because this country is mainly possessed by the MacIntoshes and MacPhersons, I shall here give a succinct account of these two Families and Clans.

MACINTOSH.

No one questions, that this is a branch of the MacDuffs Thanes and Earls of Fife. *Tosch* in Irish (from *Tus*, i. e. First or Chief) signifies Thane, and *MacIntosh* is the Thane's son. (1) Shaw MacDuff, second son of Duncan fifth Earl of Fife, who died anno 1154, is
said

said to have had a command in the army of Malcolm IV. against the Moravienses about 1160, and that, upon quelling that rebellion, the King made him Governor of Inverness, and granted him some lands near to it. This is highly probable; for when Prince Henry, only son of King David I. died anno 1152, and the King declared Malcolm the son of Henry successor to the Crown, he committed him to the foresaid Duncan Earl of Fife, to bring him through all the countries, and to have him proclaimed in all the Burroughs, Heir of the Crown *(Chron. Mil.)*. In this tour, Shaw MacDuff accompanied his father, and got into the favour of the young Prince, who afterwards preferred him as said is. Shaw fixing his residence in the North, and being called, *Mac-an-toshich*, i. e. " The Thane's son," this became the sirname of the family. By Giles Montgomery he left issue, (2) Shaw, who was thirty-six years Governor of the Castle of Inverness, which he bravely defended against the Lord of the Isles. By a daughter of Sir Hary Sandyland, he had Ferquhar, William, and Edward Ancestor of Monivard, and died 1209. (3) Ferquhar had no Issue, and was succeeded by (4) Shaw, son of William, and, by a daughter of the Thane of Calder, was father of (5) Ferquhar, who fought at the head of his Clan against Haquin King of Norway, in the battle of Largs, anno 1263. By Mora, daughter of Angus Oig Lord of the Isles, he had (6) Angus, who married Eva, the only child and heir of Dowal Dàl, Chief of the Clan Chattan, 1292. By her he obtained the lands of Locharkeg, Glenluy, and Strathlochie, which remained with the Family, till they were sold to Lochiel in 1665. Argyle paid the purchase-money, and is Superior of those Lands.

In consequence of this marriage, the Lairds of MacIntosh were (in Royal Charters, Royal Missives, Indentures, Contracts of Amity, &c. of which I have perused many) designed " Captains of Clan Chattan." In a bond of Man-rent, dated

4th

4th April 1609, and granted by the MacPherfons to MacIntofh, they name him, "Our Chief, as it was of auld, according to the Kings of Scotland, their Gift of Chieftanry of the hail Clan Chattan." *(pen. MacIn.).* But if there were fuch a Royal Gift, it is now loft. Yet it cannot be doubted, that the MacIntofhes, MacPherfons, MacBeans, Shaws, MacGilivraes, MacQueens, MacPhails, Smiths, MacInteers, &c. as one Incorporated Body, did own MacIntofh for their Captain or Leader, for about 300 years. In thofe times of barbarity and violence, Small Tribes or Clans found it neceffary, to come under the patronage of more powerful Clans. Thofe Incorporated Tribes forefaid, went by the general name of Clan Chattan; yet every Tribe retained its own Sirname and Chief.

Angus, by his Wife Eva, had a numerous Iffue, and dying, about 1346, his eldeft Son (7) William, married a Daughter of Rory More MacLeod of Lewis, and had (8) Lachlan, who fought the Camerons at Invernahavon *(Vid. Mil. Hift.),* and by a Daughter of Frafer of Lovate, had (9) Ferquhar: This Gentleman, being of a peaceable difpofition, lived a private life, and refigned the Chieftanry and Fortune in favour of his Uncle (10) Malcolm Beg, who brought a Battalion to the Battle of Harlaw anno 1411, and for his conduct there obtained the Lands of Braelohaber, in 1447. By a daughter of MacDonald of Moidart, he had Duncan, William of Thylachie, and Lachlan Badenach, and died 1457. (11) Duncan, by Florence Daughter of MacDonald Earl of Rofs, had (12) Ferquhar, who died 1514, without Male Iffue, and was fucceeded by (13) William, Son of Lachlan Badenoch, who married Ifabel MacNivan, Heirefs of Dunachtin: He was murdered in Invernefs, by one of his unruly Clan, in 1515; of him came Strone. His Brother (14) Lachlan Oig fucceeded, and married Jean, Heirefs of Line of Gordon of Lochinvar, and was barbaroufly murdered by fome of his Clan, in 1524. His Son
(15) William

(15) William married a Daughter of Findlater, and was treacherously murdered in Huntley-castle by that Earl's orders, anno 1550, for which Huntley paid a great Assythment or Compensation in Lands. His Son (16) Lachlan More was a Gentleman greatly respected, for his behaviour in the Battle of Glenlivat, 1594 *(Vid. Mil. Hist.)*. He married a Daughter of Lord Kintale, and died 1606; Of his Sons are descended the Families of Borlum, Aberarder, and Corrybrugh. His eldest son Angus went abroad to travel, and died in Padua anno 1593; by a daughter of the Earl of Argyle, he left a son, (17) Sir Lachlan, who was, for some time, a Gentleman of the Bed-Chamber to Prince Charles: He married a daughter of the Laird of Grant, and died in 1622, leaving two sons, William and Angus of Daviot. (18) William, by a daughter of Graeme of Fintrey, had a son, and dying in 1660, (19) Lachlan married the daughter of Lindsey of Edzel, and dying in 1704, his son (20) Lachlan died in 1731 without Issue, and was succeeded by (21) William son of Lachlan of Daviot. This Gentleman served some years in the army, and was finely accomplished, and dying in 1740 without Issue, was succeded by his brother (22) Angus, who married a daughter of John Farquharson of Invercauld, and died in 1770 without Issue: He was succeeded by his nephew Æneas, son of Alexander third son of Lachlan of Daviot.

For arms, MacIntosh taketh quarterly. 1. Or, a Lyon rampant Gul. for MacDuff. 2. Arg. a Dexter hand couped sessways, grasping a man's heart in pale Gules. 3. Az. a Boar's head couped, Or. for Gordon of Lochinvar. 4. Or. a Lymfad; her oars in Saltire erected, Sab. for Clan Chattan. Supporters, two wild Cats proper. Crest, a Cat saliant as the last. Motto. TOUCH NOT THE CAT BUT A GLOVE.

MACPHERSON.

An account of the original of the Clan Chattan and MacPherfons is publifhed in the *Dictionaries of Collier, Moreri,* &c. too long to be tranfcribed here. I am forry the author of it difcovereth more vanity than Hiftorical knowledge. His fetching the Clan Chattan from Germany, becaufe Tacitus mentions the Catti in that country, is a poor playing with the gingle of words. The marrying *Gillicatan-more* to the fifter of Brute King of the Picts, is mere vanity, without any foundation. The making the anceftor of the Keiths, to have ferved King Kenneth II. in overthrowing the Picts, is an unpardonable anachronifm; for the Picts were overthrown by Kenneth, about anno 842, and the anceftor of the Keiths was not heard of before the Battle of Barry anno 1010. And the fending one of the Clan on a pilgrimage through a great part of Europe and Afia, and then making him King of Leinfter in Ireland, is fuch Knight errantry, as none but the Irifh fhould commit to writing, and yet not one of their Hiftorians mentioneth it.

It is to me probable, from the names *(Muiroch, Ewan, Colum, Gilicolum, &c.)* fo frequent among the Clan Chattan, that they came originally from Ireland, and either took their name from, or gave their name to *Catav,* now Sutherland; their ancient refidence. Sutherland, in Irifh *Catav,* and Caitnefs, *Gualav,* were antiently called, *Catenefiacis et ultra montem,* viz. Ord. In Irifh *Cad* is *altus,* High; and *Guael,* is *humilis,* Low, Plain. And fo *Catav* (from *Cad,* High, and *Taobh* or *Tav,* a Side) is the high fide of the Ord; and *Gaul av* is the low fide of it. The very nature and figure of the country confirmeth the Etymology: And the inhabitants might have taken their name, *Catach,* from the country. Or, if they were fo called from Saint Cutan or Cathain, an ancient Scottifh Saint to whom the Priory of *Ardchallan* in Lorn was dedicated, and the Priory of Searinch in Lewis *ubi extreie Sancti Cattani affervantur,* "Where the remains of St Cat-
"tan

" tan are preferved." *Keith. Catal.* they might have given their name to the country. In this I fhall not determine, and fhall only add, that their antiquity in Catav was fuch, that I have not heard of any inhabitants in that country before them.

At what time, and upon what occafion, they removed from Caithnefs and Sutherland into Lochaber, I find not. The current tradition is, that they were expelled, becaufe Gillicattan, their Chief, difobeyed a call to attend the royal ftandard, probably in the beginning of King Malcolm II.'s reign, which commenced anno 1004, and who then called his fubjects into the field againft the invading Danes. The conjecture feemeth to be favoured by this, that their chief was commonly called *Gillicatan-more o' Gualav*, i. e. " The Great Gillicattan from Caithnefs," implying, that he came, or was driven from Caithnefs.

From Gillicattan More, fome of them are called MacGillichattans. The general name is Catenach: from Muirach, they are termed Clan Mhuirach, and from Gillicattan Clerach Parfon of Kingufie, they go now in Badenoch by the name of MacPherfon. The MacBains, MacPhails, Catteighs are branches of the old Clan Chattan; and the Kieths are likewife faid to have defcended from them. At what time they came from Lochaber into Badenoch, I find not. Surely it was not all at one time, and probably the forfeiture of Cummine Lord Badenoch by King Robert Bruce, made room for them in that country.

It is the common Tradition, that Gili-Cattan-More lived in the reign of King Malcolm II. Cent. XI.: and the moft probable account I find of his Defcendents, for about 200 years, is as follows. (1) Gili-Cattan More was Father of (2) Dougal, Father of (3) Gili Cattan and David Dow Anceftor of Invernahavon. Gili Cattan was Father of (4) Muirach More, who had two Sons, Kenneth and Gili-Cattan Clerach. (5) Kenneth had no Iffue, and was fucceeded by his Brother (6) Gili Cattan Clerach Parfon of Kingufie, who refigned his Pafloral Charge, married

married, and became Chief of the Clan: He had two Sons, Gili-Patrick, and Ewan-Bane. (7) Gili-Patrick was Father of (8) Doual Dâl, whose only Child Eva married Angus MacIntosh of that Ilk, about anno 1292. The direct Male Line failing thus, the Chieftanry divolved to the descendents of Ewan Bane, second Son of Gili Cattan Clerach. Ewan Bane died about anno 1296, leaving three Sons, *viz.* Kenneth Ancestor of Clunie, John Ancestor of Pitmean, and Gelis the first of the Family of Inveralbie. These and their Descendents assumed the Surname of MacPherson, from the said Parson of Kingusie; but the Posterity of David Dow of Invernahavon were called *Clan Dabhi* in my time.

In the 14th Century, the Clan Chattan possessed the greatest part of the Country of Badenoch, and lived happy and respected: But a fatal discord, between two of the Tribes, broke their harmony, and occasioned the Memorable Combat on the North Inch of Perth, in the year 1396. The Earls of Crawford and Moray, by Commission, attempted to reconcile them, but without success: wherefore they proposed, that thirty on each side should decide the Quarrel by the Sword, in presence of the King and Nobility. (Who the Combatants were, and what the difference between them was, see *Mil. Hist. Pag.* 216.) The Parties, like the Roman Horatii and Curatii, accepted the motion: but when they were met on the day appointed, one of the Clan Chattan had absented through fear, and a smith, named Henry Wyne, offered to supply his place for a Crown of Gold, about 7sh. 6d. value. The conflict was fierce and desperate: Of the Clan Cay twenty nine were killed, and the thirtieth escaped by swimming the Tay: and of the Clan Chattan nineteen were killed. The victory was much owing to Henry Wyne, which gave rise to the Proverb, "He did very well for his own hand, as Henry Wyne did." His Posterity

(called

(called *Sliochd a Gune Chruim*, the Issue of the Stooping Smith) were incorporated with the Clan Chattan.

The Family of Clunie, from Ewan Bane, continued the Succession, but I cannot pretend to give the names of the Representatives before the last Century. I know, that, in 1660, Andrew was Laird of Clunie, whose Son Ewan was Father of Duncan, who died in 1722, without Male Issue. The Direct Line thus failing, the nearest Collateral Male was Lachlan MacPherson of Nuid (Son of William, who was Son of Donald, whose Father John was Brother to the foresaid Andrew of Clunie). Lachlan, in 1722, had the Designation of Clunie, and, by Jean Daughter of Sir Ewan Cameron of Lochiel, was Father of a numerous Issue, of which the Eldest Son, Ewan of Clunie, rashly engaged in the Rebellion 1745, and was forfeited. He left a Son, by Janet Daughter of Simon late Lord Lovate, called Duncan.

Clunie beareth for arms. Parted per Fess. Or. & Az. a lymphad, sails trussed and oars in action, of the first. In the dexter chief point, a hand couped fessways, grasping a dagger, point upward, Gul. And in the sinister, a cross croslet fitchie, of the last. Crest, a Cat sejant proper. Motto, TOUCH NOT THE CAT GLOVELESS.

The Parish of ALVIE.

The parish of Alvie, i. e. *Rockie*, from *Ail*, a Rock. It lieth, a part on each side of Spey. On the West side, it extendeth from Craig Elachie seven miles in length, and little above half a mile in breadth, from the river to the hills. The church standeth near to a mile from the North end of the parish, in a peninsula of a lake called Loch-Alvie, six miles South of Duthel, a mile and a half West of Rothemurchus, two miles and a half North of Inch, and six miles North of Kingussie.

Kingussie. In the North end is Lenevulg, the property of the Duke of Gordon. Next Southward is Delraddie, a part of the estate of MacPherson of Invereshie. Below Delraddie on the side of the river, is Kinrara, for some generations the heritage of MacIntosh of Kinrara and Balnespic, and now a wadset pertaining to Rothemurchus. South from Delraddie are Dillafoure, Pitcherin and Pitaurie: The first, a feu property of MacPherson of Dillafoure: The other two, the property of the Duke of Gordon. Farther South is the Barony of Dunachten, the property of the Laird of MacIntosh, which came into his family, about anno 1500, by marrying the heiress. Here MacIntosh had a seat; but being burnt in 1689, it has not been rebuilt. Next thereto are the lands of Rait, the seat of Shaw MacIntosh of Borlum, a feu holding of the Duke of Gordon, as all Badenoch doth. On the East side of the river, the parish extendeth a mile and a half on the river, and about three miles into Glenfeshie S. E. all the property of the Lairds of MacIntosh and Invereshie. Of the woods in this and the other parishes I speak elsewhere, and so go on to

The Parish of KINGUSIE and INSH.

I begin with INSH, which is situated below Kingussie, on the the East side of the river. Here the river passeth through a lake one and a half mile long, and near to a mile broad, called Loch-Insh: And when the river swelleth, a branch of it runneth on each side of a small hill on which the church standeth, thereby making it an Island; and hence is the name *Insh*. The church is two and a half miles south of Alvie, and 3 and a half miles north of Kingusie. This parish extendeth near to 3 miles every way, betwixt the waters of Feshie and Tromie. Feshie falleth from the Grampian hills, and being swelled by many brooks,

after

after a course of about 15 miles, dischargeth into Spey below the church, and it boundeth the parishes of Alvie and Insh. Tromie likewise runneth out of the Grampian hills a course of about 14 miles, and falleth into Spey, a mile north of Ruthven, and boundeth the parish of Insh to the South. All betwixt these two rivulets is the property of George MacPherson of Invereshie, Chief of one of the principal Tribes of that name. Close by the church of Insh, are the lands of Balnespick, holding of Grant of Rothemurchus, which had been the property of MacIntosh of Kinrara and Balnespick, but were sold to Invereshie about the year 1749. An half mile up the water of Feshie, is the seat of the proprietor, who has a salmon-fishing on Loch Insh, and a passage-boat on Spey at the church.

The parish of KINGUSSIE on the East side of Spey, stretcheth about 6 miles from Tromie to Truim. This rivulet riseth in the hills of Drumochter, and running from S. W. to N. E. betwixt the parishes of Kingussie and Laggan, after a course of about 15 miles, falleth into Spey at Invernahaven. Near the mouth of Tromie is Invertromie, the heritage, for several generations, of a branch of the MacPhersons of Pitmean, and in 1758 purchased by John MacPherson of the family of Invereshie. A mile up the river is Ruthven, a small village having a post-office. Close by it, is a green mount jutting into a marshy plain; the mount about 20 yards high, and the area on the top of it about 120 yards long and 60 broad. Here Cummine Lord Badenoch had his seat and fort, (See my Mil. Hist. p. 208.) The lands of Ruthven are the Duke of Gordon's property. Next up the river is *Neid*, a part of Clunie's estate, now forfeited to the Duke of Gordon his superior, by the Clan-Act. At the mouth of Truim, is Invernahaven, the heritage of John Macpherson Chief of the Clan Dabhi or Davidsons. And two miles up the side of

Truim

Truim are *Phoiness* and *Etterish*, the property of a Gentleman of the Family of Invereshie. I pass to

The West-side of the River, on which the Parish extendeth four and a half Miles. The Church standeth near the North-end, 6 Miles South of Alvie, and near to 15 North of Laggan. The Lands are Laggan, Ardbrylach, Kingusie, Pitmean, Strone and Bealids; and are the property of the Duke of Gordon. Coulinlin is the heritage of Donald MacPherson, of the Family of Clune. Clune is now the Feu-hold of Andrew MacPherson of Benchar, holding of MacIntosh as Superior, and this Gentleman holdeth Benchar in Mortgage off MacIntosh of Borlum.

The Parish of LAGGAN.

This Parish lieth on the Head of the River Spey, and extendeth on both sides of the River, about ten miles in length. In the North-end it is about 4 miles broad, besides Delwhinny that is two miles in the hill of Drumochter.

On the West-side of the River, 6 miles above Kingusie, stood the fine modern house of Clunie, which was burnt in 1746; and the estate of Clunie forfeited, by the Clan-act, to the Duke of Gordon Superior. Six miles above Clunie is Garva, at the foot of the hill *Coryerack*, where the military-road leadeth to Fort Augustus. At Garva there is a stone-bridge over Spey, and beyond it there is no land inhabited on the West-side of the River, which hath a course of about 8 miles further into the hills.

On the East-side of the River, 6 miles above the Water of Truim, is *Strathmasie*, the heritage of MacPherson of Strathmasie. And here the Rivulet of Massie falleth into Spey. Four miles farther South is *Laggan*, likewise *Aberarder*, and other lands pertaining to the Laird of MacIntosh, and Galagie pertaining to the laird of Grant. All the rest of the parish is the property of the Duke of Gordon. The church of Laggan standeth here at the North end of Loch Laggan. But, as this is beyond the bounds of the province of Moray, and the river of *Spey* issuing out of Lochlaggan runneth into Lochaber, I here break off. And having run over the valley of Spey that covereth the whole province, I now return to the mouth of that river, to describe the Low Country; And begin with

The Parish of SPEYMOUTH.

This parish extendeth in length, four miles and a half, from the sea southward on the bank of the river, and generally it is but a half mile broad, except the south end that is a mile in breadth. The church standeth near the river, over against the church of Bellie, and about a half mile west from it; three miles east from Urquhart, and three miles and a half north from Dundurcrofs. Till the year 1731 *(vid. Ecclef. Hist.)* this made two parishes, viz. Essil and Dipple. Essil *(Iafal,* i. e. Low) in the north end. At the mouth of the river is the harbour and town of *Germagh*. The harbour receiveth no ships of burden, being chocked with sand and shut up by a barr. The town of Germagh is a Burgh of Barony, consisting of about sixty dwelling houses. It was long the property of the family of Innes, and now belongs to the Earl Fife, and feued out to small heritors. South of the town are the lands of Essil, for several generations the heritage of Geddes of Essil, disponed in 1698 to Duff of Dipple, father of the late Earl Fife. Dipple *(Dubh* or *Du-pol,* i. e. The Black or Deep Pool, viz. in the River) was church land, for some time the heritage of the family of Innes, and now of Earl Fife. The Duke of Gordon has a farm or two in this parish, and for the space of about four miles above the mouth of the river is one of the best

salmon

salmon fishings in the kingdom, belonging to the Duke of Gordon, the Earl of Moray and Earl Fife.* West from Speymouth lieth,

The Parish of URQUHART.

This parish stretcheth upon the frith to the river Lossie four miles, and two miles in breadth. The church standeth near the south end three miles west from Speymouth, one mile north from Langbryde, and three east from Elgin; the south and east parts are called the Lordship of Urquhart. They were a part of the lands of that Priory, and were created into a temporal Lordship, in favour of the son of Lord Winton Chancellor of Scotland and Earl of Dunfermline, anno 1591. *(Vid. Eccles. Hist.)* and were purchased by the Duke of Gordon about the year 1730. North from the church is the barony of Innes. The house of Innes is a fine modern building, surrounded with gardens, inclosures and planting. In the year 1737, it was all consumed by Lightning, but is now for the most part repaired and well finished. West of Innes is the barony of Leuchars. This was anciently a part of the Earldom of Moray, and came to Sir Alexander Dunbar of Westfield, as a part of his patrimonial estate. About the 1570, a daughter of Westfield, married to Innes of Crombie, brought Leuchars, and a half coble of fishing on the Spey, into the family of Innes; and now it is the heritage of Captain John Innes a branch

---

* The Duke of Gordon's fishing, is partly a perquisite of the Lordship of Urquhart, and partly purchased from Cumine of Ernside. The Earl of Moray's fishing formerly belonged to the Bishop of Moray, and came to the Regent Earl of Moray with the lands of Dipple, about anno 1567, from Patrick Hepburn the last Popish Bishop. And when the lands of Dipple were sold, the fishing was retained, and the Earl Fife's fishing came to him with the lands of Germach, from the family of Innes; and with the lands of Essil, from Geddes of Essil.

branch of the family. Here let me give some account of the name and family of Innes.

The Family of INNES.

This is a local firname. *Inis* in Irish fignifieth an Ifland, or a Peninfula, fuch as a part of the lands of Innes very probably was. The antiquity of this family, poffeffed of the barony of Innes for 600 years, appeareth from the original charter (Append. No. XIV.) Beroaldus Flandrenfis, who obtained this charter, either was a Flandrian, according to Sir James Dalrymple, or was one of the ancient Moravienfes, and having been for fome time in Flanders, was called the Flandrian. Thus the anceftor of Frafer of Foyer, having been for fome time in France, was called Hutcheon Francach. Many fuch inftances are obvious. I incline the rather to this opinion, becaufe the Morays, Sutherlands, Inneffes and Brodies have all the fame paternal arms, viz. ftars differing only in the tincture: Whence it is probable, they were anciently Moravienfes. The charter now mentioned was granted by King Malcolm IV; and though the original is loft, there is extant a tranfcript of it under the fubfcription of Gavin Dunbar clerk regifter in the reign of King James V. The form of this charter fheweth it ancient. Our Kings had at that time (and not before King William) ufed the plural, *Nos;* and ancient charters had no particular date; yet the date of this charter may be nearly fixed, by obferving that William Bifhop of Moray was made Legate, anno 1159, and died anno 1162, *(Chron. Melr.)* which bringeth the date within three years. King Alexander II. by his charter, 1ft January, anno regni 12mo, 1226, confirmed the lands of Innes, Waltero filio Joannis filii Berwaldi *(Pen. Inn.).* (4) Sir Alexander Innes fucceeded.

succeeded his father Walter, whose son (5) William was the first of this family, designed *Dominus de Innes* in an Indenture betwixt him and Simon prior of Pluscardine, in or before the year 1298. This son (6) William de Innes, is one of the witnesses to an agreement betwixt the town of Elgin and the monks of Pluscardine, dated the 4th of December 1330. He is therein designed *Baro de Innes*. His son (7) Robert de Innes is designed *Dominus ejusdem*, in a charter of King David the II. of the Forrestry of Boyne. This charter is without date; but it appears, by the other witnesses mentioned in it, to have been granted before the year 1360. His son (8) Alexander had three sons and a daughter: Sir Walter the eldest son died unmarried: John third son was, on January 23. 1406-7, consecrated Bishop of Moray, and died in April 1414. He advanced the rebuilding of the Cathedral, and began the building of the great Steeple. On his Tomb is this inscription: " Hic jacet Reverendus in Christo Pater et D. D. " Johannes de Innes, hujus ecclesiæ Episcopus, qui hoc no- " tabile opus incæpit, et per septennium potenter ædificavit." The daughter Giles was married to Ferquhard M'Intosh of that Ilk: The second son (9) Sir Robert Innes succeeded his brother. He married Dame Janet daughter and heiress of Sir David Aberkerder Thane of Aberkerder, now Marnoch, with whom he got a great accession to his estate. By this lady he had a son (10) Sir Walter Innes, who got a charter of confirmation of his mother's lands, from King James the II. anno 1450. He married, 1st, Eupheme daughter of Hugh first Lord Lovat, by whom he had three sons and two daughters: Sir Robert his heir: Beroaldus Innes of Hatton, from whom several of this name in Caithness are descended: His third son John was Bishop of Caithness: Isabel eldest daughter was married to James Dunbar Earl of Moray: Margaret the second to Patrick

trick Maitland of Netherdale. Sir Walter, by his second lady, had a son John Innes of Ardmilly, from whom several families of the name are descended. (11) Sir Robert Innes succeeded his father, and was infeft in all his father's lands anno 1456. He was a man of great personal bravery, and remarkably distinguished himself in the service of his King on many occasions, particularly at the battle of Brechin anno 1452. His lady was a daughter of the Baron of Drumlanrig, by whom he had three sons and two daughters: James his heir; Walter second son, ancestor of the families of Innermarkie, Balvenie, Coxtown, Innerbrakie, Ortown, Auchintoul, &c. Robert third son, progenitor of the Innesses of Drence: His eldest daughter Margaret, was married to Sir James Ogilvie, ancestor of the Earls of Findlater: The second was married to Barclay of Towie. (12) James Innes of that Ilk succeeded his father, to whom he was retoured heir anno 1464. He married lady Janet Gordon, daughter of Alexander Earl of Huntly, and with her had a numerous issue. The male issue of Alexander the eldest son failed in the person of his grandson John, who was succeeded by the grandson of (13) Robert Innes of Cromby, second son of James; which Robert was father of (14) James Innes of Rathmakenzie, who died fighting gallantly in the defence of his country at the battle of Pinkie, anno 1547; and was succeeded by his son (15) Alexander, who, by right of blood, as well as by mutual entail, succeeded to the representation and estate of this family. By his lady Isabella, daughter of Arthur Forbes of Balfour, and niece of John eighth Lord Forbes, he had a son (16) Robert Innes of that Ilk, who succeeded him; and by Elizabeth daughter of Robert third Lord Elphinston, he had two sons; Sir Robert his heir, and Sir John father of Sir Robert Innes of Muirton. (17) Sir Robert Innes of Innes was a great favourite of King Charles I. who created him a Baronet of NOVA SCOTIA, with destination

tion to his heirs male whatever, by Patent dated at Whitehall the 29th of May anno 1625. He afterwards fided with the Covenanters, and was appointed one of the Committee of Eftates anno 1641. He married Lady Grizel Steuart, daughter of James Earl of Moray, by whom he had three fons and five daughters: Sir Robert his heir: James of Lochnet fecond fon: William a captain in the guards: His eldeft daughter Elizabeth was married to John Urquhart of Craigtown: The fecond daughter Mary was married to James Steuart of Rofyth: His third was married to Sir Robert Innes of Muirton: His fourth Barbara to Robert Dunbar fheriff of Murray: His youngeft daughter was married to Alexander firft Lord Duffus. He died before the Reftoration, and was fucceeded by his eldeft fon (18) Sir Robert Innes of Innes, who married Mary daughter of James fifth Lord Rofs of Halkhead; by whom he had (19) Sir James Innes of Innes; who, by his lady Margaret daughter of Henry Lord Kerr, apparent heir of Robert Earl of Roxburgh, had his fon and fucceffor (20) Sir Henry Innes of Innes Baronet, who married Jean daughter of Duncan Forbes of Culloden Efq; by whom he had Sir Henry his heir, and John Innes of Inchbroom Efq; an officer in the army, and two daughters. (21) Sir Henry Innes of Innes Baronet married Anne daughter of Sir James Grant of Grant, by whom he had James his heir, and Robert who went to the Eaft Indies; He had alfo five daughters, Anne, Jean, Margaret, Sophia, and Ludovica. (22) Sir James Innes of Innes Baronet fucceeded his father Sir Henry. He is the fixth Baronet of this family; the twenty-fecond generation in a direct male-line from Beroaldus; and the fecond in precedency of the order of Baronets of NOVA SCOTIA.

This family had, for many years, a very opulent eftate. They were proprietors of the Baronies of Innes, Luchars, Kelmalemnock, in Moray county; Crombie, Rothmakenzie and Abercherder

cherder in Banff county, and much land in the County of Caithness. They early embraced the Reformation of religion, and William Laird of Innes was a Member of the Parliament in 1560, which established that happy change.

Sir James Innes (son of Sir Harry who died in 1762) sold the estate of Innes in 1767, to James Earl Fife.

The arms of Innes are, Argent, three stars, each of six points azure, with the badge of Nova Scotia in the center. Crest, Within an Adder disposed circleways, a castle triple towered Proper. Motto, PRUDENTIA ET VI. Supporters, two grey hounds Argent, each having a collar azure, charged with three stars of the first.

The Parish of LANBRIDE.

This parish is so called, either from the British, *Lhan* a church, and Bride or Brigida, i. e. St Brigida's church: Or (it being written in some ancient manuscripts, *Lambnabride*) because a Lamb, an emblem of meekness, was taken up and decorated with many ornaments on St Bride's day, as a memorial of her. This parish lieth south of Urquhart, and is a mile in length, and as much in breadth. The church standeth a mile south of Urquhart; two and a half miles S. E. from Elgin. In the east end of the parish is Pitnaseir, a part of the lands of the Preceptory of Maison Dieu, and now the heritage of Ogilvie of Pitnaseir, holding of the Town of Elgin. In the south end is Cotts, for some generations the heritage of a branch of the family of Innes, and in 1757 sold to Alexander Bremner merchant in Portsoy; holding of the Earl Fife. Below Cotts is Cockstoun, a barony that had long been the property of a branch of the family of Innes of Invermarkie. Cockstoun was created a Baronet in 1687, whose grandson Sir Alexander married the

heiress

heirefs of Barclay of Towie. The whole barony of Cockftoun now belongeth to the Earl Fife. Next to Langbride is,

The PARISH and ROYAL BURROUGH of ELGIN.

The meaning of the word ELGIN, is uncertain. In Britifh, *Hely*, i. e. To hunt, and *Fin*. i. e. *Fair*, q. a pleafant Forreft or Hunting place. Or, in Saxon, *Hely*, i. e. Holy, and *Dun*, a Hill. So *Helgun* (throwing out D to foften the found) is a Holy Hill. In the repofitory of the town, there is an old iron feal, with the infcription, *Helgun*. And at the end of the town there is a green mount called *Our Lady's hill*. Whether thefe hints may lead to the true etymology, I determine not. Paffing fuch curiofities,

The town ftandeth on the fouth bank of the river Loffie, in the Northern extremity of the parifh, on a plain, and the ground floppeth a little to the north. This fiuation is dry, pleafant, and well aired. The river has taken a winding turn northward from the centre of the town; whereas it antiently run by the foot of the gardens, and was the boundary of moft part of the cloffes on that fide. The town is one long ftreet from fouth weft to north eaft, croffed about the middle by the fchool wynd or lane to the fouth, and by Loffie wynd to the north. The Crofs ftandeth near to the middle, and near the eaft end ftandeth the Little Crofs; from which the High Street divideth into two branches, whereof one runneth due eaft, and the other leadeth north by eaft into the College. The High Street is, for the moft part, broad, beautiful, and well laid or cawfewayed, On the middle of the ftreet near the Crofs, ftandeth the High Church: A large and beautiful edifice, furpaffed by few in the kingdom. It ftandeth on two rows of arched pillars, and is fixty feet broad, and above eighty long within walls.

No church can be better furnished with seats and lofts of wainscot, and a pulpit of curious workmanship. It is lighted, besides several windows in the side walls, by a Venetian window of three arches in the western gavel, whereof the middle arch is about 15 feet high. It has four hearses of brass of curious work, each having 12 sockets, hung in the middle of the church. To the east end is joined, the Little Church, where worship is performed on week days, and betwixt these two churches is the steeple, with bells and a clock. The High Church, dedicated to St Giles, stood on two rows of massy pillars, and was all vaulted and covered with thick and heavy hewed stone instead of slate. On the 22d of June, being the Sabbath day, anno 1679, (the very day on which the battle of Bothwell-bridge was fought), when the people had returned from worship in the forenoon, the whole fabrick fell down, except the four pillars and vault that support the steeple. The rebuilding was finished in 1684, at the expence of the heritors of the parish, merchants and tradesmen of the town, and some private contributors. I have before me an account, charge and discharge, by James Winchester some time treasurer of the town, of what money he received, and how it was applied. The charge amounts to L. 1485 : 9 : 2 Scots, and the discharge to L. 4003 : 15 : 0 : Scots. The Laird of Grant, in payment of his stent, and by a voluntary contribution, furnished the whole timber necessary. The Laird of Muirton, besides his stent, contributed L. 266 : 13 : 4 : Scots. The Bishop contributed L. 133 : 6 : 8 : Scots, and Mr Alexander Todd minister at Elgin L. 66 : 13 : 4 : Scots. The kirk Session paid out of the penalties L. 151 : 6 : 8 Scots. Alexander Douglas of Spynie gave sixty bolls of victual, which, at L. 3 : 6 : 8 per boll, amounted to L. 200 Scots. The building of the pulpit (besides the price of the wainscot) cost L. 244, and the glazng of the windows and wire cost L. 400 Scots. I find nothing paid out of the common good of the Town.

Westward of the church standeth the tolbooth, ornamented with a high steeple vaulted to the top, and with bells and a clock. The Town is also accommodated with a large and well finished council chamber, a court house, and several strong prison rooms. The houses in the Town are all built of free stone, and many of them stand on pillars to the street. No Town can be better accommodated with gardens; and there are few closses but have draw-wells. This Town stood formerly farther to the west, than now it doth; for this *See my Military History*; and for the Cathederal, College and religious houses, *See my Ecclesiastical History*.

The Town standeth two miles north from the church of Bernie, one mile and a half south east of New-Spynie, and one mile and a half west from St Andrews. The parish to landward extendeth eighth miles from east to west, and three miles from north to south, and is situated on both sides of the river Lossie, which rising in the hills betwixt Knockando and Edinkyle runneth north three miles to the church of Dallas, thence turneth east about three miles, and then running north west, and watering the parishes of Bernie and Elgin, it passeth north, and after a course of about fifteen miles falleth into the frith. A half mile west from Elgin, there is a bridge of one large arch, built anno 1636; on the east side of the river, a mile from the town to the south, are the lands of Maine, the property of David Brodie, M. D. *. South east from Maine, are the

---

* The lands of Maine are a part of the ancient Earldom of Moray, and in 1471 were the property of Hays of Maine, of the Hays of Park and Locbloy, in which name they remained till some time after the 1621. I find Maine pertaining to the Laird of Innes in 1630, to Gordon of Maine in 1635, to Mr Joseph Brodie minister of Forres in 1654, to Alexander Brodie (son of Mr Joseph and grandfather to Brodie of Muir-house) in 1666. Then they came to Brodie of Lethem, who conveyed them to his nephew Thomas Brodie of Pitgavenie, and his son David sold them to Dr Brodie writer of Pitgvanie.

the lands of Langmorn, Whitewreath and Thornhill, formerly a part of the estate of Cockstown, and now the property of the Earl Fife. Further east is Blackhills, the heritage of Robert Innes of Blackhills.

On the west side of the river, is the barony of Mosstowie, in the north west end of the parish. The Town of Elgin are superiors of it, by the gift of King Alexander II. and now the Earl Fife has possession of it, by an adjudication against William Sutherland of Rosscommon, son of the late Lord Duffus, who held it in feu of the said Town. South east of Mosstowie is the barony of Milntown, which, for about an hundred years, was the heritage of a branch of the family of Brodie, and by Joseph Brodie of Milntown sold to Lord Braco, about 42 years ago. It was church land. South and east of Milntown, is the barony of Pittenrich and Monbein. Pittenrich was a part of the Earldom of Moray, and long the property of Douglas of Pittenrich, from whom the Earl of Moray purchased it, in the end of the last century. Monbein Upper and Nether, Bogside, the Haugh, &c. are the lands of the Preceptory of Maison Dieu, and hold of the Town of Elgin (Appendix, No. XXIV.) These baronies are now the property of Colonel Francis Stewart, uncle to the present Earl of Moray, except Upper Monbein, that pertaineth to baillie John Laing of Elgin. Westward lieth the Glen of Pluscarden, a valley extending three miles in length, and surrounded with hills, except to the east. It is (with the old mills near the town of Elgin) the property of the Earl Fife, except a few farms that Watson of Westertown holdeth of him in feu. Elgin giveth title to Braco, Lord Kinloss, and Earl of Elgin. Next up the river is,

The Parish of BIRNIE.

The parish of Birnie, anciently *Brenoth*, i. e. a Brae or High Land. It extendeth on the east bank of Lossie, three miles from north to south, and a mile from east to west. The church standeth near the river, a half mile above the north end of the parish, two miles south from Elgin, and four miles north east of Dallas. The whole parish was a part of the Bishop-lands of Moray; and when Patrick Hepburn, the last Popish Bishop, harboured his out-lawed nephew James Earl of Bothwell, anno 1566, he resigned these and other lands to the Earl of Moray Regent; and this parish is a part of the estate of the Earl of Moray, but held in feu by the Earl Fife, William King of Newmiln, Leslie of Finrossie, Coupland of Stackhouse, Duff of Tomshill, &c. But of late the Earl of Findlater has purchased, and is now sole proprietor of this parish.

The parish of DALLAS.

The parish of Dallas (*Dale-uis*, i. e. a Watered Valley) is surrounded with hills, except to the east towards Bernie, and a small portion of it to the north west. The church standeth on the west bank of Lossie, about four miles south west of Bernie, and near five miles north of Knockando. In the lower end of the parish is Killess, church land, for above an hundred years the heritage of Farquharson of Killess now extinct, and the lands are the property of the Earl Fife. Above this is the barony of Dallas. I know not, if from this valley Dallas of that Ilk had its name and designation. But I find Willielmus de Doleys, a witness to Hugo Herok's donation, anno 1286 (Appendix, No XVI.) " Johannes de Dolais, Thanus de
" Cromdale

"Cromdale anno 1367", (Appendix, No XX.) and Elizabeth, daughter and heiress of Archibald Dallas of that Ilk, with consent of her husband Duncan Fraser, in 1428, disponed her right of Dallas, to John Dallas of Easter Foord, her uncle, and the heir male of that family, who, in exchange of his lands in the south, got from David Earl of Crawford, the lands of Budzet in Calder parish anno 1440, *(Hist. Kelr.)*. This barony had been long the property of Cumine of Altyre, before it was sold to Sir Ludovick Gordon of Gordonstoun, in the end of the last century. Sir Robert Gordon, by ditching, draining and manuring, has improved this place, and built a convenient house, adorned with much planting. A mile north west from the church is Brenchil, some time the property of Grant of Brenchil, but lately of Cumine of Craigmiln, who, about anno 1752, sold it to James Grant of Knockando. I now return to the mouth of the river Lossie.

KENEDAR Parish.

The Parish of Kenedar *(Cean-edir,* i. e. a Point betwixt the Sea and the Loch) is two miles in length and one in breadth, westward from Lossie-mouth, betwixt the Frith and the Loch of Spynie. The church standeth near the centre, a mile east from Duffus; two and a half miles almost north from New Spynie, and two miles and a half north west from St. Andrew's. At the mouth of Lossie is a harbour, but so barred as to admit only small craft. It is the property of the Town of Elgin, where they have some fishing boats †. Next thereto are the lands of Kenedar, granted by Patrick Hepburn Bishop of Moray, to the
Earl

---

† The harbour of Lossie and the fishing houses, were the property of the family of Brodie, from whom the Magistrates of Elgin purchased it, and pay a small feu-duty. The harbour, which is now repairing, will be of great advantage to the merchants and other Inhabitants of the Town.

Earl of Moray Regent, and purchased from that family by the Lord Brodie. Here there is a fishing of white-fish at Stotfield. West from Kenedar is Drainie, once the heritage of Innes of Drainie now extinct, from whom Sir Robert Gordon purchased it anno 1636, as he did in 1638 the adjacent lands of Ettles from Innes of Pathnack, and in 1639 the lands of Plowlands, Ogstoun and Bellormie, from the Marquis of Huntley. Here is a fine seat called Gordonstoun, and a large modern house, with gardens, ponds and planting. At Cave-Sea there is a good white fishing.

The Family of GORDONSTOUN.

Sir Robert Gordon the first of Gordonstoun, was second son of Alexander 15th Earl of Sutherland. He was a gentleman much, and deservedly respected. In the year 1606, he was made Gentleman of the King's Bed-chamber, with a pension of L. 200 for life. In the year 1634, he was appointed one of the Lords of the Privy Counsel of King Charles I. and by the Parliament 1642, was made a Privy Counsellor for life. He married, anno 1613, Louisa, only child of John Gordon Lord of Glenluce and Dean of Salisbury, by whom he had, Ludovick his heir, Robert ancestor of the Gordons of Clunie, and two daughters; Katharine married to Colonel David Barclay of Urie, by whom she was mother of the ingenious Author of the *Apology for the Quakers*; and Jean married to Sir Alexander M'Kenzie of Coull. (2) Sir Ludovick Gordon of Gordonstoun Baronet, succeeded his father Sir Robert, anno 1656: He married Elizabeth, daughter and co-heiress of Sir Robert Farquhar of Manie, by whom he had Robert his heir, and three daughters; Lucy, married first to Robert Cumine of Altyre; secondly, to Alexander Dunbar of Kinloss; Katharine married to Thomas Dunbar

Dunbar of Grange; and Elizabeth married to Robert Dunbar of Westfield: They all had issue. (3) Sir Robert Gordon succeeded his father Sir Ludovick: By his lady, Elizabeth only daughter of Sir William Dunbar of Hemprigs, he had Sir Robert his heir, and a daughter Lucy married to David Scott of Scotstarvet, Esq; (4) Sir Robert succeeded his father anno 1701: He married Agnes, only daughter of Sir William Maxwell of Calderwood, by whom he had two sons, Robert and William, and a daughter Christian who died young. (5) Sir Robert Gordon, the fifth Baronet of Gordonstoun, succeeded his father Sir Robert: He is yet unmarried.

Arms of the family of Gordonstoun. Quarterly 1st and 4th grand quarters, the quartered coat of Gordon, 2d and 3d Gules, three stars Or, all within a border of the last. In the centre of the shield the badge of NOVA SCOTIA. Crest, a cat, a mountain saliant, argent, armed azure. Motto, SANS CRAINTE. Supporters, on the dexter, a deer hound argent, collared Gules, and thereon three buckles Or: And in the sinister, a savage wreathed about the head and middle, with laurel proper.

In the year 1621, Sir William Alexander of Menstry undertook to plant a colony in NOVA SCOTIA in North America, and was joined in that undertaking by the Earls Marshal, Melrose, and Niddisdale, Viscount Dupplin, and the Lairds of Lochinvar, Lesmore, Clunie and Gordonstoun. For their encouragement the King granted them severally, large districts of land in that country, and proposed to create a new title of honour that should be hereditary. This Order was erected in 1625, and Sir Robert Gordon is the First Knight of it, whose Patent beareth date at Whitehall, the 28. May 1625.

KNIGHTS.

KNIGHTS-BARONETS.

Having perused this Patent, I shall set down the Honours and Priviledges granted to *Knights Baronets* in Scotland, and, (1.) In all writings, they are stiled Knights and Baronets. (2.) In addressing them, they are called *Sir*. (3.) Their wives have the honour of *Lady*. (4.) They have precedency of all Knights, Lairds, Esquires and Gentlemen, except the King's Commissioners, Counsellors, and Knights Bannerets, dubbed in the field of war under the Royal Standard, REGE PRESENTE. (*N. B.* The Order of the Thistle or St. Andrew, was not revived at that time.) (5.) Their wives, sons, daughters, and sons wives, have precedency as themselves have. (6.) Their eldest sons, when twenty-one years of age, in their father's life, shall receive the honour of Knighthood, if they ask it, upon paying only the fees of the servants. (7.) In Royal armies, they shall have place near to the Royal Standard. (8.) No other degree of honour shall ever be created betwixt them and Lords, nor any degree equal to them, and inferior to Lords. (9.) The honour is by patent under the Great Seal, and hereditary as that of Peerage. (10.) There shall not be in Scotland, at any one time, more than 150 such Knights. (11.) They may bear the arms of NOVA SCOTIA in a Canton, or Shield of pretence: And the same enamelled on an oval Medal of Gold on their Breasts, hanging at a broad Orange Ribband round their Necks; as by Royal Warrant (Appendix, No LIII.) from King Charles I. dated at Whitehall 17. November 1629, and recorded in the Lord Lyon's Registers. (12.) They are allowed two gentlemen assistants of their body, *ad supportandum vetamen*; and at their funerals they are allowed one principal mourner, and four assistants.

Besides

Besides these priviledges common to the Order, Sir Robert Gordon's Patent beareth, That he is the First Knight in the Order, and that no one has had, or ever shall have the precedency of him. And he had 16,000 acres of land in Nova Scotia disponed to him and his heirs, with ample priviledges. The like priviledges had also the rest of the Baronets, till the French took possession of that Province; after which there is no mention of lands in any of the Patents.

The arms of this Order are. An Escutcheon Arg. charged with a saltire, Az. The Field and Cross of St. Andrew, the tinctures counterchanged, and thereon the Royal Arms of Scotland, with an Imperial crown above this last Shield. Motto, FAX MENTIS HONESTÆ GLORIA. This (without the Motto) may be placed in a Canton, or a Shield in Surtout.

DUFFUS Parish.

The Parish of Duffus (*Dubh-uis*, i. e. Black or Stagnating water) lieth west of Kenedar, between the Loch of Spynie and the Sea. It extendeth about three miles from east to west, and one mile from south to north. The church standeth in the east end, a mile west of Kenedar, one and a half mile north west of New Spynie, and three miles north east of Alves. The whole parish (except a small feu pertaining to Sutherland of Keam) is the property of the Duke of Gordon, Sir Robert Gordon of Gordonstoun, and of Alexander Dunbar of Thunderton. This last has far the greater share, and resides here. His seat is close by the church: The house is neat, convenient, and well finished; and the gardens, avenues and inclosures are

well

well laid out. A half mile south east stood the house and fort of old Duffus, *(Vid. Milit. Hist.)* and two miles west is the *Burgh-head,* a remarkable Danish Fort *(Vid. Milit. Hist.).* Close by which, is the village of the *Burgh-Sea,* where Gordonstoun and Thunderton have a good fishing of white fish, upon which the Town of Elgin have a servitude, whereby the fish must be brought to their market. Here about 300 people live by fishing, and have no corn land, and little garden ground. At this village there is a good harbour for small craft. And I cannot but observe, that the people on the coast westward having plucked up the bent-grass on some small hills, the loose sand is driven so thick by the west wind, that much land in Duffus and Gordonstoun has been covered by it: But of late years, there has not been much hurt done in this way, the Strata on these hills becoming probably more firm, and the sanded land is again tilled. In this parish there is much free stone, and rich quarries of lime stone. Before I describe the south-side of the Loch of Spynie, I shall take a view of the ancient

MORAYS of DUFFUS.

Duffus gave title to a Noble Lord, but is more remarkable for having been the seat of the principal Family of the ancient Moravienses. (1.) Friskinus, stiled *De Moravia,*[*] (for particular sirnames were not at that time fixed) was Dominus de Duffus, in the reign of King David I. *(Chart. Morav.)* His son (2) Willielmus *de Moravia* Filius Friskini had a charter from King William, about

---

[*] It is observed, that Sir Robert Douglas often calls this person *De Moravia;* but it is much doubted if he had any authority for calling him so. It is supposed, that he gave him this appellation, because his son William is called *De Moravia.*

about anno 1169, of the lands of Duffus, Roflile, Kintrae, Infkele, &c. " Quas terras, Pater fuus Frifkinus tenuit tempore " Regis David Avi mei" *(Ibid)*. He had feveral fons; as Hugh his heir, mentioned in a Charter by Richard Bifhop of Moray, to the Abbey of Kinlofs *(Ibid)*. Hugh † is fuppofed to have been anceftor of the Sutherlands, who dropt the name *De Moravia*, and affumed a firname from their country, for both Sutherland and Caithnefs were anciently called *Catanefia*, afterwards divided into *Auftralis* and *Borealis;* Sir John fheriff of Perthfhire, the undoubted progenitor of the family of Tullibardine, reprefented in the direct male-line by his Grace the Duke of Athole, who is the twentieth generation in defcent from this Sir John; Willielmus Filius Willielmi Frifkini, Dominus de Pettie, Brachlie and Boharm, and father of Walter of Pettie, of whom came Sir Andrew Moray Lord of Bothwell Governor of Scotland, who died anno 1338; and Sir John de Moravia, whofe reprefentative in the right male-line is Mr Moray of Abercairny; Andrew Bifhop of Moray; Gilbert Bifhop of Caithnefs; and Richard of Coulbin. (3) Hugh was father of (4) Walterus de Moravia, filius quondam Hugonis de Moravia, fo called in an agreement, anno 1266, with Archibald Bifhop of Moray, about a part of the wood and moor of Spynie. His fon (5) Frifkinus filius Walteri *(Ibid)* had two daughters coheireffes, viz. Hellen, married to Sir Reynold Cheyne, and Chriftine married to William de Federeth. The family of Cheyne of Duffus ended likewife in two daughters; viz. Mary married to Nicholas Sutherland, fecond fon of Kenneth Earl of Sutherland,

---

† Hugh, the anceftor of the family of Sutherland, was called Hugh Frifken; *(See Addition I Cafe for Laby Elizabeth Sutherland, page 8.)* It is doubted, whether he was the fon of William, or his brother, and father of the perfons after mentioned.

Sutherland, who was killed at Halidon hill anno 1333; and the other daughter married to John Keith, younger son to Sir Edward Keith Marshall of Scotland, and with her got Inverugie lands in Buchan, and a part of Duffus. This Duffus was divided into, the King's part, Duffus's part, and Marshall's part. Alexander Sutherland, grandson of Nicholas, married Morella the heiress of Chisholm of Quarrelwood, which greatly increased his fortune; and the family purchased Marshall's Third, and had an opulent estate. Alexander, the fifth in descent from him, was raised to the dignity of the Peerage, by the title of Lord Duffus, by King Charles II. 8. December 1650. James the second Lord, who died anno 1705, sold the greatest part of the estate to Archibald Dunbar of Thunderton, (a branch of the family of Kilbuiak and Hempriggs) whose grand-nephew now enjoyeth it. Kenneth, third Lord Duffus, who was a Commander in the Royal Navy in Queen Anne's time, in which station he signalized himself in several engagements, had the misfortune to enter into the Rebellion anno 1715, and was attainted. His grandson James Sutherland Esq; had it not been for the forfeiture, would have been the fifth Lord Duffus. He now represents that family.

The original arms of Moray are, Az. 3 stars. Arg. And of Sutherland, Gul. 3 stars. Or.

Arms of the family of Lord D U F F U S. Quarterly, 1st and 4th, Gules, three stars, Or. 2d, Azure, three cross crosslets fitched, Argent. 3d, Azure, a boar's head erazed, Argent. Crest, a Cat Sejant proper. Motto, W I T H O U T F E A R. Supporters, two Savages proper, each armed with a baton over his shoulder, and wreathed about the head and middle, Vert.

The Parish of St. ANDREWS.

St Andrews parish lieth north of the town of Elgin, on both sides of the river Lossie, about two and a half miles in length, and near a mile in breadth. The church standeth on the north bank of the river, one and a half mile east from Elgin, two miles E. S. E. from New-Spynie. This parish was formerly called, the Barony of Kilmalemnock, and was the heritage of Sir Gilbert Hay of the family of Lochluy or Park: Afterwards it came to the family of Innes. And Alexander of Innes, having killed a gentleman on the street of Edinburgh anno 1576, purchased a remission from the Regent Morton, at the expence of resigning this barony (which comprehended Pitgavenie, Bareflathills, Dunkentie, Kirkton, Fosterseat and Scotstonhill) in his favour *(M. S. Hist. of Innes.)*. East of the river, at the lower end is, Insh, pertaining to the family of Innes. Above which is Dunkentie, which once belonged to Alexander Gordon, son of Alexander of Strathdon, who, with his two sons, was killed in Glenavon, by a party of thieves about anno 16 . and the lands came to the family of Gordon. Dunkentie is now the heritage of John Innes of the family of Leuchars: And Fosterseat is the property of the Duke of Gordon. Farther south is Barmukatie, lately pertaining to a branch of the Dunbars, and now to George Duff Esq; the third son of the late Earl Fife. Above which is Linkwood, which pertained to the Gibsons, from whom it came to Dunbar of Bishopmiln, whose nephew, John Dunbar of Burgie, sold it lately to James Anderson Provost of Elgin, and his son Robert sold it in 1767 to the Earl of Findlater.

West of the river, at the lower end, is Pitgavenie, a part of the Bishop's lands. It was purchased by Alexander Brodie of Lethin,

Lethin, who, in 1657, difponed it in favour of a younger fon; and the male heirs failing, it was purchafed in 1747, from the co-heireffes, by Alexander Bremner merchant in Portfoy, from whom James Brander bought it.

Next above it, is Caldcotts, Kirktoun and a part of Newmiln, pertaining to Innes of Dunkintie; the other part of Newmiln belongeth to William King of Newmiln. Next weftward is,

The Parifh of S P Y N I E.

The parifh of Spynie, is fituated betwixt the river of Loffie, and that Loch to which it giveth name. It was formerly three miles in length; but now by drains and banks, it is much confined. At the eaft end it is near an Englifh mile broad, but narrower and of unequal breadth weftward. It abounds with Pykes or Gidds, and is in winter haunted by Swans, that yield fine diverfion in killing them. The Loch (except a few pits) in fummer is not above five feet deep, and might be eafily drained, could the gentlemen proprietors agree about the rich foil that would be recovered. The hard chinlie beach at the eaft end, makes it probable that once the fea flowed into the loch.

This parifh ftretcheth about three miles from eaft to weft, and one mile in breadth. The church ftood in the extremity to the eaft, and anno 1736 was tranfplanted to, and built at, Quarrelwood, and called New-Spynie. It is one mile and a half north weft from Elgin, about three miles eaft from Alves, and two miles weft north weft of St Andrews. This parifh was moft part Bifhop's land, and in the eaft corner, on the bank of the Loch of Spynie, ftood the Bifhop's palace. In 1590

Sir

Sir Alexander Lindsay, son of the Earl of Crawford, was created Lord Spynie, whose grandson dying 1670 without issue, the lands reverted to the Crown, and were granted to Douglas of Spynie, from whom the Barony was purchased by James Brodie late of Whitehill, and is now the property of James Brodie his grandson. But the castle and precinct (paying about L. 12 Sterling annually) belong to the Crown.

Next westward is Myreside, which lately pertained to Laurence Sutherland of Greenhall, and was purchased from him by the Earl of Findlater. Farther west is Finrossie, the property of a branch of the family of Lesly of Rothes, the first of which was Robert, fourth son to George 5th Earl of Rothes, by Margaret daughter of the Lord Crichton Chancellor of Scotland. Robert was succeeded in his lands of Finrossie, by his eldest son Robert; who, by Margaret daughter of Alexander Dunbar of Grange a Lord of Session, had Robert his successor, who married Isabel, daughter of Forbes of Blackston, by whom he had George, fourth of this family, laird of Finrossie, who married Mary, daughter of Bannerman of Elsick, but died without issue. I shall not dip into the question, Who was the true heir of Earl George, after the disinheriting the eldest son Norman; whether Andrew who succeeded, or the first mentioned Robert of Finrossie, for whom much may be said.

Westward is Quarrelwood, so called from a rich Quarry of free stone in the adjacent hill, which was once covered with a large oak wood, whereof there are yet some remains. In the year 1334, Sir Robert Lauder of Quarrelwood was Governor of the castle of Urquhart *(Abercrombie)*. His grandson, by his daughter and heir, Sir Robert Chisholm succeeded him, whose daughter and only child, Janet, was married to Hugh Rose of Kilravok

ravok anno 1334* *(MSS. Hist. Kilr.).* And John, brother to Sir Robert, succeeding in the estate, his grand daughter (heiress to his son Robert) married Alexander Sutherland of Duffus, and brought Quarrelwood, Kinsterie, Brightmonie, &c. into that family. Now Quarrelwood and its pertinents, are the property of the Earl Fife. Below Quarrelwood is *Kintrae (Cean-traidh,* i. e. the Head of the Strand or Shore, for it was the end of the loch) a part of the estate of Duffus, now pertaining to the Duke of Gordon. On Lossie side is Bishopmiln Barony, purchased by James Robertson late Provost of Elgin, from John Dunbar of Burgie, about 1752, and the late Earl of Findlater purchased it from Mr Robertson. Next up the river, is Moraystoun, purchased by Lord Bracco in 1756, from the heirs and creditors of Martin of Moraystoun. And further up the river is Aldruchtie, probably a part of the estate of Quarrelwood, and for generations pertaining to Nairn of Aldruchtie, but now to the Earl Fife.

Below Quarrelwood on the plain next to Duffus is Westfield, the seat of Sir William Dunbar of Westfield, from whose son-in-law, Captain Thomas Dunbar, Sir Ludovick Grant of Grant purchased the Barony of Westfield and his lands about Forres, anno 1767. The mention of the family of Westfield, leads me to speak of

The

---

* It is incredible, that Sir Robert Lauder should be Governor of the castle of Urquhart in the year 1334, when his great-grand-daughter was married to Kilravock. Abercrombie in his History Vol. II. page 38. in the life of King David II. calls him *Robert Lauder captain of Urquhart.*

The DUNBARS.

The name of DUNBAR is plainly patronimic, taken from Bár their progenitor, and Dunbar is, Bar's hill. The Highlanders do not use the word Dunbar, but *Barridh*, i. e. the Descendants of Bar. Our History favours this, and mentions Bar a general in King Kenneth MacCalpin's army about anno 842, who, from his name, called his residence Dunbar. In the battles of Cullen anno 961, and Mortlich anno 1010, Dunbar Thane of Lothian was a commander. Earl Patrick de Dunbar lived about anno 1061 *(Buchann. & Hume)*. And anno 1072 King Malcom III. gave to Gospatrick Earl of Northumberland, " Dunbar cum " adjacentibus terris in Lodonio" *(Sim. Dunelm.)*.

Of him came the noble family of the EARLS of DUNBAR and MARCH, in a direct line, to the year 1434, when Earl George was, in an arbitrary manner, forfeited, and the direct line became extinct, through the ambition of the rival house of Douglas. Of this great family came the Homes, Dundasses, &c. but the name was continued in the family of Moray.

John DUNBAR, (2d son of George eleventh Earl of March, who died anno 1416, whose mother was Agnes Randolph, daughter of Thomas Earl of Moray) married King Robert II.'s daughter, who, March 2d (anno regni 2*do*) 1372, gave the Earldom of Moray (except Badenoch, Lochaber and the castle of Urquhart) " dilecto filio nostro Joanni de Dunbar & Mariotæ Sponsæ ejus " filiæ nostræ charissimæ" *(Publ. Archiv.)*. Their sons were, Earl Thomas and Alexander of Frenderet. Earl Thomas, leaving no male issue, was succeeded by his nephew Earl James son of Frenderet, who married, 1st, Isabel daughter of Sir Walter Innes of Innes who brought him a son Alexander; and, 2dly, Janet Gordon daughter of Huntley, by whom

whom he had Janet, married to James second Lord Crichton, Lord Chamberlain of Scotland; and Elizabeth, married to Archibald brother to the Earl of Douglas. Earl James died about anno 1446, and his son ought to have succeeded him; but, because his mother Isabel Innes (who stood in the 4th degree to her husband) died before a dispensation was obtained, the power of the Douglasses got Alexander declared illegitimate, made his eldest sister renounce her right, and Archibald Douglas, husband of the younger sister, was made Earl of Moray anno 1446. Thus was Alexander, son of Earl James unjustly deprived: But, to make some compensation to him, he was knighted, made heritable sheriff of Moray, and got an opulent estate. And Archibald Douglas, having joined in his brother's rebellion, was slain in the field of battle, and the Earldom of Moray was forfeited, and annexed to the Crown anno 1455, where it remained, till King James IV. bestowed it on his bastard son James, by Jean daughter of John Lord Kennedy in the year 1501. Who dying in the year 1544 without male issue, it again reverted to the Crown, where it remained till the 10th of February 1562, when Queen Mary conferred it on her base brother James, afterwards Regent; whose eldest daughter, Lady Elizabeth, conveyed it to her husband James Lord Down, whose issue at present enjoy it, as will be more fully shown afterwards.

The DUNBARS of WESTFIELD.

(1) Sir Alexander Dunbar of Westfield, only son of James fifth Earl of Moray, had great possessions in lands. Beside the barony of Westfield, he had the lands of Carnousie, Pitterhouse, Kilbuyack, Conzie, Durris, Tarras, Balnagath, Fochabers, Clunies, Moyness, Clavack, Golfurd, Barlow, &c. By Isabel, daugh-

* *Nota. The Account of this Family having been printed off with several Errata, the Reader is desired to adopt the following as more exact.*

The DUNBARS of WESTFIELD.

(1) Sir Alexander Dunbar of Westfield, had, by Elizabeth Sutherland daughter of Duffus, six sons and one daughter: i. Sir James. ii. Sir John, who by marrying Margarete co-heiress of Cumnock, obtained the lands of Mochrum, and of him is descended Mochrum, (*Dal. Col. p.* 346.) Baldoon and Grange. iii. Alexander of Kilbuiack, represented now by Alexander Dunbar of Thunderstoun. iv. Gavin Bishop of Aberdeen. v. David of Durris, which was sold, and Grange-hill bought. vi. Patrick, of whom is Dyke-side. vii. Janet married to Keith of Inverugie, and of her Marshall and Forbes are descended. (2) Sir James, by marrying Euphemia the eldest co-heir of Cumnock, obtained that Barony; and his son (3) Sir James, by a daughter of Deskford, had (4) Sir Alexander, who married a daughter of Leslie of Parkhill; and dying 1576, his son (5) Patrick, by a daughter of the Earl of Sutherland, had James and Patrick of Boghall; and dying 1577, (6) James, by a daughter of Carmichael of that Ilk, was father of (7) Alexander, who left no male issue; and was succeeded by (8) Alexander, son of Patrick of Boghall (This Patrick of Boghall was killed with the Earl of Moray at Dunibristle anno 1592) who had no male-issue; and was succeeded by his brother (9) John, who died 1622; and by a daughter of Lovate, had (10) Alexander, who died 1646 without issue; and was succeeded by his brother (11) Thomas, who married a daughter of Spence of Kirktoun, and had by her (12) Robert.

(12) Robert, who by a daughter of Sir Robert of Innes, had Robert and Alexander of Moy, and died 1661. (13) Robert, by a daughter of Gordonſtoun, had (14) Alexander, who married a daughter of Sir James Calder of Muirtoun, and had James, Robert, and Elizabeth. He died in 1702. (15) James died in 1720 unmarried, and was ſucceeded by his brother (16) Robert, who died 1721 a batchellor; and was ſucceeded, in the Collateral Line, by (17) Ludowick, ſon of Alexander of Moy: He ſold the ſheriffſhip to the Earl of Moray, and diſponed the eſtate to the Heir of Line; and dying in 1744, was ſucceeded by (18) Elizabeth, daughter of Alexander (N° xiv.) She married Sir William Dunbar of Hempriggs, ſon of Sir James Sutherland ſecond ſon of James Lord Duffus, and Sir William aſſumed the name of Dunbar; and their daughter (19) Janet, married Captain Thomas Dunbar of Grangehill, by whom ſhe has (20) Alexander and other children.

Arms of DUNBAR of Weſtfield. Quarterly, 1. and 4. Gules, a Lyon rampant within a border Argent, for Dunbar; 2. and 3. Or, three Cuſhions pendent by the corners, within the Royal treſſure, Gules. Creſt, A Sword and Key diſpoſed in Saltyr proper. Motto, SUB SPE.

Moray. She married Captain Thomas Dunbar of Grangehill now of Weſtfield, with whom ſhe had iſſue two ſons, (13) Alexander the eldeſt, William-Henry ſecond ſon, and a daughter Elizabeth.

It is obſervable, that when Ludovick of Weſtfield died anno 1744, I could not find a male that could inſtruct his propinquity to him, without going back two hundred and fifty years, and tracing down the deſcendents of Sir John Dunbar the firſt of Mochrum.

Arms of DUNBAR of Weſtfield. Quarterly, 1. and 4. Gules, a Lyon rampant within a border Argent, for Dunbar; 2. and 3. Or, three Cuſhions pendent by the corners, within the Royal treſſure, Gules. Creſt, A Sword and Key diſpoſed in Saltyr proper. Motto, SUB SPE.

The Pariſh of ALVES.

This Pariſh lieth to the weſt of Spynie, extending three miles from N. to S, and as much from E. to W. The church ſtandeth near the centre, four miles W. of Elgin, above two miles W. of Spynie, and above two miles E. of Kinloſs. The ſouth part of the pariſh ſtretcheth along the hill that divideth it from the glen of Pluſcarden. Here the lands of Cleves, Monachtie, and Aſliſk have been, for above a hundred years paſt, a part of the eſtate of Brodie, formerly belonging (as they were church lands) to the Earls of Moray, ſince the reformation of religion. In the middle of the pariſh, to the Eaſt, are Newtown and Ardgaoidh, once a part of the eſtate of Duffus, now the property, the firſt of the Earl Fife, and the other, of the Duke of Gordon. Next weſtward is Alves,
pertaining

pertaining to the Earl of Moray, and a part of that ancient estate.*

Close by the church is Kirktown, the seat of Harry Spens D. D. and of his family for several generations. West from which is Ernside, which had been successively the heritage of the Cummines and MacKenzies for some centuries, and now is the property of Mr Spens of Kirktown. In the north part of the parish, near the coast, is Coltfield, formerly pertaining to William Brodie, grandson of the family of Brodie, upon whose death without issue, the lands reverted to that family, and now they are the property of James Brodie of Brodie, and of Watson of Westerton. Westward is Hemprigs, which, with the lands of Kilbuyack in the middle of the parish, was the heritage, for several generations, of a branch of the Dunbars. Kilbuycak was sold to Brodie of Lethen; and Sir William Dunbar of Hemprigs dying without male issue, and his daughter and heiress marrying a son of Sir James Sutherland's, (vid. p. 84.) the honour of Baronet, obtained on the 10th of April 1700, came to his brother Sir Robert, father of Sir Patrick of Bowermaden, who died without male issue, and the lands of Hemprigs were purchased by William Dawson Provost of Forres, and with his two daughters co-heiresses came to Alexander Tulloch of Tanachie and Alexander Brodie of Windy-hills. Windy-hills in the west end of the parish, was long the heritage of

---

* Those parts of this parish that now belong to the Earl of Moray, have so long been the property of that noble family, in all the revolutions of it, that, I am told, about 40 years ago, a tennant gave to Mr Russel late factor, a discharge of rent granted by Thomas Randolf Earl of Moray to that tenuant's ancestor in that land. A remarkable evidence this of the benevolence and goodness of that family, in continuing the farmers in their tenements from one generation to another for above 400 years.

of the Dunbars: From them they were purchased by Francis Brodie (son of John, a natural son of David of Brodie), whose grandson John, who dyed a captain at Carthagena in 1741, having no issue, disponed his lands to Major George Brodie, son to Milntown; by whose death in 1748, they came to his brother Alexander Brodie of Windy-hills, the fourth in descent from David Laird of Brodie, who is now Baron of Windy-hills and Hemprigs.

The Parish of KINLOSS.

The parish of Kinloss, i. e. the Head of the Loch or Bay, from the burgh of Findhorn, runneth within land a mile and a half, and near a mile in breadth. Here the river Erne emptieth into the Frith. It riseth in the hills betwixt Badenoch and Stratherick, and watering Strathern and the Streins from S. W. to N. E, at Doulasie in the parish of Ardclach, a bridge of two arches was built in the year 1754; thence it runneth N. and after a course of more than 30 miles, enters into the bay of Kinloss.

The parish of Kinloss lieth on the east side of the Bay. The church standeth near the head of the Bay, about two and a half miles west from Alves, a mile and a half north of Forres, and near three miles north of Rafford. At the mouth of the Bay is Findhorn, or Inverern, a Burgh of Barony. The barr at the mouth of the river allows no ships of burden to enter the Bay, yet a good trade is carried on by small merchant ships and fishing boats. It is the sea-port of the town of Forres; and about sixty years ago, the sea cut off from the land, and covered the town now called Old Findhorn. The present town, with the barony of Muirton, lying south on the Bay, was the property of Hugh Rose of Kilravock, who, in

1766,

1766, sold the barony of Muirton to Colonel Hector Munro of Navarre. In 1656 it came to Sir Robert Innes of Innes, who disponed it to Sir James Calder. Sir James was created a Baronet of NOVA SCOTIA, by Patent dated the 5th of November 1686, and was son of Thomas Calder of Sheriff-miln, of the Calders of Assuanly. About the year 1710, Sir James disponed his estate, with the burden of the debts, to Hugh Rose of Kilravock, James Sutherland of Kinsterie, William Brodie of Coltfield, and Alexander Dunbar of Moy, and they disponed with absolute warrandice to Kilravock. The value of the estate fell short of the debts, and the disponees bore the burden. Kinloss gave title to Edward Bruce (of the family of Clackmannan) created Lord Kinloss 8th July 1604, and his son Thomas, Earl of Elgin 19th June 1633. From this last, Alexander Brodie, the first of Lethen, purchased the Abbey lands in Kinloss, and the superiorities of such lands elsewhere, and they are now the property of the eldest daughter of the late Alexander.

The south end of the parish was Abbey land, now the property of Dunbar of Grange, except the Struthers sold to Colonel William Grant of Ballendalach about 1730. On the bay of Kinloss, Lethen has a salmon fishing. Next southward is,

The Parish of FORRES.

The parish of Forres, *Far-uis*, i. e. Near the water. The parish extendeth from the Bay of Kinloss southward upon the river, three miles, and from the east to the river two miles. The town standeth two miles north west of Rafford, one mile and a half south of Kinloss, and two miles east from Dyke. It is situated in a pure and wholesome air, on a rising ground, slopping to the south and north, and commandeth a charming

ing view of the Frith and the adjacent country. It consists of one street from east to west, of well built and convenient houses. In the middle standeth the Tolbooth, adorned with a steeple of modern work, and a clock. Near the west end standeth the church, and beyond it the castle-hill, which with some lands about it has been the property of the Dunbars sheriffs of Moray, since about the 1450, and belongs now to Sir James Grant of Grant.

In the parish to landward, the house of Tanachie standeth at the head of the Bay, the seat of Alexander Tulloch of Tanachie, whose family have enjoyed these lands above 250 years. A part of the lands of Tanachie have lately been sold to Urquhart; and Loggie, in the South of the parish, formerly the property of Tulloch of Tanachie, now belongs to Sir James Grant of Grant, and is called Cot-hall. Here there is a neat house and valuable improvements. Near to Tanachie, is Bogtoun, the small heritage of a cadet of Tanachie's family. Close by Bogtoun, is West Grange, a part of the estate of Dunbar of Grange. To the west of the town is Bennageth, a small feu belonging to Alexander Lesly; and west thereof is Mundole, which has often changed Masters, and now pertaineth to Sir James Grant of Grant. Below Mundole on the side of the river, is the *Grieship*, purchased by David Laird of Brodie, from Sutherland of Duffus, about the year 1620, and is now the property of the Laird of Brodie. It was anciently a part of the estate of Lauder of Quarrelwood, whose heiress brought it to Chisholm, and his heiress to Sutherland. A half mile south of the town is the house of Sanchar, the seat of Duncan Urquhart of Burds-yards. This is an ancient branch of the Urquharts of Cromarty. I find in an indenture between William Thane of Calder, and Hucheon Rose Baron of Kilravock, dated at Forres 21. June 1482, Alexander Urquhart of Burds-yards is a witnefs. The family is ftill in a flourifhing way. Weft of Sanchar are the lands of Benneferry, Cnockomie, and fome others belonging to the Family of Moray.

The Parifh of RAFFORD.

Rafford parifh lieth South-eaft from Forres. The church ftandeth near the centre, two miles South eaft of Forres, and five miles North-eaft of Edinkyllie. In the North-eaft end is the barony of Burgie, and the feat of Jofeph Dunbar of Grange, a branch of the Dunbars of Mochrum. Mr Alexander Dunbar Dean of Moray (and very probably fon of Mochrum) was one of the Lords of Seffion anno 1567 *(And. Col.)*. He married Katherine Reid, daughter of Thomas and niece of Robert Reid abbot of Kinlofs and bifhop of Orkney, and with her got a part of the abbey-lands, fuch as Burgie, Grange, &c. His fon Thomas Dunbar was father of Robert of Grange by a firft marriage, and of Robert of Burgie by a fecond. About 1680, (Burgie having run deep in debt to his coufin) Grange got poffeffion of Burgie by adjudication, and made it his feat. Below Burgie lieth Tarras, which (with Clunie in the upper end of the parifh) pertaineth to the Earl of Moray. Weft from Burgie is the barony of Blarvie, a part of the church or bifhop's lands. It was long the heritage of the family of Dunbars. In the beginning of this Century, it was purchafed by Alexander MacIntofh fon of John MacIntofh baillie of Invernefs; and from him it was purchafed by William late Earl Fife, and is now the property of his fon Captain Lewis Duff. South from the church a mile and a half, ftands the houfe of Altyre, the feat of Cummine of Altyre, reputed Chief of that name. And this leads me to fpeak of

The

The Family of CUMMINE.

CUMMINE is a surname of great antiquity in Scotland; but the origin of it is not agreed on. Some deduce it from Hungary, others from Normandy with William the Conqueror; but I incline to think that the name is a Scottish patronimick.

It was antiently the custom to assume a surname from reputed saints, or eminent men; as Anderson from St Andrew; Cuthbertson, from St Cuthbert; Catanach, from St Catan, &c. and the learned Primate USHER *(Antiq. Ecclef. Brit. cap.* 15. p. 694, and 701.) shews, that Comineus Albus, anno 657, was the sixth Abbot of I. ColumbKill; from whom I would deduce the name: And the frequent mention of the Cummines, in the 11th and 12th centuries, is a presumption of a higher original than the days of William the Conqueror.

The direct line of the family of Cummine, from father to son, is as follows: (1) Comes Robertus Cummine was killed in the battle of Alnwick anno 1093. His son (2) John, whose brother William, was chancellor to King David I. was father of (3) Sir William, who married Hexilda, grand daughter of King Donald the Usurper, and was father of (4) William, Lord Chamberlain to King William. His son (5) Sir Richard, was father of Sir John, the *Red Cummine* Lord Badenoch, and of Sir Walter Earl of Montieth, and Sir William Earl of Buchan. (6) Sir John Lord Badenech, was father of (7) John, the *Black Cummine* one of the Governors of Scotland in 1286, who married Marjory sister of King John Baliol, which wrapped him into the Baliol interest, to the ruin of his family. His son (8) John, Lord Badenoch, was killed by Robert Bruce in the church of Dumfries, anno 1306, leaving a son

son (9) John, who died without iſſue, anno 1326; and in him failed the direct line of a family, once the moſt populous and powerful in Scotland.

Tradition bears, that the family of Altyre is come off a ſon of the direct line; but at what time I find not. They reſided for ſome generations in Strath-Dallas, and built the tower there: How early they aſſumed the title of Altyre, I know not. But I find in a contract between William Thane of Calder and Hutcheon Roſe of Kilravock, 21ſt June 1482, Thomas Cummine of Altyre is arbiter. I have not ſeen the writes of this family, and therefore will not offer to deduce the genealogy of it.

They carry the paternal arms of Cummine, without any mark of cadency, viz. Az. 3 Garbs of Cummines, Or.

Arms of the houſe of ALTYRE, Azure, three garbs of wheat, Or. Creſt, a Lyon rampant, Or. holding in his dexter paw a Dagger proper. Motto, COURAGE. Supporters, two Horſes at liberty, Argent; Their manes, tails and hoofs, Or.

Following the courſe of the river Erne, I now proceed to

EDINKYLIE PARISH.

The Pariſh of EDINKYLIE, i. e. the Face of the Wood, or a Wood in the face of the Hill. I incline to think, that here was the *Cawood*, and *Logiefoidikenach* mentioned Appendix No X. and that moſt part of this pariſh was anciently a foreſt. It now lieth on both ſides of the river Erne. The church ſtandeth on a brook, called Duvie, five miles South of Forres, three miles North Eaſt of Ardclach, and ſeven miles North of Cromdale. In the South Eaſt of the pariſh, a part of the eſtate of Altyre, viz. Phorp, Brylac, Dallasbrachtie, &c. lye in the
face

face of the ridge of hills towards Strathſpey. Weſt-ward on the river is Sluie, pertaining to James Cummine (grandſon of Mr David Cummine Miniſter at Edinkyllie) of the family of Rylucas. Above which, on the river, is Logie, the heritage, of Robert Cummine, a branch of the Houſe of Altyre. Next up the river, and South of Duvie-water which here falleth into the river, is Rylucas, the heritage of Dr PATRICK CUMMINE, Miniſter at Edinburgh, whoſe family have enjoyed that eſtate for ſeveral generations, and of which family I ſhall here give ſome account.

The Family of CUMMINE of RYLUCAS.

It cannot be queſtioned, that Cummine of Rylucas is deſcended off the family of Lord Badenach. It is ſaid, that they poſſeſſed the lands of Preſley, above three hundred years ago; and I think it probable that their anceſtor was a ſon of Cummine of Glenchernich, a direct branch from Lord Badenach. The lands of Rylucas were purchaſed by James Cummine of Preſley, ſon to William Cummine of Preſley. This James was father of a numerous family, who were much and juſtly reſpected, and were firm adherers to the religion and liberties of their country, in the reigns of the Royal Brothers. James of Rylucas was much eſteemed in the country of Moray: He was ſucceeded by his eldeſt ſon John Cummine of Rylucas: His ſecond ſon William was profeſſor of philoſophy in the Univerſity of Edinburgh: John the third ſon was miniſter of Aldern, and Dean of Moray, a man of great piety and benevolence: In the year 1681, he, with many more of the clergy, ſubſcribed the Teſt with an explication; but, upon reflexion, he retracted and demitted his charge in 1682; yet ſo much was he regarded, that the Earl of Findlater, to whom he was related, called him

to

to the parish of Cullen, where he lived undisturbed: David the 4th son was minister of Edinkylie, a man of such knowledge and prudence, that his house was a little academy, in which the children of the best families in the neighbourhood had their education: Patrick the 5th son was minister of Ormieston; and Duncan the youngest was a Doctor of Medicine, and was physician to King William's army at the battle of the Boine anno 1690: Afterwards he settled in Dublin, where he died anno 1724. So great was his desire to propagate the knowledge of the Christian religion, that he made a contribution in Ireland, of which he himself gave L. 100 Sterling, and upon this three Schools were established in Edinkylie. John was succeeded by his eldest son James Cummine of Rylucas, who, by Jean daughter of Robert Cummine of Altyre, had two sons; Robert his heir, and John a physician in Irvine. Robert Cummine of Rylucas, by Magdalane Frazer of the family of Kinkell a cadet of the house of Lovat, had two sons; Patrick his heir, and John. Robert was succeeded by his eldest son, the reverend Mr Patrick Cummine of Rylucas, D. D. Regius Professor of Divinity and Ecclesiastical History in the University of Edinburgh, and one of the Ministers of that City.

Arms of the Family of RYLUCAS. Azure, a Strawberry Leaf Argent, between three Garbs, Or. Crest, a Lyon rampant Gules, holding in his dexter paw a Dagger proper. Motto, C O U R A G E.

From Rylucas to the South-east on both sides of Duvie water, is the barony of Dunphail, which was the heritage of Dunbar of Dunphail, descended of West-field, for near 250 years, and about 1738 purchased by Colonel Ludowick Grant, brother to Sir James Grant of Grant. The Colonel dying in 1742, in the expedition to Carthagena, the barony is now the property of Sir James Grant. In the South end of the parish, on a brook called Dava, are the lands of Knock, Tombain, Kerraw, &c. the property of the Earl of Moray. On the West side of the river Erne, the parish runneth North to the gates of Tarnua Castle. The lands of Dunduff, in this parish, were the heritage of William Falconer, son of Alexander of Hakerton and Lethin, and Father of Colin Bishop of Moray; but now all this part of the parish is the property of the Earl of Moray, and the whole parish was anciently a part of that Earldom. Next is,

ARDCLACH Parish.

The parish of Ardelach (i. e. a Stonnie high ground) on both sides of the river. The church standeth on the South-west bank of the river, three miles South-west of Edinkylie, nine miles South-east of Moy, and five miles East of Calder. On the East side of the river are the lands of Ardrie, Logie, Fernes, and Aitnach, pertaining to Hugh Rose of Kilravock; and above these is Dunern, the property of the family of Brodie of Lethin. Close by the church of Edinkyllie, on the opposite side of the brook, is Glenernie, a small feu possessed, for several generations, by a branch of the Frasers, descended of Hugh laird of Beaufort, who died anno 1450. In 1526, Dallasbrachtie, Craigroy, Glenernie [N. these now belong to Altyre] Ardrie and Logiegown, were the feu-property of James Dunbar of Cunzie and Kilbuyack (*pen. Cald.*). Mr James Grant of Ardnellie, son of Duncan Grant of Grant, purchased Logie and Arderie; and his son John of Logie having purchased Moyness, his brother William had Logie, from whose heirs it came to Kilravock. The Lands of Fernes and Aitnach were sold by Bishop Patrick Hepburn to Mr John Wood of Tilliderie, who disponed them to Kilravock.

On

On the West side of the river, and close by it, is Daltulick and Culmonie, purchased from Bishop Hepburn anno 1545, and ratified by the Pope's bull 1548. At Culmonie, Kilravock has built a neat summer-house, and adorned the place with planting and inclosures. North-west is the barony of Bellivat and Middle Fleenes, which, for several generations, were the heritage of Rose of Bellivat (afterwards Blackhills), and about the year 1605 were sold to Falconer of Lethin, and they are now the property of Brodie of Lethin, and so are the lands above Culmonie, on the side of the river, above three miles. These were a part of the estate of Lethin *(Vid. Aldern. Par.)*. The lands of Keppernack and Boath, in the South-west end of the parish, and Benhir in the Streins, are the property of John Campbell of Calder. Anno 1236, *regni Alexander* II. 22° Alexander de Horstrot obtained a charter of Boath and Benchir *(pen. Cald.)* and from him the Thane of Calder purchased it. In 1568, Fleenes and Keppernach was the property of Mr Alexander Campbell son of Sir John Campbell of Calder, sold to Sir John 25th June 1545, by Patrick Hepburn Bishop of Moray, *(pen. Cald.)*. And Alexander's great grandson, John Campbell of Moy, sold these lands to John Hay of Lochloy anno 1665, who disponed them to Sir Hugh Campbell of Calder, anno 1669 *(Ibid)*. Two miles above the church, is the bridge of Doulasie, and for four miles farther the strath or valley is very narrow, inclosed with high hills, and called the Streins, consisting of three Davachs of land, the lower in Ardclach, the middle in Calder, and the upper in Moy parish, all the property of John Campbell of Calder. This leads me to,

The

The Parish of MOY.

The united parish of Moy and Dalarasie. *Moy*, from the Irish *Magh*, signifies a Meadow or Plain; and *Dale-Fergusie* is Fergus's Valley. This parish stretcheth on both sides of the river about fifteen miles, and is strictly called *Strathern*, a part of the antient Earldom of Moray. On the South-west of the river, above the Streins, the Davach of Moy jutteth North-west among the hills above two miles, in the middle of which is the Loch of Moy, a mile long, and a half mile broad. Here, in an island, the Lairds of MacIntosh had a house, as yet entire, where they resided in times of trouble. Now they have Moy-hall, a good house and convenient Summer-seat, at the west end of the Loch. So rich is the Loch of delicious red bellied trouts, called Red-wames, that I have seen near 200 taken with one draught of a small net. The lands of Moy were purchased from the Bishop of Moray: And MacIntosh took a new right from Bishop Hepburn in October 1545 *(pen. MacInt.)*. Above Moy, on that side of the river, are Tomatin, pertaining to a gentleman of the name of MacQueen; Free or Forest, belonging to MacIntosh of Holm; and the lands of Kylachie (all holding of the Earl of Moray) the property of Alexander Mac-Intosh of London merchant, the 9th in descent of the family of Kylachie. Above Kylachie is Invermasran, the property of Kilravock from the year 1460.

On the North-east of the river, in the lower end of the parish, is Pollochack, the property of MacQueen of that place. Next up the river is Corebruch, the heritage of MacIntosh of Corebruch; above which is Corebruch MacQueen, the property of Donald MacQueen, Chief of that branch of the Clanchattan. Some miles further up is Delmigvie. This was a part of the estate eftate of Weft-field, given by Sir Alexander Dunbar, to his fon David in 1495, difponed to Campbell of Calder in 1608, and feued by him to Lachlan MacIntofh of Kylachie in 1614, whofe great grandfon Donald MacIntofh now enjoyeth it. Above Dalmigvie, on both fides of the river, is the Davach of Sevin, which was a part of the caftle lands of Invernefs, *(Vid. Milit. Hift.)* and given by the Earl of Huntley, as a part of the affythment for the murder of MacIntofh in 1550, and it is the property of MacIntofh. The church of Moy ftandeth on the Weft bank of the Loch of Moy, three miles South of Deviot, and nine miles South-weft of Ardclach. Having travelled over the valley of Strathern, I return to the coaft, to defcribe

DYKE PARISH.

The parifh of Dyke and Moy, which is three miles in length and as much in breadth, bounded by the river to the Eaft, by the fea to the North, by Aldern parifh to the Weft, and by the Foreft of Tarnua to the South. The church ftandeth near the centre, two miles Weft of Forres, and four miles Eaft of Aldern. At the mouth of the river is the barony of Caulbin, the antient inheritance of a branch of Moray of Duffus. Giles, daughter and heirefs of Moray of Caulbin, married Kinnaird of that Ilk. About the year 1705, the houfe, gardens, and a great part of the lands were quite covered with fand blown from Maviefton hills, and the barony was fold to Alexander Duff of Drummuir. Next up the river is Kincorth, formerly pertaining to Falconer of Lethin, and given by Alexander of Lethin and Hawkerton, to his natural fon Mr Samuel Falconer (father of Mr William minifter of Dyke) who fold it to Dunbar of Durn; and Durn fold it, it, in 1758, to Sir Alexander Grant of Dalvey. Farther up is Easter Moy. This was purchased from the Earl of Ross by Donald Thane of Calder anno 1419 *(pen. Cald.)*. It was the heritage of a branch of the family of Calder during six generations, and John Campbell of Moy sold it to Alexander Dunbar son of West-field, whose son, Ludowick, disponed it to Alexander Duff of Drummuir, who conveyed Moy and Caulbin to his second son John Duff, and from his creditors Major George Grant made the purchase about 1732; upon whose death in 1755, without issue, these lands came to his nephew, Sir Ludowick Grant of Grant. Moy holdeth of Calder. Next is Wester Moy, pertaining to the late Archbald Dunbar of Dykeside. Farther South is the barony of Grange hill: Here the Prior of Pluscardine had a Grangier, or farm, and a cell of monks to manage it. With the other lands of that priory, it came to the Earl of Dunfermline, who sold it to Mark Dunbar of Durris about the year 1608, from whose descendants, Sir Alexander Grant of Dalvey purchased the barony anno 1749, and in his charter changed the name Grangehill into Dalvey.

In the South end of the parish is Tarnua Castle and Forest, the seat of the Earl of Moray. The castle is a large, but irregular pile, built at different times. The Hall is a curious room, very large in all dimensions, eighty feet long, and thirty-six broad, and built (or rather the foundation of it was laid for a hunting house) by Thomas Randolph Earl of Moray. It standeth on a green mount, and the Great wood or Forest close by it make it a situation romantic and delightful. In ancient writs it is called *Tarnua*; in Irish *Taranich*, probably from *Taran* or *Tarnach*, i. e. Thunder, because there Jupiter Taranis might have been anciently worshipped *(Vid. Eccles. Hist.)*.

North from Tarnua, is the Barony of Brody. Brody-house,

house, the seat of the family, is a large and convenient old building. The improvements, by inclosures, planting, avenues, vistas through the adjacent wood, and a large pond, make it a delightful seat. A mile North-west close by the Frith, are two small pyramidical mounts, called the Hills of Mavieston which being quite stripped of all sward or turf, and nothing but quick-sand remaining, are the source from whence the sand has covered much land in Caulbin, Duffus and Gordonstoun. Before I proceed further, I shall give a sketch of

The EARLS of MORAY.

This Earldom continued long feudal, reverting to the Crown in default of male issue in the direct line. The first I have found signed Earl of Moray is, OEngus Comes de Moravia interfectus est cum suis, *(Chron. Melr.)* anno 1130. Mr Myles makes him descended of King Duncan the bastard. Others will have the descendants of Duncan Earls of Moray, as followeth (1) Duncan, bastard son of King Malcom III. He usurped the throne anno 1094; and his charter *(Appendix* No. XVII.) sheweth, that he hoped to transmit it to his posterity; but he was cut off anno 1095. His son, by Ethelreda daughter of Gospatrick son of Criman Earl of Northumberland, *(Myles)* (2) William Nepos Comitis David et Nepos Regis, *(Dalr. Col.).* Dugdale says, if my memory doth not fail, that he was Earl of Moray, and married Ailtze de Rumelli. This is the more probable, because he was much in favour with King David I. and was one of his generals. His son was (3) Dovenald. Hovedan says, He was called MacWilliam, MacWilliam being son of William, the son of Duncan, and was killed anno 1187. This is agreeable to *Chron. Melr. ad ann.* 1186. " Cumque
" Rex esset apud oppidum Inverness cum exercitu, Comites
" Scotiæ

"Scotiæ miserunt suos homines ad prædandum, inveneruntque
"MacWilliam cum suis super Moram quæ dicitur *Mamgarvia*
"prope Mureff, & mox cum eo pugnarunt, et Deo opitulante,
"cum multis aliis interfecerunt." His son was (4) Dovenald,
of whom the *Chron. Melr. ad ann.* 1215 observeth, that Dovenald son of MacWilliam invaded Moray, but was cut off by *Mac-in-Tsagairt* ancestor to Ross Earl of Ross, and his head brought to the King. Possibly from these MacWilliams, came the MacWilliams in Boharm, &c.

The next Earl of Moray I have met with, is Sir THOMAS RANDOLPH great grandson of Ranulfus, who is a frequent witness in King William's Charters. His son Thomas died anno 1262, and was interred in the Abbay of Melrose. His son, Sir Thomas, Lord Chamberlain, married Isabel sister of King Robert Bruce: And their son, Sir Thomas, was created Earl of Moray anno 1313 or 1314 (*Appendix* No. I.). Although the charter or patent beareth no date, yet it is certain, that in the convention at Ayr 1315, he was Earl of Moray, (*Anderson Indep.*) Thomas died anno 1331, and his son Thomas, second Earl of Moray, succeeded him. He was, according to Fordun, " paternæ probitatis imitator." He was slain fighting gallantly against the enemies of his country, at the fatal battle of Duplin anno 1332; and having no issue, he was succeeded by his brother Earl John, who was a strenuous asserter of the liberties of his country. He had the misfortune to be taken prisoner at the battle of Kilblain anno 1335, and was confined, first in the castle of Nottingham, afterwards in the Tower of London, till he was released by the mediation of the King of France, and exchanged for the Earl of Salisbury anno 1341. He was immediately constituted Warden of the West marches. He accompanied King David II. in his unfortunate expedition into England, and was killed at the battle of Durham

ham anno 1346, leaving no issue, and the Earldom reverted to the Crown. But Patrick Dunbar, Earl of March, in right of his wife Agnes, daughter of Thomas Randolph first Earl of Moray, was designed " Comes Marciæ et Moraviæ."

John Dunbar, second son of Earl Patrick, marrying the Princess Marjory King Robert II.'s daughter, was made Earl of Moray 1372, but Badenoch, Lochaber and Urquhart were excepted out of the grant. And upon the demise of Earl James Dunbar, the last of that name,

Archibald, brother to the Earl of Douglas, was Earl of Moray, about 1446 : But having joined in his brother's rebellion in 1452, he was forfeited, and was killed in 1455.

Upon the forfeiture of Archibald Douglas, the title was assumed by Janet Dunbar, daughter of James Earl of Moray, and wife of James Lord Crichton. In 1454, there are several charters granted by Janet Dunbar Countess of Moray, and lady Frenderet, to Alexander Dunbar of Westfield her brother, (*pen. West.*) but she gave up her pretensions to the Earldom of Moray, and obtained that of Caithness to her son George.

In 1501, James Stewart, natural son of King James IV. got the Earldom of Moray. He was called the Little Earl, and died in 1544 without male issue.

In 1548, the Earldom was conferred on George Earl of Huntly ; but that grant was recalled in 1554, and it remained in the Crown till the year 1562.

It was then granted to James Stewart, natural son to King James V. In the acts of Privy Counsel 12th February 1561, he is designed Earl of Mar ; but in the Counsel held at Aberdeen 15th October 1562, he is designed Earl of Moray (*Keith's Hist.*). His eldest daughter, Elizabeth, married James Stewart Lord Downe, who, in her right, became Earl of Moray. Lord Downe was descended of Robert Duke of Albany, third son to
King

King Robert II. James, son of Murdac Duke of Albany, had four sons; viz. Andrew, James, Walter and Arthur, who, because they were born out of the country, were legittimated anno 1472. Andrew was created Lord Evendale 1459; and having no issue, was succeeded by his nephew, Alexander son of Walter, whose son Andrew third Lord Evendale, with the consent of the Crown, exchanged that title for Ochiltree. In his father's life-time, he married Margaret, daughter of Sir John Kennedy of Blairquhan, with whom he had three sons, Andrew second Lord Ochiltree, whose male-line is now extinct; Henry Lord Methven, whose male-line is also extinct; and Sir James of Beith, who was a great favourite of King James V. and was by him made one of the Gentlemen of his Bed-chamber, Lieutenant of his Gards, Constable of the castle of Down, and Stewart of Mentieth and Strathgartny. He was killed in Dumblain by the Laird of Duntreath, and his two brothers, out of a grudge for his having obtained the Stewartry of Mentieth, which was formerly in their family 1547, and his son James was created Lord Downe anno 1581, † whose son, James, married Elizabeth Countess of Moray, and from them the present family is descended.

Arms

---

† The form of creating Lord Downe a Peer, is by an Act of Parliament, 7th of James VI. anno 1581, bearing, That the lands of Downe, &c. were feued by Queen Mary to Sir James Stewart of Downe Knight, his heirs, &c. and the said Sir James being descended of the Royal Blood : " Therefore his Highness, with " the advice of his Three Estates, erects, creates, and incorporates, all the foresaid " lands, offices, &c. in an Lordship, to be called The Lordship of Downe, who " shall have the dignity and place of a Lord of Parliament, with his arms effeiring " thereto." This was an usual form (possibly for the greater solemnity, the King being under age) in imitation of the old form of creating an Earl, by creating his lands into a County. (*Essay on Brit. Antiq.*).

Arms of RANDOLPH Earl of MORAY.

Or, three Cuſheons pendent by the corners within the royal treſſure, Gules.

Arms of DUNBAR Earl of MORAY.

Quarterly, 1ſt and 4th, The Arms of Randolph Earl of Moray above blazoned. 2d and 3d Gules, a Lyon rampant within a Border Argent, charged with eight Roſes of the Field.

Arms of DOUGLAS Earl of MORAY.

Quarterly. 1ſt and 4th, The Arms of Randolph Earl of Moray above blazoned. 2d and 3d, Argent, a Man's Heart enſigned with an Imperial Crown proper, on a chief Azure, three Stars of the Field.

Arms of JAMES Earl of MORAY natural ſon of King James IV.

Quarterly, 1ſt and 4th, The Imperial Arms of Scotland bruiſed with a Baton Siniſter, counter charged of the field and charge. 2d and 3d, The Arms of Randolph Earl of Moray above blazoned.

Arms of JAMES Earl of MORAY, Regent of Scotland in Queen Mary's time:

The ſame as the laſt.

Arms of the preſent EARL of MORAY.

Quarterly, 1ſt and 4th, The Imperial Arms of Scotland within a Bordure gorbonated, Azure and Argent. 2d, Or, a Feſs checkie Azure and Argent. 3d, The Arms of Randolph Earl of Moray above blazoned.

Above the ſhield is placed his Lordſhip's Coronet, over which is ſet an Helmet befitting his Quality, with a Mantling Gules, the doubling Ermine. On a wreath of his Liveries is ſet for a Creſt, a Pelican feeding her young. Or, in a Neſt Vert. In an Eſcroll above the Creſt, this Motto. SALUS PER CHRISTUM REDEMPTOREM. And on a compartment below the ſhield, are placed for ſupporters, Two Grey Hounds Argent Collared, Gules.

I shall now give some account of

The Family of BRODIE.

This name is manifestly local, taken from the lands of Brodie. In ancient writings, it is called Brothie, softened into Brodie. In the old Irish, *Broth* signifies a Ditch or Mire; the same as *Dyke* in Saxon, and *Digue* in French. And the Mire Trench or Ditch, that runneth from the village of Dyke to the North of Brodie-house, seemeth to have given this place the name of Brodie. Be this as it will; the antiquity of this name appeareth from this, that no history, record, or tradition (that I know of) doth so much as hint, that any other family or name possessed the lands of Brodie before them, or that they came as strangers from another country. I incline much to think, that they were originally of the ancient Moravienses, and were one of these loyal tribes, to whom King Malcolm IV. gave lands about the year 1160, when he transplanted the Moray rebels. At that time surnames were fixed; and the MacIntoshes, Innesses, Rosses, then assumed their names; and probably so did the Brodies. And their arms being the same with these of the Morays, sheweth that they were originally the same people.

The old writs of this Family were either carried away by Lord Gordon when he burnt Brodie-house in 1645, or were destroyed in that burning; and yet the descents of the family may be traced up about 500 years. (1) Malcolm was Thane of Brodie in the reign of King Alexander III. (2) Michael filius Malcolmi, Thanus de Brothie and Dyke, had a charter from King Robert Bruce about 1311, (*Hist. of Kilr. and Sir G. Mk. MS.*). (3) Joannes de Brothie, accompanied the Earl of Mar Lord Lieutenant, about the year 1376, (*Hist. Kilr. and MacInt.*) (4) John

(4) John of Brodie, assisted the MacKenzies against the Mac-Donalds, in the conflict at Park, anno 1466, (*Hist. of Sutherl. &c.*). (5) John of Brodie, witness in an indenture between the Thane of Calder and the Baron of Kilravock, anno 1482, (*Pen. Cald.*). *(Here two or three Descents are wanting, which I could not find out.)*

Alexander of Brodie father of (9) David, who died anno 1627, leaving six sons; viz. David who succeeded him; Alexander who purchased the lands of Lethin, Kinloss and Pitgavenie; Mr John who was Dean of Moray, and whose son William Brodie of Whitewreath was father of Mr William Brodie Advocate, who died a Batchelor in 1741; Mr Joseph, the fourth son, was Minister of Forres, and purchased the lands of Maine near Elgin, which his son Alexander disponed to Pitgavenie, and bought the lands of Muirhouse near Turriff, which Alexander's grandson sold of late; Francis, the fifth son, purchased the lands of Milntoun and others near Elgin, which his grandson sold to Lord Braco, and his great-grand-son is Alexander Brodie of Windyhills; William, the sixth son, was proprietor of Coltfield, and his son William dying without issue, the lands came to the house of Brodie. (10) David had two sons; Alexander who succeeded him, and Joseph of Aslisk: This Joseph of Aslisk, was father of George of Brodie, and of James of Whitchill, who purchased Coltfield and Spynie; and whose son, James Brodie of Spynie, Advocate and Sheriff-depute of Moray and Nairn, died in 1756, leaving a son and heir, James a minor, who now enjoys the estate, and represents the family of Brodie: (11) Alexander was a man of eminent piety and prudence, and was chosen a Lord of Session in 1649; but soon resigned. He was one of the Commissioners who were sent to treat with King Carles II. at the Hague and at Breda. He died in 1679, leaving issue, by a daughter of Sir Robert Innes,

Innes, a son James, and a daughter married to Sir Robert Dunbar of Grangehill. (12) James married Lady Mary Kerr daughter of Robert Earl of Lothian, and dying in 1708, left nine daughters: viz. Ann married to Lord Forbes; Catharine married to Robert Dunbar of Grangehill; Elizabeth married to Cummine of Altyre; Grizzel married to Dunbar of Dumphail; Emilia married to Brodie of Aslisk; Margaret married to James Brodie of Whitehill; Vere married to Brodie of Muirhouse; Marry married to Chivez of Muirtoun; and Henrietta the youngest who died unmarried. (13) George of Aslisk succeeded, and dying in 1716, left two sons, James and Alexander; and two daughters, one of which was married to Sinclair of Ulbster in Caithness, and the other to Munro of Navarre. (14) James succeeded his father; and dying in 1720, was succeeded by his brother (15) Alexander, who was appointed Lord Lyon in 1727: He married Margaret daughter of Major Sley; and dying in 1754, left a son Alexander who succeeded him, and a daughter who was married to John younger of MacLeod. (16) Alexander died a Batchelor in 1759; and was succeeded by (17) James Brodie son of James Brodie of Spynie, and grand-son of James Brodie of Whitehill. He married Lady Margaret Duff, daughter of the late Earl of Fife.

The Arms of the FAMILY of BRODIE.

Argent, a Cheveron Gules between three Stars Azure. Supporters, two Savages proper wreathed about the Head and Middle with Laurel. Crest, a Right Hand holding a Bunch of Arrows: All proper.   Motto, UNITE.

ALDERN Parish.

The parish of Aldern, (*Ault-Jaran*, i. e. the Iron Coloured Brook,) is about three miles from East to West, and as much from North to South. The church standeth about a mile from the sea, and from the East end of the parish, about four miles West from Dyke, two miles East from Nairn, and four miles East from Calder. In the lower part of the parish, towards the Frith, is the Barony of Inshoch, with a large old house, the seat of the Hays of Lochloy and Park. This was a very ancient branch of the house of Errol, and were Lairds of Park about 400 years. By their declining, the lands of Inshoch and Park came into the family of Brodie about the beginning of this century. The lands of Park (in the West end of the parish) were sold about the year 1724 to Hugh Hay, after whose death they were, at a judicial sale in 1755, purchased by Sir Alexander Grant of Dalvey. South-east of Inshoch is the house of Penick, the seat of, and built by Alexander Dunbar Dean of Moray, or by his son. This was a part of the priory lands of Urquhart, and the residence of the Dunbars of Grange, till about the 1680, when they sold Penick to the Laird of Brodie, and resided at Burgie. Next Westward is Kinsterie, which (with Brightmonie contiguous to it) came from the Lauders to the Chisholms, and from them to the Sutherlands of Duffus. A branch of the family of Duffus were heritors of Kinsterie, which they sold about 50 years ago, and purchased Burrowsbridge and Myreside in Spynie parish, and took the title of Greenhall. James Sutherland late of Kinsterie, was a surveyor of the customs: The lands were long under sequestration for debt, but lately purchased by John Gordon of Clunie.

Close by the church is the Barony of Boath, the property of

of Alexander Dunbar, the oldest branch of the family of Durris, and possessors of that Barony above 150 years. West from Boath is Kinudie; this was a part of the estate of Park, and in 1741 and thence to 1621, Hay of Kinudie had the lands of Maine near Elgin. From the Hays, Kinudie came to the Urquharts, and in 1670 Hugh Rose of Kilravock purchased Kinudie, Hunterbog, &c. from Alexander Urquhart; and in 1767 they were sold by Kilravock to Mr James Russel.

The upper part of the parish is high ground, and in the East end of it, is the Barony of Moyness and Boghol. This was a part of the estate of Westfield, given to John Dunbar, a second son of that family, about the year 1584. And in 1634, Robert Dunbar, son of the said John, disponed these lands to John Grant of Loggie, whose son, James Grant, sold them to Sir Hugh Campbell of Calder in 1668, and they are now Calder's property. West from Moyness is the Barony of Lethin; this was a part of the estate of Falconer of Hawkerton as early as the year 1295, (*Appendix* No XVIII.) and continued so, till soon after the year 1600, it was sold to John Grant of Fruechie, who about the 1613, built a large house, and there resided. His son Sir John Grant, after he came to the estate in 1622, sold this Barony to Alexander Brodie, second son to David Laird of Brodie. This gentleman likewise purchased the Abbay lands of Kinloss, from Bruce Lord Kinloss, and in 1630 purchased the lands of Pitgavenie from Alexander Hay of Kinudie. There has of late been built at Lethin, a fine modern house, which, with the gardens, inclosures and planting, makes a delightful seat. I now come to

The

The Parish of NAIRN.

The Parish and Burough of NAIRN, in Irish *Invernairn*. The river Nairn riseth in the hills between Stratherick and the Braes of Strathern, and running North-east through the parishes of Dunlichty and Deviot, it turneth almost due North, and dischargeth into the Frith at the town of Nairn, after a course of above twenty miles. It is called Nairn, from the Alder trees growing on the banks of it. *Uisge-Nearn*, is the Water of Alders.

The Town standeth at the mouth of the river on the West side, and is one street from East to West. At the East end there is a bridge of three arches upon the river, built by William Rose of Clava in the year 1631. In the middle of the town standeth the Tolbooth and Town-house; and at the West end, Kilravock has a good house of modern architecture. A little above the bridge, on the bank of the river, is the castle-hill, where stood a royal fort (now quite demolished), whereof the Thanes of Calder were the hereditary Constables. Within the flood-mark are some vestiges, called the Pier end; but the mouth of the river is now so barred, that no vessels, but fishing boats for salmon and white fish, can enter. The church standeth on the bank of the river, two miles West from Aldern, five miles East from Arderfier, three miles North from Calder, and four miles North-north-east from Croy. The lands contiguous to the town, are the property of Rose of Kilravock, Rose of Newton, and Rose of Clava. Mr Rose of Clava, in 1768, sold all his lands in Nairn, Croy and Ardelach, to Sir Alexander Grant of Dalvey. Westward on the coast are the lands of Delnies, held, in mortgage, by Alexander Campbell of Delnies, of the Laird of Calder. These were a part of the church-lands

of

of Rofs, and David Panitar bishop of Rofs, difponed Denlies and Arderfier, anno 1556, to his brother uterine Robert Lefly, from whofe fon, John Campbell of Calder purchafed them anno 1575. On the fide of the river, a mile South of the town is Kildrummie, the feat of Hugh Rofe of Brae; thefe lands were fold by Patrick Hepburn Bifhop of Moray, to Hugh Rofe of Kilravock, in 1545, (*Pen. Kilr.*).

On the Eaft fide of the river near the coaft, is Belmakeith, the property of Alexander Dunbar of Boath, and holding feu of Calder. William Thane of Calder, was infeft in Belmakeith anno 1442 (*Pen. Cald.*). Next up the river is Braidley: This was, for fome generations, the property of Rofe of Braidley. John Rofe the laft of that family (and father of Jean Rofe, late lady dowager of Kilravock) having no male iffue, fold his lands to Alexander Gordon of Ardach, from whom they were purchafed, about the year 1726, by Hugh Rofe of Kilravock. Further up the river is the Barony of Geddes, the patrimonial eftate of Rofe of Kilravock and Geddes, (*Vid. Rofe of Kilravock*). Clofe by Geddes is Raite-caftle: Here is an old fort, built in the form of a fquare, which was anciently the feat of Raite of that Ilk, who, having killed Andrew Thane of Calder about the year 1404, was banifhed that county, and founded the family of Raite of Halgreen in the Merns. A part of Raite was Calder's property in 1442 (*Pen. Cald.*); another part of it with Meikle Geddes, was the property of Ogilvie of Carnoufie, from whom Sir John Campbell of Calder made the purchafe anno 1532 (*Ibid.*). South of Raite lye the lands of Urchany, once a part of the eftate of Park. John Hay of Kinnudie fold them to Chifholm of Comer, in 1620; and Sir Hugh Campbell of Calder purchafed them in 1660. Following the courfe of the river Nairn, I now come to

The

The Parish of CALDER.

The Parish of CALDER, so called from *Cale*, a Wood, and *Dur*, Water; for here is a fine wood, with a brook of water on each side of it. The parish is bounded by the river Nairn to the West, and by the hills towards the Streins to the South-East; the church standeth near the centre, from North to South, and is a neat little fabrick, ornamented with a steeple and a clock. A furlong East from the church, is the house of Calder, the seat of John Campbell of Calder. The Thanes of Calder, as Constables of the King's house, resided in the castle of Nairn, and had a country seat at what is now called Old Calder, a half mile North from the present seat. There they had a house on a small moat, with a dry ditch and a draw-bridge, the vestiges whereof are to be seen. But, by a royal licence, dated 6th August 1454, they built the tower of Calder that now standeth; It is built upon a rock of free stone, washed by a brook to the West, and on the other sides having a dry ditch, with a draw-bridge. The Tower stands between two courts of buildings. Tradition beareth, that the Thane was directed in a dream, to build the tower round a Haw-thorn tree on the bank of the brook. Be this as it is will, there is in the lowest vault of the tower, the trunk of a Haw-thorn tree, firm and sound, growing out of the rock, and reaching to the top of the vault. Strangers are brought to stand round it, each one to take a chip of it, and then to drink to the *Haw-thorn tree, i. e.* " Prosperity to " the Family of Calder." This house, with spacious inclosures, fine gardens, a park of red deer, and a large wood close by the house, make a grand and delightful seat. A small pendicle in the South of the parish, called Drumurnie, is the property of Rose of Holm. The lands of Meikle Budzeat, West of the church,

church, the lands of Torrich a mile to the East, and the lands of Clunies two miles to the South-east, are mortgages pertaining to the descendants of this family, and all holding of Calder. I shall here give some account of

The Family of CALDER.

The surname of CALDER is local, taken from the place; and the Family has been among the most ancient, and the most considerable in the North. About the year 1040, the tyrant Macbeath cut off the Thane of Nairn (*Buchan.*). This, no doubt, was the Thane of Calder; for no history or tradition mentioneth a Thane of Nairn, distinct from the Thane of Calder, who, as Constable, resided in that town: And Mr Heylin in his Geography, expresly calleth him Thane of Calder. But not to deal in uncertainties, (1) Dovenaldus Thanus de Calder was one of the estimators of the Baronies of Kilravock and Geddes, anno 1295, (*Append.* No. XVIII.). His son (2) William had from King Robert Bruce, 7mo Augusti anno regni 4to 1310, " Thanageum de Kaledor, infra vicecomitatum de " Inner Nairn, propter servitia debita et assueta tempore Alex- " andri Regis predecessoris nostri ultimo defuncti," (*Pen. Cald.*) His son (3) Andrew was killed by Sir Alexander Raite, whose son (4) Donald was served heir to his father Andrew in 1405, and saised in the offices of Sheriff and Constable of Nairn in 1406 (*Ibid.*) He purchased the lands of Dunmaglass from William Menzies of Balwhonzie in 1414; the lands of Moy in Moray from the Earl of Ross in 1419; and Urchany-beg in Calder from Henry Bishop of Moray in 1421 (*Ibid. and Append.* No. XIX.) His son (5) William was in 1442 infeft in the Thanage of Calder, the Sheriffship and Constableship of Nairn, in Boath, Benchir, half of Raite, and six merks out of Belmakeith

P   (*Pen.*

(Pen. Cald.). In 1450, he built the Tower of Calder by a royal licence. His son (6) William, in 1471, bought from Andrew Lesly master of the hospital of Spey, with consent of the Bishop of Moray, the miln of Nairn with its pertinents *(Ibid.)*; and in 1476, the Thanage of Calder, Baronies of Clunie and Boath, Belmakeith, half of Raite, Moy, Dunmaglass, two Kinkells, Kindess, Invermarkie, Mulchoich, Drumurnie, Ferintosh, &c. were united in one Thanage, and such lands as lye in Inverness or Forres shires, to answer to the Sheriff Court of Nairn *(Ibid.)*: Hence Ferintosh, Moy, Dunmaglass, are a part of the shire of Nairn.

This Thane had five sons, viz. William, John, Andrew, Alexander, and Hucheon, on whom he entailed his estate, allowing the immediate succession to John, to which William (who was lame and weak) consented, and had L. 20 annually and the viccarage of Ewan; all this was settled by charter anno 1488 *(Ibid.)*. This Thane lived to about the year 1500; his son (7) John married Isabel Rose, daughter of Kilravock, in 1492, *(Pen. Kilr.)* and dying in 1494, left one posthumous child, a daughter (8) Muiriel or Marion. Kilravock intended this heiress for his own grand-son, her first cousin; but Kilravock being pursued in a criminal process for robbery, in joining MacIntosh in spoiling the lands of Urquhart of Cromarty, Argyle the Justice General made the process easy to him, got the Ward of Muiriel's marriage of the King anno 1495, and she was sent to Inverary in the year 1499, *(Penn. Kilr.)*.

In Autumn 1499, Campbell of Inverliver, with sixty men, came to receive the child, on pretence of sending her South to school. The lady Kilravock her grand-mother, that she might not be changed, seared and marked her hip with the key of her coffer. As Inverliver came with little Muiriel, to Daltulich in Strath Nairn, he was closs pursued by Alexander and

Hugh

Hugh Calders her uncles, with a superior party. He sent off the child with an escorte of six men, faced about to receive the Calders; and to deceive them, a sheaf of corn, dressed in some of the child's cloathes, was kept by one in the rear. The conflict was sharp, and severals were killed, among whom were six of Inverliver's sons. When Inverliver thought the child was out of reach, he retreated, leaving the fictitious child to the Calders. And Inverliver was rewarded with a grant of the L. 20 land of Inverliver; it is said, that, in the heat of the skirmish, Inverliver cried, *'Sfada glaodh o' Lochow, 'Sfada cabhair o' chlan Dhume,* i. e. " 'Tis a far cry to Lachaw, and a distant " help to the Campbells:" Now a proverb signifying, *Imminent danger, and distant relief.* All this I give on tradition.

Muiriel was married in 1510, to Sir John Campbell third son of Argyle. In memory of which, in the old hall of the house of Calder, is cut S. I. C. and D. M. C. with this inscription, " Ceri mani memineris mane." (1) Sir John Campbell of Calder, in 1533, purchased from John Ogilvie of Carnousie, Meikle Geddes, Raite, and the fort of it, (*Pen. Cald.*) and in 1535, purchased from David Earl of Crawford, the Barony of Strath Nairn, Fortalice of Castle Davie, and the patronage of Lundichty, now Dunlichty (*Ibid.*); and in 1545 he bought, from Patrick Bishop of Moray, the lands of Fleenefsmore (*Ibid.*): He died in 1546; and his son (2) Archibald, married Isabel the daughter of the Laird of Grant; and dying in 1553, his son (3) John, purchased Arderfier and Delnies (*Vid. Nairn Parish.*), and was murdered in 1592 by Lochinel's brother. His son (4) Sir John got from the Earl of Moray a renounciation, &c. (*Vid. Daviot. Par.*). He purchased the Baronies of Durris and Borlum (*Vid. Dur. Par.*); and in 1609, took a charter of Little Budzet, Little Urchany and Croy, from Alexander Bishop of Moray (*Ibid.*); but in 1614, he feued

out

out Delmigvie and Holm; in 1617 he sold Croy to William Dallas of Cantray, and in the same year disponed Ferintosh to Lord Lovat, and mortgaged other lands; and all this in order to purchase, or rather to conquer the island of Ilay. His son, by Glenurchie's daughter, (5) John Dow, had all his lands in the North, by a charter under the Great Seal anno 1623, erected into a Barony, called the Burough of Campbelltown, with power to create Baillies, Constables, Serjeants and other officers; liberty to have a Town-house and a market cross, a weekly market on Wednesday, and a fair to begin on July 15th and to hold eight days; and that all infeftments may be taken at the Castle of Calder (*Ibid.*). Lord Torphichen had some Temple-lands in Arderfier, which he sold to Mr Thomas Rollock Advocate, with the office of heritable Baillie and a priviledge of regality, which he disponed to Calder in 1626, (*Ibid.*). In 1626, Calder granted the feu of Dunmaglas to Ferquhard MacGillivray; and in 1639, he disponed all his lands in favour of his eldest son (by Cromarty's daughter) viz. Colin. I find that this John was seized with melancholy in 1639, and yet was living in 1650. His son (6) Colin died at the university of Glasgow a batchelor; and was succeeded by (7) Sir Hugh, son of Colin of Boghol, who was brother to the last John. This gentleman purchased Moynefs and Urchany, as formerly observed: In 1678, he purchased Raite Castle and Raite Lone from John Hay of Lochloy, and redeemed some mortgages; but mortgaged other lands, and feued out Kinchyle in 1685. In 1688, he disponed his whole estate in favour of his son, reserving the life-rent of his estate in the North; and died in 1716. His son, by lady Henriet Stewart, (8) Sir Alexander, married Elizabeth, sister to Sir Gilbert Lord of Stackpole in South Wales, and died in 1700. His eldest son (9) Gilbert died in 1708, and was succeeded by his brother (10) John Campbell, now

now of Calder, born in 1695; he fold Ilay and Muckarn, to disburden his estate of debt. He married Mary Pryse heiress of Gogirthen in North Wales; by whom he has three sons, and three daughters: The first daughter Ann married Lord Fortescue, Mary died unmarried, and Elizabeth married Captain Adams: Pryse, the eldest son, married in 1752 Sarah Bacon, daughter of Sir Edmund of Garboldisham first Baronet of England, and dying in 1768, left four sons, viz. John, Alexander, George, and Charles; and three daughters, Mary, Sarah, and Henrietta: John, the second son, was in 1754 appointed Lord Lyon for Scotland; he married Eustachia, daughter of Basset of Heaton: Alexander, the third son, is a Lieutenant Colonel, and married Frances daughter of Philip Meadows.

Arms of the Family of CALDER.

Four Coats Quarterly, 1st, Or. A Hart's Head cabossed Sable, attired Gules, for CALDER. 2d, Gyronne of eight, Or, and Sable, for CAMPBELL. 3d, Argent, a Galley with her Oars in action Sable, for LORN. 4th, Parted per Fess, Azure and Gules, a Cross Or, for the name of LORT. Crest, a Swan proper crowned Or. Supporters, on the Dexter, a Lyon rampant Guardant Gules, armed Or: And on the Sinister, a Heart proper. Motto, above the Crest, CANDIDUS CANTABIT MORIENS: And below the Shield, BE MINDFUL.

CROY Parish.

The parish of Croy is next above Calder, on both sides of the river. It stretcheth twelve miles in length on the West side of the river, and four miles on the East side, and is generally two miles in breadth. The church standeth on the West-
side,

side, a mile from the river, four miles West from Nairn, two miles West-north-west from Calder, three South-east from Petty, and four North from Deviot. The North part of this parish, to the West of the river, viz. Kildrummie, Flemington, and the Baronie of Kilravock, are a part of the estate of that Family.

ROSE of KILRAVOCK.

The surname of ROSE cometh from the Hebrew, *Rosh* a Head, and *Rhos*, or *Ros*, signifying a Promontory or Head-land jutting out into Water. In many nations, places are called Rose, or compounded with it. And the country be-north Inverness is called Ross, because it stretcheth out into the sea. I question not, but Ross Earl of Ross took his surname from the country. But Kilravock's family being descended of the Rosses in the South country (as their paternal arms shew) and the name being anciently written *de Roos*, which we found much as Rose, they have changed Roos into Rose, to distinguish them from the Earl of Ross's family. And yet I have found this family in ancient writs, called Roos, Ross, Rosse, Rose.

Had not the writings of this family been destroyed, (as we shall see) in the burning of the Cathedral of Moray in 1390, few families could have better instructed their antiquity; and even, with that misfortune, few can exceed it. The Barony of Geddes, in the parish of Nairn, was their ancient inheritance: Hugo de Roos Dominus de Geddes is a witness in the foundation charter of the Priory of Beaulie, anno 1230 (*M. S. Hist. Kilr.*). Sir John Bisset of Lovat had three daughters Co-heiresses, viz. Mary Domina de Lovat, married to Sir David Graham; Cecilia Domina de Beaufort, wife of Sir William of Fenton; and Elizabeth Domina de Kilravock, married to Sir Andrew

drew de Bosco (Wood) of Red Castle; and Mary, daughter of Sir Andrew, was married to (1) Hugh Rose Baron of Geddes, and she and her husband obtained a charter of the Barony of Kilravock from King John Baliol anno 1293 (*Pen. Kilr.*); and in 1295, the Baronies of Kilravock and Geddes were estimated by an inquest, the first to L. 24, and the other to L. 12 yearly rent (*Appendix*, Nº XVIII.). Their son (2) William married Morella, daughter of Alexander de Downe, and had Hugh, and Andrew, of whom came Rose of Achloffin in Mar, (3) Hugh ii. died about 1363; his son (4) Hugh iii. married Janet, only child of Sir Robert Chisholm, Constable of the Castle of Urquhart anno 1364, and with her he got the lands of *Cantra-nabruich* in Strathnairn, (*Ibid.*): He died about 1388. His son (5) Hugh iv. died in 1420, whose son (6) John, obtained a charter of de Nova Damus under the Great Seal, 30th May 1433, "pro eo, quod Chartæ suæ, tempore combustionis Ecclesiæ "de Elgin, in Ecclesia prædicta fuerunt vastatæ et destructæ." (*Ibid.*). He got from his grand-uncle, John Chisholm, the lands of Little Cantray and Ochterurchll, in 1420 (*Ibid.*). His son, by Isabel Cheyn daughter of Esslimont, was (7) Hugh v. who, in 1482, purchased the lands of Coulmore in Ross (*Ibid.*). He married More or Marion daughter of MacIntosh; his second son Alexander founded the family of Holm: Hugh died in 1494; and his eldest son (8) Hugh vi. by Margaret Gordon daughter of Huntley, had Hugh, John progenitor of the Rosses of Bellivat, and Alexander of whom came the family of Insh in the Garioch, and died in 1517. (9) Hugh vii. by Agnes Urquhart daughter of Cromarty, had Hugh and John of Wester Drakies, and died anno 1543. (10) Hugh viii. purchased from Bishop Hepburn, in 1545, the lands of Kildrummie, Coulmonie and Daltulich. His facetious humour appeareth in a submission between him and two neighbours,

his

his subscription to which is, " Hutcheon Rose of Kilravock, an " honest man ill guided between you baith." He died in 1597, leaving, by Catharine daughter of Hawkerton, a son (11) William ii. who, by Lilias Hay daughter of Dalgatie, had Hugh, William of Clava, John of Braidley, and David of Earlsmiln; and died anno 1611. (12) Hugh ix. purchased Flemington from the Earl of Moray in 1639; he married Magdalene Frazer daughter of Strichen, and died in 1643. His son (13) Hugh x. married a daughter of Sinclair of Dunbeth, who brought him Hugh and John, of whom is Hiltoun, and he died in 1649. (14) Hugh xi. purchased Kinudie, &c. (*Vid. Aldern. Par.*) sold Coulmore, and purchased Coulefs and Rarichees in Rofs anno 1681 (*Ibid.*). By Margaret daughter of Innes of that Ilk, he had Hugh his successor, and other sons. (15) Hugh xii. added to his estate the Barony of Muirton near Kinlofs, and the lands of Brae in Rofs. He was five times married: 1st, with Margaret daughter of Sir Hugh Campbell of Calder, by whom he had a son Hugh, and two daughters, Henrietta married to Sir John MacKenzie of Coul, and Mary to Duncan Forbes of Culloden, afterwards Lord President; 2d, Joan only child of Mr James Frafer of Brae, and had by her a son James of Brae; 3d, Jean daughter of Cuthbert of Castlehill, who brought him Magdalene, married to MacKenzie of Dachmaluack, and Jean to Robertson of Glafgoego; 4th, Elizabeth daughter of Sir James Calder of Muirton, who had Margaret married to Sir Charles Campbell son of Sir Archibald; 5th, Katharine daughter of James Porteous of Invernefs, who left two sons, Arthur and Alexander. He died in January 1732. (16) Hugh xiii. sold the lands of Brae in Rofs, and purchased Braidley near Nairn; he died 28th May 1755, leaving, by his first lady Elizabeth daughter of Sir Ludowick Grant of Grant, two sons, viz. Hugh and Ludowick of Coulmonie:

monie: And by his second lady, Jean Rose daughter of Braidley, several children. (17) Hugh xiv. born in 1705; in 1739 he married the daughter of Collonel William Clephan, nephew of Carslogie in Fifeshire; He was sheriff-depute of Ross and Cromarty, and died in 1772, leaving a son Hugh, and a daughter Elizabeth. His son (18) Hugh xv. of this name, is present Baron and Laird of Kilravock.

It is observable, that, in the course of eighteen generations in this family, the representation did not once diverge from the Direct line to the Collateral.

KILRAVOCK's Paternal Arms are: Or. 3 Water Budgets, Sab.

Now to describe the parish:

The house of Kilravock standeth on a rock, on the West bank of the river. It is a large pile of building, with a strong tower built in 1460, by a patent from the Earl of Ross. (*Ibid.*) The river, gardens, inclosures, and adjacent Birch-wood, make it a very agreeable seat. South-west on the river is Holm, the property of John Rose of Holm, the 9th descent in a direct line; the small heritage is a part of the Barony of Strathnairn (*Vid. Daviot. Par.*). Next up the river is Cantray, which, with Galcantray and Bellaffresh on the East side of the river, and the lands of Croy near the church, are the property of Mr Davidson, who lately purchased them from Dallas of Cantray. Croy was purchased from Campbell of Calder in 1617; but Cantray (and Budzet in Calder) has been the seat of Dallas for many generations. North-west from Cantray, on the top of the hill, standeth the Castle of Dalcross, built in 1621 by Lord Lovate, whose property the land was at that time: It came afterwards to Sir James Frazer of Brae, who gave it as a portion with his daughter Jean Frazer to Major Bateman. The Major fold it to James Roy Dunbar Baillie of Inverness, and from him MacIntosh of MacIntosh purchased it in 1702. About four miles farther, on the West brae of the hill, is Easter Leys pertaining to Robertson of Inches, (*Vid. Invernefs Par.*) Next is Mid Leys, the property of George Baillie son of John Baillie late writer to the signet in Edinburgh, who was son of James Baillie Sheriff-Clerk of Invernefs, of the family of Dunean. Farther is Weft Leys, the heritage of Alexander Shaw of Tordaroch, who fold it lately to Sir Ludowick Grant of Grant, (*Vid. Daviot Par.*). These Leys hold of Lord Lovate, as a part of the ancient estate of that family.

To return to the side of the river Nairn. Above Cantray, are Little Cantray, *Contra-na-bruich*, Orchil, &c. pertaining to Kilravock; and further up is the Barony of Clava, the heritage of Rose of Clava; of which branch, Hugh of Clava is now the 6th in descent, This Barony is situated on both sides of the river. And in the upper part of the parish is Daltulich, a mortgage possessed by a branch of the Frasers for five generations past. Following the river, I come to

DAVIOT Parish.

The parish of Daviot and Dunlichtie stretcheth on both sides of the river Nairn, about ten miles in length, and in few places two in breadth. It is inclosed with hills except towards Croy. The church standeth on the West bank, a mile above the North end of the parish, three miles North from Dunlichtie, which is united with it; four miles South from Croy, four miles South-east from Invernefs, and three miles North-west from Moy. The Barony of Strathnairn was the free-hold of the Earl of Crawford

Crawford before the year 1500. David Earl of Crawford married Catharine daughter of King Robert II. and with her got the Barony of Strathnairn, &c. anno 1378 (*Rot. Rob.* II.); and he difponed it in feu to Ogilvie Laird of Findlater, who refided at Hall-hill in Pettie, and was defigned Laird of Strathnairn. Sir John Campbell of Calder purchafed Crawford's right in 1535, and thereafter Findlater conveyed his feu-hold to the Earl of Moray. This Earl, unwilling to hold of Calder, privately obtained a charter from the chancery, by which he was to hold of the Crown. Sir John Campbell, great-grandfon to the former mentioned, carried on a reduction of the Earl of Moray's right, and obtained from Earl James an ample renounciation, dated 17th November 1608, acknowledging, " That he held of Sir John Campbell of Calder, the lands of Meikle Davie, cum Fortalicio, Budzeat, Little Davie, Coul-
" clachie, Meikle and Little Craggies, Inverarnie, Gafk, Wefter
" Larg, Aberchaladers, Aberarders, Dalcrombie, Letterwhiln,
" Brinns, Fleechtie, Far, Holm, Failie, and Drumornie ;" *(pen. Cald.).* Thus the Earl of Moray holdeth this Barony of Mr. Campbell of Calder as his fuperior.

On the Weft fide of the river, in the lower end of the Parifh, is Coulclachie, a fubvaffalage of Angus MacIntofh who now reprefenteth the MacIntofhes of Connidge. Next South-ward is Davie, the property of the Laird of MacIntofh ; here was a fort built by David Earl of Crawford, and after him called Davie fort. Next is Failie, the heritage of MacBean of Failie, a branch of the old Clan Chattan, who have long poffeffed this fmall eftate. South thereof is Gafk, which, with Dunmaglafs, are the property of William MacGillivray of Dunmaglafs. This laft was purchafed by the Thane of Calder in 1414, and feued to Ferquhard MacAlafter in 1626; but they had immemorial

Duchus or possession of it. Dunmaglass is Chief of the ancient Clan of MacGillivrey.

On the East side of the river, the first Northward is Craggie, the property of the late William Shaw of Craigfield, cousin to Tordaroch. South of which is the Barony of Largs, a part of MacIntosh's estate. Further South is Inverarnie, a mortgage from Rose of Kilravock, who is the Earl of Moray's subvassal. MacPhail of Inverarnie is the Chief of that ancient tribe of the Clan Chattan. Above Inverarnie, on the brook of Fearnie, is Far, the property of MacIntosh of Far, a branch of the family of Kylachie. Above Inverarnie, on the side of Nairn, is Tordaroch, the seat of Alexander Shaw, an ancient branch of the Shaws of Rothemurchus. This Family's heritage is Wester Leys in the parish of Croy; but they hold Tordaroch in lease of MacIntosh, and have resided in it above 200 years. In the South end of Dunlichtie parish, is Aberarder, the heritage of William MacIntosh of Aberarder, a branch of the family of MacIntosh; and West of Aberarder, is Dunmaglass, of which I have spoken. There are in this Brae-country, some other subvassals of the Earl of Moray. But I return to the coast.

ARDERSIER Parish.

The parish of Ardersier lieth on the West Coast from Nairn. It is a promontory running into the Moray Frith, from South-east to North-west, and is about two miles in length, and little more than a half mile in breadth at the South-east; and at the North-west it terminates in a narrow point, on which the Fort is built. The whole parish is the property of John Campbell of Calder, and was a part of the lands of the Bishop of Ross, with some Temple lands formerly belonging to the Knights Templar. More than a third part of the whole bounds was purchased.

chased about 1746 by the Government, for a precinct of the Fort. The church formerly stood within the precinct; but of late, there is a new church built a little without it, about five miles West from Nairn, three miles North from Croy, and four miles North-east from Pettie. Whether the precinct shall be Intra-parochial, or Extra-parochial, is not as yet determined.

Westward on the Coast is,

PETTIE Parish.

The parish of Pettie is pleasantly situated in a plain, betwixt the Frith and the hills towards Strathnairn. It is in length from East to West near five miles, and in breadth not above a mile and a half; the church standeth on a rising ground, a furlong from the sea, almost two miles from the West end of the parish, five miles North-east from Inverness, four miles South-west from Arderfier, and near three miles North-west from Croy.

The Barony of Pettie was antiently a part of the Earldom of Moray; but upon the death of Earl Archibald Douglass, anno 1455, " The castles of Inverness and Urquhart, and the " Lordships of them, the water mails of Inverness, the Lord- " ship of Abernethie, the Baronies of Urquhart, Glenurchan, " Boneich, Bonochar, Pettie, Brachlie and Strathern, with the " pertinents, were annexed to the Crown," (*Act Parl.* 1455). Some time after this, the Laird of Findlater held the Barony of Pettie of the Crown, and afterwards of the Earl of Moray. I find, that Elizabeth, daughter of Sir James Dunbar of Cumnock, who died in 1505, was married to John Ogilvie of Strathnairn, (*Pen. Westf.*) Ogilvie resided at Hall-hill in Pettie. Lachlan Laird of MacIntosh being murdered by some of his Clan in 1524, James Earl of Moray committed the young Laird of

MacIntosh

MacIntoſh (who was his nephew) to the care of the Laird of Strathnairn. The MacIntoſhes reſented this as an indignity, demoliſhed the houſe of Hall-hill, and killed twenty-four of the Ogilvies about the year 1531, (*M. S. Hiſt. MacInt. and Kilr.*) It is probable, that this barbarous treatment induced Findlater to diſpone his right of Strathnairn, Pettie and Borlum, to the Earl of Moray.

In the Eaſt end of the pariſh is Calder's Brachlie, a ſkirt of the Thanedom of Calder. Near to it is Eaſter Brachlie, pertaining to Kilravock. All the reſt of the pariſh is the property of the Earl of Moray, except a ſmall feu in the Weſt end, called Alterlies, which pertaineth to Forbes of Culloden. Near the church ſtandeth Caſtle-Stewart, one of the Seats of the Earl of Moray, but now out of repair; and near thereto is a Corn-miln ſet a-going by the Sea water.

Next to Pettie Weſtward, is

The Town and Parish of INVERNESS.

The Town ſtandeth on the Eaſt bank of the river Neſs, a little above the mouth of it. It confiſteth of two ſtreets, cutting one another, from South to North and from Eaſt to Weſt. The buildings are good and convenient, all of ſtone: In one of the angles, at the interſection of the ſtreets, ſtandeth the Tolbooth and Court-houſe, adorned with a lofty ſteeple and a Clock; and in an oppoſite angle, is the Town-houſe, a large building of modern work. The Churches ſtand on the river bank, at the North end of the Town; and near to them is Dunbar's Hoſpital, a large houſe with a garden, mortified by Proyoſt Alexander Dunbar. Below the Churches is the Harbour, which receiveth merchant ſhips, but ſtandeth too open to the ſtrong Weſt wind; and cloſe by the harbour are the veſtiges of

Cromwell's

Cromwell's Fort. In the middle of the Town is the Bridge, of seven arches, and beautiful architecture, with a prison room in one of the pillars: Formerly there stood here a Bridge of wood, supported by pillars of oak, some of which are yet to be seen; It fell on the 28th September 1664, and though more than a hundred persons, who stood on it, dropt all into the river, no life was lost, (*M. S. Hift. of Lovat*). The present Bridge was finished about the year 1686. Several gentlemen contributed liberally for it; and by an Act of Privy Council, there was a collection for it through the Diocess † (*Syn. Reg.*). On the West bank of the river, there is a large suburbs of two streets; and a little above the Town, there is a pleasant little island in the river, where the magistrates entertain strangers with salmon killed in their presence with spears. The Town is very populous, and the houses being too much crowded, and the streets narrow, under the Castle-hill and Barn-hill the air is thick and moist.

The parish lieth on both sides of the river. On the West side, it extendeth eight miles, and on the East four miles. The Town standeth five miles South-west from Pettie, five miles almost East from Kirk-hill, five miles North from Durris, and four miles West-by-North from Daviot. The Town lands lye adjacent to it (*Vid. Civ. Hift.*); and the country parish is full of Gentlemens seats.

On the East side of the river, two miles North-east of the Town, is Culloden, a good old house, gardens well laid out, with much planting, which make it an agreeable seat.

---

† The Council's Act and Recommendation was for a general collection throughout the whole Kingdom, and no doubt brought in a considerable sum. Sir Hugh Campbell of Calder gave L. 400 Scots, the Laird of MacLeod L. 800, the Ministers of the Diocess of Moray L. 500, (*Syn. Reg.*). Others likewise contributed liberally.

seat. This land belonged to a gentleman of the name of Strachan, who married the daughter of Hugh Rose of Kilravock that died anno 1543. Of that marriage there were only two daughters portioners, and the Laird of MacIntosh purchased from them and their husbands the rights of that Barony. MacIntosh built a part of the house of Culloden, and his successor sold the Barony about the year 1626, to (1) Duncan Forbes, son of Tolquhon and Provost of Inverness, whose son (2) John of Culloden, purchased Fairentosh and Bunchrive anno 1673. His son (3) Duncan, was father of (4) John, who had no issue, and of Duncan Lord President of the Session, who died the 10th December 1747. His son (5) John, has left (6) Arthur now of Culloden. Of this Family is Forbes of Pitnacrief.

<small>FORBES of CULLODEN.</small>

South-west is Easter Drakies, the property of Hugh Falconer merchant in Inverness; and Wester Drakies pertaining to the estate which belonged to Cuthbert of Castle-hill, both holding of the Town of Inverness. Next is the Barony of Castle-hill: In the reign of King David II. Susanna and Adda were sisters and heiresses of Castle-hill, and a gentleman of the name of Cuthbert marrying Susanna, became thereby Baron of Castle-hill *(M. S. Hist. of Kilr.)* From that time the Cuthberts have been in possession of these lands.

<small>ROBERTSON of INCHES.</small>

Further is the Barony of Inches, the first of which family was a son of Robertson of Strowan, who married the widow of Cuthbert of Castle-hill, about 1548; and his son became Laird of Inches which was a part of the Barony of Castle-hill. Arthur Robertson of Inches now represents the family.

The lands of Essich are the farthest South, and are a part of MacIntosh's estate. Below Essich towards the river, are Coulduthil, Knocknagial, and Torbreak, all Castle lands. Torbreak was the property of Captain William Baillie, and by a judicial sale

sale in 1758, became the property of Doctor James Frazer son of Phopachie. And on the side of the river is Holm; this is the Fief of Alexander MacIntosh of Holm, a branch of the family of Kylachie, who have possessed this small estate ever since the year 1614, and hold it mainly of Campbell of Calder.

I pass now to the West side of the river Ness. At the mouth of it is Markinsh: This for 150 years was the property of Rose of Wester Drakies and his descendants, and has lately been purchased in a judicial sale by James Frazer of Phopachie. Next is the Barony of Muirtown, a part of the estate of Lovat, sold about the year 1620, to Thomas Skivez for 2,000 merks Scots, (*M. S. Hist. of Lovat*). His descendants lately sold it to Sir Ludowick Grant of Grant, who disponed it to William Duff third son of Alexander Duff of Drummuir. Farther South is Kylmiles, a part of the Bishop's lands of Orkney, purchased by Thomas Lord Lovat from Bishop William Tulloch about the year 1464; it was afterwards sold to Colonel Hugh Frazer of Kinerries, who disponed it to Mr David Polson; From him it was purchased by Alexander Frazer (son of David Frazer Baillie of Inverness) of Fairfield, who lately sold it to George Ross of Pitkerries merchant in London. Next up the river is the Barony of Dunean: This family has enjoyed this Barony about 300 years; the first of it was a son of Baillie of Hoprig and Lamington, who, for his brave behaviour as a Volunteer in the battle of Brechin anno 1452, was soon after rewarded by the Earl of Huntley, with this and other lands, a part of the Castle lands of Inverness. South of Dunean is Dochgarach, the property for some generations, of a branch of the MacLeans. Next to which is Dochfoure, pertaining to Baillie of Dochfoure, a branch of the family of Dunean. The very upper end of the parish is Aberiachan, in the face of the hill, at the side of Loch Ness. This is a part of the Barony of Urquhart,

Urquhart, pertaining to Sir James Grant of Grant, of whom Ewan Baillie fon of Dochfoure holdeth it in mortgage.

Following the courfe of the river, I now come to

DURRIS Pairifh.

The parifh of Durris, from *Dur*, i. e. Water, becaufe the parifh lieth on the fide of the river and the Loch of Nefs.

Before I proceed further, I fhall fhew the courfe of the RIVER NESS; and if we trace it to its fountain, we fhall find the fprings of it in the hills of Knoidart, and its courfe thus: To Loch Queich, four miles; Loch Queich, feven; to Loch Garie, nine; Loch Garie, five; to Loch Eoich, two: All this courfe is from Weft to Eaft, and Garie falleth into the middle of Loch Eoich, which is four miles long; fo to the end of Loch Eoich, two miles; to Loch Nefs, four; length of Loch Nefs, twenty-two; to Invernefs, five: In all fixty miles. The courfe from Loch Eoich is from South-fouth-weft to North-north-Eaft; from the Moray Frith at Invernefs, to Fort-William, is one continued valley of forty-eight Scots miles, running from North-north-eaft to South-fouth-weft, without any bending, except that it turneth one point towards the Weft, from Loch Lochie to Fort-William. It is called *Glean-mor-na-halben*, i. e. the Great Valley of Scotland. Loch Nefs lieth in this valley, and is in length about twenty-three Englifh miles; At the North end it is three miles broad, and thence gradually tapereth, fo that at the South end it is not two miles broad; it has no bending, no bay, except a fmall one at Urquhart. The high hills on both fides, are fo variegated with hanging rocks, fhady groves of wood, murmuring cafcades, and ftreams of water, and fome plots of corn land, that, to one who fails the Loch in the fummer feafon, they prefent a moft charming landfkip.

This

: This parish extendeth about six miles from North to South, and as much from East to West. The church standeth at the North-east corner of the Loch, five miles South of Inverness, seven miles North of Bolesken, and six miles South-west of Daviot. The lower and champaign part of the parish comprehendeth the Baronies of Borlum and Durris. Above Inverness, three miles on the river, is Borlum: This was a part of the estate of the Earl of Moray; and after the forfeiture of Earl Archibald Douglas, the Laird of Findlater obtained this Barony and held it of the Crown, and his son was designed Ogilvie of Cardale. Findlater conveyed his right to Stewart Earl of Moray, and Earl James disponed "Borlum " cum Fortalicio, with the fishing on the river Ness, the lands " of Coulard and Kinchyle, the Loch of Lochindorb, the " houses within the same, cum adjacentibus shelingis, to Sir " John Campbell of Calder, 31st October 1606, (*Pen. Cald.*)." Borlum was thereafter given in feu to William MacIntosh of Borlum.* Kinchyle lying South of Borlum, was, in 1685, feued to William MacBean, whose ancestors had the Duchus or possession thereof for many generations. Tradition beareth, that Bean-mor, son of Maolmuir MacGilonie, of the ancient Clan Chattan, came to this country with Lady MacIntosh heiress of Clan Chattan, soon after the year 1291, and was the ancestor and Chief of the MacBeans, now represented by the

---

* The Barony of Borlum, was feued by Shaw MacIntosh late of Borlum, to his cousins William and Angus MacIntoshes Baillies of Inverness, but redeemable by him in a certain term of years. At the expiring of that term, the Barony was brought to a public sale, and was purchased by Simon Fraser, merchant in Gibraltar, son to John Fraser (*MacTavish*) late merchant in Inverness, who lately sold the lands to John Fraser writer to the signet his brother.

the son of Giliose MacBean who was killed in the battle of Culloden anno 1746.

Next thereto, and on the Loch, is the Barony of Durris. This was a part of the estate of Sir Alexander Dunbar of Westfield " who disponed Durris, half of Holm, Little Bel- " lacheranich, Tirchirochan, and Dalmigvie in Strathern, in " favour of his son David Dunbar, 27th October 1495; and, " by a charter under the Great Seal 17th December 1569, " these lands were erected into a free Barony, of which Lopan " (the seat of the Family) was the principal messuage. Like- " wise, Alexander Earl of Dunfermline sold the Kirk lands of " Durris (a part of the lands of the priory of Urquhart) to " Mark Dunbar anno 1592, reserving the patronage and " tiends; and Mark Dunbar disponed the whole Barony to " Sir John Campbell of Calder, 4th August 1608, who, in " 1610, purchased from Dunfermline the patronage of Dal- " cross, and the patronage and tiends of Durris." (*Pen. Cald.*)

Durris and Aldaurie, were sold by Calder in feu to Mac- Intosh of Kylachie, who conveyed his right to Baillie John Barbour of Inverness, whose son disponed in favour of Wil- liam Fraser writer in Edinburgh, and son of Balnaine.

South of the church are the lands of Drummin, possessed long by the MacBeans, and now the property of Angus MacIntosh merchant in Inverness, and grand-son to Borlum.

Next thereto, is Erchit, the property of the said William Fraser writer in Edinburgh. In the hilly part of the parish, are the lands of Bochrubin, Dundelchag, &c. pertaining to MacIntosh, and other lands, a part of the estate of Lovat: Which leads to

BOLESKIN

BOLESKIN Parish.

The Parish of Boleskin and Abertarf, which lieth on the East side, and the South end of the Loch. Boleskin parish (*Baloician*, i. e. the Town over the Loch, for the church standeth on the face of the hill, Over the Loch Ness,) is properly Sratherik, or *Strathfarigack*, scattered in the valleys betwixt Loch Ness, and the hills towards Badenoch.

The church standeth near the Loch, seven miles South of Durris, and twelve North of Kilhuiman. Here entering the country of the FRASERS, I shall speak of

The FAMILY of LOVAT.

I shall not attempt to assign the origin, or to determine the antiquity of the name of FRASER. Some would fetch the Frasers from Frieseland, and it favours this conjecture, that, in ancient writings, they are called Frisele, in Irish *Friselech*, and not Fraser. Others bring them from France, as early as the reign of Charlemaigne, and derive the name from the French, *Frasier*, a Strawberry plant: But passing these conjectures, I may say with Buchanan, that in Scotland they were right early, "Gens numerosssima, et de re Scotica bene merita."

The late Lord LOVAT caused publish in NISBET's *Heraldry* Vol. II. An account of his Family, "disclaiming his ancestor's "marriage with a daughter of Bisset of Lovat, and affirming "that Sir Simon Fraser (who was executed in London after "the battle of Methven, anno 1307) had a son, Simon, "that was killed at Haledon-hill, anno 1333, leaving a son "Hugh, who got the Barony of Lovat from King David II. "and the three Crowns, as Arms of Concession." But this, whole wholly unvouched, account will not bear a trial. It is uncertain, if the Great Sir Simon had a son; and if he had, he certainly left no issue: For the Families of Tweedale and Wigtoun quarter the Frasers Arms, because their Ladies (daughters of Sir Simon) were Co-heiresses, which they could not be, if their brother had issue and succession. Besides, it cannot be instructed, that the Barony of Lovat was in the King's gift; nay, the contrary is apparent from *Char. Morav. and the M. S. Hist. of the Family of Kilravock*. Nor were the three Crowns Arms of Conceffion; Lovat's ftricking them out, fhews that he confidered them as the Arms of Biffet, with whom he difclaimed a connection; for had they been a royal Conceffion, they ought to poffefs the firft place in the Field, as the moft honourable. Lovat's apparent defign was, to eftablifh a right of Chieftainry in his Family, which no Hiftory, or Genealogy I have feen, will admit.

I incline to think, that Sir Simon of Tweedale or Olivercaftle, called Simon Pater by Mr Rymer, William Bifhop of St Andrews, and Gilbert Sheriff of Traquair (*Reg. Kelso*) were brothers. Simon Pater, fon of Bernard, is allowed to have been Chief of the name, and had two fons, viz. Sir Simon and Sir Alexander *(Life of King Robert Bruce)*. Sir Simon was put to death, and his daughters were married as above mentioned. Sir Alexander then became Chief, was made Lord Chamberlain anno 1325, married Mary Bruce, fifter of King Robert, and widow of Sir Neil Campbell, and that King gave him the Thanedom of Cowie, and other lands *(Rotul. Rob.)*. Sir Alexander's fon was Sir William of Cowie and Dores; whofe fon, Sir Alexander, married Janet, daughter of William Earl of Rofs, by whom he got the lands, and took the title of Philorth in Buchan. He died about 1412, leaving two fons, Sir William and Alexander of Dores; Sir William of Philorth

lorth died anno 1441; whose son Sir Alexander was, 14th April 1461, served heir to Sir Alexander of Cowie, the Laird of Lovat being one of the inquest. His lineal descendant, Alexander of Philorth, in 1598, married Margaret daughter of George Lord Abernethie of Saltoun; and their grand-son, Alexander, upon the death of Alexander Lord Saltoun in 1669 without issue, served heir to Lord George, and in parliament 1670 had the honour and rank of Saltoun confirmed to him: And, in my opinion, Lord Saltoun is undoubted Chief of the Clan.

Gilbert Sheriff of Traquair probably was ancestor of the family of Lovat. His son Sir Andrew was father of Simon Fraser, who married the daughter (or grand-daughter) of Sir John Bisset of Lovat. The three daughters, Co-heiress of this gentleman, were, according to their birth, Mary Lady Lovat, Cecilia Lady Beaufort, and Elizabeth Lady Kilravock. Mary the eldest was married to Sir David Graham, second son of Sir David of Kincardine; and Sir David Graham was alive anno 1294, and had a son, Patrick Graham. If therefore Mary Bisset was married to Simon Fraser, it must have been some time after the 1294, and she must have been of an advanced age; for Mary Wood, daughter of the youngest sister Elizabeth, was married to Hugh Rose of Geddes before that year 1294. Either then, Simon's wife was Mary Bisset, widow of Sir David Graham, and well stricken in years; or the daughter of Sir David became heiress of Lovat, upon the death of her brother Patrick without issue: Leaving this uncertain. The first of this name I find designed "Of Lovat," is Hugh Frisele, who does homage to the Bishop of Moray, anno 1367, for some lands in the Aird (*Appendix* N° XX.). I shall now deduce the succession, according to the *M. S.* account of the Family.

In the law suit in 1730 by the late Lovat, for obtaining
the

the Peerage, it was acknowledged, that it does not certainly appear, by any writing or record, in what year the dignity of a Lord was conferred on that Family; and that Lord Lovat is marked in the Rolls of Parliament in 1540, and not more early. But in the Additional Cafe of Elizabeth Countefs of Sutherland in 1771, I find that the Retour 1430 calls him Hugh Frafer de Lovat; and in a Royal Charter in 1480, he is defigned " Hugo Frafer Dominus de Lovat," and thus the Family was ennobled, betwixt the year 1430 and 1480, and the third or fourth defcent feems to have been the firft Lord.

(1) Simon Frifele, was father of (2) Hugh, who married Margaret, daughter and heirefs of William Fenton of Beaufort, fon of Thomas of Dounie, and by her got the lands. He died about 1420, leaving three fons, viz. Hugh, Alexander of whom is Feralin, and James anceftor of Craigray and Glenerhie. (3) Hugh ii. married Janet, daughter of Thomas Dunbar Earl of Moray, and with her got the lands of Abertarf. His fon (4) Hugh iii. married a daughter of Lord Glammis, and was killed at Flouden anno 1513, leaving a fon Thomas, and a baftard fon; who, having been fome time in France, was called Hutcheon Franchoch, of whom is Frafer of Fohir. (5) Thomas feems to have been the fecond who was advanced to the Peerage; he married Janet Gordon, daughter of Sir Alexander of Midmar, brother to Huntley, and in his favour Huntley renounced all right he had to Stratherick; he died anno 1526, leaving a fon Hugh, and a baftard fon Hutcheon Bane, anceftor to Relick. (6) Hugh iv. married a daughter of John Grant of Freuchie, and by her had Hugh; and by his fecond Lady, a daughter of Belnagawn, he had Alexander and William of Strawie. Lord Hugh and his eldeft fon were killed in the battle of *Cean-Lochlochie,* anno 1544. (7) Alexander married Jean, daughter of Sir John Campbell of Calder, and had Hugh,

Hugh, Thomas of Strichen, and James of Ardachie. Lord Alexander purchased Strowie, Coulgaran, Kilwadie, Crochils and Comer, from William Forbes of Kinaldie; and his son Thomas married Isabel Forbes widow of Chalmers of Strichen, and purchased the lands of Strichen in Buchan, about 1580. Lord Alexander died 1588. (8) Hugh v. married Elizabeth Stewart, daughter of John Earl of Athole, and purchased from Sir Walter Reid, Prior of Beaulie, the lands and tythes thereof, about 1569, and died 1576. His son, (9) Simon ii. by his first wife daughter of Kintail, had Hugh; and by his second wife, daughter of the Earl of Moray, had Simon of Inveralachie, and Sir James of Brae. He sold Glenelg to MacLeod, and mortgaged Kilmiles, Fanellan, and Kingylie, to Strichen, and Phopachie to Coulbokie. In 1617, he purchased Ferintosh and Inveralachie, and disponed these and Bunchrieve to his second son. He died 1633. (10) Hugh vi. by his Lady a daughter of Weemys, had Hugh, and Thomas of Beaufort. He sold Abertarf to Glengary for 5,000 merks, and Muirtoun to Thomas Shevez for 2,000 merks; he died in 1646. (11) Hugh vii. by a daughter of the Earl of Leven, had (12) Hugh viii. who sold Kilmiles to Fraser of Kinaries, Kingyle to Coulbokie, Belladrum to Hugh Fraser, and Buntaite to Chisholm of Comer; and Sir James of Brae gave Dalcross, as a portion with his daughter to Major Bateman. Lord Hugh died about anno 1672, leaving, by the daughter of MacKenzie of Tarbet, a son, (13) Hugh ix. who married Emilia, daughter of John Marquis of Athole, who brought him three daughters; viz. Emilia, married to MacKenzie of Prestonhall; Anne to the Laird of MacLeod, and again to Pourie; and Catharine to William Moray son of Achtertyre. By his marriage articles, this Lord provided his estate to heirs whatsoever: He died in 1696. (14) Simon iii. son of Thomas of Beaufort, by Sybilla daughter of MacLeod, being out-lawed, out-lawed, lived in exile till the year 1714. He then obtained a remiſſion, next year got the life-rent Eſcheat of Preſtonhall, and an annual penſion of L. 300. In 1730, the honours were adjudged to him by the Court of Seſſion; he was made Captain of an independant highland regiment; paid a ſum of money to Preſtonhall's ſon, for his right to the eſtate: But his behaviour, in 1745 and 1746, brought him to the block, 9th April 1747; and his eſtate was forfeited, and honours extinguiſhed. By his firſt wife, daughter of Ludowick Grant of Grant, he left iſſue, Simon now a Colonel, Alexander, Janet married to MacPherſon of Clunie, and Sybilla: By his ſecond wife, daughter of Campbell of Mamore, he left a ſon Archibald. Simon, the eldeſt ſon, having been, againſt his inclination, driven by his father into the late rebellion, ſoon obtained a remiſſion; and having ſerved in the military in America and Portugal, he was advanced to the degree of a Major General: And by an Act of Parliament in 1774, the King granted to him the lands and eſtate of his father, upon certain terms and conditions.

The above mentioned *M. S.* gives an account of a branch of the Fraſers, called the Family of Fruid in Tweedale; of which John Fraſer Biſhop of Roſs, in 1485, was a ſon. In 1492, Anne Wallace, widow of Fruid, with her ſeven ſons, came into the North. Paul and Almond, the two eldeſt, were Clergymen; of John, the third ſon, is deſcended Fraſer of Dunbalach; Alexander, the fourth ſon, was anceſtor of Phopachie; James, the fifth ſon, was anceſtor of Mr Robert Fraſer Advocate, and Mr Michael Fraſer Miniſter of Daviot; of Duncan, the ſixth ſon, is deſcended Fraſer of Daltulich, in the pariſh of Croy; and of Robert, the ſeventh ſon, came the Fraſers called *MacRobie Friſelich*.

The proper Arms of FRASER are: Az. three Fraifes Arg. Motto, JE SUIS PREST. The Family quartered the Biffets Arms, viz. Gul. three antique Crowns, Or. But the late Lovat ftruck out thefe, and having come peaceably to the poffeffion of the eftate, added another Motto, viz. SINE SANGUINE VICTOR.

I now return to the parifh of Bolefkin. Stratherick was the ancient feat of the Grants before they came into Strathfpey; they left fome veftiges behind them to confirm this, for we find the fame names of country feats in Stratherick; as Gartmore, Gartbeg, Dellachaple, &c. which they gave to the places where they fettled in Strathfpey. The above mentioned *M. S.* of the Family of Lovat affirms, that, in the fifteenth century, there were many Grants and Kerans, or *Clanchiaran*, living in Stratherick: And that Thomas, Lord Lovat, having married the daughter of Alexander Gordon of Midmar, brother to the Earl of Huntley, that Earl, in 1493, renounced in Lovat's favour, all his right to the lands of Stratherick: What right Huntley had, or claimed, I know not; but it is certain, that the Frafers have poffeffed that country, for many generations.

The water of Faragack, which giveth name to the country, runneth through the North of the parifh, from Eaft to Weft, and falleth into the Loch two miles North of the church; and the water of Feachlin runneth through the middle of the parifh, emptying into the loch at Fohir, a little South of the church. Upon thefe waters, and the branches of them, ftand the feats of many gentlemen of the name of Frafer; fuch as, Fohir, Gortuleg, and Balnaine, feuers; Taralin, Gartmore, Gartbeg, Drumyample, Kinbrylie, Kilchoinlim, Drummin, &c.

Abertarf came to the Family of Lovat by marriage, and was fold to MacDonald of Glengary, as above related. A fmall glen,

glen, or valley, called Glendoe, runneth up into the hills near the South end of the Loch; and upon the banks of the water Doe, are Molagan, Glendoe, &c. but the main part of this parish lieth upon the rivers of Tarf and Eoich. Tarf, a rapid stream, riseth in the hill of Corryarack, near Gamrvaore in Badenoch, and running North-west, falleth into the South end of Loch Ness. On the banks of it, in the face of the hill, are some corn lands, and at the mouth of it is Kilhuiman, Borlum, &c. The river Eoich is the great source of the Ness, rising out of Loch Eoich, and running four miles North-east, falleth with a deep stream into Loch Ness. In the point between Eoich and Tarf, standeth Fort-Augustus. On the West side, at the mouth of the Eoich, is Inshnakirdich, the seat of Fraser of Coulduthill; and South from it, are the lands of Pitmean. I now go on to

KILMANIVACK Parish.

A small part only of this parish lieth within the PROVINCE of MORAY, viz. Glengary and Achadrom. From Loch Ness, to Loch Eoich, are four miles, a part of Abertarf. Loch Eoich is four miles long, from North to South, and one mile broad. From the South end of Loch Eoich, to the North end of Loch Lochie (the utmost boundary of Moray) is one mile, called Achadrom; a fertile little valley, not above a half mile broad, betwixt chains of high hills. Here are Lagan-Achadrom, Dunan, Kylerofs, &c. The country of Glengray lieth on the West bank of Loch Eoich, and stretcheth into the hills Westward, on both sides of Loch Garie, seven miles. It is a rough, unequal valley, full of Birch Wood, but warm and fertile; at the mouth of the river Garie, where it falleth into Loch Eoich, is Invergary, the seat of Alexander MacDonald of Glengary: And, in this Glen, are the seats of several gentlemen, such as

Lic,

Lic, Lundie, Ardnabee, &c. The inhabitants of Achadrom are Kennedies, called Clan Ulric, from one Ulrick Kennedy, of whom they are said to have descended.

Glengary is planted by MacDonalds, a branch, it is said, of the Clan Ranold, or MacDonalds of Moidart. Lord MacDonald of Aros, (descended of MacDonald Earl of Ross) having died in 1680 without issue, the honours became extinct, and his estate (by a marriage connection) came to Glengary; by which means the fortune of the family lies in Glengary, Abertarf and Knoidart, and is very considerable.

MACDONALD of Glengary.

The MacDonalds derive themselves from Colla Uais King of Ireland, in Century IV. and are said to have come to Scotland in the reign of Malcolm Canmore: They have spread into many branches, of which the Family of Glengary (descended of the Clan Ronalds of Moidart) are as follows:

John, Lord of the Isles, had a son Ranold, who, by a daughter of MacDougal of Lorn, had two sons, viz. Allan of Moidart, and Donald of Glengary. (1) Donald was father of (2) Alexander, father of (3) Alexander, who married Margaret heiress of MacDonald of Loch Alsh, and had Alexander and Angus ancestor of Lord MacDonald of Aros, and died about the year 1515. (4) Alexander married a daughter of MacKenzie of Kintail, and dying about 1550, was succeeded by his son, (5) Alexander, who married a daughter of Lachlan More of MacIntosh; and dying anno 1604, his son (6) Æneas married a daughter of MacIntosh, and had Alexander and Angus of Scothouse; and having been killed by the MacKenzies, before his father's death, (7) Alexander succeeded his grandfather, and by a daughter of Lord Lovat, had Donald Gorm, and Alexander; and upon the demise of Lord MacDonald,

anno

anno 1680 without issue, Alexander obtained his estate, and died about 1685. (8) Donald Gorm, was killed at Killicrankie 1689, unmarried: His brother (9) Alexander married a daughof Seaforth, by whom he had John, Ranald, and Donald: His loyalty led him into the battles of Killicrankie 1689, Cromdale 1690, and Sheriffmuir 1715, and dying in 1724; (10) John, by   MacKenzie, had Alexander, and Angus of Tyindrish; and by a daughter of Glenbuckit, had James and Charles: And dying 1754, (11) Alexander being a prisoner in London in 1745, his brother Angus led the Glengary men to that rebellion, and was himself killed at Falkirk, in January 1746, by an accidental shot: Alexander returned home, and died unmarried, anno 1761, and was succeeded by the son of Angus, by a niece of Struan, viz. (12) Duncan now of Glengary, who married Marjory, daughter of Sir Lewis Grant of Dalvey, and has issue.

From the frequency of the name ALEXANDER, the Chief of this Family is called *Mac-Mhic-Alifter*.

I now return, by the West side of Loch Ness, to

URQUHART PARISH.

The Parish of Urquhart and Glenmoriston, which lye on the West side of the Loch, over against Stratherick. Urquhart stretcheth up into the hills Westward towards the Aird, about five miles, and is a warm and fertile valley: The church standeth near a mile West from the Loch, twelve miles South-west from Inverness. The castle or fort stood on the edge of the Loch: In the valley is Corimonie, a feu-holding pertaining to a branch of the Grants; Shoglie, a mortgage of a Cadet of Corimonie; Achmonie, the heritage of a gentleman of the name of MacKay, or rather MacDonald. All the rest of the parish is the property of Sir James Grant of Grant: Urquhart

quhart was probably a part of the estate of Cummine Lord Badenoch, upon whose forfeiture it was granted to Randolph Earl of Moray. The *M. S.* history of the Family of Sutherland bears, that, in 1359, King David II. gave the Barony, and Castle of Urquhart to William Earl of Sutherland, and his heirs: If so, the grant was afterwards revoked. It is true, Urquhart was excepted out of the grant to John Dunbar Earl of Moray, anno 1372 *(Vid. page* 102*)*; and upon the forfeiture of Earl Archibald Douglas, anno 1455, Urquhart was annexed to the Crown. In a decreet arbitral, betwixt Duncan MacIntosh Captain of Clan Chattan, and Hutcheon Rose of Kilravock, anno 1479, the possession and Duchus of Urquhart is adjudged to Kilravock, *(Pen. Kilr.)*; and in 1482, the Earl of Huntley gave Kilravock a discharge of the rents of Urquhart and Glenmoriston *(Pen. Kilr.).* What right Huntley had to these lands, I know not, if it was not as factor for the Crown. I incline to think, that after the death of Earl John Randulph, in 1346, the Barony of Urquhart was the salary of the Governor of that fort, until it was no longer garrisoned, *(Vid. Milit. Hist.)* Be this as it will, the Laird of Grant purchased Urquhart and Glenmoriston, in the reign of King James VI.

Glenmoriston is distant from Urquhart Southward, eight miles of hills. The river Moriston riseth in the hills of Glensheil, near Kintail, passeth through Loch Clunie, watereth Glenmoriston, and after a course of above thirty miles, emptieth into Loch Ness, four miles below Fort-Augustus. The inhabited glen extends eight miles in length, from the mouth of the river, but the breadth is inconsiderable. The whole valley is warm, fertile, and well inhabited. It is a part of the Barony of Urquhart, and has been the heritage of Grant of Glenmoriston, for above 200 years; that family has a good house at Invermoriston, on the bank of Loch Ness, Urquhart and Glenmoriston are separated from Kirkhill and Kiltarlatie, by a ridge of hills. I now return to the Moray Frith, near Invernefs, to take a view of

KIRKHILL Parish.

The Parish of Kirkhill, formerly called *Wardlaw*, because the Garrison of Lovat kept Ward or Watch, on this Law or Hill. In Irish it is called *Knock-Mhuire*, i. e. Mary's Hill, dedicated to the Virgin. This Parish stretcheth about three miles and a half on the side of the Frith, to the head of it at Beaulie; and from the head of the Frith about one mile and a half, up the East side of Beaulie river; and a ridge of hills to the East, separate it from the parish of Inverness. The church standeth an half mile from the sea, and as much from the river; near five miles West from Inverness, and near three miles North-east from Kiltarlaty. In the East end of the parish, on the Frith, is Bunchrive, sold by Inveralachie to Forbes of Culloden, (as also sold to him Ferintosh) anno 1673: Next Westward on the Frith is Phopachie: A branch of the Frasers had this land in mortgage near 150 years, but it was redeemed by the late Lord Lovat. A mile farther West, on the Frith, is Newtoun, the seat of Fraser of Dunballoch, a gentleman of a good fortune, and a Baron. At the mouth of the river Beaulie, stood the Tower and Fort of Lovat, anciently the seat of the Bissets of Lovat, and afterwards of the Frasers, pleasantly situated on a rich and fertile soil. South of the church is Achnagairn, the heritage of Duncan Fraser Doctor of Medicine, descended of Fraser of Belladrum. At the foot of the hills Eastward, is the Barony of Relick, where James Fraser lately of Relick built a neat and convenient house at Easter Moniack. And close by it is the Tower of Wester Moniack, once the

seat

seat of Fraser of Strichen, and the land continued to be the property of that family, until it was lately sold to the last Lord Lovat. The whole of this parish is a rich soil, fertile in corn, and pasture ground. Next South and West, is

KILTARLATIE Parish.

The Parish of Kiltarlatie stretcheth on the East side of the river Farar, about fourteen miles in length. This river riseth out of Loch Monar, in the Western hills of Ross, passing through Glen-Strath-Farar, the river of Glasater joineth its stream with it at Comer, and having watered the parishes of Kiltarlatie, Kelmorack, and Kirkhill, it falls into the head of the Moray Frith at Lovat, after a course of above forty miles. This river divides Kiltarlatie from Kilmorak parish to the West, and a range of hills runneth between Kiltarlatie, and Urquhart, and Glenmoriston, to the East. The church standeth on the bank of the river, a mile above the lower end of the parish, near three miles South-south-west of Kirkhill, six miles North-west of Urquhart, and about a furlong East-north-east of Kelmorack church, that standeth on the opposite bank.

A half mile below the church is Downie or Beaufort, the seat of the late Lord Lovat, pleasantly situated on a rising ground near the river, and commanding a delightful view, but not improved by art, as it is capable. This was a part of the estate of Sir John Bisset of Lovat, whose second daughter married Sir William Fenton, and brought him this Barony of Beaufort or Downie, and their grand-daughter heiress of Beaufort married Hugh Fraser. A mile East of Downie, is Belladrum, the seat of a gentleman of the name of Fraser, descended of Fraser of Coulbokie; and of Belladrum, are come the Frasers of Achnagairn, Fingask, &c. At the confluence of the rivers above mentioned, is the seat of Fraser of Strawie, of

T whom

whom Fraser of Eskadale, &c. is descended. The rest of this parish is planted by the Clan of Fraser, except Strathglass, that is inhabited by the Chisholms.

Strathglas is a valley watered by the river Glas or Glassater, into which another river, flowing out of Loch Assarig, falleth at Comer, the seat of Roderick Chisholm of Comer or Strathglas Chief of that name. I have not learned upon what occasion the Chisholms sold their lands in Teviotdale, and made a purchase in the North, if it was not upon being made Constables of the Castle of Urquhart. Sir Robert Lauder was Governor of that Castle, anno 1334, (*Abercrombie*). His daughter and heiress was married to Sir Robert Chisholm, also Governor of the said Castle, (*Hist. Kilr.*) and by her he got the lands of Quarrelwood, Kinsterie, Brightmonie, &c. and their daughter married Hugh Rose of Kilravock (*Ibid.*). John Chisholm of Quarrelwood succeeeded his brother Sir Robert, and was father of Robert Chisholm, whose daughter, and only child, Morella, married Alexander Sutherland of Duffus, and brought into that Family the lands of Quarrelwood, Brightmonie, Kinstarie, &c. and the heir male of Chisholm enjoyeth the paternal estate of Strathglass.

The frequent changes of the Proprietors of Land, verify Horace's observation.

> Nam propriæ Telluris Herum Natura, neque illum,
> Nec me, nec quemquam statuit.
> Nunc ager *Umbreni* sub nomine, nuper *Ofelli*
> Dictus, erit nulli proprius; sed cedet in usum
> Nunc mihi, nunc alii.

I have now delineated the Geographical Face of this Province, and proceed to

PART III.

THE

NATURAL HISTORY of MORAY.

Of the Climate and Weather——the Mountains and Valleys——the Soil——the Productions of the Country——the Waters——Animals ——Rarities.

ALTHOUGH this Country is in a climate confiderably **The Air.** Northern, being in the 12th Climate, and from about 57 degrees to 57—40 North latitude, the longeft day being about feventeen hours, forty-fix minutes, and the fhorteft fix hours fourteen minutes; yet no Country in Europe can boaft of a more pure, temperate and wholefome Air. No part of it is either too hot and fultry in Summer, nor too fharp and cold in Winter: And it is generally (and I think juftly) obferved, that in the plains of Moray they have forty days of fair weather in the year, more than in any other country in Scotland. The wholefomnefs of the Air appears in the long lives of its inhabitants: In the year 1747, William Catanach in Plufcardine died at the age of 119 years; in the 1755, Sir Patrick Grant of Dalvey died 100 years old; in 1756, Thomas Frafer of Gortuleg

Gortuleg in Stratherick died aged 97: And generally 80 years are reckoned no great age to the sober and temperate.

The Light. 'Tis observed in this, as in all Northern Countries, that, in the beginning of the year, the Day-light encreases with remarkable celerity, and decreases in a like proportion, at the approach of Winter, which is owing to the inclination of the Earth towards the Poles. And in the Winter nights, the Aurora Borealis (from its desultory motion, called *Merry-dancers* and *Streamers*) affords no small light. Whether this proceeds from nitrous vapours in the lower region of the air, or from a reflection of the rays of the sun, I shall not enquire: It is certain that the *Ignis Fatuus* or *Ignis Lambens* that shineth in the night, is owing to a thick and hazy atmosphere, and a clamy and unctuous dew; for in riding, the horse's maine, and the hair of the rider's head or wig, shine, and by gently rubbing them, the light disappears, and an oily vapour is found on the hand.

The Cold. The Cold in this Country is never found too sharp and severe. In the winters of 1739 and 1740, the frost was not by much so strong in Moray, as it was at Edinburgh and London, and during the continuance of it the water-milns at Elgin were kept going. The warm exhalations and vapours from the sea dissolve the icy particles in the air, and the dry Sandy Soil doth not soon freeze, or retain these particles: And if, among the mountains, the Cold is more intense, it is an advantage to the inhabitants; for by contracting the pores of the body, the vital heat is kept from dissipating, and is repelled towards the inner parts, keeping a necessary warmth in the whole body.

The Heat. The Heat is pretty strong in Moray; for in summer, the Sun's absence under the horizon is so short, that either the atmosphere, or heated soil, has little time to cool. And often, the Heat is greater

greater in the glens and valleys, than in the champaign ground, for the rays of the Sun are pent in and confined, and reverberated from the rocks.

Rains in this Country are seldom hurtful, or occasion inundations. Usually we have the Lambmass Flood in the beginning of August, and sometimes a Michaelmas storm; but the Soil is generally so sandy and dry, that Drought is more hurtful than Rain. *The Rain.*

Snow seldom lieth a long time, even in the glens and valleys; and when it continueth, the benefit of it is considerable, especially if it is attended with Frost; for it mellows and manures the ground, and renders it more fertile, impregnating it with nitre and other principles of vegetation, which improve both corn and grass. *The Snow.*

The Winds that prevail here, are the South-west, the North and North-east. From January to June they generally blow between North-west and North-east, and from June to November between South-west and North-west. In winter they are more various and inconstant: By these periodical changes, the barley seed-time in April and May is cool, and the Harvest is fair and dry. Hurricanes are seldom known in this Country. *The Winds.*

The Mountains and Desarts in the Highlands of Moray, are incomparably more extensive than the areable ground. A chain of the Grampian Mountains runneth on the South side of Spey, and another chain, though lower than the former, stretcheth on the North side, from the mouth to the head of the river. And the straths of the other rivers, Erne, Nairn, Ness and Farar, are, in like manner, inclosed by ranges of hills. Although, to the taste of some travellers, these may seem to disfigure the Country; to others, their diversifying figures form the most agreeable landskip. And certainly, the benefit of *The Mountains.*

these

these Mountains is very great; they collect and dissolve the clouds into rain, and from the reservoires in their bowels, form the rivers and brooks that water the valleys and plains. The Mountain-water being impregnated by the earth, through which it is filtrated, has a vegetable power, which appears in the fertility of the grounds at the foot of Mountains. Their surface affords rich and wholesome pasture, necessary for the inhabitants, whose property consists mainly in cattle. Let me add, that these Mountains, as natural fences inclosing the valleys, make a fresh stream of air fan them, and drive away all noxious vapours: And hence the inhabitants are so sound, vigorous and wholesome, as to know few diseases, except such as are contracted by intemperance, or communicated from other countries.

The Hills and Valleys. In distant ages, and in times of tumults and war, much of the corn land was on the tops and sides of the lower hills. The ridges and furrows, are as yet discernable in many places, and the great heaps of stones gathered out of the corn-fields still remain. Their safety from the incursions of enemies, made them chuse these high places to dwell in; and at that time, the valleys were all covered with woods, and haunted by Wolves; and by burning the woods many glens and valleys are become swamps, marshes and mosses, by the water stagnating in them. When more peaceable times encouraged agriculture and trade, men found the produce of corn in the hilly ground turn to small account. They destroyed the woods in the valleys (of which many roots, and trunks of oak and fir are daily digged up), drained swamps and marshes, cultivated the rich ground, and removed their houses and habitations into more convenient situations, and more fertile land in the valleys.

The

Part III.   The NATURAL HISTORY of MORAY.   151

The Plains of Moray below the hills, extend the whole *The Plains.* length of the Country, from Spey to Farar; but of an unequal breadth, not above fix miles where broadeft. And although the Country is champaign and level, it is fo cultivated, that there is no ftagnating water or fens, to render it unwholefome by exhalations and vapours.

The Soil of this Country is generally, either a light Sand, or *The Soil.* a deep Clay. The Sandy Soil in the plains, is called Moray-coaft, two or three feet deep of a light fandy earth, below which is a ftratum of free-ftone, or of hard compacted gravel. This compofition makes it very warm, and the ftrong re-action of the fun-beams fo heats the Soil, that, without frequent fhowers in Summer, the produce of it is burnt up. The Clay Soil is ftrong and deep, and when well manured with hot dung or fea-ware or weeds, it yieldeth a rich increafe; but it requireth moderate rain, as much as the Sandy Soil doth, for heat and drought bind the Clay, and the circulation of the fap and moifture from the root is ftopt: Hence the common obfervation is,

A mifty May and a dropping June,
Brings the Bonny Land of Moray *aboon.*

The Soil in the Highlands is better watered, and by the fides of rivulets and brooks is deep and fertile, and needeth not much rain; and the valleys running from North-eaft to South-weft, the South fide is always moft fertile, becaufe it is better watered, and lefs dried up by the heat of the fun.

The Corn grain produced by this Soil, is, Wheat, Barley, *The Corn.* Oats, Rye, Beans and Peafe. The low lands are fo plentiful in thefe forts of grain, that they not only have enough for home-confumpt, and fupplying fome parts of the Highlands, but they export annually good quantities into other kingdoms.

And

And if some parts of the Highlands have not plenty of grain for their consumpt, it is not that the Soil is less fertile, or worse manured; but the Barley and Oats are of a smaller body, and a thicker hool, Providence wisely so ordering, to guard the tender grain, which in cold valleys is apt to be chilled and blasted by clamy mill-dews, and sometimes by hoar frost: And though their grain doth not yield so much meal as in the low lands, it yields more and better straw, which to them is no less useful. But the principal cause why they fall short in Corn, is, that the inhabitants are too many for the small extent of land, in so much, that I have often seen ten persons on a poor farm of twenty pounds Scots. And what is wanting in Corn, is abundantly made up in Cattle, which are their main property.

FLAX and HEMP.
Of late Flax and Hemp are propagated, the former especially in great plenty, which is manufactured both for home-consumpt, and for exportation; and no Soil in the kingdom is more proper for Flax, than a part of the low lands of Moray. And it is no less proper, both in the low lands and Highlands for Hemp; but the want of shipping discourages the propagation of it.

POTATOES.
The Potatoe, almost unknown in this Country eighty years ago, is now every where planted with great success, and thereby the poor are supplied, and much barren ground is cultivated, to the no small advantage of the proprietors.

MUSTARD.
Mustard is likewise propagated in the fields, and might be made a profitable article, in its quality not inferior to any in the Kingdom.

GARDEN FRIUTS.
There are no Garden Fruits or Herbs in any part of Britain, but can be brought to as great perfection in the low lands of Moray, by the same or less culture. Gentlemens Gardens yield, in plenty, Nectarines, Peaches, Apricotes, Apples, Pears, Plumbs,

Part III.   The NATURAL HISTORY of MORAY.   153

Plumbs, Genes, Cherries, Straw-berries, Rasps, Goose berries, Currants, &c. all of the best kinds. And the kitchen garden affords the greatest plenty of kitchen Herbs and Roots.

Nor are the Wild Fruits and Herbs less various and plentiful, especially in the Highlands, in woods and heaths, such as Hasle-nuts, Service berries, Sloes, Rasps, Bramble-berries, Hip-berries, Bug-berries, Blae-berries, Averans, or Wild Straw-berries. Wild Herbs of the Medicinal kind abound every where: As Valerian, Penny-royal, Maiden-hair, Scurvie grass, Sorrel, Gentian, Brook-lime, Water-trefoil, Mercury, Germander, Worm-wood, Liver-wort, Sage, Centaury, Buglos, Mallows, Tormentil, Scordium, &c. I cannot here omit the Root and Herb Carmile, which abounds much in heaths and birch woods. DIO *in Severo*, speaking of the ancient Caledonians, says, " Certum cibi genus parant ad omnia, quem si ceperunt quantum est unius fabæ magnitudo, mineme esurire aut sitire solent.*" Dr Sibbald observes, from *Cæs. de. Bel. Civ. lib. 3.* That Valerius's soldiers had found a kind of Root called *Chara*, " quod admistum lacte multum inopiam lævabat, id at " similitudinem panis effeciebant, ejus erat magna copia.†" Theophrastus calls it *Radix Scythica*, and says, That the Scythes could live on it and mare's milk for many days. To me it is probable, that Cæsar's *Chara*, and our *Carmile* (*i. e.* the Sweet-root, for it tastes like Liquorish) are the same, and are Dio's *Cibi Genus*. It grows in small knots on the surface of the ground, and bears a green stalk four or five inches long, and a small

WILD and MEDICINAL HERBS.

CARMILE.

U

---

* " They provide a certain kind of food, of which if they take the bigness of
" a Bean, they use not to hunger or thirst."

† " Which, mixed with Milk, greatly relieves hunger: They prepared it
" like Bread, and had great plenty of it."

small red flower. I have often seen it gathered, dried and used on journeys, especially on hills, to appease hunger; and being pounded and infused in water, it makes a pleasant wholesome balsamick drink, and is so used sometimes in the Highlands.

FORRESTS.   If we view the Forrests, we shall not find them, as in England, large woods inclosed for holding the King's game. Such woods, but not inclosed, there seem to have been in this country, as the Forrests of Rothemurchus, Tarnua, Inverculan, &c. (*Appendix* N° XII.). And now Forrests are such parts of the Mountains and Glens, as are appropriated to the pasturing of Deer and other game. The King is properly the Superior and Master of all Forrests, and Gentlemen in whose lands they lie are but the hereditary keepers of them. The Duke of Gordon has large Forrests in Glenavon, and in Badenoch, in which I have seen three hundred Deer in one flock or herd. Lovat, Grant, Rothemurchus, MacIntosh, Glengary, have fine Forrests; but they are now every where laid open for pasturing Cattle; and few Deer (which love a clean pasture) are to be found in them, but have removed into the Forrest of Athole which is carefully kept.

WOODS.   Notwithstanding the visible destruction of Woods in this Province, by burning, felling, clearing of Valleys and Glens, no Country in Scotland is more plentifully served than this is. In the parish of Duthel, Sir James Grant has a Fir Wood several miles in circuit. And in the parishes of Abernethie, Kinchardine, Rothemurchus, and Alvie, the Duke of Gordon, Grant, MacIntosh, and Rothemurchus, have an almost continued Fir Wood, fourteen miles in length, and in some places more than three miles in breadth. In Glenmoriston, there is a good Fir Wood, and in Strathglas a very large one. Parts of these Woods are often burnt by accidental fire; and in the

year

year 1746, the Wood of Abernethie suffered some miles in circuit, by which some millions of trees, young and old, were destroyed. Here I cannot but observe, as peculiar to Fir Woods, that they grow and spread always to the East, or between the North and the South-east, but never to the West or South-west. The cause of this seemeth to be, that in the months of July and August, the great heat opens the Fir apples then ripe, and the winds at that season, blowing from South-west to West-south-west, drive the seed out of the open husks to the East and the neighbouring Earths. Almost all the Glens and Valleys abound in Birch, Hasle, Alar, Aspine, Saugh or Sallow, Holly, Willows, Haws, Service-tree, &c. And in the Plains, are the Forrest of Tarnuay, and the Woods of Inshoch, Kilravock, and Calder; and in this last, and in Inveravon, Alvie, and Urquhart, are large Oaks. I incline to think, that these Woods are the remains of the Sylva Caledonia, which Ptolemy extends, "A Lelalonio Lacu ad Æstuarium Vararis," from Loch-Lomond to the Moray Frith.

With this abundance of Wood, there are Materials for Building found in great plenty. Throughout the Plains of Moray, there are rich quarries of Free-stone, easy to hew and dress, and yet durable. And in the Highlands, there is the greatest plenty of Lime-stone, besides some quarries of it near Elgin, in Duffus, at Tarnua, &c. Slate-stones are found both in the Highlands and Lowlands; and good Clay almost in every parish within the Province.

<small>MATERIALS for BUILDING.</small>

There are no mines of Coal as yet discovered in this Country; yet I doubt not but such there are, and in a few generations the exigencies of the people will require their digging for them. In the Highlands, there is an inexhaustible store of Turf and Peats; and the Lowlands (except the parishes on the coast, from Spey to Findhorn) are as yet well served in these,

<small>FUEL.</small>

and

and in Broom, Heather, and Furz. I have not observed any Furz or Whins in Strathspey or Badenoch; and only in the low Country: But the Moss ground is much exhausted, and will soon become very scarce.

MINES. No Gold, Silver, Copper, Brass, or Tin, has as yet been discovered in this Country. But there are rich Mines of Iron-ore in several parts; and at Coulnakyle in Abernethie parish, a Forge was set up lately, which made very good Iron, but through the extravagance and luxury of the Managers was given up. At Achluncart, in the parish of Boharm, there is a quarry of fine Whet-stone; and in Glenlivat, and other places, there is great plenty of rich Marle for Manure.

DYEING. Let me add, that there is in this Country, several materials for Dyeing, which the people use with success. With the top of Heather they make a Yellow colour; with a red moss growing on stones, and called Korkir, they dye Red; with the bark of the Alder or Allar-tree, they dye Black; and a Gentleman in the parish of Kirkmichael has several hands employed in gathering, in the hills, Materials for Dyeing Blue, Ingrain, Purple, &c. I have seen some of the Indigo he has made, and it proves very rich and good. This invention, if successful, may be a great benefit to the Country. But the Gentleman died lately; and with him, that useful art.

Salt Water. Having surveyed the Land, I shall now look into the Waters. The Moray Frith is the only Salt Water in this Province, and extendeth the whole length of it. It is somewhat remarkable, that though from Buchan ness to Beaulie, the Frith is about seventy miles in length, and in some places twenty in breadth, there is not any one island in it. The North shore of this Frith, in Ross and Cromarty, is high and rocky; but the opposite Moray shore is low and sandy: Hence, by the Water rebounding from the Ross-side, it encroacheth much, in some places,

places, on the Moray-fide. On the confines of the parifhes of Duffus and Alves, there is a fmall Bay, which about fixty years ago or little more, was a mofs, in which they digged up great roots of trees, and abundance of peats, and now a five hundred ton fhip may ride at anchor in it. And when fome years ago, I viewed it, I found, that, if the fea fhall encroach further, and rife about four feet higher, it will overflow and drown all the plains of Duffus, Kenedar, and Innes. The like encroachment it begins to make, at the Town of Findhorn; for as it formerly cut off the old Town, it is not improbable that it will furround this new Town, and endanger the lands of Muirtoun and Kinlofs.

The Frefh Waters are, the Rivers already named, and the Lakes. The Water in all thefe is light and wholefome; and not to mention here the Salmon taken in the rivers, Spey ferveth to float down much of the Oak and Fir Woods to Germach, where they are fawed and fhipped for export. The Loch and River of Nefs likewife are very ufeful, not only in keeping a communication by Water to Fort-Auguftus, but in floating much Wood from Glenmorifton and Urquhart to Invernefs. The Firs of Strathglas are in like manner brought down the River Farar to Beaulie. I fhall afterwards fpeak of Loch Nefs and Lochindorb: The other Lakes have nothing remarkable, but what fhall be obferved in treating of FRESH WATERS.

The Animal produce of this Country, whether on the Land or in the Waters. ANIMALS

Among the Tame Land Animals, the Horfe claims the preference: In the Low-lands, they have got of late a brood of Horfes, much ftronger than they formerly had, and very fit both for the faddle and draught; yet in the Highlands, their fmall Horfes are more proper for rough and hilly ground. They are fmall, ftrong, and durable; and being paftured TAME BEASTS.

among

among hills and rocks, they are very sure footed; when they come to a mire or bog, they smell to it, and sound it with one foot, and if they find not a firm bottom, they will not go forward; They live and work in winter upon a little straw, without any corn. The Oxen and Cows are small, owing to the climate; but their flesh is more delicious, than what is stall-fed: In the Plains where they sow grass-seeds, they have Cows of a bigger size; but in the Highlands, the small Cattle are more serviceable, where their pasture in Summer is in woods and hills. The Sheep, though of a small size, are broody, and their flesh is tender and delicate; the Wool in Strathspey and Badenoch is little inferior in fineness to the English Wool. The Highlands are well stored with Goats, whose flesh, though dry and strong, is very wholesome; their Milk and Whey are medicinal restoratives, as they brooze upon the finest herbs among the rocks; their Skins are a good article of trade. Hogs are not plentiful in this Country, but the few that are fed about milns and barns are very good. The Dogs are of various kinds, some small and mild, others large and surly: Some Terriers, to ferret the Fox out of his hole; But the most remarkable is the Greyhound, so swift and strong as to catch and kill the Red Deer in the Forrest.

Wild Beasts. The Woods and the Hills shelter many Wild Beasts, as well the useful as the hurtful. The Red Deer in our hills are allowed to be of the largest size, and, if the Forrests were duely kept, would be very plentiful; they are of the Gregarious kind, and go in herds; they always brooze in the hills, and move forward against the wind, and never with it, but when they are chaced; they shed their horns annually until they become old; the young horns for some months are covered with a skin as fine and soft as velvet, to preserve them against the inclemency of the weather; as the Deer keep the open hills,

the

the Roes are seldom found except in woods; the Foxes destroy so many of their young, that now they are but few in number. Hares are to be met with every where, even in the high hills, where in Winter they change their colour into white. We have very few Rabbits in this Country. These are the useful Wild Beasts in this Country, and fit for food. The rapacious and hurtful beasts are but few: I cannot find, that ever there were in this Country any Lyons, Tygers, Leopards or Bears. It appears by the names of several places, and by statutes made for destroying them, that there were Wolves in this Country about 300 years ago; but now there are none. There are still in this Province, Foxes, Badgers, Martens, Squirrels, Wesels, Whitreds, Wild Cats. Of these the Fox is the most hurtful, and destroys not only much of the Game, but also Lambs, Kids, Fawns, &c. and notwithstanding the many arts used to destroy them, they find such shelter in woods and rocks, that they are very numerous. The Badger is a harmless animal, and lives upon grass; he is so strong in the back, that no stroke will kill him, but a small stroke on the forehead lays him flat. The Marten is of the Cat kind, but the head is small and long, and the colour a dark brown, and the fur nothing inferior to sable; it haunts the woods, lives on mice, birds, &c. and is quite harmless, but defends fiercely when attacked, or when it has its young. The Squirrel is a pretty, sportive, harmless creature; it is a kind of a Wood-Wesel, haunts the fir trees, if you toss chips or sticks at it, it will toss pieces of the bark back again, and thus sports with you; if it is driven out of a tree, and skipping into another finds the distance too great, it turns back to its former lodge, its bushy tail serving for a sail or wings to it. The Wesel, a kind of Pole-cat, and the Whitred are well known. In the Highlands they change their colour into white in time

of

of snow: The Wild Cats are no other than the house Cats that leave their home, and lodge in rocks and woods, and in this Country do little hurt. To these let me add the Mice and Rats, that are well known, yet not so destructive here as in other places. I have never seen any Rats in Strathspey or Badenoch, although I have lived long in these Countries.

VIPOROUS ANIMALS. Of the Viporous or Poisonous Animals, there are few in this Country. The Serpents are small, few of them a yard long, and their bite is commonly cured by a bath of the leaves buds and tender bark of the Ash-tree: They cast their slough or epidermis annually: It is a common opinion, that Serpents have a power of charming and bringing down into their mouths, Birds, Squirrels and other animals; whether this is done by poisonous effluvia breathed out by the Serpent, and affecting animals within the sphere of these effluviæ, so that they are stupified, and fall down; or if, as the eye of the setting dog makes the patridges stand confunded, so the Bird, knowing the Serpent to be his natural enemy, is stupified with fear seeing the Serpent's eye fixed upon him, and so falls; or what else may be the cause, I shall not determine, nor enquire.

Lizards are frequent, generally about five inches; but I have seen some a foot in length. They are of a dark yellow colour, run swiftly in the heaths, and are very harmless. Toads and Frogs are not very numerous. Catterpillars in April and May, often destroy the fruit of trees and shrubs. But we have few of those Gnats, which in other Countries are extremely troublesome.

FOWLS. The number of Feathered Animals, which are either Natives of this Country, or Birds of passage, that visit us annually, is considerable. The Tame or Barn-door Fowls, as Pea-Cocks, Turkies, Geese, Ducks, Pidgeons and Poultry, are plentiful.

The

The Ravenous and Carniverous Wild Fowls are numerous. Among these, the Eagle is, with us, called the King of Birds: He destroys not only much of the small game, but also Lambs, Kids, Calves and Foals: He nestles commonly in high rocks, difficult to come at; but indulgent Nature has provided that the ravenous Eagle and Hawke should have but few young, and seldom more than two in the year; when the harmless little Wren has ten or twelve. Hawkes, Gleds, Stenchils, Ravens, Crows, Rooks, Magpies, &c. are numerous. The harmless Wild Fowls are, the Swan, Caperkylie, (called also the Cock of the Wood) in Latin *Capricalea*, as if he infested the Goats, but properly in Irish *Capal-Coil*, i. e. the Wood Horse, being the chief Fowl in the Woods: He resembles, and is of the size of a Turkey Cock, of a dark grey, and red about the eyes; he lodges in bushy Fir trees, and is very shy: But the Hen, which is much less in size, lays her eggs in the Heather, where they are destroyed by Foxes and Wild Cats, and thereby the Caperkylie is become rare: His flesh is tender and delicious, though somewhat of a resinous Fir taste.

The Water Animals in this Country, are common to it with other places. In, and near to the Moray Frith, is found, Cod, Ling, Haddock, Whiting, Scate, Flounders, Makarel, Prawns: And of the Testaceous kind, Oisters, Cockles, Muscles, Lobsters, Crabs, in such plenty, that there is not in Britain a cheaper Fish Market. The nearness of this Frith to the Northern Ocean made it antiently much frequented by Whales; insomuch, that Orkney had its name from that Fish: For in Irish, *Orc* is a species of Whale, and *I* an Island; and so *Orcy*, is the Island of Whales. As yet Whales follow Shoals of Cod, or Herring into this Frith; In 1719, a Whale upwards of fifty feet in length, was left by the tide at Phopachie, near Inverness; another of the like dimensions was stranded in the Barony

WATER ANIMALS.

rony of Innes; and one in the Barony of Infhoch, about the year 1754: They were all of the *Cetus Dentatus* kind, and yielded much *Spermaceti*. Young Whales, Porpoifes, Seals, are frequent in the Frith, and fometimes plenty of Herring. The rivers of Spey, Findhorn, Nefs, and Farar, abound in Salmon of the beft kind: And in all our Rivers and Brooks, are delicious Trouts and Eels. I have feen in Spey, fome Lampreys, which feem to be of the longer Eel kind, above four feet in length, and of a great thicknefs. In all our Lakes there are Pikes of a very large fize, and in many Lochs, particularly in the Loch of Moy, near MacIntofh's houfe, there is fo great plenty of a fat Trout, called Red-wame, (becaufe the belly of it is of a vermillion red) that at one caft of the net, there will be taken out fometimes upwards of two hundred. In the river of Spey, there are Pearl Shells, in which I have feen many ripe Pearls, of a fine water, and great value.

RARITIES. I fhall now conclude this part, with an account of the Rarities, whether of Nature or Art, found in this Country. And,

1. The only Rarities of Art I fhall take notice of, are: The Chapter Houfe, called the *Apprentice Ifle*, in the Cathedral at Elgin; For which, fee Part VI. Ecclefiaft. Hiftory, § 3. The Obelifk near Forres: See Part V. Military Hiftory. The Sea Burgh: See Part V. Military Hiftory. And the Druid Circles and Cairns: See Part VI. Ecclefiaft. Hiftory, § 2.

2. As to Natural Rarities, the Loch and River of Nefs merit our notice. Thefe never freeze, but retain their natural heat in the moft extreme froft: Upon the Banks of the Loch, Snow feldom lies two days; and Corn ripens much fooner than in other places. This quality is probably owing to Mines of Sulphur in and near to the Loch. This Loch, tho' about twenty-two miles in length, has no Ifland in it; in fome

parts,

parts, it has been founded with a line of about three hundred fathoms, and no bottom found. This depth, with the lightness of the Water, makes waves rise very high, yet not broken upon it. What Mr Gordon writes in his Geography, on the authority of Sir George MacKenzie Advocate, concerning the Hill *Meal-fuor-vonie*, is a mistake. That Hill is not two thirds of a mile of perpendicular height from the surface of the Loch, neither is there any Lake on the Top of it.

3. The Loch of Dundlechack, in the parish of Durris, does not freeze before the month of February; but in that month, it is in one night covered with Ice. This I have been assured of, by the inhabitants near to it.

4. The Cascade, or Water Fall neer to Fohir in Stratherick. Here the River Feachlin, contracted between Rocks, falls down a precipice about an hundred feet high, as I conjecture from a bare view of it, and breaking on the rocky shelves, the Water is dissipated and rarified, and fills the great hollow with a perpetual mist.

5. The Carngorm Stones. This Mountain, of a great height, is in Kinchardine in Strathspey; about the top of it, Stones are found of a chrystal colour, deep Yellow, Green, fine Amber, &c. and very transparent, of a Hexagon, Octagon, and Irregular figure. They are very solid, will cut as well as Diamond, and being now in great request, are much searched for, on this, and other hills; they are cut for Rings, Seals, Pendants, Snuff Boxes, &c.

6. In the Parishes of Kinnedar and Duffus, there are several Caves; some are ten or twelve feet high, and it is uncertain how far they extend; they open to the sea, in a Hill of Free Stone, and probably were formed by the impetuous waves washing away the Sand and Gravel between the Strata of Stone.

7. Chalybeat.

7. Chalybeat Mineral Water, at Teynland in Lanbride; at Achterblair in Duthil; at Achnagairn in Kirkhill, and other places; an unctuous Mineral at Miltoun of Rylugas in Edinkylie: Thefe are much frequented, and found Medicinal in feveral Difeafes.

8. The Black Cock, called by fome Writers of Zoology *Gallus Scoticanus* as peculiar to Scotland. It is the moft beautiful Fowl of our country, larger in the body than any Capon, of the colour of the Pea Cock, but wanting the proud train, which would retard his flight; he haunts the birch woods in the hills, and is very fhy; although he is not fo large in the body as a Goofe, he has more flefh, and is more delicious.

9. I may reckon among our Rarities, the Hill of Benalar on the South fide of Spey, in the braes of Badenoch. It is not improbable, but this is the higheft ground in Scotland; for Brooks from it fall into Spey, Lochie, and Tay, and fo enter into the Sea at Germach, Fort-William, and Dundee.

10. Let me add, as now become a Rarity, the *Courach*. This nautic veffel was antiently much ufed; SOLINUS, *Cap.* 22. fays of the Irifh in his day, " Navigant autem vimi- " neis alveis, quos circundant ambitione tergorum bubulorum," a fhort, but exact, difcription of the *Courach*. It is in fhape oval, near three feet broad, and four long; a fmall keel runs from the head to the ftern; a few ribbs are placed acrofs the keel, and a ring of pliable wood around the lip of it. The whole machine, is covered with the rough hide of an Ox or a Horfe; the feat is in the middle, it carries but one perfon, or if a fecond goes into it to be wafted over a river, he ftands behind the rower, leaning on his fhoulders; in floating timber, a rope is fixed to the float, and the rower holds it in one hand, and with the other manages the paddle; he keeps the float in deep water, and brings it to fhore when he will; in returning
home,

home, he carries the machine on his shoulders, or on a horse. In Irish, *Curach* signifies the Trunk or Coat of the Body; and hence this vessel had its name, and probably its first model.

11. I shall add but one Rarity more, not indeed natural to this Country, but adventitious; I mean the Locust; which came to our coast in July 1748, and for ought I know was never before seen in it. This flying insect is full two inches long in the body, and half an inch round, consisting of several rings or cartilages; the head is in the form of a Lobster's head, broad and covered with strong scales, with two antennæ; the mouth wide, and armed with sharp teeth; the neck and shoulders covered with a scale like a helmet; the eyes large and lively; it has three pair of legs, the nearest to the head about an inch in length, the next pair somewhat longer, and both armed with sharp claws; the third pair, with which it leaps, are two inches long, besides the foot that is near half an inch; the leg has an inflexure or joint in the middle; the upper part or thigh, is in form like a bird's thigh; the lower half is smaller, but serrated or like a saw; the foot has three glands in the sole to tread softly, and is armed with three claws on the heel, and as many at the point, to take a firm hold; the body is covered with two pair of wings, the under wing is finer, and of a silver colour, and the upper is stronger, and spotted of silver and brown; when the wings are folded, the whole length of the Locust is two inches and a half. From what Country they came here I know not, but they found this Climate too cold to generate in.

PART

PART IV.

THE

CIVIL and POLITICAL HISTORY of MORAY.

Of the Inhabitants, their Manners, way of Living, and Genius—Agriculture and Improvements—Manufactures, Trade and Commodities for Export—Civil Government—Feudal Customs—Titles of Honour—Counties; Inverness, Nairn, Moray or Elgin—Regalities—Baronies—The abolishing the Heretable Jurisdictions—Courts of Judicature—Roll of Barons—Royal Burroughs; Inverness, Elgin, Nairn, Forres—Burghs of Barony, &c.——

The Inhabitants.

IT cannot well be doubted, that the ancient Inhabitants of this Province, were the Picts and Scots; the one inhabiting the Low-lands on the coast, the other the Highlands among the hills. The Romans called the former *Picti*, because they painted their bodies; but their true name was *Phichtiad*, i. e. Fighters, because they were brave and valiant. The antient writers bring them from the European Scythia; BEDE, *Lib.* 1. says, " It happened that the Picts from Scythia, " as it is said, entered the ocean in long ships. Coming to
" Britain,

"Britain, they began to reside in the Northern parts of the Island, for the Britons had possessed the Southern." And NENNIUS, Sect. 9. writes, "The Picts came and possessed the Islands called the Orcneys, and afterwards from the adjacent Islands wasted many large Countries in the left, i. e. Eastern side of Britain, and there remain to this day."

The Picts thus coming from Scandia, about the mouth of the Baltic Sea, had an easy course to Shetland and Orkney, and thence to the Continent, where, it is by all acknowledged, they possessed the Eastern coast, Southward to Tweed, and consequently they inhabited the Plains of Moray. The Scots were so called by the Romans, from *Scuot*, i. e. in Celtic, a Shield or Target, which they much used; They were unquestionably Celts, and the same with the ancient Britains, and were driven by the Picts (as NENNIUS hints) out of the Grampian coast, into the glens and valleys; When the Pictish kingdom was overthrown about anno 842, the Picts were not extirpated as some authors write; It is certain, they made a part of King David's army in the battle of the Standard anno 1138 (*de Bello Standardi*). And when in the reign of King Malcolm IV. many of the Moravienses were transplanted into the South (*Vid. Milit. Hist.*), Lowlanders, no doubt of a Pictish descent, were brought to replace them; and so the inhabitants of the Lowlands of Moray were, and as yet are, of a Pictish origin.

This is confirmed by the Language of the Country; for though Gentlemen, and all who have any liberal education, speak the English tongue in great propriety, yet the illiterate Peasants use the broad Scottish or Buchan Dialect, which is manifestly the Pictish. And the Pictish, English, Saxon, Danish, Swedish, Icelandish, and Norwegian, are but the various dialects of the Gothic and Teutonic languages; as the British, Welsh, Cornish, Scottish, Irish, are Dialects of the Gallic and Celtic.

Language.

Now

Now that, since the Revolution in 1688, Schools are erected both in the Highlands and Lowlands, the English Tongue spreads and prevails; insomuch, that in the parishes of Inveravon, Knockando, Edinkylie and Nairn, where, in my time, Divine Worship was performed in Irish, now there is no occasion for that language.

Way of Living and Manners.

What the Manners and Way of Living of the ancient Inhabitants were, we can know only by the short hints the Roman Writers give us, of the ancient Caledonians, Scots and Picts, which I shall not here transcribe. But what TACITUS, *De Mor. Germ.* writes, is true of this Country in its ancient state; " They do not dwell together in Towns, but live separate, as " a fountain of water, a plain, or a grove pleased them." SIDONIUS APOLLINARIUS, *Epist.* 20. in describing a Gothish Gentleman, gives a lively picture of a Highland Scotsman. " He covers his feet to the ankle with hairy leather, or rul-" lions, his knees and legs are bare, his garment is short, " close, and parti-coloured, hardly reaching to his hams, his " sword hangs down from his shoulder, and his buckler covers " his left side." Nay, Dr SHAW's Account of the Arabs and Kabyles of Barbary is a plain description of the more rude parts both of the Lowlands and Highlands. They are, says he, " the same people, if we except their religion, they were 2000 " years ago, without regarding the novelties in dress or beha-" viour, that so often change; Their *Gurbies*, i. e. Houses, are " daubed over with mud, covered with turf, have but one " chamber, and in a corner of it, are the Foles, Kids, and " Calves; The *Hyke*, i. e. Blanket or Plaid, six yards long " and two broad, serves for dress in the day, and for bed and " covering in the night; by day, it is tucked by a girdle. " Their milns for grinding corn, are two small grind-stones, " the uppermost turned round by a small handle of wood,

" placed

" placed in the edge of it. When expedition is required,
" then two perfons fit at it, generally women." This explains
Exod. ii. 5. *Matth.* xxiv. 41.

One would imagine the Doctor had been defcribing the way
of living in Glengary. It might be eafily made appear, that the
ancient Moravienfes, though bold and brave, were contentious,
proud, turbulent and revengeful, and upon the fmalleft pro-
vocation run to arms, and butchered one another; and this
wicked difpofition ran in the blood, from one generation to
another.

But now that fierce and wild temper is done away, and no
Country in the Kingdom is more civilized than the Low-
lands of Moray. Their education fince the Revolution verifies,
That

> *Ingenuas didiciffe feliciter artes,*
> *Emollit mores, nec finit effe feros.*

And even the Highlands, except Glengary, and fome other
fkirts, are more peaceable and induftrious than other Highland Countries. In a word, one will not find, in the common people of this Country, either the rufticity of the Lowlanders, or the rudenefs of the Highlanders in fome other Countries; and the Gentry are not exceeded by any of their neighbours for politenefs and civility. In no Country are the people more hofpitable; both the gentry and the peafants have a
pleafure in entertaining ftrangers, in which they rather exceed than fall fhort; and this hofpitable temper is remarked
in the Highlands, where there are but few inns to accommodate
travellers, and where the natives, in looking after their cattle,
often travel from one country to another; yet I muft own,
that fome other focial virtues are rather on the decline; that
benevolence, in fupplying the wants and relieving the dif-
treffes

tresses of relations and neighbours, and mutually assisting one another in their necessary affairs, that once shined in this country, is degenerated into Selfishness. The laudable custom of accommodating debates and differences, by an amicable arbitration, is become obsolete, through the craft of the chicaning tribe: And to the same set of men it is much owing, that there is less of ingenuity and plainness, of trust and confidence in social dealing, than I have seen.

GENIUS. The Skill of this People in Mechanics, and their Genius for Arts and Sciences, is not inferior to any other corner of the Kingdom. The Peasants build Houses, make all their Instruments for Agriculture, frame their Corn and Saw-milns, and many of them are Tanners, Shoemakers, Weavers, Joiners, &c. nor is their capacity for Arts and Sciences inferior to their skill in Mechanics. No people sooner learn the art of War, or make more eminent Officers and brave Soldiers. It is true, in later ages the Lowlanders, formerly brave, by their continual labour about their farms, and by the disuse of Arms, have become more heavy and phlegmatic; and yet when brought young into the Military, are exceeded by no soldiers in bravery and fidelity. The Highlanders have always had a peculiar advantage for martial exercises: The fresh and wholesome air they breathe, their plain and homely diet, their continual motion and exercise, render them vigorous, healthy, and lively. They are inured to cold and fatigue, and accustomed to arms from their child-hood, which, with the rugged rocks they daily traverse, inspires them with a contempt of dangers and difficulties; and their freedom from Slavery and Vassalage, (except a dependence on their Chiefs who encouraged their manliness) gave them a sprightliness, and generosity of mind, elevated above the boorish and mean spirit of the common soldiery. The generous, brave, and

and steady behaviour of the Highland Regiments in the late Wars, abundantly evinces that they were an honour to their Country: How long they shall continue so, I shall not pretend to guess. The Highlanders being disarmed, and stripped of their native dress, appear not only aukward and slovenly in the Lowland garb, but dejected and dispirited: But if this change of Dress makes them less fit for the field, it may render them more fit for the farm, and the useful arts of life.

In brief, the Genius of the Inhabitants of this Country will appear from the following list of Men, eminent in the State and in the Field, on the Bench and in the Church, all of them Natives of, or residing in Moray.——viz. Sir John Cummine Lord Badenoch, conjunct Guardian of the Kingdom, anno 1299:—Thomas Randolph Earl of Moray, Governor in 1329:—Sir Andrew Moray, Lord Bothwell, of the Family of Duffus, conjunct Governor in 1332:—John Randolph Earl of Moray, General in 1346:—Gavin Dunbar, grandson of Sir Alexander of Westfield, Chancellor in 1528; and one of the Regents in 1536:—the Earls of Huntley often Chancellors:—John Lesly Bishop of Ross, bastard son of the Parson of Kingusie, President of the Court of Session in 1564:—Duncan Forbes of Culloden, late President of that Court:—Alexander Brodie of Brodie; Sir Francis Grant of Cullen; Patrick Grant of Elchies; all Senators of the College of Justice:—Gavin Dunbar above mentioned, Archbishop of Glasgow 1524:—Gavin Dunbar, son of Sir Alexander of Westfield, Bishop of Aberdeen 1518:—Gilbert Moray, son of Duffus, Bishop of Caithness anno 1222:—John Innes, son of John Innes of that Ilk, Bishop of Moray in 1406:—Adam Gordon, son of Huntley, Bishop of Caithness in 1460:—Alexander Gordon, son of Huntley, Bishop of Galloway 1558:—John Lesly above mentioned, Bishop of Ross anno 1565.——Not to mention the Bishops of Moray, Natives of the Country, nor the learned Professors and Advocates of later times.

Experientia constat,
Summos sæpe viros, et magna exempla daturos
Verveeum in patria, crassoque sub aere nasci.

Agriculture

If we view the Agriculture, Improvements, Manufactures, Trade and Commerce of this Province, we will not find them such as might be expected. The people have, for ages, continued in one beaten tract of Agriculture; Their only manure, in the inland, is the raw dung of cattle, not fermented or rotten, but mixed with coarse gravel, or dry sand; near the coast, they mix sea ware in the dung-hill; if the soil were not good, it would yield little by such poor manure. Marle, a fat and unctuous earth, and limestone in abundance, is found in many places. Few parts of the dry and hot soil in the Highlands or Lowlands but may be moistened and fattened by an easy conveyance of rills of Water to them; and by inclosing the corn land, resting it, and sowing grass seeds, it would be greatly improved: But the severe exactions of Masters, and the poverty of Tenants, hinder all improvements; Tenants have neither ability nor encouragement to try experiments; some have no leases; and if they who have them shall improve their farms, strangers will reap the benefit of it; for at the expiration of the lease, they must pay an additional rent, or a high grassum, or entry-money, which, if they refuse, the farm will be put to the roup, and the improver will be removed.

Improvements.

The Country is very capable of improvement, and several branches of Police and Improvement, which might be easily made, are much wanted. In the Plains of Moray, the moss ground, from which they take their fuel, and in which the Tenants

Tenants find Fir-roots for light, and Fir and Oak timber for building, will soon be exhausted; and the price of Wood from the Highlands is become very high. But of late, the Duke of Gordon, the Earls of Findlater and Fife, Sir James Grant, Sir Lewis Grant, and some other Gentlemen, have planted millions of barren trees, and continue in such improvement; yet no care is taken to plant barren timber in the extensive heaths and muirs, or indeed any where, except a few trees about Gentlemen's Seats. In no Country can the open fields be more easily inclosed, either with a dry stone dyke or wall, or with a ditch, bank and hedges; But this is totally neglected, except about gentlemen's manours. The watering of ground is a rational and easy, and in other countries a beneficial improvement; but here not once attempted. The draining of lakes and marshy ground, would at once improve and beautify the Country; but the discords of Heretors prevent it. No Country in Scotland yields finer Wool, or may yield better Flax; yet there are no Factories, for either Woolen or Linen Cloath: And it is well known how conveniently the Country is situated for a Herring Fishery; but it is totally neglected.

In these useful branches, our Country is shamefully deficient; *Manufactures.* but in some others, a small advance has been made of late. Gentlemen have drained and inclosed their own manours, which till of late lay open and naked: Wheat is propagated in greater plenty, and of a better body, by fallowing the ground, and bringing the seed from England; Flour Milns, and Milns for sheelling Barley are set up; Flax is propagated with good success; Lint Milns and Bleach-fields are erected: And in the Highlands, the propagating Flax, and Spinning it, makes progress, by the encouragement given by the Trustees, who have settled a Factory at Invermoriston, purchased ground,
built

built the proper houses, and allow Liberal Salaries to an Overseer, Spinsters, Wheel Wrights, Flax Dressers, &c. and now the Country has Linen coarse and fine for home consumpt, and a small article for export; and though we have no Factories for Weaving, yet we have good Weavers of Plain and Figured Linen. The manufacturing of Broad Woolen Cloth is likewise improved by private hands; And, which was little known thirty years ago, Cotton Cloth is wrought and dyed with success. Let me add, that Potatoes are now planted every where, to the great benefit of the poor, and the improving of ground. Grass Seeds are sown by Gentlemen to great advantage.

Trade and Commerce. With respect to Trade and Commerce, there are many obstructions. We have no good harbours; Garmoch or Speymouth is often choaked with banks of sand; Lossie-mouth is but a creek, and receives no ship of any burden; Findhorn is much barred; and Inverness river receives but Sloops and Doggers. Were our harbours good, we have but few articles for export: Our merchants are generally men of no stock; and our landed gentlemen have no inclination to employ their money in this way. The Commodities our Country affords for export, either into Foreign Countries, or into neighbouring Countries, are these:

Commodities for Export. Barley and Oat Meal, to the quantity of about 20,000 bolls, may be exported annually; and this article may be improved to much greater extent: Salmon is a considerable article, and no Country affords better fish, than what is taken in the rivers of Spey, Findhorn, and Ness, Farar or Beaulie, to the value of several thousands of pounds yearly. The White Fishing of Cod and Ling turns to small account: Linen Cloth is an improving article, and might become a stapple commodity, did Gentlemen set up work houses, and encourage the manufacture.

nufacture. Although our Wool is not manufactured at home to any advantage, yet considerable quantities of it are sold in the Counties of Banff and Aberdeen; Beef and Pork are exported, though not to a great amount; thousands of Black Cattle are annually sold in the South of Scotland, and in England; great Flocks of Sheep are driven to Dee-side, and other Countries; and some Horses are likewise sold. No small benefit arises from the Woods in the Highlands, which furnish the neighbouring Countries with Plank, Deal, Board, Joists, and all kinds of Timber for building Carts, Waggons, Labouring Instruments, Bark for Tanning, Pipe Staves, &c. To which, let me add, that the Highlands furnish much Peltrie, Raw Hides, Skins of Deer, Roe, Fox, Hare, Otters, Wild Cats, Goats, Badgers, &c.

For Home Consumpt, we have in plenty, Corn, Fleshes and Fishes, Butter, Cheese, Honey, Fruits, Fowls Tame and Wild, Tallow, &c. In a word, would Gentlemen live at home, and improve the Country; would they encourage the Tenants, and exempt them from slavish servitude; would all ranks live frugally and wisely; small as the produce of our Country is, it may be called

Terra suis contenta bonis, nec indiga mercis.

But the luxury and vanity of our times, know no bounds. Even they that live on alms are infected by it: It must be restrained or the Country will be impoverished: In few Countries do the peasants live more poorly; and though many of the gentry do grind the faces of the poor, they do not enrich themselves; they multiply exactions upon the people, who dare not complain; and they exhaust their own fortunes, by the expence of imitating the manners and luxury of their more wealthy neighbours.

Civil Government.

I shall now take a view of the Civil Government of this Country, as it is divided into Counties and Boroughs: And as it may be thought that a general view of the Feudal System may throw some light on this, I shall, from Mr DALRYMPLE's accurate Essay on Feudal Property, extract a few lines:

Feudal Customs.

The Goths and Vandals having over-run the Roman Empire, settled the Feudal Law in the Countries they conquered; They went abroad, though under a General, as Independant Clans, to find a Settlement; And when they settled in any conquered Country, they must fall into some subordination. Their General naturally became their Prince or King; and all must be ready, at a Military Call, to maintain their Conquest. Of the Conquered Land,

1. Some part would be reserved for the Prince or King.
2. The rest would be parcelled out among the Chieftains.
3. Such of the ancient inhabitants, as were allowed to remain in the Country (for it was not their way to extirpate them) kept their lands on the ancient footing: And,
4. Such Intruders and Followers, as were not attached to any Chieftain, taking possession of any vacant land, enjoyed it on the same footing. The King judged, and led out to war in his own lands; the Chieftains did so in their lands; and the King sent his officers to judge in the third and fourth classes. In France, lands held on the ancient footing, were called *Alleux*, or *Allodial*; the officer sent to command in them, was termed *Count*; those living under his jurisdiction, were named *Liberi* and *Milites*, i. e. who owned no Superior in a Feudal, though subject to the King in a Political way. Lands held on the Feudal footing, were called *Feodaux*; these holding them, were named *Leuds*, i. e. Lords, and they judged their own people, led them to war, and were no way subject to the Counts. Among the Saxons in England, lands granted to the Thanes

or

or Lords, were called *Thain-Land*, and if held by charter *Boc-Land*: Hence the proprietors of Boc-Land were called *Thegen*, i. e. Lords; and those under them *Theoden*. Allodial lands, over which the King's Officer, called *Reve*, and *Sherive*, had jurisdiction, were called *Reve-Land*, and being held without writ *Folkland*; the Governors of such lands were called, *Coples*, i. e. Counts, and those under them *Ceorles*. At first, grants of conquered lands were made only during pleasure, afterwards for life; and because men would not serve in war, if by their death their families would be ruined, therefore grants were made hereditary.

In all the Gothic constitutions, Honour and Dignity, (such as Count, Earl, Thane, Lord) were originally annexed to lands and offices. An Earl was the Governor and Judge of a Province, and only during pleasure, or for life. William the Conqueror made these offices hereditary and feudal. Then Earls, too great to bear the fatigue of business, appointed Deputes, Vice-comites, or Sherives. This left an Earldom, not so much a territorial office, as a territorial dignity. Afterwards, though the estate was lost, the honour was allowed to continue with the family; or lands were erected into an Earldom, in favours of the grantee and his heirs, and this conferred on him the territorial dignity, though he had neither office nor property in these lands.

In Scotland, and in other nations, the feudal system was established by degrees. King Malcolm II. made advances to it. The outlines of it consisted, in making the crown-vassals hold by military service; in certain profits paid on change of heirs; in granting the Superior the incidents of ward and marriage; and in making the King, not a Supreme Magistrate, but a Paramount Superior, invested in the whole property of the kingdom, and his vassals attached to him by homage and Fealtie.

tie. To subject themselves to feudal service, to surrender all their lands to the King during the minority of the heirs, and to pay a year's rent at the entry of every heir, were perquisites the Nobles and Cheiftains would not yield without a valuable compensation; And this granted,

(1.) A part of the Crown lands was given, on condition of military service; and if the gift was confiderable, the receiver could not handfomely refufe to allow his own eftate to be engroffed in the charter.

(2.) Titles of Honour were conferred on many. And,

(3.) Whereas lands were formerly held by poffeffion only, without writ; charters were granted, as the moft folemn and fure title to land. By thefe baits they were gradually allured to give up their independency, and to accept of their own eftates as a gift from the King, holding of him by military tenure.

COUNT OF EARL.
The only COUNT or EARL anciently in this Province was, the EARL of MORAY. The charter to Thomas Randulph, is fet down (Append. No. I.) Before that time, the Earls of Moray were probably officers or governors, during pleafure, or for life. But Randulph's dignity was manifeftly territorial, and hereditary. The privileges granted to him were ample, fuch as a regality in the whole county; the fuperiority of Baronies and Freeholders, and of the Boroughs of Elgin, Forres, and Nairn; the patronage of Parifh Churches; and the military command of the whole county. But the patronage of prelacies, the town and caftle of Invernefs, and the reverfion of the whole county were referved to the Crown.

This charter beareth no date, though granted Anno 1313. *(Char. Mor.)* Ancient charters often wanted the date of time and place, as King Duncan's charter (Append. No. XVII.) Some name the place, but no time. In fome a remarkable fact is related inftead of the time, as in the charter of Innes (Append.
No.

No. XIV.) I do not find, that any of our Kings before the eighth year (1221) of King Alexander II. used the Plural NOS, in their charters. And in England, King Richard I. or his immediate predecessors, first used that stile. And how soon Kings us'd it, the Nobles and Prelates copied from them.

Our Kings never did subscribe their charters and grants, but only affixed their seals to them, and of late they superscribe them. And though the names of witnesses to royal deeds were inserted in the body of the writ, yet they never did, nor as yet do manually subscribe; but of old they affixed their seals to it. The crosses subjoined to King Duncan's charter, were drawn by the writer, or rather the King and witnesses drew the crosses, and the Scribes wrote the names: The foundation charter of the Abbey of Scone, by King Alexander I. Anno 1115, thus ends: "Ego Alexander Dei Gratia Rex Scotorum, propria manu mea hæc confirmo.—Ego Sybilla Regina confirmo." These names were written by the Scribe, and the Roman Letter E was in Red, or in Gold: And with respect to the deeds of subjects, it was not necessary, before the year 1681, that either the writer, or the witnesses, should be designed in the write; or that the witnesses subscribing should be the only probative witnesses. *Vid. Act. Parl.* 1681.

King Malcolm III. was the first who affixed a Seal to his deeds, but without any armorial figures. His son Duncan used Cross and Seal. King Alexander I. introduced counter-sealing; and King William, (whose reign commenced Anno 1165.) first used armorial figures on his seal. The figures formerly on royal seals were, as on King Edgar's, viz. The King on the Throne, a Sword in one hand, and a Sceptre in the other, with this inscription; "Ymago Edgari Scottorum Basilei." In England, King Richard I. who began to reign anno 1189, first used armorial figures. The

Barons and Gentry had their seals likewise early charged, (not with armorial figures, but) with " Quilibet Baro, vel " alius tenens de Rege, habeat Sigillum proprium, et qui " non habuerit, incidet in Amerciamentum Regis. Et quod " sigilla sint, et non signeta sicut ante ista tempora fieri con- " suevit," *(Stat. Rob.* III.*)* In observance of this law, Gentlemen sent their seals to the Court in lead, which the clerk kept by him. *(M'Kenz. Herald.)* To seal Bonds, Deeds and Conveyances was the custom, till Anno 1540. Then besides sealing, the granter's manual subscription, or that of a notary, was made necessary. *(Act. Parl.* 1540. *Pref. to Diplom. Scot.)* To return from this digression.

THANES.
We had several THANES in this Province. Concerning these, FORDUN, *Lib.* iv. *Cap.* 45. Writes, " Antiquitus consueve- " rant Reges suis dare militibus, plus aut minus de terris " suis in Feodifirmam, alicujus Provinciæ portionem vel Tha- " nagium ; nam eo tempore, totum pene regnum divideba- " tur in Thanagiis: De quibus cuique dedit prout placuit, " vel singulis annis ad firmam, ut agricolis ; vel ad decem " annorum, seu viginti, seu vitæ terminum, cum uno saltem, " aut duobus heredibus, ut Liberis et Generosis; Quibusdam " itaque, sed paucis, in perpetuum, ut militibus, Thanis, prin- " cipibus." Probably these Thanes were at first the King's servants, (so the word signifies,) or officers in provinces and countries, and during pleasure only, or for life. But afterwards the title and the lands granted to them were made hereditary. In the Highlands they were termed, *Mormhaor*, i. e. a Great Officer ; and hence probably, came *Marus comitatus Regis*. They were likewise called *Tosche,* (from *Tus.* i. e. First) that is, " Principal Persons, Primores."

In this Province we had—The THANE of MORAY ; of whom I know no more, but that the lands of Ligate, Newton, Ardgaoith

gaoith, &c. in the parishes of Spynie and Alves, are called the Thanedom of Moray.—The Thane of Brodie and Dyke was probably the ancestor of the Family of Brodie.—Thanus de Moithes, (probably Moy or Moyness) is one of the Inquest, in estimating the Baronies of Kilravock and Geddes, (Ap. No. XVIII.) But I know no more of that Thanedom.—In the year 1367, Joannes de Dolais was Thane of Cromdale, (Ap. No. XX.) Whether or not he was the Earl of Fife's stewart or factor of these lands, I know not.—An account of the Thanes of Calder, is given. The succession of these Thanes, always so designed, continued to the year 1500; and in this family, the title of Thane was honorary, and not official; at least since the time of King Alexander III. I question not but the title of Thane was more ancient with us, than the titles of Honour that now obtain. DEMPSTER, page 120. says, " Mal- " columbus tertius, sublato Maccabæo tyranno, regnum le- " gitime sibi debitum occupavit ; quod ut ornaret unica cura " incubuit : Tunc et a Prædiis nobilibus nomina quisque sump- " sit ; et cum magna frequensque nobilitas S. Margaretam " ex Hungaria et Anglia secuta in Scotia confedisset, splendo- " rem suo principatui additurus, Barones et Comites creavit."

The first Duke we had in Scotland, was David son of King Robert III. so created about the year 1397. DUKES.

The first Marquisses were, John Marquis of Hamilton, and George Marquis of Huntley, so created in one day ; viz. 19th April 1599. MARQUIS.

The first Earl is said to have been Duncan M'Duff, made Earl of Fife about the year 1057; but the laws of King Malcolm II. mention Comites, in his reign. EARLS.

The first Viscount was, Thomas Lord Erskine, created Lord Viscount Fenton; anno 1606. VISCOUNTS.

How early we had Lords or Barons, either by tenure or by LORDS.
writ,

writ, I find not. It is certain, we had such named, *Leg. Malc. cap.* 8. But Lords by Patent we had not before the Reign of Queen Mary, or of King James VI.

COUNTIES.   I now come to consider our Counties.

In France the King's Officer who judged in allodial lands, was called COMES, and the District in which he judged COMITATUS, and his Depute VICECOMES. In England, the King's Officer was called REVE and SCHEREVE, and the district SHIRE. In Saxon, *Scire* (from *Scyran*, to divide) is a division; and *Sherif*, *Scirgerf*, is the *Gerif*, *Reve*, or *Officer* of a *Shyre*. Hence probably, some lands of Elgin, Forres, &c. are called *Greſhip Lands*, because they were the salary of the *Gerif* or *Sheriff*. How early this province was divided into shires or counties, I find not. It now takes in a part of the shire of INVERNESS, the whole shires of NAIRN, and of ELGIN, and a part of the shire of BANFF.

INVERNESS County.   The Shire or County of INVERNESS within this Province, comprehends the parishes of Inverness, Kirkhill, Kiltarlartie, Urquhart, Boleskin, Durris, Cromdale, Alvie, Rothemurchus, Kingusie, Laggan, Arderſier, and the greatest part of Petty, Croy, Daviot, Dunlichtie, Moy and Dalarasie, and a part of Duthel. It stands the nineteenth in the roll of Parliament. It appears from *Reg. Maj. Lib.* 1. *Cap.* 16, 20, That there were Vicecomites, or Sheriffs, of Inverness, in the reign of King David I; and all the Countries benorth the Forth being divided into Districts, for the more regular administration of justice, Inverness was one of the " Loca Capitalia Scotiæ Comi-
" tatuum, per totum regnum." The other capital places were, Scoon, Dalginsh, Perth, Forfar, and Aberdeen. Ross, (including Sutherland and Caithness) and all Moray, answered at Inverness. We cannot infer from the words, " Loca Capita-
" lia

" lia Comitatuum," that the Counties were erected at that time, as they now are. Comitatus, as that of Randulph Earl of Moray, comprehended several of the present counties; and *Loca Capitalia* were the Towns, in which the *Comites* kept their Courts. *Parl.* 6. *James* IV. *Anno* 1503. it is ordained, " That
" the Justices and Sheriffs of the North Isles have their seat
" and place in Inverness or Dingwall; that Mamore and
" Lochaber come to the Aire or Justice-court of Inverness.
" And because the sheriffdom of Inverness is too great, that
" there be a Sheriff made of Ross, who shall have full juris-
" diction, and shall sit at Tain or Dingwall. And that there
" be a Sheriff at Caithness, who shall have jurisdiction of the
" hail Diocess of Caithness, and shall sit at Dornock or Wick,
" and the shires of Ross and Caithness shall answer to the Ju-
" stice Aire of Caithness."

The Sheriff-ship of Inverness was granted heretably to the Earl of Huntley by the King's Charter anno 1508, with a power to name Deputes within the bounds of Ross, Caithness, Lochaber, and other distant parts (*Falcon. Decif.*) And in 1583, the Earl of Huntley disponed to the Earl of Sutherland, the Sheriff-ship of Sutherland, in exchange for the lands of Aboyne and Glentanir, the Patrimonial estate of Adam Gordon son to Huntley, who married the Heiress of Sutherland. And the Marquis of Huntley, having resigned the Sheriff-ship of Inverness into the King's hands anno 1628, there was a mutual contract between the King and the Earl of Sutherland in 1631, whereby the Earl resigned the Regality and Sheriff-ship of Sutherland for a sum of money; but retained possession by way of mortgage, untill the money should be paid: And the King dismembered the Sheriff-ship of Sutherland from that of Inverness, and erected Sutherland into a separate County, comprehending the lands of Sutherland, Assint, Strathnavir, Edirdachaolis,

dachaolis, Diurness, Strathaladale, and Ferincoscarie in Sliofchaolis, and appointed Dornoch to be the Head-Borough of the shire; which was ratified in Parliament, anno 1633 (*M.S. Gordon of Straloch.*)

K. CHARLES I. under pretence of the general revocation in the beginning of every reign, made an attack upon all the heretable offices and jurisdictions that had been granted posterior to the Parliament 1455. And the Marquis of Huntley resigned the Sheriff-ship of Inverness and Aberdeen in 1628, for a compensation of L.5000 Sterling: But the shire of Ross was not divided from that of Inverness, and the bounds of it fixed, before the year 1661. (*Unprint. Acts of Parl.* 1661.)

The Legal Valuation of the Shire of Inverness now is, L.73,188 : 9 Scots.

Nairn County.

The County of NAIRN lies all within this Province, and comprehends the Parishes of Nairn, Aldern, Calder, and Ardclach, and some parts of the parishes of Croy, Pettie, Daviot and Moy. The lands of Ferintosh in Ross are likewise within this county, having been a part of the Thanedom of Calder. (*Ferina Toshe*, signifies the Thane's land) which, by a special privilege, was all in the county of Nairn, *Vid. page* 111. And on this account Culloden, as Baron of Ferintosh, votes in elections of Parliament for the County of Nairn. This County stood the twentieth in the Roll of Parliament.

At what time Nairn was erected into a distinct County, I find not. In a Charter of the Thanedom of Calder anno 1310, it is called *Thanagium de Calder infra vicecomitatum de Innernarn.* (*Pen. Cald.*). Donald Thane of Calder, as heir to his father Andrew, was infeft in the office of Sheriff of the shire, and Constable of the castle of Nairn, anno 1406. (*Ibid.*). In the year 1442, Alexander de Yle Earl of Ross directed a Precept to the Deputy Sheriff of Inverness, his Bailiff in that part, for infefting William de Kaldor, as heir to his father Donald, in the

the Sheriff-fhip of Nairn, held of him *in capite* (*Ibid.*). The Earl of Rofs being forfeited in the year 1476, the Thane of Calder held the Sheriff-fhip of the King *in capite*, and that office continued heretably in the Family of Calder till the year 1747. The legal valuation of the County of Nairn, is about L. 16000 Scots.

The County of MORAY, or of ELGIN and FORRES, is all within this Province, and the Parifhes it comprehends, in whole or in part, may be feen in the valuation Roll (*Append.* No. XXI.). But though Eafter Moy, in the parifh of Dyke, pays Cefs in the County of Moray, it is a part of the County of Nairn, and Thanedom of Calder. The County of Moray was the thirtieth in the Roll of the Scot's Parliament.

MORAY COUNTY.

I find not, at what time this County was erected, or how early it had Counts and Sheriffs. In a Charter granted by Eva Morthac Domina de Rothes to Archibald Bifhop of Moray, Anno 1263, " D. Gilbertus Roule miles Vicecomes de Elgyn" is a witnefs (*Append.* No. XXII.). Sir Thomas Randulph Earl of Moray was Hereditary Sheriff of this County; and fo were his fucceffors in the Earldom, till upon the demife of Earl James Dunbar, his fon Alexander of Weftfield, unjuftly deprived of the Earldom, was made Hereditary Sheriff of Moray; and the office continued in his Family till the year 1724, when Ludowick Dunbar of Weftfield fold it to Charles Earl of Moray for L. 25,000 Scots. The Earls of Moray were principal Sheriffs from that time till the year 1747.

The Legal Valuation of this Shire is, about L. 65,603 Scots.

I do not find that any one within this Province had an Heretable Jufticiary. But Hereditary REGALITIES, both Ecclefiaftical and Civil, were numerous. I fhall in the Ecclefiaftic part confider the former, and here only the latter. REGALITY

Regalities.

is

is a Jurisdiction, which the Lord thereof has in all his own lands, equal to the Justiciary in Criminals; for he judges in the four pleas of the Crown, and equal to the Sheriff in Civil causes. Randulph Earl of Moray, had the whole Comitatus erected into a Regality in his favours, as his Charter bears. George the first Duke of Gordon had all his lands erected into a Regality, and this engrossed in his Patent of Duke, Anno 1684, by which his power of jurisdiction was great and extensive. Ludowick Grant of Grant got a power of Regality in all his lands, in the year 1690. The Earl of Moray claimed the office of Lord of Regality over the Citadel of Inverness. Lord Lovat was Lord of the Regality of Lovat. The Ecclesiastic Regalities of Spynie, Kinloss, Pluscarden, Urquhart, Grangehill, and Arderfier, came after the reformation into the hands of Laics.* And even in time of Popery, Noblemen and Gentlemen got themselves made Hereditary Bailives of Regality in church lands. The Family of Gordon claimed the Bailiery of the Regality of Spynie, because this office was, by King James VI. conferred on Lord Spynie; and when that Family became extinct, King Charles II. as *Ultimus Hæres*, disponed the Regality to the Earl of Airly, who conveyed it to the family of Gordon. Several such claims will be mentioned, when I speak of the abolishing Hereditary Jurisdictions in the year 1747.

BARONIES.
The Jurisdiction of BARONS or FREEHOLDERS was very ancient. By the *Leges Malcolmi*, Barons had their Courts, and might judge of Lith and Limb; and in Capital Crimes they got the escheat of their Vassals, except in the four pleas of the Crown. And the Milites or Vassals of Freeholders, even Sub-vassoles,

---

* King James VI. gave to the Earl of Dunfermline Chancellor, the Regality of Urquhart, which the Duke of Gordon obtained.

vaffoles, or Vaffals of the Milites, had their Courts, but could not judge of Lith and Limb, but only of wrong and unlauck. If a Baron be infeft *cum Curiis et Bloduitis*, he may Judge of Riots and Blood-wits; and if he holds of the Crown *cum Furca et Foffa*, i. e. " Pit and Gallows," his power is very ample. We had likewife in this Country, Hereditary Conftables, of whom I fhall fpeak in the *Military Hiftory*.

Thus we have feen, that our Kings very early gave away the Crown Lands, which made them dependent on their Nobles: And the want of Property was attended with the want of JURISDICTION. They made Hereditary Sheriffs, Chamberlains, Conftables; erected Hereditary Regalities and Jufticiaries; and at laft, by one Grant, made the office of the Jufticiar of Scotland Hereditary in the Family of Argyle. When our Kings became fenfible of their error, they gradually weakened the Feudal Courts. King James V. inftituted the Court of Seffion; James VI. appointed Juftices of the Peace; Charles I. purchafed back the Jufticiary of Scotland, when the Court of Jufticiary was erected. Yet there remained many Hereditary Jurifdictions, and too much power in the hands of Great Men, and Chiefs of Clans, which was often abufed, in perverting Juftice, and encouraging infurrections and rebellions. This was fo manifeft in the rebellion 1745, and 1746, that the Earl of Hardwick Lord Chancellor, planned the Jurifdiction Act in 1747, which has abolifhed fome, and limited others of fuch of the Territorial Jurifdictions as were found dangerous to the Community, and made the power of Judging in the General Official.

Jurifdictions Abolifhed.

It was referred to the Lords of Seffion by the Parliament, to confider the validity of the claims for Heretable Jurifdictions, and to determine the Compenfation that fhould be given to the Proprietors. They rejected many claims, becaufe:

I. Some Regalities were erected since the year 1455, but not granted in Parliament, or confirmed by it, as the Act XLIII. that year requires.

II. Some Jurisdictions were lost, *non utendo*, and prescription took place.

III. Some Jurisdictions were found split into parts, which the Lords of them had no right to do: And,

IV. The Sheriff-ship of Invernefs was resigned to the Crown, anno 1628, for L. 2500 Sterling: And it was presumed the price was paid. What the Proprietors of Jurisdictions within this Province asked, and what the Lords of Session judged should be given, and was actually given, in Compensation, is as follows:

		COMPENSATION SOUGHT. Sterling.			COMPENSATION GRANTED.		
		L.	s.	d.	L.	s.	d.
Duke of Gordon	For the Justiciary and Regality of Huntley	10000	0	0	4000	0	0
	For the Sheriff-ship of Invernefs	2500	0	0	0	0	0
	For the Regality of Urquhart	1000	0	0	300	0	0
	For the Bailiery of the Regality of Spynie	2000	0	0	500	0	0
	For the Bailiery of the Regality of Kinlofs	1500	0	0	182-19		6
	For the Conftabulary of Invernefs Caftle	300	0	0	0	0	0
Earl of Moray	For the Sheriff-ship of Moray	8000	0	0	3000	0	0
	For the Regality of Invernefs Citadel	1000	0	0	0	0	0
Laird of Calder	For the Sheriff-ship of Nairn	3000	0	0	2000	0	0
	For the Conftabulary thereof	500	0	0	0	0	0
	For the Regality of Arderfier	500	0	0	0	0	0
Earl of Sutherland	For the Regality in Strathnaver	100	0	0	0	0	0
Lord Braco	For the Regality of Pluscarden	1000	0	0	68	18	5
Sir Ludowick Grant	For the Regality of Grant	5000	0	0	900	0	0
Catbol	For the Bailiery of Regality there	1000	0	0	0	0	0
Lovat	For the Regality of Lovat	166	4	0	0	0	0
Lethin	For the Regality of Kinlofs	4000	0	0	0	0	0
Grangehill	For the Regality of Grangehill	500	0	0	0	0	0
	L.	42066	4	0	10951	17	11

Courts of Judicature.

The Heretable Jurisdictions being taken out of the hands of Subjects, and being annexed to the Crown; the Courts of Judicature kept now within this Province are:

I. The Circuit or Justiciary Court, which sits twice every year, and the Judges remain six days in the Town, at each Circuit.

II. The

II. The Sheriff Court. The King appoints the Depute, who muſt be an Advocate, of at leaſt three years ſtanding, and muſt reſide four months in the year within his diſtrict; the Depute may appoint Subſtitutes. The Sheriff of Inverneſs is allowed a ſalary of L. 250; one Sheriff for Moray and Nairn Counties, at L. 150 of ſalary; and the like for the Sheriff of Banff; the Depute pays the ſalary of his Subſtitutes. No fine, forfeiture, or penalty ſhall belong to the Sheriff, but his ſhare belongs to the King, and no ſentence money ſhall be taken: But by this the ſubject has no eaſe, for the fees allowed to Clerks and other Officers, by acts of Sederunt, are very high.

III. The Juſtice of Peace Court.

IV. The Baron Court, for receiving and enrolling Barons.

V. The Court of the Commiſſioners of Supply, for regulating what concerns the Land Tax, and Window Tax, for ordering the Highways and public Roads, for granting ſalaries to Schools, &c.

VI. The Commiſſary or Conſiſtorial Court, at Elgin and Inverneſs: And,

VII. The Baron Court, of thoſe who hold their land *cum curiis*: Such have no Juriſdiction in any Criminal Cauſes, except ſmall Crimes, for which, the puniſhment ſhall not exceed a fine of 20 s. Sterling, or three hours in the ſtocks in the day-time, or a months impriſonment, on not paying the fine; Nor in Civil Cauſes exceeding 40 s. Sterling, except in recovering rents and multures: No perſon ſhall be impriſoned without a written Commitment, recorded in the Court Books: And the Priſon ſhall have ſuch Windows and Gates, as that any friend may viſit the Priſoner, &c.

I ſhall now conclude what regards the Counties, with a liſt of the Barons enrolled, who have votes in electing Members of Parliament.

Roll of Barons.

In the SHIRE of BANFF within this PROVINCE.

The Earl of Fife
Sir Ludowick Grant of Grant
William Grant of Bellindalach
Alexander Grant of Achomonie

In the SHIRE of MORAY.

The Earl of Fife
James Viscount MacDuff
Sir Robert Gordon of Gordonstoun
Sir Harry Innes of Innes
Sir Ludowick Grant of Grant
Sir William Dunbar of Westfield
Sir Alexander Grant of Dalvey
William Grant of Bellindalach
James Grant of Knockando
James Grant of Wester Elchies
Alexander Brodie of Brodie
Alexander Brodie of Lethin
Alexander Brodie of Windy Hills
James Brodie of Spynie
Colonel Francis Stewart of Pitenriech
Archibald Dunbar of Newton
James Robertson of Bishop Miln
Robert Anderson of Link-wood
John Innes of Leuchars
Mr James Spence of Kirktown
George Cummine of Altyre
Alexander Tulloch of Tanachie
Duncan Urquhart of Burdsyards
Joseph Dunbar of Grange
Hugh Rose of Kilravock

In the SHIRE of NAIRN.

John Campbell of Calder
Pryse Campbell of Bogbole
Alexander Brodie of Brodie
James Sutherland of Kinsterie
Alexander Brodie of Lethin
Alexander Dunbar of Boath
Hugh Rose of Kilravock
Hugh Rose of Clava
John Forbes of Culloden

In INVERNESS SHIRE in this PROVINCE.

Æneas MacIntosh of MacIntosh
Sir Ludowick Grant of Grant
James Grant of Rothemurchus
John Campbell of Calder
Pryse Campbell of Durris
John Forbes of Culloden
Roderick Chisholm of Comer
John Cuthbert of Castle-hill
John Robertson of Inches
George Ross of Kilmyles
William Duff of Muirton
Hugh Fraser of Dunbalach
Fraser of Fohir
Alexander MacDonald of Glengary

This was the Roll in 1760; since that time there have been considerable alterations. With respect to BARONS lately made, and

and who take the Oath of Truſt, I pretend not to know their names, their number, their deſignations, nor the tenure of their holding; therefore I paſs them over, To conſider the Burroughs both Royal and Barony.

The Royal Burroughs within this Province are: Inverneſs, Elgin, Nairn, and Forres. The *Leges Malcolmi*, deſcribe the office of the Chamberlain, who had Juriſdiction over the Burroughs; he had at that time for his ſalary, " Ducentas libras " per annum, de Eſchetis Burgorum, Toloneis et cuſtomis " Burgorum" *(Leg. Malc. Cap. 4.).* In the year 1579, the Parliament appointed Commiſſioners to determine the antiquity and priority among the Burroughs, *(Vid. unprint. Acts)*; but what their determination was I know not. In the Roll of the Burroughs, Inverneſs is the ſeventeenth in order, Elgin the thirty-fourth, Nairn the forty-third, and Forres the forty-fourth.

The antiquity of the Burrough of INVERNESS cannot be queſtioned, though we pay no regard to BOETIUS' *fabulous* ſtory, that it was founded by King Fergus I. What I obſerved from the Regiam Majeſtatem ſhews, that this Town was conſiderable in the reign of King David I. BUCHANNAN ſpeaks of it a hundred years before that time, viz. That King Duncan was murdered in Inverneſs, by MacBeath anno 1039; but in this he differs from FORDUN, who writes, that King Duncan was wounded at Logiſnan (Forte Loggie in Brae-Moray) and was carried to Elgin, where he died. An older Author than either of them writes, " Dunchath filius MacTrivi Abthani de " Dunkeld et Bethoc filiæ Malcomi MacKinat, interfectus eſt a " MacBeath, MacFinleg in Bothgouanan" *(Excerp. ex Reg. S. And.)*; but where this place lies, I know not. This Town has an ample Charter from King James VI. before his acceſſion to the Crown of England, referring to Charters granted by the

Burroughs.

INVERNESS.

Kings,

Kings, William, Alexander II. David II. and James I. ratifying and confirming all the Rights, Privileges, Liberties, and Immunities granted by these Kings to the Burrough, particularly the power of constituting a Sheriff in the Town, who may appoint Deputes, and of naming a Coroner: I have placed an abstract of this Charter in *(Appendix* N° XXIII.). This Town being the Key of the Highlands, has a great resort, and a considerable trade. It received an addition of buildings and trade, upon Cromwell's raising a Fort there, in 1652, and keeping a numerous Garrison, to awe the neighbouring Highlands; and when, in 1662, to gratify the Highland Chieftains, that Fort was demolished, some of the best houses in Town were built out of the materials found there.

The Town is governed by a Common Council of twenty-one members; viz. a Provost, four Baillies, a Treasurer, Dean of Guild, Deacon Conveener, ten Merchant Councellors, and three Deacons of Trades: The Sett of this Town, is much the same as of the Town of Elgin, afterwards described. They have a weekly market on Friday, and several public annual Fairs, as at Martinmass, Candlemass, Mid-Summer, Mary-mass in August, Rood-mass in September, &c. and every Fair continues for three days.

Their revenues are about L. 300 Sterling yearly, arising from Feu duties, petty Customs; upon building the Bridge of Inverness, the Parliament in 1681, empowered them to receive a small Toll to keep it in repair, *(Vid. unprint. Acts* 1681). The Town is the Seat of the Courts of Justice; the Justiciary, the Sheriff, the Commissary, the Justices of Peace, the Commissioners of Supply, keep their Courts there: Here likewise are the Customs and Excise Offices.

The Arms of the Burrough are: A Camel, supported by two Elephants. Motto, FIDELITAS ET CONCORDIA.

Part IV.   HISTORY of MORAY.   193

The Burrough of ELGIN appears to have been a considerable Town, with a Royal Fort, when the Danes landed in Moray, about anno 1008 *(Vid. Milit. Hist.).* The earliest Charter of Guildrie I have seen in favours of this Burrough, was granted by King Alexander II. as follows: " Alexander Dei gra-
" tia Rex Scotiæ, omnibus probis hominibus totius terræ suæ
" salutem. Sciatis Nos concessisse, et hac Carta nostra con-
" firmasse Burgensibus nostris de Elgyn, ut ipsi ad meliora-
" tionem Burgi nostri de Elgyn habeant in eodem Burgo
" Guildam suam mercatoriam, adeo libere, et sicut aliqui Bur-
" gorum nostrorum in toto regno nostro Guildam suam habent.
" Testibus Alano Hostiario, Regmaldo de Cheyn Camerario,
" Hugone de Abernethie, Willielmo et Bernardo de Monte
" Alto; Alexandro de Moravia, et Willielmo Bisset; Apud Elgyn
" vigesimo octavo die Novembris, anno regni nostri vigesimo
" 1234;" *(Archiv. of Elgin).*

This Town was the Manour of the Comitatus, and was subject to the Earls of Moray, as Constables of the King's Fort. John Dunbar Earl of Moray, by his Charter May 1st 1390, discharged to the Town for ever, the assize or quantity of ale which they were bound to pay to him, as Constable of the Castle of Elgin. Thomas Dunbar Earl of Moray, by Charter the 23d July 1393, granted to the Town of Elgin, all the Wool, Cloth, and other things that go by Ship out of his Harbour of Spey uncustomed. And the same Earl Thomas, by his Charter of the 22d October 1396, confirmed King Alexander's Charter of Guildrie; and so did Earl Archibald Douglas by his Charter, of October 27th 1451, *(Ibid.).* King Charles I. by his Charter, dated October 8th 1633, ratified and confirmed to this Burrough, the Charters granted by the Kings Alexander II. Robert I. James II. and James VI. with ample Privileges, Liberties, and Immunities, of which I have given

B b

an abstract (*Appendix* Nº XXIV.). King James VI. by Charter dated 29th February 1620, resumed or narrated his Charter, of date 22d March 1594, to the Magistrates of Elgin, of the Hospital of Maison Dieu, with the Patronage thereof, and all the lands belonging to it, for sustaining the Poor in the said Hospital, and sustaining a qualified Master of Music, and performing the ordinary services in the Church of the Burrough (*Ibid.*).

The Government of the Burrough, will appear from the Sett or rule of Government, ratified by the Convention of Burroughs July 8th 1706; in the heads and articles following:

I. The Town Council shall consist of seventeen Members, including the Deacon Conveener and two Deacons of Trades.

II. These two Deacons shall be chosen by the Council.

III. The New Council shall be elected annually, on Monday immediately preceeding Michaelmass.

IV. The Magistrates, and other Office Bearers, shall be elected on Tuesday thereafter.

V. There shall be annually put off, three of the Guildrie, and two of the Trades.

VI. One Provost, four Bailies, a Treasurer, and other Office Bearers shall be chosen.

VII. The Provost shall not continue in Office above three years, nor the Bailies, Dean of Guild, or Treasurer above two, and they may be changed yearly.

VIII. When these are put off their Offices, they shall be continued on the Council for the next year.

IX. The Old Council shall chuse the New, and both the Old and New shall chuse the Magistrates and Office Bearers. In the week preceeding, the Incorporate Trades chuse their Deacons, and on Saturday three of every Trade meet, and leet three of their number, of which three the Council on Monday chufes one for Conveener.

X. None may be elected but Refidenters and Burgeffes, who bear Scot and Lot.

XI. The Councellors fhall chufe annually out of their own number, five Affeffors to the Dean of Guild, whereof three with the Dean fhall be a *quorum*.

XII. The Council fhall chufe fifteen perfons, not of their own body, whereof two of the Trades, for Stent Mafters, who fhall be fworn *de fideli*, and nine make a *quorum*.

XIII. No Stent, except the public Cefs, fhall be impofed, without the confent of a Head Court.

XIV. On the fecond Tuefday of September yearly, a Head Court fhall be called, and the ftate of the Burrough, and the Magiftrates management of the Common Good, fhall be laid before them, and the books and accounts fhall lie on the Council table for twenty days, preceeding the Head Court; for the fatisfaction of all concerned.

The Town is the feat of the Courts of Juftice, where the Sheriff, Commiffary, Juftices of Peace, Commiffioners of Supply, and the Barons hold their public meetings and Courts. They have a weekly market on Friday, and annual Fairs at Faften's-Eve, Pafch, Trinity, St James's Day, Michaelmafs, and Anderf-mafs: They have the fuperiority of feveral lands, as may be feen in the abftract of King Charles's Charter, and a fervitude on the Burgh Sea in Duffus, by which, the fifhers there are oblidged to bring their fifh to market in Elgin: They have fome fifhing boats at Loffy-mouth; and yet for want of a good Harbour, that might encourage Trade and Commerce, their Revenue, or Common Good is but fmall. By immemorial practice, though not by a fpecial grant, the Magiftrates have a Sheriff-fhip within the Town's Liberties. If we may take the

City of Edinburgh for a pattern, this Town, in which the Cathedral of Moray stood, may be called a CITY; for King Charles I. in his Charter, erecting the See of Edinburgh, dated 29th September 1633; says, " Nos animo nostro revolventes, Bur-
" gum nostrum de Edinburgh esse principale Burgum Regni
" nostri Scotiæ, idemque maxime idoneum ut sit Capitalis
" Civitas dicti noviter erecti Episcopatus; Igitur Nos ereximus,
" tenoreque præsentis Cartæ nostræ erigimus, dictum nostrum
" Burgum de Edinburgh in Civitatem, et ordinamus eandem
" fore principalem et Capitalem Civitatem dicti Regni nostri,
" ac predicti noviter erecti Episcopatus, ac damus et concedi-
" mus eidem omnes libertates, et privilegia Civitati debita."
But nothing is more uncertain than what constitutes a City; whether its being the Capital of a Province, or being a Walled Town, or being a Royal Burrough, or being a Bishop's See.

The Arms of the Town of ELGIN are: Saint GILES in a Pastoral Habit, holding a Book in the right hand, and a Pastoral Staff in the left. With this Motto, SIC ITUR AD ASTRA.

NAIRN. The Burrough of NAIRN is of considerable antiquity. We find it mentioned as early as the year 1008: And as long as it had a good Harbour, and the King's Constable residing in the Castle of it, no doubt it flourished and made a good figure; now the want of Trade has brought it much into decay. The constitution of the Town is much the same with that of Elgin, except that Gentlemen in the Country are admitted upon the Common Council, because the Town cannot afford the necessary annual changes. It has a weekly market, and some annual Fairs, and the Courts of Justice for that County sit there. The Common Good is but small. The inhabitants are about six hundred.

The Arms of the Town are: Saint NINIAN in a proper Habit, in his right hand a Cross Fitchie; in the left a Book open.

The earliest mention I have found of the Burrough of FORRES. Forres is, "Dovenaldus filius Constantin occisus est in oppido "Fothir anno 904." *(Chron. de Regibus Scotiæ)* Fothir is supposed to be Forres, and King Duffus was murdered in Forres, about anno 966. How early this Town was erected into a Royal Burrough, I find not. A Charter of "De novo damus," by King James IV. dated June 23d 1496 bears, That the ancient Charters granted to this Burrough had been destroyed by fire and other accidents, and therefore the King erects it of new into a free Burrough, with all the privileges of a Royal Burrough; I have placed an abstract of this Charter *(Appendix* No. XXV.)*. The constitution of this Burrough

is

---

* The Charter of the Town of Forres grants to them; "Aquam et Piscaturam "de Findhorn, tam in aqua dulci quam salsa." This Right is to be understood as follows: 1*st*, The Fishing of the Sluie-pool pertains to the Earl of Moray; and he claims and possesses this Fishing, from that Pool down the River as far as the Forrest of Tarnua extends. 2*dly*, By King James I. Charter anno 1425, the whole Fishing of Findhorn, was granted to the Monks and Abbot of Kinloss; and King Robert's Charter to them *anno Regni 4to*, of the whole fishing of the River, was confirmed *(Pen. Lethen.).* 3*dly,* By Charter December 2d 1505, the whole Fishing, except the Sluie-pool, was granted to the Abbot, *(Ibid.).* 4*thly,* By Contract betwixt Thomas Abbot of Kinloss, with the Convent, and the Town of Forres, Alexander Urquhart of Burdsyards, and William Wiseman, of date February 15th 1505—6, the Town, Burdsyards, and Wiseman, renounced all title to the Fishing of the River. (It is probable the Town obtained this Charter anno 1496, unknown to, and to the prejudice of the Abbot) And the Abbot and Convent did sett heretably, and in feu-farm to the foresaids, the Fishing on the fresh water, from the Sluie-pool, to the entering of the burn of Masset into the Sea *(Ibid.).* 5*thly,* The Lord of Kinloss and Earl of Elgin, came in the room and right of the Abbot and Convent, to whom the whole Fishing, from the Sluie-pool downward, both in fresh and salt water, did originally belong. And by Charter of date February 26th 1664, under the Great Seal, (Thomas Earl of Elgin having resigned) Alexander Brodie of Lethen acquired a right to all the Fishing

that

is much the same with that of Elgin. The only Sett they have,
is the following indistinct one: " At Forres 20th September
" 1711, in presence of the Town Council of the Burgh, a
" letter being read, directed by the Agent of the Burroughs
" to the Magistrates of the said Burgh, anent their making a
" true account and return to their Agent, of their Sett in elec-
" ting yearly. In obedience to which, the said Magistrates
" declare, That the number of their Council exceeds not
" seventeen, Provost, Bailies, Dean of Guild, and Treasurer
" included; and that at Ilk Election, the Old Council chuses
" the New, and are changed yearly as occasion offers; and to
" that effect, timeous premonition is made to the whole Bur-
" gesses, Heretors and Inhabitants, of the day prefixed for
" election of the said Magistrates and Town Council, by tuck
" of drum, and placading on the cross, and by other advertise-
" ments used and wont; and that the New Council chuses the
" Magistrates, and puts off, and takes on, or continues them
" as the circumstances of the place need and require. And
" this our Sett has been unaltered for many years; and or-
" dains our Clerk of Court to send an extract hereof to the
" Agent of the Burroughs. Signed in our name, and by our
" order, by Robert Tulloch our Common Clerk; *sic subscrib.*
" Robert Tulloch Clerk." This Sett leaves room to admit Gentlemen in the County upon the Council, which accordingly
is the practice.

The Town has a Jurisdiction of Sheriff-ship by their Charter

---

that had belonged to the said Earl and Abbot (*Ibid.*). And now, 6thly, The Town of Forres holds off Lethen; Tanachie and Durn hold off Forres; the Earl of Moray and Burfyards hold off the Crown; and the estate of Grangehill, pur-chased in 1749, by Sir Alexander Grant of Dalvey. The F shing upon that estate lay partly in the Priory lands of Pluscarden, and partly in the Abbay lands of Kinlofs.

ter; a weekly market, and feveral annual Fairs. Their Revenue is about L. 1000 Scots. The number of inhabitants is about nine hundred.

The Town's Arms are: Saint LAURENCE in a long habit, ftanding on a Brander; a Chaplet round his head; at his right fide a Crefcent; and at the left a Star of fix points; holding in his right hand a Book. Motto, JEHOVAH TU MIHI DEUS, QUID DEEST.

Every one of thefe Burroughs has a Poft Office, and a regular return of pofts three times in the week. And fince the Union of the two Kingdoms, Forres, Nairn, Invernefs, and Chanonrie in Rofs, make a Diftrict; and Elgin, Cullen, Banff, Inverurie, and Kintore make another. Each Diftrict fends a Member to the Britifh Parliament. And each of the Counties of Banff, Elgin, and Invernefs, chufes a Commiffioner; But the County of Nairn being fmall, chufes only alternately with the County of Cromarty.

Befides thefe Royal Burroughs, there are in this Province, feveral Burghs of Barony. Thefe are erected by Royal Patents or Charters. What their privileges and immunities are, will appear from the following inftances: Germach was erected into a Burgh of Barony, by a Patent anno 1537; the Kirktoun of Spynie, an Ecclefiaftic Barony anno 1452; the Town of Findhorn made a Barony, and the erection ratified in Parliament 1661; (*Vid. unprint. acts*) the Town of Geddes in the parifh of Nairn, was erected into a Burgh of Barony by Charter anno 1600; " cum poteftate creandi Balivos et Bur-" genfes, et vendendi et vinum et cervifiam, et mercemonia " quæcunque;" with a weekly market, &c. (*Hift. Kilrav.*)

By a Charter anno 1635, in favour of John Grant of Loggie, Moynefs, Broad-land, and Aldern, were erected into the

BURGHS of BARONY.

Barony

Barony of Moyness, with a weekly market on Saturday, and an annual Fair at Michaelmass (*Pen. Calder*). By Charter anno 1476, the Thanedom of Calder, Barony of Duris, &c. were erected into one Barony, called Campbelltoun, with power to create Bailives, Constables, Serjeants, and other Officers therein, with liberty to buy and sell within the freedoms thereof, and to have a Town House, and a market Cross, with a weekly market on Wednesday, and an annual Fair on July fifteenth; the Castle of Calder being the principal Messuage, at which Infeftments and Seasins may be taken, &c. *(Ibid.)*. The Town of Fochaber, the Kirktoun of Duffus, Blackstob in Muirtoun, the Town of Cromdale in Strathspey, and no doubt other villages within this Province, were Burghs of Barony.

PART

PART V.

THE
MILITARY HISTORY of MORAY.

Royal Forts; At Elgin, Forres, Nairn, Inverness, Urquhart, Cromwell's Fort at Inverness, Fort George at Inverness, Fort Augustus, Ruthven-Barrack, Fort George at Arderfier. Fortalices; At Duffus, Raite, Abernethie, Ruthven, Lochindort.—Battles; At Forres, with a description of the Obelisk or Sueno's Stone at Forres, and an elegant Engraving of its present appearance; At Mortlich, anno 1010; At Spey, anno 1078; At Spey, anno 1110; At Urquhart, anno 1160; At Invernahaven, anno 1386; At Perth, anno 1396, as having a connection with the History of this Country; At Drumnacoal anno 1427; At Elgin, anno 1452; At Clachnaharie, anno 1454; At Cean-Loch-Lochie, anno 1544; At Glenlivat, anno 1594; At Aldern, anno 1645; At Cromdale, anno 1690; At Inverness, anno 1715; At Culloden, anno 1746.—Military Roads.—Military Officers, Customs, &c.——

IT does not appear that the Romans had any Military exploits within this Province, nor have they left any monument of such actions. Though Severus forced a march into the

the Northmost bounds of Scotland, yet he fought no battle, but lost 50,000 of his army, in strugling with cold, hunger, and fatigue (*Xiphil. in Sev.*); and Agricola's ships which sailed round the North, and first discovered Britain to be an Island, gave names to people and places, but left no Military monuments. As little can I find any certain account of the Military actions of the Picts in this Country; their Battles and Skirmishes, whether with the Scots or the Saxons, were in the Southern Provinces: But since the overthrow of the Pictish Kingdom, we have traces of some memorable Battles and Conflicts, of which I shall give the most genuine account I could learn.

The Character which Tacitus gives of the German *Catti*, may, I doubt not, be applied to the ancient inhabitants of this Province, particularly to the Highlanders, viz. " Duriora genti " corpora, stricti artus, minax vultus, et major animi vigor; " nec arare terram, aut expectare annum, tam facile persuaseris, " quam vocare hostes, et vulnera mereri ; Pigrum quin imo et " iners videtur sudore acquirere, quod possis sanguine parare."

The great men and Chiefs of Clans in Scotland, for many ages, lived independent of the Kings ; they held their land by no other tenure than a forcible possession. In the year 1590, there was brought to the Exchequer, an account of 250,000 merks yearly rent (a large sum in these days), to which the Chieftains in the Western Isles had no other right but *Duchus* or possession.

The few Royal Forts through the Kingdom, were not sufficient to awe the Country and maintain peace ; and our Kings were necessitated to grant large powers, and extensive Jurisdictions to great men, with liberty to build Fortalices on their own lands, and to garrison them for the maintaining peace and order. By this, the power of the Crown was weakened, and
the

the Nobles and Chieftains became factious and ungovernable; and insurrections, tumults, and riots were frequent in every corner.

The Royal Forts in this Province were: Royal Forts

A Fort at Elgin; This Fort stood on a small hill, now called At Elgin. the Lady-hill, at the West end of the Town, on the North side: The plain area on the top of the hill, is eighty-five yards in length, and forty-five in breadth: There are some remains of the walls of this Fort yet standing, but such as do not shew the form or extent of the buildings. Generally these Forts were a square, or an oblong square; the walls about twenty feet high, and four feet thick, with towers in the angles, all wrought with run lime: Within the walls, were rooms and barracks of wood; the gate or entrance was guarded by an iron grate, and a port-cullis; and some Forts had parapets on the top of the wall: Within the Court there was a draw-well, and the whole Fort was environed with a fosse, over which was a draw-bridge. Vestiges of all these things are to be seen at this Fort at Elgin. The strength of such Forts were considerable before great guns came into use. The Randulphs, Dunbars, and Douglas Earls of Moray, were Constables of this Fort, and had the customs of the Town, the assize of ale, and probably the sixty-auchten parts, and the moss wards, now belonging to the Town, for their salary. They had a Jurisdiction within certain bounds round the Fort, and judged in riots and trespasses committed within these bounds; I am not certain, if after the death of Archibald Douglas anno 1455, any Earl acted as Constable of this Fort; But the Castle-hill, or Lady-hill, has always been the property of the Earls of Moray, and is so of the present Earl.

The Fort at Forres was pleasantly situated on an eminence, Forres. at the West end of the Town; and was fortified as that of Elgin. It was in this Fort that King Duffus was barbarously murdered, anno 965 or 966. Donald, grand-uncle of Bancho Thane of Lochaber, and anceſtor of the Family of Stewart, (*Mr. Simſ.*) was Governor of the Fort, and much truſted when the King came to Forres, in order to puniſh ſome villains. The King was a ſtrict Juſticiar, and would not grant a remiſſion to ſome Criminals, for whom Donald and his wife had warmly ſolicited; wherefore they cauſed ſtrangle him in his bed, and hid his corpſe under a bridge near Kinloſs. Donald, conſcious of his guilt, fled from Cullen ſucceſſor to Duffus; But his wife being put to the torture, confeſſed the whole ſcene: Donald was ſeized, and with his accomplices juſtly put to death, and the Fort was razed (*Ford. Buch.*). I know not if this Fort was rebuilt, and uſed as a Royal Fort; but it is certain, there was a Caſtle where it had ſtood, of which the Dunbars of Weſtfield had the property, with the Caſtle-lands; but I do not find that they acted as Conſtables.

Nairn.

The Royal Fort at Nairn ſtood on the bank of the River, a little above the preſent bridge. The River, with a rocky precipice, guarded one ſide of it, and it was ſtrongly walled, and ditched about on the other ſides. The Thanes of Calder were hereditary Conſtables of this Fort, and ſo was the preſent John Campbell of Calder, till the Juriſdiction-act anno 1747.

Inverneſs.

At Inverneſs we find in our Hiſtories a Fort or Caſtle very early: It ſtood on a hill cloſe by the River, and commanded the Town. What was the form of the old Fort, I find not: But it appears that it had a ditch, and an agger or rampart of earth on three ſides. The Governor of it was appointed during pleaſure, or for life, for ſome ages; but about the beginning of the ſixteenth Century, if not ſooner, the Earl of Huntley was made hereditary Conſtable of it, and for his fee or ſalary had the following lands, called the Caſtle-lands: viz. The three Davachs of Dunachtin, and the two Davachs of Kinrara and Delnaford in Badenoch,

Badenoch, the Davach of Shevin in Strathern, the lands of Tordarach, Bochruben, and Dundelchack in Strathnairn and Stratherick (thefe lands are the property now of the Laird of MacIntofh); likewife the Davach of Effich in the parifh of Invernefs, now belonging to MacIntofh; the lands of Porterfield, Little Hilltoun, Albnafkiach, and Haughs, all near the Town of Invernefs; the three Davachs of Caftle Leathers, and Coulduthil, the two Davachs of Upper and Nether Torbrecks, and Knocknagial; the two Davachs of Dunainmore, Dunaincroy, and Lagnalane; the two Davachs of Dochgarach and Dochnahuirg; the lands of Dochfoure, Dochcharn, and Dochnacraig, all in the parifh of Invernefs; and the lands of Bunachtin and Drumbuie in Strathnairn. The above-mentioned lands, now belonging to MacIntofh, were granted to that Family, as an affythment for the death of the Laird of MacIntofh, whom the Earl of Huntley caufed to be barbaroufly murdered in the Caftle of Huntley, in the year 1550. Thefe lands were held Ward, but MacIntofh purchafed the Freeholding of them; the other Caftle-lands hold of the Duke of Gordon.

There was likewife a Royal Fort in Urquhart. It ftood on a rock on the Weft fide of Lochnefs, twelve miles from Invernefs, and as many from Fort-Auguftus. The Loch wafhed the Eaft-wall of it, and the other three fides were fortified with a ftrong rampart, a ditch, and a draw-bridge: There were within the walls fome good buildings, and accommodation for a battalion of foldiers. In the year 1303, King Edward I. of England reduced this Fort, and bafely put to the fword Alexander Bois and his garrifon, who had bravely defended it (*Abercro.*). In 1334, Robert Lauder Governor maintained this Fort againft the Englifh (*Ibid.*); Sir Robert Chifholm was Governor of this Fort in 1364 (*Hift. Kilr.*); but who fucceeded him I know not. Thefe old Forts were a good defence againft the military weapons

Urquhart.

pons at that time in use; but when Cannons and Mortars were invented, they were soon reduced.

Oliver's Fort.

The Citadel of Inverness, called Oliver's Fort, from Oliver Cromwell, was a modern regular building. It was begun in 1651, and next year finished. It stood on the East bank of the River Ness, near the mouth of it; was a regular pentagon, with bastions, ramparts, a wet ditch, a covered way, and a glacis; one side of it was washed by the River, and it could lodge 2000 men. But it had several inconveniencies; the foundation was bad, and brandered with oak, the water was breakish, the air was moist, approaches to it were easy, and the Town was a shelter for an enemy. In the year 1662 it was demolished, because it was a relict of usurpation, but chiefly because it was a check upon the adjacent Highlands then esteemed Loyal.

Fort-George at Inverness.

Fort-George stood on the Castle-hill of Inverness, and the building was begun soon after the rebellion in 1715; the old Castle was repaired for lodging the Officers; a fine house was built for the Governor; a pile of barracks stood as wings to the Castle; a chapel, magazine, and store house were built; the old draw-well was opened, and the whole surrounded with a strong wall, proof against any artillery except battering Cannon. But the hill, being a heap of quick sand, could be easily sapped or undermined; and it is strange that so much money was thrown away upon it. On the 19th February 1746, this Fort was taken and reduced by the Rebels.

Fort-Augustus.

Fort-Augustus, so called from Frederic Augustus then Prince of Wales, stands at the South end of Lochness, in the point betwixt the rivers Eoich and Tarf, where they empty into the Loch. The Loch and Tarf wash two sides of the Fort, which was built about 1730. The Rebels likewise demolished this Fort; but it has been since rebuilt, and surrounded with

with a ditch and ramparts. A small Galley is kept on Lochness, for the service of this Fort, and to convey stores to it.

The Barrack of Ruthven in Badenoch was begun to be built in 1718. It stood where the old Castle had been, and consisted of two large houses standing parallel, and joined by ramparts, and two bastions in the diagonal angles: It had convenient lodging for two companies of men, a draw-well, and a large stable. In August 1745, all the company lodged here joined General Cope, except Serjeant Mulloy and fourteen men, who maintained the Barrack against two hundred of the Rebels: And in February 1746, Serjeant Mulloy with twelve men only defended it for three days, and obtained an honourable capitulation, for which gallant behaviour he was preferred to be a Lieutenant. The Rebels burnt the barrack. Ruthven-Barrack.

Fort-George at Aderfier stands on a point of land that jutts into the Frith: The land is near a half mile broad to the continent, and tapers to a narow point: On this point the Fort is built in form of a triangle, whereof the sea covers two sides, and the ditch, which may receive the sea at pleasure, makes the third. It is invironed with high ramparts and bastions, with a reveline, a covered way and glacis; It is well served with sweet water, and can have a fine harbour. For an English mile no high ground commands it, and no lines of approach can be digged in the hard channel, without great labour. The air is pure and wholesome, and it will accommodate 2000 men. Fort-George at Arderfier.

Besides these Royal Forts, there were in this Country several Fortalices built by Gentlemen for defence. Of these the following five were ancient, and built in the old form: viz. Fortalices.

The Castle of Old Duffus, which stood on a green mote, on the bank of the Loch of Spynie. It was square, the wall about twenty feet high, and five feet thick, with a parapet, ditch and At Duffus.

and draw-bridge: Within the square, were buildings of timber built to the wall, with stables and all necessary offices. I question not but this Fort (the walls whereof were built with run lime, and as yet stand pretty entire) was built as early as the time, if not sooner, of Friskinus de Moravia, in the reign of King David I.

Raite. The Castle of Raite in the parish of Nairn, was of the same form, and was probably the seat of Raite of that Ilk.

Abernethie. The Red Castle in Abernethie, the walls of which stand, was of the like form, and was the seat of Cummine Laird of Abernethie.

Ruthven. The Castle of Ruthven, the seat of Cummine Lord Badenoch, stood on a green mount, jutting into a marshy plain. The mount is steep on three sides, and tapering to the top, as if it were artificial; the area on the top, about an hundred yards long and thirty broad; the South wall was nine feet thick, through which the arched entry was guarded by a double iron grate, and a port-cullis; the other walls were sixteen feet high, and four thick, and in the North end of the court were two towers in the corners, and some low buildings, and a draw-well within the court. I have seen this Fort entire.

Lochindort. In Lochindort, in the hills betwixt Strathspey and Brae-Moray, stand in a small island the walls of a strong Fort as yet entire. In the year 1335, when the Earl of March defeated and killed David de Strathboggie Earl of Athole, at Kilblain, and raised the siege of Kildrummie Castle, the Earl of Athole's Lady fled to the Castle of Lochindort. Sir Alexander Gordon laid siege to it; but next year King Edward of England obliged him to raise this siege. This Fort, and the adjacent forrest belongs to John Campbell of Calder; for " James Earl of Moray, " 31st of October 1606, disponed to Sir John Campbell of Cal-
" der,

A representation of the Staty of Moray Scotland.

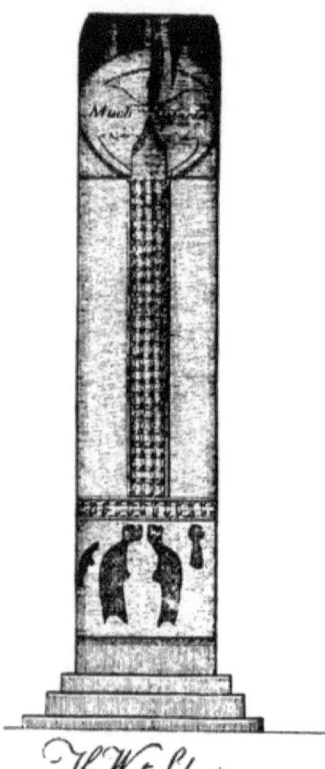

The West Side.

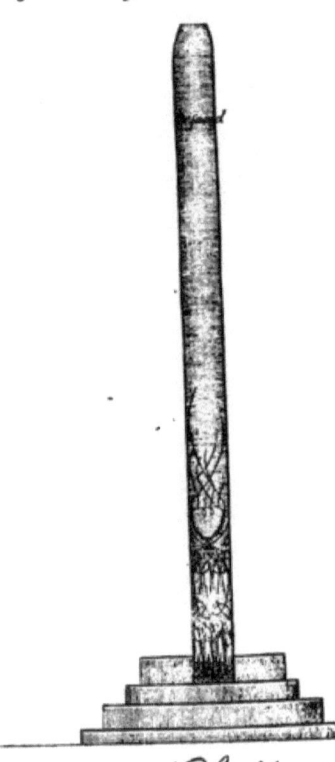

North Side.

" der, the lands of Borlum, Coulards, and Kinchylie, cum
" Lacu de Lochindorb, domibus in eo, et adjacentibus Shelingis
" (*Pen. Cald.*)."

The other Fortalices were strong Towers; at Calder, Kilravock, Daviot, Lovat, Borlum, Ernside, Dallas, &c. These were for the most part built in the reign of King James II. when the rebellion of the Earls of Douglas, Crawford, Ross, &c. had run the Kingdom into confusion.

I now come to give some account of the Military actions, whether Battles, Skirmishes, or Rencounters, within this Province; The earliest of which was: BATTLES, &c.

The Battle of Forres. Sueno, son of Harald King of Denmark, having defeated the English, and driven their King Ethelrad out of the Kingdom, sought to be revenged of the Scots, who had aided Ethelrad; for this end, he sent a great army into Scotland, under the command of Olaus and Enecus, who landed in Moray anno 1008, and committed great ravages. King Malcolm II. being informed of this, marched against them with an army of new Levies, and gave them Battle near the Town of Forres; But the unexperienced soldiers, rushing on with more courage than conduct, and the King being wounded in the head and carried out of the field, the enemy got an easy victory, which they improved, as might be expected from such barbarians, with cruelty, blood-shed, and plunder. They soon reduced the Castles or Forts of Elgin, Forres, and Nairn. Flushed with this success, they sent for their wives, children and families, hoping they should quietly possess the pleasant and fertile plains of Moray, and from thence extend their conquests (*Ford. Buch.*). At Forres.

A furlong or two East of Forres, stands an Obelisk, called *Sueno's Stone* which is one of the most curious and stately monuments of that kind in Britain. Some years ago, the corn land OBELISK at Forres.

land round it being always plowed up, it was like to fall ; But Lady Ann Campbell, late Countess of Moray, caused it to be set upright, and supported with several steps of free-stone. The height of this Stone cannot now be certainly known; It is about twenty-three feet above ground, and said to be twelve feet under ground ; Its breadth is about four feet. What is above ground, is visibly divided into seven parts, whereof the lowest is almost wholly hid by the supports. The second division contains many figures, but much defaced. In the third are figures of men, and some of beasts, with human heads. The fourth contains Ensigns and Military weapons, carried by figures much worn out; And in the fifth, sixth, and seventh, the figures are scarce discernible. On the reverse is a Cross, beneath which, are two human figures of a Gothish form. Mr Gordon, in his *Itinerarium Septentrionale*, will have this Obelisk erected after the Battle of Murthlac, and in memory of the Danes leaying the Kingdom : But why should there be erected at Forres a monument of a Battle, fought at more than twelve miles from it? And after the Battle of Murthlac, the Danes fought at Balbryde, Aberlemno, Gemri, and Cruden in Buchan, where they engaged to leave the Kingdom ; which places were more proper for such a monument, than at Forres.

BURGUS.   The Danish families sent for, arrived ; upon which they fortified a small Promontory in the parish of Duffus, which our Historians call BURGUS. This Promontory jutts into the Frith, and rises above low-water about sixteen yards; To the West and North it is a perpendicular rock ; To the East the ascent is steep, and covered with grass ; At the South the ascent is more easy ; The top forms nearly a rectangular-figure, in length about one hundred yards, and in breadth about thirty. This area they surrounded with a strong rampart of Oaken-logs, laid deep in the earth, of which some pieces are as yet digged up, up, and the burnt remains appear in the earth. The neck of and towards the South being small, they cut a deep trench, and brought the sea round the Promontory; and within this, they cut other trenches, with a rampart of stone and earth. At the foot of the Promontory, to the East, is an area about forty yards long and twenty broad, of which the hill makes one side, and the other three were well fortified with a high rampart. This Fort served them for a place of arms, for a safe retreat if defeated, for an Asylum to their wives and children; and it guarded the harbour at the foot of the rock, where the transports lay. Our Historians, not acquainted with the Geography of the Country, place this Fort at Nairn; But no such Promontory or Fort was there, nor any Tradition of it. As the Danes called it *Burgh*, it still retains that name, and is called *Burgh-sea*, or surrounded by the Sea. The Sea near it has retired, by the reflection from the rock, and it is no longer an Island.

After the Battle of Forres, King Malcolm II. returned South, and finding that the Danes purposed to settle in Moray, raised a powerful army, with which he marched in the beginning of the year 1010, to drive out the Invaders. How soon the Danes were certified of the road by which the King marched, they moved forward to meet him, wisely chusing to Fight at a distance from their projected settlement. A little East of the house of Carron, there are manifest vestiges of a Camp, where it is thought the Danes encamped, till by their speculatories or scouts, they had certain intelligence of the King's approach; Then they marched to Mortlich, and the King's army came to Achindun, two miles from the enemy. The King, having learned that the Danes lay on both sides of the water of Dulenan near the Church, was advised to use a Stratagem, viz. A mile above the Church, the water runs in a narrow channel betwixt high rocks: here it was dammed up, and made

At Mortlich anno 1010.

made to flow back into a spacious plain; and the army about the dawning of the next day having attacked the enemy, he caused break the Dam, and the torrent separated the two parts of their army, so that the one could not assist the other; those on the South side, who were the smaller number, were all cut off; but upon the falling of the water, the great body of the Danes charged the Scots with great fury, yet were entirely broken, and fled precipitately towards Moray. Enecus their General was killed, as was another General named Magnus or Manus, from whom *Bal-vanie*, i. e. Manus's Town, takes its name. The Scots lost three Generals, Kenneth Thane of the Isles, Dunbar Thane of Laudian, and Græme Thane of Strathern. In memory of this victory, the Episcopal See of Murthlac was erected. After this, the Danes had repeated defeats at Balbryde, Aberlemno, Gemrie, and Cruden, and left the Kingdom about the year 1012 (*Buch.*).

At Spey, Anno 1078.

King Malcolm III. having concluded a peace with the King of England, was soon after disturbed by insurrections at home. The inhabitants of Moray, Ross, and Caithness, made a revolt, and raised a powerful force; MacDuff Earl of Fife was detached to quell this tumult: But when he had come to Dee, and was certified of the enemy's strength, he halted till the King came up with a considerable reinforcement; The army then marched to the River Spey, where the rebels on the other side were ready to obstruct their passage: The Standard-Bearer and others, declined to enter a River so deep and rapid, in the face of a numerous and desperate enemy; Upon which, one Alexander de Caron, taking the Standard, stepped into the River, and his boldness encouraged the army to follow him: The enemy observing the resoluteness of the Royal army, laid down their weapons, were pardoned, and peace was restored. Alexander Caron was made hereditary Standard-Bearer, and Constable of the

the Castle of Dundee: Having defeated a bold English Bully or Fencer, he got the name of *Scrimger*, i. e. Hard Fighter, which became the surname of his Family. One of his descendants was created Viscount Dundee; but the male line failing, the honours became extinct, (*Buch.*).

In the year 1110, the 4th of the Reign of King Alexander I. some young Gentlemen in the Merns and Moray, whose licentious life the King had restrained, conspired to cut him off. The conspiracy was happily discovered, and then the villains placed their safety in an open rebellion, and got a great number of desperadoes to join them. The King raised an army and pursued them into the Country of Moray: At the River Spey the rebels halted, determined to dispute the passage; But the King immediately rode into the River, the army followed, and he ordered Alexander Scrimger, son of Alexander Caron, to charge the enemy, which he did so gallantly, that many being killed, the rest betook themselves to a precipitate flight. The King pursued them through all Moray, and at the Stock-foord above Beaulie, followed them into Ross; Some were apprehended and punished, and others found shelter from inaccessible mountains and rocks. This resolute action, in the beginning of his reign, rendered the remainder of it peaceable, (*Wint. Major. Buch.*).

At Spey, anno 1110.

King Malcolm IV. was a Prince of two mild and peaceable a disposition for the time in which he lived; and suffered the English to robb him of those Counties in England, which his predecessors had possessed for some generations. This made his own subjects contemn his authority, and disturb his reign; Somerled (*Somharle MacGilbhride*) Thane of Argyle and the Isles, was reduced by Gilchrist (ancestor of the Ogilvies) Earl of Angus; The same Earl defeated MacDowal Lord of Galloway. But the Moravienses, or people of Moray, were not so easily

At Urquhart, anno 1160.

easily reduced; These, under the command of (*Gildomhnich*) Gildominic, laid waste the neighbouring Countries, and so little regarded the Royal authority, that they hanged the Heralds sent to require them to lay down their arms. Earl Gilchrist was sent to reduce them, but was defeated and chased over the Grampian mountains. These insults upon authority, and the cries of his people, roused the indolent King. About the year 1160, he marched with a powerful army, and found the enemy on the muir of Urquhart near the Spey, ready to give him battle; Having passed the river, the Noblemen in his army reconnoitered the enemy, and found them flushed with their late victory, and become desperate by rebellion; To Fight against such men, and under a Prince of no military character, would make the event doubtful; and should they succeed, the victory would only destroy their fellow subjects, and weaken the force of the Kingdom. Wherefore, they advised the King to promise the Rebels, that, upon their submission, all their lives should be spared. The Rebels finding the King's army superior, and resolute; and considering that their own crime was such, as, if defeated, left them no room to hope for favour, they accepted the King's offer, and laid down their arms. The King performed his promise to them; but in regard that they were, as Buchanan says, " Homines inquie- " to semper ingenio," of a turbulent and unpeaceable disposition, He, with the advice of his Nobles, ordained that every family in Moray, that was engaged in this rebellion, should, in a limited time, remove out of Moray into other Countries, where possessions would be assigned to them; and that people of such Countries should be placed in Moray. For performance of this, they gave hostages; and at the time appointed, transplanted themselves, some into the Northern, but the greater number into the Southern Counties.

Our

Our Historians say, That there was here an obstinate Battle, in which the Moray-men were (pene internecionem) almost totally cut off, and strangers brought into their place. But the account given in the Register of Paisley (*Vid. Innes's Critic. Essay*) is, as I have here written, and seems more probable: The consequences confirm it; for the Moray-men, at that time transplanted into the South, did assume, and their posterity use the Surname of Moray, and are numerous in all the Counties Southward to the English borders. In the Northern Counties, some retain the name of Moray, and others have taken that of Sutherland; But in the Province of Moray, there have been very few of the name of Moray, since the time of that action. I likewise incline to think, that as at that time the MacIntoshes, and probably the Roses of Geddes, came into Moray, so the Calders and Innesses, whose ancestors were Moray-men, but not concerned in that rebellion, assumed surnames from their possessions.

The next Battle or Fight, in order of time, does, I confess, as to the circumstances of it, depend on Tradition; but such as is unvaried. *Buchanan, in vita Jac.* I. mentions this Fight, but out of the order of Chronology, for it happened anno 1386; "Catanei et Cameronii, orto inter ipsos dissidio, tanta contentione animorum et virium pugnarunt, ut multis Cataneorum trucidatis, Cameronii pene omnes extincti fuerunt." The occasion of the Conflict was as follows: The lands of MacIntosh in Lochaber being possessed by the Camerons, the rents were seldom levied, but by force and in cattle: The Camerons, irritated by the poinding of their cattle, resolved to make reprisals, and marched into Badenoch about four hundred men strong, commanded by Charles MacGilony. MacIntosh informed of this, in haste called his friends and Clan to meet together; The MacIntoshes, MacPhersons, and Davidsons, soon made a force superior to the enemy; but an unseasonable difference was

At Invernahavon, anno 1386.

was like to prove fatal to them: It was agreed by all, that MacIntosh, as Captain of the Clan Chattan, should command the centre of their army; but Cluney and Invernahavon contended about the command of the right wing. Cluney claimed it as Chief of the ancient Clan Chattan, of which the Davidsons of Invernahavon were but a branch. Invernahavon pleaded, that to him, as the oldest branch, the right hand belonged, by the custom of Scottish Clans. The contest was spun out, till the enemy were at hand; and then MacIntosh, as Umpire, imprudently gave it in favour of Invernahavon. The MacPhersons, in whose Country they were met, and who were as numerous as both the MacIntoshes and the Davidsons, being greatly offended, withdrew as spectators. The Conflict was very sharp, by the superior number of the Camerons; many of the MacIntoshes, and almost all the Davidsons were cut off. The MacPhersons could no longer bear to see their brave neighbours and friends overpowered: They rushed in upon the Camerons, and soon gave them a total defeat: The few that escaped, with their leader, were pursued from Invernahavon, the place of Battle, three miles above Ruthven in Badenoch, over the River Spey; and Charles MacGilony was killed in a hill in Glenbenchir, which is still called *Cor-Harlich*, i. e. Charles's Hill (*Hist. MacIntosh*).

At PERTH. anno 1396. This Fight, in my opinion, gave occasion to the memorable Conflict on the Inch of Perth, in presence of the King and Nobility anno 1396. *Buch. lib.* x. *Cap.* 2. and 3. gives a particular account of it, but does not name the combatants. Boetius calls them " Clan Cattani et Clan Caii:" But though we read of those of the name of *Cay* or *Kay*, in the Lowlands, they are never reckoned among the Clans, nor had the Clan Chattan any intercourse with them. The combatants, thirty of a side, were the MacPhersons, properly Clan Chattan, and the Davidsons

Davidsons of Invernahavon, in Irish called *Clan-Dhai*, which is commonly sounded *Clan-Cai*; and our Historians, ignorant of the Irish, made them a Clan different from, and at enmity with the Clan Chattan; whereas they were a tribe of them. I mentioned above the rash judgement of MacIntosh in their favour, giving them the right wing in Battle, and Clunie's resentment of this injurious decision: After which decision, the MacPhersons and Davidsons, for ten years, miserably slaughtered one another. The judicious author of a M. S. History of the Family of Kilravock, says, That a contest about precedency was the occasion of this Conflict, and the Fight at Perth was constructed a Royal sentence in favour of the MacPhersons. I have mentioned this Conflict, though it was not in Moray, because the Combatants were of this Province; and our Historians have not sufficiently explained who they were, or what was the cause of the combat.

Although it may be reckoned a digression, I shall mention another Conflict, which was not within this Province, that I may rectify a mistake in our History. *Buch. in vita Jac.* I. writes, " Emiserat Rex e custodia duos Angusios, Duffum " et Moravium, latronum duces. Hi, furore in se verso, pari " fere numero congressi (alebat enim e rapinis latrones quis- " que ad 1200) adeo pertinaciter conflixerunt, ut vix superessent " cladis nuncii." The translator would make this a Conflict between the Duffs and the Morays; But it was anno 1427, betwixt Angus *Dubh*, or Black Angus MacKay, ancestor to Lord Rae; and Angus Moray of Pulrossie (son of Alexander Moray of Coulbin in Moray) at Drumnacoub near Tung in Strathnaver, where both the Anguses were killed. (*M. S. Hist. of Suther.*) — At Drumnacoub, anno 1427.

The next Military action, in order of time, was near the Town of Elgin, anno 1452. When the Earl of Huntley was at — At Elgin, anno 1452.

at the Battle of Brechin in May 1452, Archibald Douglas Earl of Moray took advantage of it, entered the lands of Strathbolgie, burnt the Castle of Huntley, and committed many outrages through that Lordship. The account of this stopped Huntley from improving his victory, and made him return in order to preserve his own lands: Douglas returned into Moray, and Huntley followed him with a considerable force, especially of Cavalry; Douglas with six hundred foot, but few horses, stood on the heights of Whitefield, not daring to face Huntley in the plains. This provoked the Gordons to plunder Douglas's lands, and finding that one half of the Town of Elgin had joined Douglas, they burnt that half, which gave rise to the Proverb, " Half done, as Elgin was half burnt." But in the evening, as a troop or two of the Gordons were spoiling the lands of Kirkhill in the parish of St Andrews, a superior detachment of Douglas's men suddenly attacked, and drove them over Lossie, and some of them were killed in the bogs and fens, which occasioned this rhyme,

> *What's come of thy men, thou Gordon so gay?*
> *They're in the bogs of Dunkintie mowing the hay,* &c.

The Earl of Huntley, however, drove Douglas into the South, where he was killed in the year 1455: It is the tradition of the Country, that the half of the Town of Elgin, at that time burnt, stood Westward of the present Town, and was never rebuilt; but the buildings were continued Eastward to the precinct of the Elgin College: And it is thought, that at that time the Earl of Moray gave to the Town of Elgin the sixty Auchten-parts (or eight parts) of land near Pittenriech, to compensate the loss of burning the half of the Town. The Town enjoys these lands by immemorial possession, without any particular charter or right that I know of: But I incline to think that

that these were Castle-lands, granted to the Earls of Moray as Constables; and that as, after Douglas, no Earl appears to have officiated as Constable, or to have resided at Elgin, and the Earldom remained long in the hands of the King, the Town's possession was fixed by prescription, and I find not that any of the subsequent Earls questioned it. (*Buch.—Hist. of Douglas*).

A shameful and bloody Conflict, happened betwixt the MacIntoshes and the Munroes in the year 1454. The occasion was this: *At Clachnaharie, anno 1454.*

John Munroe tutor of Fowles, in his return from Edinburgh, rested upon a meadow in Strathardale, and both he and his servants falling asleep, the peevish owner of the meadow cut off the tails of his horses. This he resented, as the Turks would resent the cutting off their horse's tails, which they reckon a grievous insult: He returned soon with three hundred and fifty men, spoiled Strathardale, and drove away their cattle; in passing by the Loch of Moy in Strathern he was observed.

MacIntosh, then residing in the Island of Moy, sent to ask a *Stike Raide*, or *Stike Criech*, *i. e.* a Road Collup; a custom among the Highlanders, that when a party drove any spoil of cattle through a Gentleman's land, they should give him part of the spoil. Munroe offered what he thought reasonable, but not what was demanded; MacIntosh, irritated by some provoking words given to his messenger, convocated a body of men, pursued the Munroes, and at Clachnaharie near Inverness, they fought desperately; Many were killed on each side, among whom was the Laird of MacIntosh; John Munroe was wounded and laimed, and ever after called John Bacilach. The Munroes had great advantage of ground, by lurking among the rocks; whilst the M'Intoshes were exposed to their arrows. How rude and barbarous was the spirit of men in those days?

days? And upon what trifling, nay shameful provocations, did they butcher one another? *(Hist. of Lovat.—Hist. of MacIntosh).*

At Cean-Loch-Lochie, an. Do 1544.

The Next, in order of time, was the battle of Cean-Loch-Lochie in the year 1544. The minority of the infant Queen, and the disturbance raised in the South by the Queen mother and Cardinal Beaton, encouraged the Highlanders to break loose, and to hope for impunity: Particularly the Clan Ranald became very unruly. Ranald, son of Donald Glas of Moidart, was sister's son of Hugh Lord Lovat; and the Clan-Ranald, conceiving a prejudice against him much upon Lovat's account, dispossessed him, and put John MacRanald his cousin in possession of the estate. Lovat resented this injustice, and repossessed his own nephew, but the unruly Clan dispossessed Ranald again, and laid waste a part of Lovat's lands in Glenelg. Then George Earl of Huntley, Lieutenant of the North, was ordered to march against the Clan Ranald, and to reduce them to a peaceable behaviour. He set out in the end of May 1544, attended by the MacIntoshes, Grants and Frasers; and when they arrived in Lochaber, all differences were composed in a seemingly amicable way, by the mediation of the Earl of Argyle. Ranald was put in possession of the estate. Huntley returned home. The MacIntoshes and Grants conveyed Lovat to Gloy, now called the Nine Mile Water, and offered to escort him into his own country. But Lovat, apprehending no danger, declined it; and they marched home by Badenoch. Lovat soon came to see his error; for at Leterfinlay, he was informed, that the Clan Ranald were at hand, in full march, to intercept him. He dispatched Bean Clerach, with 50 men to secure an important pass; But Bean either losing his way, or playing the knave, kept out of danger. As Lovat came to the North end of Loch-Lochie, the Clan Ranald appeared, coming down

the

the hill from the West, about 500 in seven companies. Lovat had about 300 who all stript to the shirts, the day (July 2d) being very hot: And hence the battle was called *Blar-nan-Lein, i. e.* The Field of Shirts. The fight was very obstinate, first with arrows, and next with sword and target. In the heat of action, Simon Master of Lovat came up with a few men, and rushed in to find his father; but soon received a mortal wound. His father observing it became desperate, and both were killed. The fight continued till night; and tradition bears, that only four of the Frasers, and ten of the Clan Ranald, remained alive.

Buchanan, and the M. S account of Lovat's Family, blame the Earl of Huntly for this barbarous conflict; that he had privately stirred up the Clan Ranald to intercept Lovat. The character of that Earl, and the resentment of his treachery, long entertained by the Frasers, found a suspicion that he was guilty, and the author of the History of that Family makes but a poor defence for him. One remarkable circumstance is observed by our Historians, That 80 gentlemen of the Frasers, killed in this conflict, had left their wives pregnant, who all brought forth male-children, which contributed much to recruit the Clan. *(Buch.—Hist. of Lov.—Hist. of MacInt.)*

The battle of Glenlivat, was so called, because it was fought in that Glen. It was likewise called the battle of Altchonlachan, from a small brook of that name, betwixt Glenlivat and Glenrinnes, on the banks of which it was fought. The occasion of this battle was, the Earl of Huntley, having basely murdered the Earl of Moray at Dunibristle anno 1592, became, on that account, odious to all Protestants. And he, with the Earls of Errol and Angus, entered into a conspiracy against both church and state, and invited the King of Spain to invade the Kingdom. The church at length excommunicated, and the King (unwillingly) forefeited these Noblemen, and gave commission

At Glenlivat, anno 1594.

mission to the Earl of Argyle, a youth of nineteen years of age, and of no military skill, to reduce them. The Earl of Athole, Lords Forbes and Lovat, the MacNeils, MacLeans, MacKenzies, MacIntoshes, Grants, Munroes, Irvines, and the Lesleys of Balquhan were summoned to join Argyle, and the King promised to follow him in person, with another army. The rebel Lords were not afraid: They knew the King's favour for them, and that he would make no haste; They also knew Argyle's want of experience, and that many in his army were Roman Catholics, and would not heartily promote the Protestant interest; and that all his army were a raw militia: Wherefore they prepared a body of horse all gentlemen, and some Field-pieces; They likewise corrupted the Grants and Campbell of Lochinel.

Argyle marched in the beginning of September 1594, and on the 27th laid siege to the Castle of Ruthven in Badenoch. But the MacPhersons, Huntley's vassals, defended it so bravely, that he soon raised the siege; and marching thro' Strathspey came to Drummin on 2d October. The Earls of Huntley and Errol (for Angus had not come up) were that day at Auchindun. Argyle's council advised him to wait for the King, at least till the Frasers and Mackenzies should join them, and till the Irvines, Forbesses and Lesleys, should come up with their horse, and make a ballance against the enemy's horse. But upon the enemy's approaching October 3d, he determined to fight. The numbers are not agreed upon. Some give Argyle 10,000 and Huntley but 900. Straloch gives Huntley 1320. Calderderwood makes Huntley's army 1400, and Argyle's 5000. Huntley and Errol could raise a far greater number: And considering the five Clans that had not come up to Argyle, tho' the other Clans had made 500 each, which certainly they did not, they would not make 5000. The field of battle was, the declivity of a hill betwixt Glenlivet and Glenrinnes. The MacIntoshes

toshes and MacLeans made Argyle's right wing: The Grants, MacNeils and MacGregors the left; and the Campbells, &c. the centre. Huntley's field pieces, which many had never seen before, put the Highlanders into disorder; and his horses rushing in, increased it. Campbell of Lochinel (whose brother Argyle had put to death, for murdering Campbell of Calder anno 1592. and who himself was Argyle's nearest heir) had wrote to Huntley to point his artillery against the Yellow Standard. This was done; and Lochinel falling, all his men fled. (*Calderw.*) John Grant of Gartinbeg, Huntley's vassal, had concerted, that the Grants whom he commanded should retreat, how soon the action began; and they did so. (*Hist. of Gord.*) Thus the centre and the left wing were broken by treachery. The right wing stood firm after the rest had fled, and retreated with order and safety: And MacQuaire observes, that had they been sustained, they had certainly carried the victory. Argyle attempted in vain to rally his men. The victory was complete. On Argyle's side 500 were killed, besides MacNeil of Bara, Lochinel and his brother. On the other side Errol was wounded; Sir Patrick Gordon of Auchindun Huntley's uncle, and Gordon of Gight, with twelve more, were killed; and many more were wounded.

The King in his usual dissimulation was glad of Argyle's defeat, and jested him upon it. " Magnis itineribus ad Regem " tendit, qui, quod omnes sciunt, Argadi adversum casum non " indigne tulit, sed potius per jocos et prælii irrisionem, de " eventu cum eo sæpius egit." (*MacQuaire*) Gordon of Straloch, in his account of this battle, says " On the fourth night, after " the King's return, I saw Lennox, Huntley and Balquhan at " supper privately in my father's house, which could not be " without the King's knowledge." And Burnet of Crimond, in his M. S. History, declares. " That he saw, among Huntley's
papers,

"papers, a private remission to him for the battle of Glenlivat, granted in that same year 1594." All these circumstances considered, it was no wonder that Argyle was defeated.

At Aldern, anno 1645.
I come now to give some account of the battle of Aldern. MONTROSE having, on the 2d of February 1645, in the night surprised the Campbells at Inverlochie in Lochaber, and thereby defeated them, wrote a vaunting letter to King Charles I. which he thus concludes: "Give me leave, after I have reduced this "country to obedience, and conquered from Dan to Beersheba, to say to your Majesty, as David's General to his Ma-"ster, Come thou thyself, least this country be called by my "name." This vain letter made the King break off the treaty of Uxbridge, which proved his ruin. (*Welw.*)

MONTROSE marched into Moray, and was soon joined by Lord Gordon, the Earl of Aboyne, Lord Napier, and others. The Covenanters in the mean time, had called over 1000 of their troops from Ireland, to join their raw militia, and Baillie remaining in the South, Hurry marched into the North, and came to Inverness, understanding that Montrose was reinforced with 1000 foot, and two hundred horse of the Gordons, and was marching back from Strathboggie. Hurry called in the assistance of the Frasers, MacKenzies, Rosses, Sutherlands, and Brodies, and made an army of about 3500 foot, and 400 horse. Montrose's army consisted of about 3000 foot, and 400 horse, made up of Gordons, MacDonalds, MacPhersons and Irish. On May 4th 1645, they engaged near the village of Aldern, immediately above the house of Kinnudie. The fight was, for a little, obstinate and dubious; till Lord Gordon bravely charging with his horse, Major Drummond called the *Crowner*, who commanded Hurry's horse, wheeling about unskilfully, broke the foot-ranks of their own men, and then Lord Gordon soon put them to a precipitate retreat. To this bad conduct

conduct of Drummond, the defeat was greatly owing, for which he was tried at Inverness and shot. About 800 of the Covenanters were killed, among whom were Campbell of Lawers, and Sir Hugh and Gideon Murrays. The loss on Montrose's side was considerable, and among the killed was William MacPherson of Invereshie. This, and the two following victories at Alford, too much elated Montrose, who understood better how to gain, than how to improve a victory. This appeared at the total defeat at Philliphaugh, Sept. 13th this year; after which he could not bring any force into the field.

The battle of Cromdale, anno 1690, comes next to be described. The death of the Viscount Dundee in the battle of Kyllicrankie, July 16th 1689, was the ruin of King James's affairs in Scotland. Colonel Canon, with 3000 men, surprised the Earl of Angus's regiment at Dunkeld, on Sept. 1689; but the brave Colonel Cleland, with 1200, made him retire, with no small loss both of men and of reputation. Canon retired into Lochaber; and in spring 1690, Colonel Buchan, with about forty officers, was sent over from Ireland, and assumed the command. In the beginning of April, the rebel chiefs had a meeting: Some inclined to capitulate: But Sir Ewan Cameron diverted this, hoping that another compaign would retrieve their affairs. And till the seed-time should be closed, and greater numbers should be raised, Colonel Buchan, with about 1500 of MacLeans, MacDonalds, MacPhersons, Camerons, and Grants of Glenmoriston, marched towards the Lowlands to amuse and fatigue the King's troops. In marching thro' Strathspey, they plundered the country, and in passing towards Strathboggie they burnt the house of Edinglassie. But Mr Gordon made severe reprisals; for in their return he seized eighteen of their number, and hanged them on the trees of his garden.

By this time Sir Thomas Livingstone had come to Inverness

At Cromdale, anno 1690.

ness with a battalion of foot, six troops of dragoons, and two of horse. The Rebels informed of this, returned towards the Highlands, and Levingstone resolved to intercept them. Conducted by some gentlemen of the Grants, he marched on the night of April 30th with the horse and dragoons, leaving the foot to follow. By the dawning of the morning May 1. 1690, he came to the Dairirade, or top of the hill above Castle-Grant, and, that he might not be discovered, he was directed down the valley of Auchlnarrow, to cross Spey below Dellachaple. The enemy had come to Cromdale April 30th, and chusing to keep near the hill, encamped that night near Lethindie, and had some advanced guards near the Kirk of Cromdale; which guards observed the troops fording the river, and alarmed the Camp. This moved the General to mount some of the Grants on dragoon horses, and all the horse and dragoons led by these gentlemen rode smartly (the distance being about a mile, and a part of the road concealed by a Birch wood), and surprised the enemy before they could all get into their cloaths, who fled precipitately about a half mile, many of them quite naked, and at the foot of the hill of Cromdale faced about, and made a faint defence, but were soon routed; and had not the hill been so steep that the horse could not pursue, few would have escaped. There were above a hundred killed, and about sixty were made prisoners, who were found in the Castle of Lethindie, and the miln. It deserves to be remarked, That Colonel MacDonald of Keppach, who was ever keen for plunder, but never once fought for his King, would not encamp with the other rebels, but with his men quartered in Garvlin, half a mile distant, and thereby escaped without loss. Such of the Rebels as climbed up the hill, could not be pursued. But a party of Camerons and MacLeans, who next day crossed the river, were pursued, and on the Muir of Granish near Aviemore some were killed, and the

rest

rest taking shelter in Craigelachie, and Keppach, who with their banditti, attempted to reduce the Castle of Lochinelan in Rothemurchus, were by that Laird and his tenants beat off with loss.

 The Rebellion, in the year 1715, is fresh in the memory of some yet living. On November 13th that year, the Rebels at Preston in England were forced to surrender; on the same day the Battle of Sherriff-muir was fought, which in the consequences of it was a compleat victory. And likewise on that day, the Town and Castle of Inverness was surrendered. On Saturday November 12th, Arthur Rose, brother to Kilravock, a bold and daring man, with Robert Rose brother to Blackhills, and twelve chosen men, undertook to surprise the main-guard in the Tolbooth. They were in the twilight conducted by one of the Rebels, who promised to get the door opened, upon which they might rush in. The villain got access, but loudly alarmed the guard, and Arthur Rose pressing to get in was bruised betwixt the door and the door-cheek, and shot through the body, of which he died in a few hours. This so enraged Kilravock, that he summoned the Governor to surrender, else he would set the Town in fire in a few hours. Sir John MacKenzie of Coul Governor, knowing Kilravock's resoluteness, knowing likewise that Lovat, with the Frasers from the Aird, and a battalion of Grants from Strathspey, were approaching, he seized all the boats on the River, and transported his Garrison into Ross, early in the morning of November 13th; Then Kilravock and Culloden garrisoned the Town for the Government. Thus was the Town of Inverness reduced by Kilravock, although others, who had no share in it, assumed the praise. *At Inverness, anno 1715.*

 The Battle of Culloden, on the 16th of April 1746, is so recent and fresh in our memories, that I shall take no further notice *At Culloden, anno 1746.*

tice of it, than to obferve, that it has broken the charm of the Broad Sword and Target, and may convince the Highlanders, that, in the way of fighting now practifed, their undifciplined, though brave militia, cannot ftand before well difciplined troops, conducted by a proper General.

MILITARY ROADS.

I now come to give fome account of the Military ways within this Province. It was the cuftom of the Romans, to make military Ways or Roads, in all conquered Countries, for the more eafy communication between their Colonies and Forts, XIPHIL. fays of SEVERUS, " Ingreffus eft in Caledoniam, " eamque dum pertranfiret, habuit maxima negotia, quod " Sylvas cæderet, et loca alta perfoderet, quodque paludes ob- " rueret aggere, et pontes in fluminibus faceret." There are clear veftiges of thofe Ways in the Lothians and Fife, particularly one that runs from Crail to Stirling bridge, along the Coaft.

It was in the year 1724, that General WADE, commiffioned by his Majefty, to enquire into fome diforders committed in the Highlands, projected the Roads that are now fo ufeful. Next year they were begun. The firft Road was from Stirling to Invernefs and Fort-Auguftus: This Road runs in two branches; one by Dunkeld and Blair of Athole; the other by Dumblain, Glenalmond, and Aberfeldie, and they meet at Delnakerdich, and enter this Province at Dalwhinnie, where the Road again branches into two; the one leads fix miles to Caitulack, three to Gavamore, and twelve to Fort-Auguftus; The other branch is nine miles to Ruthven, ten to Aviemore, ten to Corribruch, and ten to Invernefs; At the fame time, the Road from Invernefs to Fort-William was begun. From Invernefs to the General's Lodge are twelve miles, about feven of thefe are upon the bank of Lochnefs, a part of which, called the Black Rock, was a very high precipice hanging over the Loch;

Here, for almoſt half a mile, the rock was blown up with powder, and the miners were hung by ropes in boreing into it. Now the Road is beautiful and ſafe, ſecured from the precipice below by a wall three feet high; From the General's Lodge to Fort-Auguſtus, are twelve miles; thence to Letirfinlay twelve; and thence to Fort-William twelve miles. In the year 1753, the Road from Fort-George in Arderſier to Perth was begun; It runs from the Fort to Kilravock four miles; to the river of Ern ſeven miles; to Caſtle Grant five miles; to the river of Avon ſix miles; to Corrigarf ſeven miles; and thence by Caſtletoun of Braemar, Glenſhee, and Blair of Gourie to Perth. There are likewiſe Roads from Fort-Auguſtus and from Inverneſs to Bernera in Glenelg.

Theſe Roads are from twenty to twenty-four feet broad, run in ſtreight lines where the hills permit, are annually repaired, have aquæducts and ſide drains, great ſtones are ſet up on end on the Road-ſide, as guides in ſnow or miſt. And beſides bridges on rivers, every brook and rivulet has a bridge over it. In a word, this is a work that might have added luſtre to the Roman name; By means of theſe Roads, ſoldiers have a ſtreight and eaſy rout; Artillery is carried into all the Forts; Waggons, Coaches and all kinds of wheel-carriages, can paſs from South to North; The weekly poſts make quick diſpatch; Commerce and Intercourſe are made eaſy; Convenient lodging is found at every ſtage, and the Highlands will be gradually civilized and improved.

I ſhall now conclude this part, with an account of ſome ancient Cuſtoms, chiefly Military, obſerved in this, and other Provinces. MILITARY CUSTOMS.

Anciently, every Chief of a Clan was, by his dependents, conſidered as a little Prince, not abſolute, but directed by the Gentlemen of his Clan. As the *Primores Regni*, and all who
held

held off the King *in capite*, were his Grand Council or Parliament; so the Gentlemen and Heads of Families, were to the Chief, by whose advice all things that regarded the Clan in common, or particular Families, were determined, differences were removed, injuries were punished or redressed, law suits prevented, declining Families supported, and peace or war with other Clans agreed upon.

YOUNG CHIEFS. Young Chiefs and Heads of Families were regarded, according to their military or peaceable dispositions. If they revenged a Clan-quarrel, by killing some of the enemy, or carrying off their cattle, and laying their lands waste, they were highly esteemed; and great hopes were conceived of them. But if they failed in such attempts, they were little respected; yea, despised if they did not incline to them.

OFFICERS. Clans had their Military Officers, not arbitrarily or occasionally chosen, but fixed and perpetual. The Chief was Colonel or principal Commander. The oldest cadet was Lieutenant-Colonel, and commanded the Right Wing. The youngest cadet commanded the Rear. Every Head of a distinct Family was Captain of his own Tribe.

ENSIGNS. Every Clan had an Ensign or Standard-Bearer, which office was at first conferred on some one who had behaved gallantly, and usually it became hereditary in his Family, and was supported by a gratuity, or a small annual salary.

BARDS. Every Chief usually had his Bard, Poet, or Orator, whose office it was (as among the Germans) in time of war to excite and animate them, by reciting the brave actions of the Clan, and particularly of their ancestors and Chiefs, as LUCAN writes,

> *Vos quoque, qui fortes animas, belloque peremptas,*
> *Laudibus in longum, Vates, diffunditis ævum,*
> *Plurima securi fudistis carmina Bardi.*

At

At marriages they recited the Genealogy of the married couple, and sung an Epithalamium; And at burials they mournfully sung the Elegy of the Chief or Great man.

Their Military Music was the Grat Pype. The office of Pyper was often hereditary, and had a small salary annexed to it: And the Pypers of several Clans had a chief Pyper who governed them; and schools in which they were instructed. *Pypers*

The most of their time being employed in Military exploits, or in hunting, every Clan had a stated place of rendezvous, where they met when called by their Chief. The manner of convocating them on a sudden emergent, was by the Fiery-Cross. *Fiery Cross*

The Chief ordered two men to be dispatched, one to the upper, and the other to the lower end of his lands, each carrying a Pole or Staff, with a Cross-tree in the upper end of it, and that end burnt black. As they came to any village or house, they cried aloud the Military Cry of the Clan, and all who heard it armed quickly, and repaired to the place of Rendezvous. If the runner became fatigued, another must take the Pole.

Every Clan had a peculiar Cry of War, by hearing which they were convocated to the place of general meeting. The Cry of the MacDonalds was *Freich*, i. e. Heather: Of the MacPhersons, *Craig-ubhie*: Of the MacKenzies, *Tullick-ard*: Of the Grants *Craig-Elachie*. And this was the Cry of him that carried the Fiery-Cross. *Cry to War.*

Every Clan had a distinguishing Badge, whereby they might be known, as they had no military habit or livery. Their Badges were natural and plain (not ribbonds, feathers, or such gewgaws), which they wore in their bonnets. The MacDonalds wore a bush of Heather; the MacIntoshes a Holly-branch; the Grants a Fir-bush, &c. &c. &c. *Badge.*

Upon

OMENS.

Upon an expedition, they much regarded Omens. An armed man meeting them, was a good Omen. If a woman barefoot croſſed the road before them, they ſeized her, and fetched blood from her forehead. If a Deer, Fox, Hare, or any beaſt of game appeared, and they did not kill it, it was an unlucky Omen, &c.

CUID-
OIDHE

The *Cuid Oidche*, i. e. A night's proviſion was paid by many tenants. In hunting, or going on an expedition, the tenant who lived near the hill, furniſhed his maſter and his followers a night's entertainment, with brawn for his dogs. This is now converted into a ſtated rent.

Paſſing other cuſtoms, I proceed to

PART

PART VI.

THE

ECCLESIASTIC HISTORY of MORAY.

SECTION I. *The Heathen or Pagan Church; containing an Account of the Druids—Their Office—Religion—Priests—Worship—Solemnities—Sacrifices and Ceremonies—Judges—Vates—Bards—Female Druids—Temples—Deities—Customs—Burials—The Origin of Druidism, &c.*

SECT. II. *The first planting of Christianity in Scotland—The Origin of the Keledees; their Purity, &c.*

SECT. III. *The Romish or Popish Church—The Regular Clergy—Abbeys; Abbey of Kinloss—Priories; Urquhart, Pluscardin, Kingussie—Convents; Black-Friars, Gray-Friars, Gray-Sisters—The Preceptory of Maison Dieu—St Nicholas Hospital—The Templars and Joannite Knights——The Secular Clergy—The Bishopric of Mortlich—The Bishopric of Moray—List of the Bishops of Moray—Extent of the Diocess—The Cathedral at Birnie, and at Spynie—The Cathedral at Elgin—Description and Dimensions of it—How demolished—The College of Elgin—The Bishop's Palace* at *Kenedar*—*The Palace of Spynie described*—*The Revenues of the Bishopric*—*Dignified Clergy*—*Inferior Clergy*—*Government of the Church*, &c.

SECT. IV. *The Protestant Church.* 1*st*, *Of the several changes in the Government of the Church, and the conduct of the Clergy since the Reformation:* 2*dly, Of the Bishops of Moray since the Reformation, their Jurisdiction and Revenues:* 3*dly, The Ministers of the several Parishes, with an account of the Patron, Stipend, School, Mortifications, Chapels, and number of Catechiseable persons in each of them: And* 4*thly, The State of Religion in the Province since the Reformation in* 1560, *to the present time.*

SECT. I. *The Heathen, or Pagan Church.*

DRUIDS.

IT cannot be doubted, that, in this Province, as indeed in all Britain, DRUIDISM was the mode of the Heathenish Religion. The remaining vestiges of their places of worship, and of their superstitious customs, put this beyond question.

Both Sacred and Profane History testify, That before Temples were built, the ancient places of worship were in shady groves, under spreading trees, and often in high places; *Gen.* xxi. 33. 1. *Kings* xiii. 14. 1. *Sam.* ix. 12. " Olim quas vellent " esse in Tutela sua Divi legerunt arbores; Quercus *Jovi*, et " Myrtus *Veneri* placuit, *Phœbo* Laurea, Pinus *Cybelæ*, Populus " celsa *Herculi*." (PHAEDR.).

And VIRGIL, says of the gardens of the *Hesperides*: Æneid. IV.

> *Hinc mihi Massylæ gentis monstrata Sacerdos,*
> *Hesperidum Templi custos, epulasque Draconi*
> *Quæ dabat, et sacros servabat in arbore ramos.*

And

Sect I. THE HEATHEN OR PAGAN CHURCH.

And in PRIAM's Palace; Æneid. II.

Ædibus in mediis, nudoque sub ætheris axe
Ingens ara fuit, juxtaque veterrima laurus,
Incumbens aræ, atque umbra complexa Penates.

The word *Druid* comes from the Greek Δρυς an Oak, or any Wood; or from the Celtic *Deru* or *Dru* an Oak: For they worshipped in groves, and under spreading trees. *Druid* was the general name of the Sect or Order; and their Literati were divided into Priests, Vates, and Bards, who were their Divines, Philosophers, Poets, Orators, Physicians, and Judges in all causes. The grand articles of their Religion were:

 I. To worship the Deity.
 II. To abstain from all evil. And,
 III. To be intrepid. This last was enforced by the belief of the immortality of the soul, and of a future state. *(Diog. Laer.)*

Whence so called.

They were the Instructors of youth in the Mysteries of Religion, Philosophy, and Morality, &c. They kept their Academies only in the sacred groves, retired from the noise of the world, and undisturbed from the hurry of business. "Dis-
"ciplina in Britannia reperta, atque inde in Galliam trans-
"lata esse existimatur; et nunc, qui diligentius eam rem
"cognoscere volunt, plerumque illo, discendi causa, proficiscun-
"tur.——Magnum numerum versuum ediscere dicuntur; Ita-
"que nonnulli annos vicenos in disciplina permanent; neque
"fas esse existimant ea literis mandare, quum in reliquis fere
"rebus, publicis privatisque rationibus Græcis literis utantur."
(CÆS. *Com. Lib.* VI.)

Their OFFICE.

They were called *Semnothei*, for their devotion *(Suidas.)* And acknowledged One only Eternal and Self-existent God, whom they worshipped without any images or statues. They own-

Their RELIGION.

G g 2   ed

ed the immortality of the foul, and a future state of retribution; They taught a warm devotion to God, and the strictest virtue and equity among men; They offered sacrifices and oblations daily, and used ablutions and purifications: In a word, the DRUIDS were at first held in great veneration, and much admired for their Piety, Virtue, and Morality; but afterwards they degenerated greatly. By the Greeks and Romans they were led into Polytheism, gross idolatry, superstition, human sacrifices, &c. which made LUCAN write with a sneer,

> *Et vos Barbaricos ritus, moremque sinistrum*
> *Sacrorum,* DRUIDÆ, *positis repetistis ab armis;*
> *Solis nosse Deos, et Cæli numina vobis,*
> *Aut Solis nescire datum.*

They committed no part of their Religious Mysteries, or Natural Philosophy, to Writing; But the Bards turned these into Clenching Rhymes, and repeated them on all proper occasions. Moral precepts called *Teagasg na Bard,* and *Foghlam na Filidh, i. e.* "The Instructions of Bards and Philosophers," are to this day repeated in the Highlands by old men.

Transmigration. The Transmigration of souls, taught, though not at first, by the Druids, seems to have given rise to a notion among many ignorant and superstitious people, viz. That when one dies of a consumption, the Fairies steal the soul out of the body before death, and animate some other person with it.

Immortality. Possibly the way in which the DRUIDS explained the immortality of the soul, and a future state, occasioned the common saying, "That at death one passes into the *Saoghal hal. i. e.* the "Yonder World," fancying, as the Americans do, that souls departed, go to pleasant regions beyond the mountains.

PRIESTS. The DRUID PRIESTS were the ordinary Ministers of Religion, and an Arch-Priest, chosen out of the College of Priests, presided in their meetings.

Their

Sect. 1. THE HEATHEN OR PAGAN CHURCH.

Their worship was either stated and ordinary; or annual and more solemn. <small>Their Worship.</small>

Their stated worship consisted in sacrifices and oblations, performed in pleasant groves, and commonly on a level plot of ground; upon which they erected one or more Circles of Stones, all on end: And in the centre stood the Altar, which was a Broad Stone laid horizontal on four Stones as Pillars; and on this, Sacrifices were offered. No Sacrifice however, was to be made without leaves or branches of the Misseltoe; and before they entered the circle to offer, they made a tour about it Sun-ways; and the like they did when they had done offering. <small>Stated Worship.</small>

These Circles, or remains of them, are found in every Country. I cannot but mention the Circle at Classernis in the Isle of Lewis; It consists of twelve stones, each seven feet high, and two broad; at South-east and West, three stones are erected in a line without the Circle; to the North point is a lane, nineteen stones in a line on each side, six feet distant from one another, the lane eight feet broad; one stone stands in the entry of the lane; and in the centre of the Circle, a stone thirteen feet high, cut in the form of a rudder *(Mr Martin)*. The Circle denotes the Sun; the twelve stones, the twelve Signs; the stones to South-east and West, the Cardinal Points; the nineteen stones in the lane, the Lunar Cycle; the stone in the entry closes the Cycle, and then it begins a-new in the other line; the Rudder shews, that the Temple was dedicated to ANVONA the Deity of the Sea. *(Toland.)* <small>Circles.</small>

In Durris, at the end of Lochness, is a Temple of three Concentric Circles; the Altar Stone is taken away, but near to where it stood is a hallowed stone, either a laver to wash in, or a bason to receive the blood of the Sacrifices; a lane leads through the Circles to the centre; in the area of the outer

Circle,

Circle, probably stood the Spectators; in the second the Offerers; and at the Altar, the Priest and servants.

Both the true worshippers of God, and in imitation of them the superstitious, at first worshipped in open fields.

The *Naos* and *Temene* of the ancient Greeks, were but allotments of ground, and sacred inclosures for worship, and not covered houses. I have seen these in corn-fields left untilled, because they were supposed Sacred: The Heathen places of worship were circular or round, because dedicated to the Sun, the emblem of their Deity. The Highlanders call them *Clachan*, i. e. a Collection of Stones: And hence they call a Church *Clachan*, as *Clachan Michel*, *Clachan Muire*, i. e. Michael's Church, Mary's Church. The Altar Stone they call *Crom Leac*, i. e. the Bowing, or Worshipping Stone; and the Priest *Cromfear*, i. e. the Worshipper. The Britains called the Sacred Grove, wherein the Circle stood, *Lhwyn*; and hence probably, they call a Church *Lhan*. And the Saxon *Kirk* or *Circ*, comes from *Circus* a Circle.

Clachan.

Lhan.

Deas-Soil.

The Tour about the Circles, is called *Deas-Soil*, from DEAS the South, and SOIL the Sun, *q. d.* South about with the Sun. I have often seen at Marriages and Churching of women, and Burials, such a tour made about the Church. This ceremony was not peculiar to the DRUIDS: We find it at the Funeral Pile of PALLAS; VIRG. Æn. Lib. XI.

> *Ter circum accensos cincti fulgentibus armis*
> *Decurrere Rogos: Ter mæstum funeris ignem*
> *Lustravere in equis, ululatusque ore dedere.*

Solemn Worship.

Their more solemn Worship was at their high Festivals; particularly in the month of March, on May-day, at Mid-Summer, and at Hallow-Eve. Their Festivals were celebrated on high or conspicuous places, where they erected Carns

or

Sect. 1. THE HEATHEN OR PAGAN CHURCH. 231

or heaps of Stones, on which they kindled great Fires, and offered Sacrifices. The Fire was forced (and accounted sacred) by rubbing one piece of dry wood against another. All the families in the neighbourhood extinguished their Fires; and upon paying a small acknowledgement to the Priest, they received of the Carn-Fire.

Their Carns were very different from the Carns or heaps of stones on high ground, gathered out of their Corn fields, and cast loose in a heap; and different likewise from the small Carns near to common roads, where men have been buried, or coffins laid down at burials, that the bearers might rest. These are called *Leacadh na Marbh*, i. e. "Stones erected in Memory of the Dead." The Druid Carns were great and broad heaps of stones, hedged in, all round with big stones placed on end in the earth, and joined close; In some of these Carns, another close Circle of such stones was placed in the middle of the Carn; and the Altar stone, one or more, on the top within the inner Circle. Such a Carn, pretty entire, is to be seen on the muir to the east of Aviemore in Strathspey; Carns are likewise on the top of the hill of Dunevan in Calder; to the East of Gateside betwixt Elgin and Forres on the muir of Urquhart in Moray; and in many other places. Round the great Carn, there were often Tumuli, or small heaps, in which, in the South, have been found Urns containing the ashes of burnt bodies; possibly the like might be found in this country. These Carns were so placed as to be within view of one another. The Druid who officiated at the Carn-Fire, was called *Carneach*. The Fire was of dry wood preserved for that use; it was an expiatory punishment for criminals to stand for a limited time betwixt two contiguous Fires, or to walk bare-footed thrice over the burning ashes of a Carn-Fire. Mr TOLAND thinks, that SILIUS ITALICUS alludes to this custom, when he makes *Equa-*

CARNS.

nus

nus the *Sabine* to pass through the Fire (if unhurt, it was a good omen, otherwise a bad) on Mount Soracte in Italy, on whose top was Apollo's Carn: as VIRGIL has it, Æneid Lib. XI.

> *Summe Deum, sancti custos Soractis Apollo,*
> *Quem primi colimus, cui Pineus ardor acervo*
> *Pascitur, et medium freti pietate per ignem*
> *Cultores multa premimus vestigia pruna.*

Possibly the trial by Ordeal, practised long in this country, had its rise from this custom of passing through the Carn-Fire.

I shall now mention such vestiges of the Druid Carn-Fires and Festivals, as I have observed in this Country.

MARCH SO-LEMNITY.

One of their great Solemnities was in the month of March, when they gathered and consecrated the Misseltoe of the Oak. On the 6th of the March Moon, a Priest, clad in white, climbed the tree, and cut the Misseltoe with a golden bill, and others in white standing round, received it; after which they offered at their Carn-Fires with mirth. (PLIN.)

> *Ad viscum Druidæ, Druidæ cantare solebant.* OVID.

In the increase of the March Moon, the Highlanders cut withs of the wood-bind that clings about the Oak. These they twist into a wreath or circle, and carefully preserve it till the next March. And when children are troubled with hectick fevers, or when any one is consumptive, they make them pass through this circle thrice, by putting it over their heads and conveying it down about their bodies. The like they do to Cattle in some distempers. This I have often seen.

MAY SO-LEMNITY.

Another grand Solemnity was on May-day. On the first of May, they offered Sacrifice for the preservation of their cattle; and that day was held sacred to PAN or BAAL, and was commonly

monly called *La Baal-Tine*, corruptly "Beltan-day" *i. e.* the Day of Baal's Fire. Clear remains of this superstition I have been present at when a young boy.

Upon *Mandy Thursday*, the several herds cut staves of Service Wood about three feet long, and put two cross sticks into clefts in one end of the staff: These staves they laid up till the First of May: On that day several herds met together; Every one had two eggs, and a bannock or thick cake of oat meal crusted over with the yolks of eggs: They raised a pile of dry wood or sticks on a hillock, and striking Fire with a flint they kindled the pile; Then they made the *Deas-Soil* thrice round the Fire; after which they roasted their eggs, and eat them with a part of the bread. The rest of the bread they brought home, to be eaten by the family; and having adorned the heads of their staves with wild herbs, they fixed them on the tops, or above the doors of their several cotes; and this they fancied would preserve the Cattle from Diseases till next May.

In the Highlands, the First Day of May is still called *La Baaltine*. In the Armoric, a Priest is called *B.lec*, probably from *Baal*: and when one is in great danger, he is said to be *Edir da theine Bheil*, *i. e.* " Between two Fires of Baal," alluding to the punishment above mentioned.

The Mid-Summer Solemnity was celebrated in honour of CERES. They made the *Deas-Soil* about their Fields of Corn, with burning torches of wood in their hands, to obtain a blessing on their Corns. This I have often seen, more indeed in the Lowlands than in the Highlands. On Mid-Summer Eve, they kindle Fires near their Corn Fields, and walk round them with burning torches. MID-SUMMER SOLEMNITY.

The like Solemnity was kept on the Eve of the first of November, as a thanksgiving for the safe in-gathering of the produce of the fields. This, I am told, but have not seen it, is observed HALLOW-EVE SOLEMNITY.

in Buchan and other Countries, by having Hallow Eve Fires kindled on some rising ground.

SACRIFICES and CEREMONIES.

In all these Solemnities they offered Sacrifices, and made the *Deas-Soil* round their Fires. It cannot be doubted, that they had Sacrifices of various sorts; as precatory, to obtain blessings; gratulatory, to shew their thankfulness; and expiatory, to attone for their sins. It appears from LUCAN, that the *Celts* and *Gauls* used human Sacrifices.

> *Et quibus immitis, placatur sanguine diro,*
> *Teutates, horensque, feris altaribus Hæsus,*
> *Et Taranis, Scythicæ non mitior ara* DIANÆ.

Cæsar, Pliny, and Tacitus assure us, that the DRUIDS used such Sacrifices. Tacitus, *Annal* XIV. writes: "The groves were "cut down, which by the DRUIDS were dedicated to sangui- "nary and detestable superstitions; for here they sacrificed "captives, and upon their altars, as an oblation, spilt human "blood." What creatures they used in Sacrifice, or what particular ceremonies, I have not learned. No doubt they used washings and purgations, and clean clothes, as other people did.

> *Casta placent Superis, pura cum veste venite,*
> *Et manibus puris sumite fontis aquam.* TIBUL.

Æneas would not touch the *Penates* or the *Sacra*, before he washed. VIRG. Æneid, *Lib.* II.

> *Tu, Genitor, cape Sacra manu, patriosque Penates,*
> *Me bello e tanto digressum, et cæde recenti,*
> *Attractare nefas, donec me flumine vivo*
> *Abluero.*

The Scots Highlanders, not only put on clean clothes on the Sabbath-

Sect. 1. THE HEATHEN OR PAGAN CHURCH. 243

Sabbath-day, as others do; but in the morning of that day, they wash (not in the house, but *Flumine vivo*) in running water, and they call it *Uifg Domhnich*, i. e. "Aqua Dominica."

The DRUID PRIESTS were Judges in all Causes, Religious, Civil, and Criminal; and were exempted from attending war, paying taxes, &c. Their authority was great, their sentence final, and the contumacious were excluded from the *Sacra*, and pronounced Profane: Hence at their religious meetings they were removed, **JUDGES.**

> *Procul, O Procul, este Profani!*
> *Conclamat Vates, totoque discedite luco.*

This punishment was so severe, that all avoided the company of the interdicted; no one would converse with them; they could enjoy no offices, nor receive honours.

CÆSAR says, In Gaul the DRUIDS, at a certain season of the year, met in a consecrated place, "in finibus Carnutum," and there decided controversies. This place was *Chartres Civitas Carnutum*, so called no doubt from the DRUID CARNS. **Their Meetings.**

Their principal seats in Britain were, the Isles of Anglesey and Man. But they administred justice in every country, and sat *sub dio* on green hillocks. Such round hillocks are found in many places. Two remarkable ones stands a little West of the Town of Elgin, and two close by the Church of Petty. The Lowlanders call them *Laws*, because there the Law was given or promulgated. Such are North-Berwick Law, Innes Law, &c. The Highlanders call them *Tom an Eracht*, and *Tom a Mhoid*, i. e. "The Court-hill." I question not but the *Mute-hill*, (rather *Moid-hill*) at Scone was of this sort: So were the *Duni pacis*, near the river Carron in Stirling-shire.

Every DRUID JUDGE carried a Rod, as a Badge of Office and authority, called in Irish, *Slaite na Druidbeachd*, i. e. "The **Rod.** **Rod**

H h 2

EGG.

"Rod of Druidism." He had likewise an Egg hung about his neck, inchafed in gold, or other precious metal. The Eggs were faid to be *Ova Anguinum,* " Eggs formed by Serpents ;" and PLINY fays, They afcribed great virtues to them. It is confidently affirmed by the common people, that in Summer a number of Serpents meet, and work a certain flimy matter into a round ball with their mouths, of the colour of their own fkin. I have feen with Jugglers round painted balls, which they called *Adder Stones,* and with them they played feats. The Welfh call them *Gleine na Druidhe, i. e.* " The Druids " Glafs." Thefe were but amulets of glafs or ftone. But the Phænicians and Egyptians made the Egg an emblem of the principle of all things, and reprefented it as coming out of the mouth of a Serpent. Hence came the DRUIDS EGG.

The VATES.

Among the Literati of the DRUIDS, next to the Priefts, were the VATES or EUBAGES, called by the Celts and Irifh, *Faidhe.* Thefe were their Diviners and Phyficians. By ftudying Natural Philofophy, the influences of the Celeftial Bodies, and the qualities and virtues of Plants and Minerals, they might cure fome Difeafes, and foretell Events that depend upon a chain of Natural Caufes; and on this account might be held in great efteem and veneration: But as the innocent name of *Magi* in the Eaft came to be taken in a bad fenfe, fo *Druidhe* and *Druidheachd* came to be abufed, even to mean " Sorcerer and Sor- " cery."

The BARDS.

The BARDS were another Order of the Druids Literati. A BARD in Celtic fignifies a *Poet and Orator.* They were not only frequent in Gaul and Britain; but Tacitus, *de Mor. Germ.* makes it probable, that they were common among the Germans. " Sunt illis hæc quoque carmina, quorum relatu, quem Bardi- " tum vocant, accendunt animos, futuræque pugnæ fortunam, " ipfo cantu augurantur." When armies were to engage, the

BARD

BARD stood on some eminence, and harangued them to rouse their courage. This was anciently much practised in Scotland. As now the General makes a speech to his army before battle; of old the BARDS did so, and it was called *Brosilughadh Cath*, i. e. "An incentive to fight." DIODORUS observes, that they were held in such veneration, that if battle was begun, and a BARD appeared and commanded it, both sides ceased from fighting. They put the religious and moral instructions into rhyme; presided in their music; acted a part at festivals; recited Genealogies at marriages and funerals; and sung the praises of their Heroes. "Bardi quidem, fortia virorum illustrium facta "heroicis composita versibus, cum dulcibus lyræ modulis can- "tilarunt. AMMIAN. lib. XV." Lucan writes the same.—But how honourable soever this Order might have been at first, they afterward became ignorant, venal, and despicable Buffoons. VALESIUS, in *Ammian. Marcellin.* lib. XV. well describes the modern BARDS. "* Ex his patet, Bardos nihil aliud fuisse quam "Parasitas, planeque similes eorum quos Latini *Scurras* voca- "bant: Ut enim *Scurræ* exercitum sequebantur, jocis ac gesticu- "lationibus milites, inter convivia, delinere soliti; ita etiam "BARDI."

There were likewise FEMALE DRUIDS, or PRIESTESSES, who might perform some ceremonies of their religion to women, in which it might not be decent to have men employed. And as all DRUIDS frequented the groves, these PRIESTESSES probably were the *Dryades* and *Hamadryades* "The Nymphs of the "groves" celebrated by the Poets. And I doubt not but these gave

FEMALE DRUIDS.

---

* "From these things it appears, that the BARDS were nothing else but Para- "sites; and like to those whom the Latines called *Scurræ* or Buffoons: For as the "Buffoons followed the Army, and used to divert the soldiers at their feast- "ing with jests and gesticulations, so also did the BARDS."

gave rise to the fancy that prevails among the ignorant, viz. That Fairy Women, or beautiful young girls, clad in green, with loose dishevelled hair, frequented the Woods and Valleys. I have often heard men affirm, that they had seen and spoken with such women.

DRUID TEMPLES. The DRUIDS seem to have had among them some Recluses and Hermites. In the Isles and on the Continent, there are many small Cells of Stone of a round figure, and each Cell capable of accommodating one single person, called *Ti na Druididhe. i. e.* "The DRUID's house." I have not observed any such in this Province: But in the Parish of Old-Deer in Buchan, I am told there is a DRUID Circle on a hill, and on the descent are the vestiges of about thirty Cells, which the people call " The Pict's Houses," possibly a convent of DRUID Hermites. These are different from the Round Stone Edifices, twenty feet high and twelve broad, in Orkney and Shetland, called *Picts houses and Burghs*. The Romans had little Towers, called *Burgus*, for keeping Military stores; and these Round Edifices might have been *Specula*, or *Watch Towers*, built by the Norwegians, when they came into these Islands: Or they might have been *Druid Temples*. For as ZOROASTRES taught the Persian Magi to build Temples, in which they kept their Sacred Fire (PRID. *Con. Vol. I.*); and as the DRUID Religion was manifestly derived from that of the Magians, the DRUIDS might have had such Fire-Temples; and it is certain that in AUGUSTUS's reign they had Temples in France. VITRUVIUS tells us, that antiently Temples were of a round form and open at top. " * Cæli naturam imitati veteres, " imprimis rotundis (sciz. Templis) sunt delectati; ædificia sub " dio hypethraque constituuntur, Cælo, et Soli, et Lunæ."

The

---

* " The Ancients, imitating the structure of the Heavens, delighted chiefly in " Round Temples, and built their Edifices in the open air, dedicated to the Hea- " vens, the Sun, and the Moon."

Sect. I.   THE HEATHEN OR PAGAN CHURCH.   247

The Round Edifice open at top, on the river Carron near Falkirk, was not the Temple of TERMINUS, as Buchanan calls it; nor a Roman place of arms and Enfigns, as GORDON in his Itinerarium thinks. There have been found near it the Horns of a Bull, and a Patera ufed in facrifices (SYB. *Hift. of Stirling-Shire*) which fhews it was a Temple; and more properly a *Druid* than a *Roman* Temple: For above Tayn in Rofs are fuch round tapering edifices, open at top; yet the Romans never built there. In that part of Rofs, Ptolemy places the *Creones*, fo called from *Cruin*, i. e. " Round.". And the Picts were called *Cruinidh*, i. e. " The round people;" becaufe their places of worfhip, their Carns, their Temples, and the Hillocks on which the DRUIDS fat as Judges, were all of a round form, as emblems of the Sun, the object of their worfhip.

The DEITIES worfhipped by the DRUIDS, are mentioned by CÆSAR. Three of them are mentioned page 234. viz. TEUTATES, HÆSUS, and TARANIS. TEUTATES was called by the Britain's *Taith Diun*, i. e. " Mercury the God of Journies:" or *Tytad*, i. e. " The Father of the Houfe;" and prefides over the Lares and Penates. HÆSUS (Heb. *Strong, Might*) was their Supreme Deity, and reprefented by an Oak. TARANIS was the Deity of the Air, as TEUTATES was of the Earth, called *Tarain Thor*, *Tor*. In Celtic and Britifh *Taran* fignifies " Thunder:" Hence Jupiter Taranis. The Earl of Moray's feat of Tarnua is in Irifh *Taranich*; probably becaufe fome Druid Carn or Circle there was dedicated to Jupiter Taranis. ANVONA was the Deity of the Water, fo called by the Gauls: And in Irifh *Anfana*, fignifies " The raging of the Sea." Let me add APOLLO CARNIUS, fo called probably from the Druid Carns; and the feaft in honour of him was called *Carnea*; and the Month of May, *Carnius Menfis*. It was ufual with the Romans, to their own names of their Gods to add the names or attributes under which they went

in

DRUID DEITIES.

in the countries where the Romans at the time dwelt: Hence also APOLLO was called *Grannus*. In the reign of Queen Mary of Scotland, there was digged up, in the lands of Merchistoun, a stone, in the shape of an altar stone, inscribed " APOLLINI " GRANNO Q. LUSIUS SABINIANUS PROC. AUG. V. S. " S. L. V. M." i. e. " Votum susceptum solvit Lubens merito." Cambden observes, that this APOLLO GRANNUS was the *Apollo Akersecomes* of the Grecians, i. e. " Having long Hair." *Grannus* may come from the Irish *Grian*, i. e. " The Sun," and in that language *Grianach*, signifies " Hairy or spreading Hair like the " scattered Beams of the Sun." The Romans, when in Britain, gave APOLLO that name.

DRUID CUSTOMS.

In speaking of the DRUID Priests, Priestesses, Vates, Bards, Circles, Carns, &c. I have all along observed, the vestiges of these, which are to be as yet met with in this Province. I shall now add an account of some Superstitious Customs still practised in this country, and which seem to have had their rise from the DRUIDS.

In HECTIC FEVERS.

In Hectick and Consumptive Diseases, they pare the nails of the fingers and toes of the Patient, put these parings into a rag cut from his clothes, then wave their hand with the rag thrice round his head crying *Deas-Soil*, after which they bury the rag in some unknown place. I have seen this done: And *Pliny*, in his Natural History, mentions it as practised by the Magians or Druids of his time.

In CONTAGIOUS DISEASES.

When a Contagious Disease enters among Cattle, the Fire is extinguished in some villages round: Then they Force Fire with a wheel, or by rubbing a piece of dry wood upon another, and therewith burn Juniper in the stalls of the Cattle, that the smoke may purify the air about them: They likewise boil Juniper in water, which they sprinkle upon the Cattle. This done, the Fires in the houses are rekindled from the Forced Fire.

All

Sect. 1. THE HEATHEN OR PAGAN CHURCH.

All this I have seen done; and it is no doubt a DRUID Custom.

They narrowly observe the Changes of the Moon, and will not fell wood, cut turf or fuel, or thatch for houses, or go upon any expedition of importance, but at certain periods of the revolution of that Planet: So the DRUIDS avoided, if possible, to fight, till after the Full Moon. (*Diodor.*)

The Moon's Changes.

They Divine by Bones; Having picked the flesh clean off a shoulder-blade of mutton, which no iron must touch, they turn towards the East, or the Rising Sun, and looking steadily on the transparent Bone, pretend to foretell deaths, burials, &c. This *Osteomateia* was much practised among the Heathens: And the DRUIDS consulted the entrails and bones of animals, even of human victims. (TACIT. *Annal* 14.) I have spoken of their regard to Omens page 240.

Osteomateia.

At burials they retain many Heathenish practices; such as Music and Dancing at Like-wakes, when the nearest relations of the deceased dance first. At Burials, mourning women chant the *Coronach*, or mournful extempory rhymes, reciting the valorous deeds, expert hunting, &c. of the deceased. When the corpse is lifted, the bed-straw, on which the deceased lay, is carried out and burnt in a place where no beast can come near it; and they pretend to find next morning, in the ashes, the print of the foot of that person in the family, who shall first die.

Customs at Burials.

They believe, that the material world will be destroyed by Fire. So general is this persuasion, that when they would express the End of Time, they say *Gu Braith*, i. e. " To the Conflagration, or Destruction."

Conflagration.

The use which the DRUIDS made of Juniper, and their regard to the changes of the Moon, shew that they were no strangers to the virtues of Plants, and the influences of the Cælestial bodies.

I i

I scarce need observe, that throughout this Kingdom, many places have their names, and some persons their surnames, from the DRUID Cards, Carns, &c. as *Baird, Carnie, Moni-bhard, Tullibardin, Carn-wath, Carn-cross,* &c.

Many more of the DRUID customs may be seen in *Cæsar, Pliny, Tacitus, Amminianus, Marcellinus, &c.* But I have mentioned only these customs, of which I have seen manifest remains in this Province:

DRUIDISM whence derived.

I shall now conclude this article with observing, that any one who reads the account given by DEAN PRIDEAUX (*Con. Vol.* I.) of the Religion of the Magians in the East, will find that DRUIDISM had a near resemblance of it: And it is to me no less apparent, that both Magianism and Druidism are borrowed, in many particulars, from the Patriarchal and Jewish plan of Religion. I shall mention a few of these particulars: They owned one Supreme Being: Used no Images or Statues: Used Sacrifices: And in high places, under spreading oaks, and with Sacred Fire, at first worshipped *sub dio:* Afterwards built Temples. Compassed their altars by going *Deas-Soil* round them. The Priests were Instructors of youth: Had their academies and schools in retired high places: They had many ablutions and purgations: They had a Rod of Office; and had mourning women at Burials. I might add several instances more in which the DRUIDS seem to have borrowed from the Patriarchs and Jews. This DRUIDISM was the Religion of the Scots and Picts, as it was of the Gauls and Britains, before the Light of the GOSPEL of CHRIST was made to shine among them: And this leads me to

SECT.

Sect. II. *The Primitive Christian Church.*

HOW early, and at what particular time, the GOSPEL of CHRIST was first made known in Scotland, I will not pretend to determine. Here the Roman writers are silent: *Gildas*, *Bede*, and *Nennius* do not touch this question. The loss of the Pictish records and writings, the want of ancient records of the Scottish Church, render it difficult to throw any light on this subject. What is said of King Donald's conversion *A. D.* 203, and of Regulus' arriving at *Muk-Ross* (now St Andrews) about anno 370, is very uncertain; and yet I see it no way improbable, that in the third and fourth Centuries CHRISTIANITY had sure footing in North Britain. "Britan-"norum inaccessa Romanis loca, CHRISTO tamen subdita." But as Pagan Druidism must have been gradually, and not all at once, rooted out; so the Christian Faith must have been gradually spread: And indeed the gross ignorance which, till of late, prevailed, and the many Heathenish customs that remained in some parts of the Kingdom, shew abundantly, that the knowledge of CHRIST advanced by very slow paces.

CHRISTIANITY planted in Scotland.

The first Teachers and Ministers of the Christian Faith in Scotland were Presbyters, or Preaching Elders, called in the Scottish language KELEDFES. Our Historians, not understanding the language, have called them *Culdei*, q. d. "Cultores Dei," and they derive *Kil*, from *Cella* the *Hut*, or "House of the "Teacher." But any one conversant with antient writings, will easily discover the mistake, and find that they are never called *Culki*, but uniformly *Keleki*; a word compounded of *Ceile* or *Keile*, i. e. "A Servant, or one devoted," and *Die* (in the genitive *De*) i. e. GOD, q. d. "A servant of GOD, or one "devoted

KELEDEES.

"devoted to him." A Church or place of Worship was called *Kil*, because it was set a-part for Divine Service. When the Church of Rome dedicated Churches to their Legendary Saints, the word *Kil* was prefixed to the Saint's name, as *Kil-Mhair, Kil-Mhilie*, i. e. "dedicated to Mary and Milesius."

Their Purity.

These KELEDEES and Primitive Christians in Scotland, were men of great Piety, and, for many ages, preserved the Doctrines of Religion, pure and unmixt with any Romish leaven. BEDE's words, though a zealous Romanist, shew this: "* Verum qualiscunque ipse (Columba, who came into Scotland, anno 565) fuit, nos hoc de illo certum tenemus, quod reliquit successores, magna continentia ac divino amore, regularique institutione, insignes. In tempore quidem summæ festivitatis, dubios circulos sequentes, utpote quibus longe ultra orbem positis, nemo Synodalia Paschalis observantiæ decreta porexerat. Tantum ea quæ in Propheticis, Evangelicis, et Apostolicis Literis, discere poterant, pietatis et castitatis opera, diligenter observantes."

This at once shows their purity and freedom from Romish errors; that they believed and taught only what is contained in the writings of the Prophets, Evangelists and Apostles. And it evinces, that the Christians in Scotland did not consider Rome as their Mother Church; otherways they would have early and fondly adopted all the innovations and usages of that Church,

from

---

* "But whatsoever he was himself, this we know of him for certain, that he left Successors renowned for much continency, the love of God, and regular observance. It is true, they followed uncertain rules in the observation of the great Festival, as having none to bring them the Synodical Decrees for the observation of Easter, by reason of their being seated so far from the rest of the world; therefore only practising such works of piety and chastity, as they could learn from the Prophetical, Evangelical, and Apostolical writings."

from which they had received their religion. But it was not without a great struggle, and not till the year 715, that the Scots submitted to the Romish innovations, as to *Pafch*, the *Tonfure*, &c. And possibly it was from the *Clerical Tonfure*, that the word *Maol* came to be prefixed to some names. The word signifies " A Servant," and also *Bare*, *Bald*: So *Maol-Coluim*, *Maol-Riogh*, is " Columba the servant, or the shaveling ;" " Re-" gulus the servant or the shaveling." The Irish likewise prefix the word, *Maith*, *i. e.* " Good ;" As *Maith Rechard*, *Maith Calen*, is the same as " St Richard, St Colen."

Maol.

Maith.

I have mentioned these things to explain the names of Churches and Chapels in this Province ; such as *Kil-Tarlatie*, *Kil-Chuiman*, *Maith-Rechard*, *Maith-Calen*.

Having met with nothing peculiar to this country in the Primitive State of the Christian Church, I go on to

SECT. III. *The Romish or Popish Church.*

IT was by slow degrees, that the CHURCH of ROME got her innovations and corruptions introduced into this Kingdom. Some few of her Superstitious Customs were adopted in the eighth century ; but before the eleventh century, we had no Diocesian Bishops except one, viz. of ST. ANDREWS; He was not properly Diocesian, for he was designed *Episcopus Scotiæ* or *Scotorum*. In the same century it was, that Romish Monks and Friars were brought in, as a militia or an army, to support the Romish Bishops, and to root out the antient *Keledees*, and propagate the poison of Popery : Yet it was not before the twelfth century, and the reign of King David I. that the Popish Clergy or Doctrines got any sure footing. Richard Prior of Hexham, writing *De bello Standardi*

The POPISH CHURCH.

anno

anno 1138 (the time when he lived), says of the Scots. " * Illi
" vero diu a Cisalpina, imo fere ab universâ Ecclesia discor-
" dantes exosæ memoriæ Petro Leoni (N. He was at that time
" Anti-Pope) et apostasiæ ejus nimium favisse videbantur.
" Tunc vero divina gratia inspirati, mandata Innocentii
" Papæ et Legatum ejus, omnes unanimiter cum magna ve-
" neratione susceperunt."

The Papists divide their CLERGY into REGULAR and SE-
CULAR: And I shall treat of both, as I have found them in this
Province; beginning with

I. The REGULAR CLERGY.

REGULAR CLERGY.   These were so called, because they were bound to live, by the Rule of St. Augustine, or St. Bennet; or by some private statutes approved by the POPE. They lived, messed, and slept under one roof. These were numerous in this Province. I shall speak of them under the distinctions of ABBEY, PRIORY, CONVENT, PRÆCEPTORY, MINISTRY and CHAPLAINRY.

An ABBEY

AN ABBEY.   Is a society of Monks or Friars, whereof the Abbot (in Heb. *Ab* or *Abba*, i. e. " Father") is the Head or Ruler. Some Abbots were independent of the Bishop, and freed from his
jurisdiction:

---

* " But they differing long from the Cisalpine, and almost from the whole
" Church, seemed to favour too much PATER LEO of abandoned memory, and his
" Apostacy. But then being inspired by Divine Grace, they all unanimously, and
" with great veneration, received the commands of Pope INNOCENT and his
" Legates."

Sect. 3.   THE ROMISH OR POPISH CHURCH.   255

jurisdiction: These were called *Abbates exempti*. Some were invested with Episcopal power, and wore a mitre, and were called "Sovereign Mitred Abbots," and had a seat in Parliament. The *Abbates Exempti* might discipline and punish their Monks; But Abbots, subject to the Bishop, must submit them to his authority. We had but one Abbey in Moray: viz. That of

KINLOSS. The Abbot of which was mitred, and had a seat in Parliament. It was founded by King David I. 12mo Kal. Januarii Anno 1150, and confirmed by the Pope's Bull anno 1174 (Append. No. XXVI.). The Monks were of the Cistertian or Bernardine order, called *Monachi Albi*, because all their clothes were white, except a black Cowl and Scapulary.   KINLOSS ABBEY.

King David endowed the Abbey with lands; and King William added many more, particularly all the lands of Stryla, or Strath-Yla, near Keith. *(Append.* No. XXVII.). I have perused a Bull in favour of this Abbey, by Honorius, anno 1216, Pontif. 3*tio*, ratifying its lands and possessions, particularly, "*Locus " in quo monasterium fixum est, cum pertinentiis ; Grange de " Kinloss, cum pertinentiis ; Grange de West, cum pertinen-" tiis ; Possessio de Crumbachin ; Possessio de Banesef; Possessio " de Invernis ; Possessio de Invernarin ; Possessio in Forres ; Pos-" sessio de Elgin ; Possessio de Aberdin ; Possessio de Berwick." Other possessions are named in the Bull; but the parchment is so spoiled, and the writing so defaced, that they cannot be read, but may be supplied as follows: The Abbey lands, out of which Mr Brodie of Lethin receives Feu Duties, are: the Ba-   Its ERECTION, and LANDS.

rony

---

* "The place in which the Monastry is fixed, with its pertinents ; Grange of
" Kinloss, with its pertinents ; West Grange, with its partinents ; a small farm in
" Crumbachin; another in Banff, Inverness, Nairn, Forres, Elgin, Aberdeen, and
" Berwick."

rony of Muirtown; the Miln of Kinlofs, Windy-hills, Coltfield, Weft Grange, and Mill; the lands of Burgie; all Hempriggs; the Crofts and Houfe of Kinlofs; Kirktoun lands of Ordies; Freefield in Elchies; all Ballendallach's lands of Struthers; Meikle and Little Tanachy; Town of Forres and their Fifhing; Burds-Yards; Kincorth's, Grangehills, and Coulbin's Fifhing; Rofe of Newton's lands near Nairn; Braco's lands in Stryla; Lands of Lichnet; Kinminitie's lands in Stryla; Lands of Edingieth; Lands of Glengerrock; feveral lands belonging to Lord Findlater; Grange in Stryla; the lands of Ellon; befides Lethen's lands of Kinlofs, and the Precinct of the Abbey.

REVENUES. The Revenues of the Abbey anno 1561, in Money, Victual, &c. were L. 1152 : 1. Bear and Meal 47 chalders 11 bolls 1 firlot 3 pecks: Oats 10 bolls 3 firlots: Wedders 34: Geefe 41: Capons 60: Poultry 125. From which was deducted, To fourteen Monks for habite; filver to each, fifty fhillings per annum: For fifh and flefh to each ten pence per diem: For fire, butter, candle, fpicery, and lentron meat L. 12: For bread and drink per annum, to each 19 bolls 1 firlot 2 pecks, and L. 40 to Mr John Ferrarius for his penfion, which he had under the Seal of the Abbey, annually during life, (*Book of Affump.* anno 1561 and 1563.). This fpecimen fhews, how fumptuoufly thefe pretendedly mortified Monks lived; and much more fo their Abbots and Priors.

BUILDING. The Abbey ftood in a fertile foil, at the head of the Loch, or Bay of Findhorn: No doubt the buildings were fumptuous, but no judgement can now be formed from the remaining ruins. In the years 1651 and 1652, Alexander Brodie of Lethin, proprietor of Kinlofs, fold the ftones to the Englifh, and with them the Citadel of Invernefs was built. (*Reg. Prefbytery of Forres.*). The Abbot had a Regality within the Abbey Lands. He had Granges or Farms, with detached Monks to overfee them, at

Eaft

East and West Grange, and at Grange in Stryla. I find in the writings of the family of Westfield, that the Abbot had a process of spulzie against Sir Alexander Dunbar of Westfield, who died 1576, for taking out of the Abbey, a Laver weighing 240 ounces of silver, and 22 feather beds, with other pieces of plate and furniture.

Upon the dissolution of the Religious Houses, Mr Edward Bruce was made Commendator of Kinloss. The King would not want the Votes of Abbots and Priors in Parliament, and therefore presented Laics to the Benefices when vacant, who, by way of Commendam, enjoyed the profits, and sat in Parliament. But this Usufructuary possession, as Titulars, gave no right to the Lands; and therefore they got them erected into Temporary Lordships. Edward Bruce was created Lord of Kinloss, and got the superiority of the other Abbey Lands. Ascelinus was the first Abbot; Renerius the second; and Robert Reid was the last. I now go to

The PRIORIES.

Of these we had three, viz. At URQUHART, PLUSCARDEN and KINGUSSIE. At first the PRIOR was but the Ruler of the Abbey, under the ABBOT who was *Primus* in the Monastery; and the PRIOR was no Dignitary. But afterwards, a Mother-Abbey detached a party of its Monks, and obtained a settlement for them in some other place; and becoming a separate Convent, a PRIOR was set over them; and their House was called *Cella Grangia*, or *Obedientia*, denoting that they depended on a Superior Monastery. This was called a *Conventual* PRIOR, and was a Dignitary; but a PRIOR in the Abbey was only a Claustral PRIOR. The oldest in this Province was,

Urquhart Priory.   The Priory of Urquhart founded by King David I. anno 1125, in honour of the Trinity. It was a Cell of Dunfermline, planted with Benedictine or Black Monks, of the Order of
Its erection.   Fleurie. King David endowed it liberally, granting "*Priori "et Fratribus ibidem Deo servientibus, Fochopir per suas rectas "divisas, et communionem pascuum animalium, et unam pis-
Lands.   "cariam in Spe, et in firma Burgi de Elgin viginti solidos, "et de dominiis hominibus eorum qui sunt in Fochopir, recti- "tudinem piscis quæ ad Thayn pertinet. et decimam Cani de "Ergathel, et de Muireff, et placitorum, et totius lucri ejusdem "Ergathel, Pethenach juxta Erin per suas rectas divisas, et "scalingas de Fethinechtin, et omnes rectitudines quas Mona- "chi de Dunfermline in Muireff habere solebant." All the lands now called the Lordship of Urquhart, the village and lands of Fochaber, the lands of Penic near Aldern, the lands of Dalcross, a fishing on Spey, pertained to this Priory; as did the patronage of Urquhart, Bellie, and Dalcross.

Revenues.   The revenues of this Priory were not given up anno 1563, so I can give no account of them. The Priory lands were
Building.   erected in a Regality. The Building stood in a hollow North East of the Church of Urquhart; but scarce any vestige thereof
Jurisdiction.   remains. In the year 1565, Alexander Seaton, son to Lord Seaton, was made Commendator of Pluscarden; and 3d Au-
Lord Urquhart.   gust 1591 he was created Lord Urquhart, and Earl of Dunfermline anno 1605: But Earl James being forfeited anno 1690,

Seaton

---

* "To the Prior and Brethren there serving God, Fochopir by its right "divisions, and commonty of pasture, and one fishing in Spey, and twenty shil- "lings in the Burgh of Elgin, and a right of the fishing which belongs to Thain, "in the lands of the people of Fochopir; and the teind of the Cain of Argyle "and Moray, and of the Pleses, and of the whole rent of the same Argyle, Pe- "nic near Erin by its marches, and the Scellings of Feehinechtan, and all the "rights which the Monks of Dunfermline were wont to have in Moray."

PLUSCARDINE ABBAY

Sect. 3.   THE ROMISH OR POPISH CHURCH.

Seaton of Barns claimed the Lordship of Urquhart; and about the year 1730 it was purchased by the Family of Gordon. Next erected was,

The PRIORY of PLUSCARDEN, which was founded by King Alexander II. 1230, in honour of St ANDREW, and named *Vallis Sti Andreæ*. It was planted by *Monachi Vallis Caulium*, a reform of the Cistercians brought into Scotland by Bishop Malvoisin of St Andrews, and settled in Pluscarden, Beaulie and Ardchatton. They were different from the Camaldulians, or *Monachi Vallis Umbrosæ*, who were properly Hermits. Of the *Monachi Vallis Caulium*, only the PRIOR and Procurator were allowed to go without the Precinct. The Monks of Pluscarden, at first independent, afterwards becoming vicious, the PRIORY was reformed and made a Cell of Dunfermline.

By the munificence of our Kings and great men, the Priory became very rich. The whole valley of Pluscarden, three miles in length, in the parish of Elgin; the lands of Old-Milns near the town of Elgin; some lands in Durris, and the lands of Grangehill belonged to it. At this last place the Prior had a Grangia and a Cell of Monks. Likewise the milns of Old-Mills near Elgin pertained to the Priory. The town lands were thirled to those Milns, and *Omnia grana crescentia cum allatis et invectis*, were to be grinded at these Milns. King Robert Bruce also gave the Priory a Fishing on the river of Spey.

The Revenue of the Priory, as given up anno 1563, was as follows: L. 525 : 10 : 1½; Wheat, 1 Chalder 1 Boll 2 Firlots; Malt Meal and Bear, 51 Chalders 4 Bolls 3 Firlots 1 Peck; Oats, 5 Chalders 13 Bolls; Dry Multures, 9 Chalders 11 Bolls; Salmon, 30 Lasts; Grassums, Cain, Customs, Poultrie, &c. omitted. Deducted anno 1563, To Ilk ane of five Monks in kething and habite, silver L. 16: And to Ilk ane in victual, 1 Charlder 5 Bolls *per annum*.

PLUSCARDEN Priory

Its Erection.

Lands.

Revenues.

BUILDINGS. The Buildings stood four miles South-west from the town of Elgin, near the entry of the valley, at the foot of the North Hill, which reverberating the Sun-beams renders the place very warm. The walls of the Precinct are almost entire, and make near a square figure. The Church stands about the middle of the square; a fine edifice in the form of a cross, with a square tower in the middle, all of hewen after. The oratory and refectory join to the South end of the Church, under which is the dormitory. The Chapter House is a piece of curious workmanship; an Octogonal Cube, whereof the vaulted roof is supported by one pillar. The lodgings of the Prior and Cells of the Monks were all contiguous to the Church. Within the Precinct were Gardens and Green Walks. In a word, the remains of this Priory shew, that those Monks lived in a stately palace, and not in mean cottages.

Jurisdiction. The PRIOR was Lord of Regality within the Priory lands, and had a distinct Regality in Grangehill, called " The Re-" gality of Staneforenoon." At the Reformation, Sir Alexander Seaton, afterwards Earl of Dunfermline, was anno 1565 made Commendator of Pluscarden. He disponed the Church lands of Durris and the patronage (Vid. page 132) and the lands of Grangehill (Vid. page 98) and the Barony of Pluscarden and Old Mills, 23d February 1595, to Kenneth MacKenzie of Kintail, who got a *Novo Damus*, dated 12th March

Conveyance. 1607, of that Barony, " * Cum omnibus et singulis decimis
" garbalibus totarum et integrarum terrarum et Baroniæ, cum
" suis pertinentiis, quæ a Stipite, le Stock, earundem nunquam
" separatæ fuere, et quarum Prior et Conventus, eorumque
" Prede-

---

* " With all and sundry the Teind-sheaves of the whole Lands and Barony,
" with their pertinents, which were never separated from the stock, and of which
" the PRIOR and Convents and their predecessors, were in possession in all times
" past."

Sect. 3.   THE ROMISH OR POPISH CHURCH.   261

" Predecessores, in possessione, omnibus temporibus præteritis,
" exstitere." May 9th 1633, George of Kintail brother and
heir of the said Kenneth, disponed the Barony to his brother
Thomas MacKenzie; From whom Sir George MacKenzie of
Tarbet evicted it, by a charter of apprising anno 1649, and
disponed it anno 1662 to the Earl of Caithness and Major
George Bateman. The Earl transferred his right to the Major
anno 1664; and the Major sold the whole Barony to Ludowick Grant of Grant anno 1677. Here let it be remarked,
that Alexander Brodie of Lethin, father-in-law to Grant, paid
the purchase money L. 5000 Sterling, and Grant possessed Pluscarden only as tutor or trustee for his second son James, and
in 1709 resigned in his favour. From the said James Grant,
(the late Sir James) William Duff of Dipple purchased it
anno 1710; and now it is the property of the Earl Fife.

The PRIORY of KINGUSIE in Badenoch was founded by KINGUSIE
George Earl of Huntley about the year 1490. Of what Order PRIORY.
the Monks were, or what were the revenues of the Priory, I
have not learned. The Prior's house and the cloysters of the
Monks stood near the Church, where some remains of them
are to be seen. The few lands belonging to it, were the donation of the family of Huntley; and at the Reformation were
justly re-assumed by that Family. I now proceed to

The CONVENTS, &c.

The CONVENTS of MONKS, FRIARS and NUNS within this CONVENTS.
Province. The MONKS and FRIARS differed in this, that the
former were seldom allowed to go out of their Cloysters; but
the FRIARS, who were generally predicants or mendicants, travelled about and preached in neighbouring parishes. MONKS,

at

at first lived by their industry, and by private alms, and came to the parish Church. But a recluse life was not so serviceable to the Romish Church; and therefore FRIARS were under little confinement. Every MONK and FRIAR used the *Tonsure* or Shaved Crown; an emblem, they said, of their hope of a Crown of Glory. They vowed chastity, poverty, and obedience, besides the rules of their respective Orders. They had few Convents in this Country.

BLACK FRIARS. The DOMINICANS, called BLACK-FRIARS, because they wore a Black Cross on a white gown, were instituted by DOMINIC a Spaniard who invented the Inquisition, were approved by the POPE anno 1215, and brought into Scotland by Bishop Malvoisin. These, with the Franciscan Gray-Friars, and Carmelite White Friars, were Mendicants, allowed to preach abroad, and beg their subsistence. The Dominicans, notwithstanding their professed poverty, had fifteen rich Convents in Scotland. And we had their Convents at Elgin, Forres, and Inverness.

GRAY FRIARS. The FRANCISCANS, called GRAY-FRIARS, wore a Gray Gown and Coul, a rope about their middle, and went about with pocks to beg. St FRANCIS an Italian established them anno 1206. King Alexander II. settled a Convent of them in Elgin, where they had a spacious Church and fine dwellings. Their principal house is now the seat of William King of Newmiln. I may add,

GRAY SISTERS. The GREY-SISTERS, or NUNS of Sienna in Italy. They wore a Grey Gown and a rochet, followed St Austin's rule, and were never to go forth of their Cloysters, after they had made their vows. They had a Nunnery at Y-colum-kill, dedicated

Sect. 3. THE ROMISH OR POPISH CHURCH.

dicated to St Oran; and at Sheens, *i. e. de Sienna*, near Edinburgh, confecrated to St Catharine de Sienna. It is probable they had a Convent at Elgin, where there are plots of land, called "St Katharine's Crofts."

The Preceptory of MAISON DIEU.

Near Elgin, was an Hospital for entertaining Strangers, and maintaining Poor Infirm People. The Hospital stood close to the town at the East, where some parts of the buildings remain. The lands of this Hospital granted to the town of Elgin by King James VI. by charter 22d March 1594, confirmed ultimo Februarii 1620, for maintaining Poor People, and sustaining a Teacher of Church Music, who shall precent in the Church. King Alexander III. mortified the lands of Monben and Kelles to this Hospital *(Appendix* N° XV.) and King Charles I. by his charter to the town of Elgin, 8th October 1633, confirms to them, " The Preceptory of Maison Dieu, with the patronage
" thereof, and all belonging thereto, with the arable lands of
" Maison Dieu, and the crofts and pertinents thereof; the lands
" of Over and Neither Monben with the haugh thereof called
" Broomtown; the lands of Bogside, with the miln thereof,
" mill-lands, adstricted multures and sequels; the lands of Car-
" dells Over and Nether, *alias* Pitcroy, Delnapot, Smiddy
" croft, with the miln, miln-lands, multures and sequels there-
" of; with the Salmon fishing on the water of Spey; and the
" lands of Over and Neither Pitinseir."

St NICHOLAS' HOSPITAL.

Another such Hospital, called St Nicholas Hospital, stood on the east bank of Spey, at the boat of Bridge, where some remains

remains of the buildings may be seen. Muriel de Pollock gave the lands of Inverorkile, for building a house there (*Appendix*, No II.) Andrew Bishop of Moray gave the Church of Rothes with its pertinents to this Hospital (*Appendix*, No IV.) Walterus de Moravia filius Willielmi granted to it the lands of Agynway (*Char, Mor.*) and King Alexander II. anno 1232, granted four merks annually of the farm of the Mills of Nairn for maintaining a Chaplain. (*Appendix*, No III.) The lands of this Hospital are now the property of several Gentlemen.

TEMPLAR and JOHANNITE Knights.

Templars. I shall add a few things concerning the TEMPLAR and JOHANNITE KNIGHTS.

The TEMPLARS were religious KNIGHTS established at Jerusalem about the year 1118, and vowed to defend the Temple, and to guard and entertain Pilgrims and Strangers. They wore a white habite with a red cross, and were called by some the *Red-Friars*. They became immensely rich, had above 9000 houses in Europe, and the Cross of the Order was on the top of every house. They had some lands in Arderfier and a jurisdiction of Regality. In 1312, the Pope and the King of France suppressed this Order, and, under pretence of abominable crimes and errors, caused destroy the KNIGHTS in one night, then shared their riches, and gave a part of the lands to the JOHANNITES. The TEMPLARS had a house in the town of Elgin: and at Kinnermonie in Aberlaure, there are the walls of an old Gothic house, and the tradition of the country is, that it was a religious house, and that all the religious in it were massacred in one night.

The

Sect. 3.   THE ROMISH OR POPISH CHURCH.   265

The JOHANNITES had their rise from some Neapolitan Merchants, whom the Calif of Egypt permitted to build a house at Jerusalem for the reception of Pilgrims. In 1104, Godfrey of Bouillon allowed a Temple and Hospital to be built in honour of St JOHN; and hence the KNIGHTS took their name. They wore a black robe with a white cross. Being driven by the Saracens and Turks out of Palestine, Cyprus and Rhodes, Charles V. Emperor, in 1534, gave them the Island of Malta; Hence they were called The KNIGHTS of MALTA. They had lands in almost all Christian countries. Their chief seat in Scotland was at Torphichen; and King Malcolm IV. gave them " Unum toftum in quolibet burgo totius terræ suæ." They had a house in the town of Elgin: But at the Reformation anno 1560, the Order was abolished.

JOHANNITES.

II. The SECULAR CLERGY.

These were so called, because, being the Parish Ministers, they lived abroad in the world, and were not shut up in Convents and Cloysters as the REGULARS were. We had two Bishop's Sees or Seats in this Province, Murthlac and Moray: And the Bishops of these, with their Inferiors, were the SECULAR CLERGY.

SECULAR CLERGY.

The BISHOPRIC of MURTHLAC.

The Bishopric of Murthlac, with the time and occasion of its erection, is mentioned by FORDUN, *Lib.* IV. *cap.* 44. *in vita Malcolm.* II. " * Novam Episcopalem constituit sedem apud " Murthlac, non procul a loco quo, superatis Norwegensibus,

BISHOPRIC of MURTHLAC.

victo-

---

* " He erected a new Bishop's See at Murthlac, not far from the place where,
" having conquered the Norwegians, he obtained a victory."

"victoriam obtinuit." This refers to the victory obtained over the Danes anno 1010; and Fordun adds, that Pope Benedict constituted Bean Bishop thereof. We have the foundation Charter of this See in the Chartulary of Aberdeen. It runs thus:

"* Malcolmus rex Scottorum, omnibus probis hominibus
" suis, tam Clericis quam Laicis, Salutem : Sciatis, me dedisse, et
" hac Carta mea confirmasse, Deo et Beatæ Mariæ, et omnibus
" Sanctis, et Episcopo BEYN de Murthelach, Ecclesiam de
" Murthelach, ut ibidem construatur sedes Episcopalis, Terras
" meas de Murthelach, Ecclesiam de Cloveth cum terris, Ec-
" clesiam de Dulmeth cum terris; ita libere sicut eas tenui, et
" in puram et perpetuam Eleemosynam: Teste meipso, Apud
" Forfar, 8vo Octobris, anno regni mei sexto." Dr NICHOL-
SON, Scot. Hist. lib. pag. 210, makes King Malcolm III. the founder of this Bishopric, but gives no reason for his opinion. It is true, in the chartulary of Aberdeen, this erection is said to have been " † Tempore Malcolmi regis Scotiæ filii Kenethi,
" per eum Malcolmum constituta est primo sedes episcopalis
" apud Murthlac, cui dotavit ecclesiam de Murthlac &c."
Yet that chartulary in another place says, that it was erected anno

---

* "Malcolm King of Scots, to all his good People, both Clergy and Lai-
" ty, Greeting: Know ye, that I have given, and by this Charter confirmed, to
" God and the blessed Mary, and all the Saints, and to the Bishop Beyn of Murth-
" lac, the Church of Murthlac, that there a Bishop's See may be erected, my
" Lands of Murthlac, the Church of Cloveth with its lands, the Church of Dul-
" meth with its lands, as free as I held them, and in pure and perpetual charity.
" Witness myself, at Forfar, October 8th, in the sixth year of my Reign."

† "The Episcopal See at Murthlac was at first erected in the time of Malcolm
" Son of Kenneth and King of Scotland, to which he granted the Kirk of Murth-
" lac."

Sect. 3.   THE ROMISH OR POPISH CHURCH.   267

anno 1070. But many circumstances concur in ascribing the erection to Malcolm II. Malcolm II, and not Malcolm III, was the son of Kenneth. Malcolm II, and not Malcolm III, defeated the Norwegians at Mortlich. It was erected anno regni 6*to*; this places it in 1010, which was the 6th of Malcolm II. But the year 1070 was the 13th, and not the 6th, of Malcolm III. If Malcolm III. had been the Founder, he would have been so called in the chartulary ; but he is mentioned only as a single Donator. And David I. would have confirmed his father's charter, had he been the Founder ; but this he does not. The transcriber, therefore, of the charter has certainly erred in writing 1070 for 1010, which is but one figure for another, 7 for 1; a mistake ready to be committed.

This See, being erected anno 1010, was the second in Scotland: And it shews how narrow and mean the extent and jurisdiction of Bishoprics were at first. This extended only over three parishes. *Diocess.*

King David I. by his charter dated at Forfar, 30th July, anno regni 18*vo, i. e.* 1142, translated the See from Murthlac to Aberdeen in favour of Bishop NECTAN, whose Diocess was declared to be, over the counties of Aberdeen and Banff (*Chart. Aberd.*). But the extent of that Diocess was afterwards altered, and much of it included in the Diocess of Moray, as we shall see. Yet the parish of Murthlac, the mother seat, remained in the Diocess of Aberdeen, until it was annexed to the Synod of Moray by the General Assembly, 9th April 1706. *Translation.*

The Bishops of Murthlac, before the translation of the See, were: 1. Bean—2. Donertius—3. Cormac: These from anno 1010 to 1122. Then, 4. Nectan was ordained, and in 1139 was brought to Aberdeen. In 114- this See was called " The Bishop-" ric of Aberdeen." (*Pref. to Dipl. et Num. Scotiae.*) I come now to *Bishops.*

L l 2   The

The BISHOPRIC of MORAY.

Bishopric of Moray.

The precife time of erecting this BISHOPRIC, or the reign in which it was erected, cannot eafily be fixt. LESLIE and BUCHANAN afcribe it to King Malcolm III. or Ceanmore; but this is uncertain. In the foundation charter of the Priory of Scone, anno 1115, Gregorius Epifcopus is a witnefs. In a char-

Erection.

ter by King Alexander I. to the faid Priory, about the year 1122, Robertus Electus Epifcopus Sti Andreæ, Cormacus Epifcopus, et Gregorius Epifcopus de Moravia, are witneffes: And in a charter by King David I. anno 1126, to the Abbey of Dunfermline, Robertus Sti Andreæ, Joannes Glafguenfis, Gregorius Moravienfis, Cormacus Dunkeldenfis, and Macbeth Roffmarkienfis, Epifcopi, are witneffes. (*Dalr. Coll.*) I think it very probable, that Bifhop Gregory, anno 1126, is the fame that is mentioned 1122 and 1115; and this brings up the erection to the beginning of the reign of King Alexander I. and higher I cannot trace it. Thus the See of Moray is fourth in order of erection; and the more ancient Sees are, St Andrews, Murthlac, and Glafgow. Let me now give an account of

Bishops.

The BISHOPS of this SEE of MORAY.——SPOTTISWOOD and others have given very imperfect Catalogues of thefe Bifhops. I have compared feveral manufcript and printed Lifts, and from them compiled the following, which I think pretty exact.

1. GREGORIUS Bifhop of Moray, anno 1115. I find not in what year he died.
2. WILLIAM. I find not when he was confecrated. He was made Apoftolic Legate 1159; next year he confecrated Arnold

Sect. 3. THE ROMISH OR POPISH CHURCH. 269

 Arnold Bishop of St Andrews, and died anno 1162. *(Chron. Melr.)* I think it not improbable, that Gregory and William might officiate from 1115 to 1162.

3. FELIX succeeded. He is a witness in a charter by King William, " Willielmo filio Freskeni," of the lands of Duffus, Rosile, &c. He died anno 1170. *(Chron. Melr.)*

4. SIMEON DE TONEI, a Monk of Melross; elected 1171, died 1184, buried in Birnie *(M. S.)*

5. ANDREW, consecrated anno 1184; died 1185. *(Chron. Melr.)*

6. RICHARD, chaplain to King William, was consecrated, *Id. Martii* 1187, by Hugh Bishop of St Andrews; died 1203 *(Chron. Melr.)*; buried in Spynie. *(M. S.)*

7. BRICIUS, brother of William Lord Douglas, Prior of Lesmahegow, was elected anno 1203; died 1222, and was buried in Spynie. He founded a College of eight Cannons.

8. ANDREW MORAY, son of William Moray of Duffus, Parson of Duffus, was consecrated anno 1223. He founded the Cathedral Church of Elgin anno 1224; added fourteen Cannons to the former eight, of which the Prebendary of Unthank was one; and he assigned to every Cannon a toft on which to build a manse, and a croft; to the Dean, Chancellor, Chantor and Treasurer, four acres of land to each; and two other acres to each of the other Cannons: Which land he bought from the Burgesses of Elgin. He died 1242, and was buried in the Choir of the Cathedral under a broad blue stone *(M. S. S.)*

9. SIMON Dean of Moray, succeeded in the year 1243, and died anno 1252. He was buried in the Choir of the Cathedral under a blue stone *(M. S. S.)*

10. ARCHIBALD Dean of Moray, was consecrated anno 1253; died 5th December 1298, and was buried in the Cathedral.

dral. He built the palace of Kenedar, and resided there. In his time William Earl of Ross had done some injury to the Church of Pettie and Prebend of Brachlie, for the reparation of which he gave the lands of Catboll in Ross, and other lands, to the Bishop and Cannons (*M. S. S.*)

11. DAVID MORAY, was consecrated at Avignion by Boniface VIII. anno 1299, and died 20th January 1325. He was buried in the Choir *(Ibid.)*

12. JOHN PILMOZE, Elect of Ross, was consecrated Bishop of Moray, 3. Kal. Aprilis, anno 1326, and died in the Castle of Spynie on Michaelmass Eve, anno 1362, *(Ibid.)*

13. ALEXANDER BAR, Doctor Decretorum, was consecrated by Urban V. anno 1362; died in Spynie 15th May 1397, and was buried in the Cathedral. In his time, viz. in 1390, the Cathedral was burnt, and he began the rebuilding of it, *(Ibid.)*

14. WILLIAM SPYNIE, Chantor of Moray, and L. D. was consecrated at Avignion, by Benedict the IX. September 13th 1397, and died 20th of August 1406. He carried on the rebuilding of the Cathedral. In his time Alexander MacDonald plundered Elgin, as we shall see.

15. JOHN INNES, Laird of Innes, Parson of Duffus, Archdeacon of Caithness, and L. L. D. was consecrated by Pope Benedict 23d January 1406, and died 25th April 1414. He began the building of the great Steeple in the centre of the Church, and was buried at the foot of the North-west Pillar of it.

16. HENRY LEIGHTON, Parson of Duffus, L. L. D. consecrated in Valencia by Pope Benedict, March 8th 1414. He was translated to Aberdeen anno 1425.

17. COLUMBA

17. COLUMBA DUNBAR succeeded. He died in Spynie anno 1435.
18. JOHN WINCHESTER, L. B. Chaplain to King James II. was consecrated in Cambuskenneth anno 1438: In 1452 he obtained the Regality of Spynie; died 1453.
19. JAMES STEWART, Dean of Moray, of the family of Lorn, was consecrated anno 1458, and died 1460.
20. DAVID STEWART, brother of the former, and Parson of Spynie, was consecrated anno 1461, and died 1475. He built that part of the Palace called " Davy's Tower," and made several good regulations; as, That no Canon be admitted except in general Covocation; That the common Kirk Lands be set to none but the Labourers of the ground; And that no Pensions should be given out of these Lands.
21. WILLIAM TULLOCH, Bishop of Orkney, was translated to Moray anno 1477, and died anno 1482.
22. ANDREW STEWART, son of Sir James Stewart of Lorn, and of the widow of King James I. Dean of Moray, and Lord Privy Seal, succeeded anno 1483. In 1488, he got a ratification of the Regality of Spynie, and died anno 1501.
23. ANDREW FOREMAN, Commendator of Drybrugh and Pittenweme, succeeded in 1501, and was translated to St Andrews 1514.
24. JAMES HEPBURN, succeeded in 1514, and died anno 1523.
25. ROBERT SHAW, son of Sauchie, and Abbot of Paisley, was consecrated anno 1525 and died 1528.
26. ALEXANDER STEWART, son of Alexander Duke of Albany, who was son of King James II. succeeded, and died anno 1535.

27. PATRICK HEPBURN, uncle to James Earl of Bothwell who murdered King Henry Stewart, Commendator of Scone, was consecrated anno 1537. He was a man of an abandoned character: Having concealed and aided his nephew, when he fled from Justice anno 1567, he purchased his own safety by yielding up a part of the Church Lands. He aliened and feued out almost all the other lands of the Bishopric. He died in the Castle of Spynie, June 20th 1573. (M. S.)

These were the BISHOPS in the SEE of MORAY before the Reformation. Let us now look into

DIOCESS. The DIOCESS in which they officiated. It was always called "The Diocess of Moray," but what the extent of it was, at its first erection, I shall not pretend to determine. In the year 1142, the Diocess of Aberdeen extended over the Counties of Aberdeen and Banff; and if the extent of these Counties was at that time, what it is now, no part of the Diocess of Moray could, in 1142, lie within them. But afterward, and right early, I find a part of the Diocess of Moray, within the Counties both of Aberdeen and Banff. In the time of Bishop Bricius, the parishes of Strathavon, Ruthven, Arntullie, and Glass (*Appendix*, No. XXVIII.); and in the Episcopate of Bishop Andrew Moray, Rynie, Dunbenan, Kinore, Inverkethnie, and Botarie (*Appendix*, No. XXVIII.) were within the Diocess of Moray. Thus it extended to the East, as far as it did any time after.

To the West, Abertarf, in the time of Bricius, (*Ibid.*) and Fernua anno 1239 (*Appendix*, No. XXXIII.) were comprehended in it. I do not find, that any part of this Diocess lay beyond the River of Farar or Beaulie, which is the bounding of Ross

Ross; for although the Bishop of Moray had lands in Ross, Strathnaver, Cullen, Banff, these were no part of their Episcopal charge.

In the Procurationes Decanatuum (*Appendix*, No. XXX.) the rural Deanrie or Archipresbyterate of Strathboggie is included; and comprehends, besides Drumblade and Inverkethnie now in the Synod of Aberdeen, the whole Presbytery of Strathboggie, as at this time, except Mortlich, Botrifnie, Bellie, and Grange.

Mortlich, the mother Church, was within the Diocess of Aberdeen till the year 1706. Botrifnie was at that time probably a part of the parish of Mortlich, or of Keith. Bellie, depending on the Priory of Urquhart, was probably exempt from the Procurationes. Grange was a part of the parish of Kieth, and was disjoined and erected into a distinct parish, in the year 1618 (*Rec. Presbytery of Strathb.*) In the Deanry of Strathspey, Laggan in Badenoch is included; and anno 1139, Laggan was in the Diocess of Moray.

How early these Procurationes were drawn up, I know not: But without regard to them it appears, that in the beginning of the thirteenth century, the Diocess extended from Rynie in the East to Abertarf in the South west, and comprehended what are now the Counties of Moray and Nairn, and a considerable part of the Counties of Inverness and Banff, and some parishes in the County of Aberdeen. Let me only add, that an enquiry made by David Prince of Cumberland (afterward King David I.) into the ancient possessions of the Church of Glasgow, Pentejacob is called one of them: And in a Charter to that Church, posterior to the enquiry, Pentejacob is said to be Glenmoriston. (*Dalr. Coll.*) But why Glenmoriston was so called, or depended on the Church of Glasgow, I know not. Such was the Diocess: Let me next give some account of

M m The

The CATHEDRAL CHURCH.

CATHEDRAL.

In the Primitive Christian Church, the Bishop sat as Præses in the Confessus or College of Presbyters, in a Cathedra, or Chair allotted to him. The pride and vanity of after-ages, when Bishops affected to imitate the grandeur of Princes, turned the humble Cathedra into a Throne. The Bishop's own Church in which he officiated, was called " The Cathedral Church of " the Diocess." It is probable, that the first six Bishops of Moray had no fixed Cathedral or place of residence, but served in Birnie, Spynie, or Kenedar, as they affected. Bishop Bricius insinuates as much (*Appendix*, No XXVIII.), and mentioning Birnie first, seems to hint that it was the Bishop's Church. It is a pleasant well-aired situation within two miles of the town of Elgin, and the fourth Bishop was there buried. The present Church of Birnie is built with a choir and nave; but it does not appear to be the fabric that was there in those early times. There are no vestiges, or tradition of a palace, except a place called " The Castle-Hill." Probably the revenues in those days were so small and so precarious, as we shall see, that they did not admit of stately Churches or Palaces.

At Spynie.

The first six Bishops having shifted from one place to another, as fancy or conveniency prompted them, Bishop Bricius, who was consecrated anno 1203, applied to Pope Innocent to have a Cathedral fixed for the Bishops of Moray. That Pope appointed the Bishops of St Andrews and Brechin, and the Abbot of Lindores, to repair to Moray, and to declare the Church of the Holy Trinity at Spynie to be the Cathedral of the Diocess, in all time coming, which they accordingly did (*Append.* No XXVIII.) But

Sect. 3.   THE ROMISH OR POPISH CHURCH.   275

But it does not appear in what year this was done; yet it must have been betwixt the year 1203, when Bricius was consecrated, and 1216, when Pope Innocent III died. Bricius instituted a College of Cannons, eight in number, at Spynie (*Append. Ibid.*)

This choice of a Cathedral did not please Bishop Andrew Moray immediate successor to Bricius; for, having come to the Episcopate in 1223, he next year represented to Pope Honorius, that Spynie was a solitary place, far from the necessaries of life, and that divine service was much neglected, while the Canons were obliged to travel at a distance to purchase the necessary provisions: And therefore craved, that the Cathedral might be translated from Spynie to the Church of the Holy Trinity, which stood a little North-East of the town of Elgin. To induce the Pontiff the more readily to comply, the Bishop signified, that it not only was the desire of the Chapter of the Diocess, but likewise of the King of Scotland Alexander II. *At Elgin.*

The Pope cheerfully granted the request; and by his Apostolic Bull or mandate, dated (4*to* Id.) the tenth day of April 1224, empowered the Bishop of Caithness, with the Abbot of Kinloss, and the Dean of Rosemarkie, or the Bishop and any one of these, to make the desired Translation, if they should find it useful. In obedience to which Mandate, the said Bishop and Dean met at the Church of the Holy Trinity near Elgin on the 14th of the Kalends of August, *i. e.* July 19th, in the said year 1224, and finding the necessity and usefulness of the Translation, as represented, declared and appointed the said Church of the Holy Trinity to be the Cathedral Church of the Episcopal Diocess of Moray, and so to remain in all time coming (*Appendix, No* XXXI.) *Determined and fixed.*

Cathedral at Elgin Founded and Built.

Bishop Andrew Moray is said to have laid the foundation stone of the Cathedral Church, on the very day in which it was declared, viz. 19th July 1224: And as he lived eighteen years after, it cannot be doubted that he greatly advanced, if not finished, the Building. It does not appear what was the model, or what the dimensions of the Church, as first built, though it is probable it was in the form common to Cathedral Churches, viz. The form of a Passion-Cross, with a spacious Choir and Nave.

Burnt.

It had stood 166 years, from the year of its foundation, when it was totally burnt and destroyed, as follows.

In the time of Bishop Alexander Barr, Alexander Stewart son of King Robert II. Lord Badenoch, commonly called "The "Wolf of Badenoch," seized on the Bishop's lands of that country, and keeping violent possession of them, was excommunicated. In resentment of which, in the month of May 1390, he burnt the town of Forres, with the Choir of the Church, and the Manse of the Arch Deacon. And in June that same year, he burnt the Town of Elgin, the Church of St Giles, the Hospital of Maison-Dieu, and the Cathedral Church, with eighteen houses of the Cannons and Chaplains in the College of Elgin. For this wickedness the Lord Badenoch was justly prosecuted, and obliged to make due reparation. Upon his humble submission he was absolved by Walter Trail Bishop of St Andrews, in the Black Friar Church in Perth, being first received at the door, and again before the high altar, in presence of the King and many of the Nobility, on condition that he should make full satisfaction to the Bishop and Church of Moray, and obtain absolution from the Pope (*Appendix*, No XXXII. *and M. S. S.*)

Rebuilt

Bishop Barr began the rebuilding of the Church; and every Canon contributed: Bishop Spynie continued the work; but though every parish paid a subsidy, yet, through the troubles of the times, it made slow advances. Bishop Innes laid the foundation

Sect. 3.   THE ROMISH OR POPISH CHURCH.   277

foundation of the Great Steeple in the middle of the Church, and greatly advanced it.   After his death the Chapter met May 18th 1414, and bound themselves by a solemn oath, that whosoever should be elected Bishop, he should annually apply one third of his revenue in repairing the Cathedral, until it should be finished.   The Church being rebuilt, it remained entire for many years; but in the beginning of the sixteenth century, about the year 1506, the Great Steeple in the centre fell down. Next year Bishop Foreman began to rebuild it, but the work was not finished before the year 1538; and then the height of the Tower, including the Spire, was 198 feet.   (*Hay of Drumboot.*)

This CHURCH, when entire, was a Building of Gothic Architecture, inferior to few in Europe.   It stood due East and West, in the form of a Passion or Jerusalem Cross, ornamented with five Towers, whereof two parallel stood on the West-end; one in the middle, and two on the East-end.   Betwixt the two Towers on the West-end was the great Porch or Entrance. This Gate is a Concave Arch 24 feet broad in base, and 24 in height, terminating in a sharp angle.   On each side of the Valves or Doors, in the sweep of the Arch, are eight round, and eight fluted Pilasters, six and a-half feet high, adorned with a chapiter, from which arise sixteen Pilasters, which meet in the key of the Arch.   There were Porticoes, or To-falls on each side of the Church, eastward from the Traverse or Cross, which were 18 feet broad without the walls.   To yield sufficient light to a Building so large, besides the great Windows in the Porticoes, and a row of Attic Windows in the walls, each six feet high, above the Porticoes; there was in the west-gable, above the gate, a Window in form of an acute angled arch, 19 feet broad in base, and 27 in height; and in the east-gable between the turrets, a row of five parallel Windows, each two feet broad, and 10 high; above these are five more, each 7 feet
high;

Described.

high; and over all, a circular Window, near to 10 feet in diameter. In the heart of the wall of the Church, and leading to all the upper Windows, there is a Channel or Walk round the whole Building. The Grand-Gate, the Windows, the Pillars, the projecting-Table, Pedestals, Cordons, &c. are adorned with foliage, grapes and other carving. Let us, after describing the body of the Church, take a view of

The Chapter House.

The CHAPTER-HOUSE, commonly called " The Apprentice's Isle," a curious piece of architecture, standing on the north-side of the Church, and communicating with the Choir, by a vaulted Vestry. The house is an exact octagon, 34 feet high, and the diagonal breadth, within walls 37 feet. It is arched and vaulted at the top, and the whole Arched-roof supported by one Pillar in the centre of the house. Arched Pillars from every angle terminate in the Grand-Pillar. This Pillar, 9 feet in circumference, is crusted over with sixteen Pilasters or small Pillars, alternately round and fluted, and 24 feet high, adorned with a Chapiter, from which arise sixteen round pillars that spread along the roof; and join at top with the Pillars (five in number) rising from every side of the octolateral figure. There is a large Window in every side of seven, and the eight side communicates with the Choir. In the north wall of this Chapter-House there are five Stalls, cut by way of nitches, for the Bishop (or the Dean in the Bishop's absence) and the Dignified Clergy to sit in. The middle Stall, for the Bishop or Dean, is larger, and raised a step higher, than the other four. They were all well lined with wainscoat.

Some

Sect. 3.   THE ROMISH OR POPISH CHURCH.   279

Some of the Dimensions of this Church may be seen as follows: *Dimensions of the Cathedral.*

	Feet.		Feet.
The length on the outside	264	The height of the Chapter House	34
The breadth on the outside	35	The diagonal breadth within walls	37
The breadth within walls	28	The breadth of every side, near	15
The length of the traverse outside	114	The circumference of the great Pillar	9
The length within walls	110	The height thereof, below the Chapiter	24
The height of the West Tower, not including the Spire	84	The breadth of the Porticoes, on the side	18
The height of the Tower in the Centre, including the Spire	198	The breadth of the West Window	19
The height of the Eastern Turrets	60	The height thereof	27
The breadth of the Great Gate	24	The height of the East Windows	10
The height thereof	24	The height of the second Row	7
The breadth of each Valve	5	The diameter of the circular Window.	10
The height of each Valve, near	10		
The height of the side walls	36		

In taking these Dimensions, I have not studied a scrupulous exactness; and in some of them, it was not possible to do so. The Spires of the two West Towers are fallen, but the stone work is pretty entire. No part of the Great Tower in the middle now stands. The two Eastern Turrets, being winding stair cases, and vaulted at top, are entire. The Walls of the Choir are pretty entire; and so is the whole Chapter House: But the Walls of the Nave and Traverse are mostly fallen.

It is a mistake, that this Stately Edifice was either burnt or demolished by the mob, at the Reformation. The following Act of Privy Council shews the contrary: viz. " Edinburgh " 14th February, 1567—8. Seeing provision must be made " for entertaining the Men of war (Soldiers), whose service can" not be spared, until the rebellious and disobedient subjects be " reduced; Therefore appoint, that the Lead be taken from " the Cathedral Churches in Aberdeen and Elgin, and sold for " sustentation of the said Men of war. And command and " charge, the Earl of Huntley Sheriff of Aberdeen and his " Deputes, Alexander Dunbar of Cumnock Knight Sheriff of " Elgin

How Demolished.

"Elgin and Forrefs and his Deputes, William Bifhop of Aber-
"deen, Patrick Bifhop of Moray, &c. That they defend and
"affift Alexander Clerk and William Birnie, and their fervants,
"in taking down and felling the faid Lead, &c. figned R. M."
(Keith's Hift.).

The Lead was accordingly taken off thefe Churches, and fhipped at Aberdeen for Holland; but foon after the fhip had left the River, it funk, which was owing, as many thought, to the fuperftition of the Roman Catholic Captain. Be this as it may, the Cathedral of Moray, being uncovered, was fuffered to decay as a piece of Romifh vanity, too expenfive to be kept in repair. Some painted rooms in the Towers and Choir remained fo entire about the year 1640, that Roman Catholicks repaired to them, there to fay their Prayers, *(Rec. Prefbytery of Elgin)*. The Great Tower in the middle of the Church, being uncovered, the wooden work gradually decayed, and the foundation failing, the Tower fell, anno 1711, on a Peace Sunday in the morning; feveral children were playing, and idle people walking within the Area of the Church, and immediately as they removed to breakfaft, the Tower fell down, and no one was hurt.

COLLEGE   The COLLEGE of ELGIN, was an Appendage of the Cathedral, and properly falleth to be next defcribed. A College is an incorporated Society, having particular Rules or Canons for their government. If the College was not annexed to the Cathedral Church, but to an ordinary Church, it was called a Collegiate Church, and the Head or Ruler of the College was called Provoft, or Dean: But in a Cathedral with a College, the Bifhop was the Ruler. Thefe Colleges were inftituted for performing Divine Service, and finging Maffes for the fouls of their Founders, or their Friends. They confifted of Canons or Prebendaries, who had their Stalls for orderly finging the Ca-

nonical

Sect. 3. THE ROMISH OR POPISH CHURCH. 281

nonical hours, and were commonly erected out of Parish Churches, or out of the Chaplainries belonging to Churches.

CANONS, or CHANONS SECULAR, (so called to distinguish them from the REGULARS in Convents) were Ministers or Parsons within the Diocess, chosen by the Bishop, to be members of his Chapter or Council, lived within the College, performed divine service in the Cathedral, and sung in the Choir, according to rules or canons made by the Chapter. They were called PREBENDARIES, because each had a Prebendum or portion of land allotted him for his service. Canons and Prebendaries differed chiefly in this, That the Canon had his canonica or portion, merely for his being received, although he did not serve in the Church; but the Prebendary had his prebendum, only when he served. CANONS.
PREBEN-
DARIES.

The COLLEGE of CANONS annexed to this Cathedral, was first instituted by Bishop Bricius in Spynie, when the Cathedral was there. He instituted eight Canonries, i. e. eight parishes, whose Ministers or Parsons should be Canons and Members of the College, viz. 1. For the Deanry, the church of Auldern, with the chapel of Nairn. 2. For the Chantry, Langbryde, Alves and Rafford. 3. For the Thesaury, Kenedar and Essil. 4. For the Chancellary, Fortherves, Lythenes, Lunyn, and Duldavie. 5. For the Archdeaconry, Forres and Logyn Fythenach. 6. Strathavon and Urquhart beyond Inverness. 7. Spynie. And, 8. Ruthven and Dyple. (*App*. Nº XXVIII.) Let me here observe, COLLEGE
erected.

1st, That Bishop Bricius had nominated the five Dignitaries, viz. The Dean, Chancellor, Archdeacon, Chantor, Treasurer, and assigned and fixed their seats.

2dly, That each Dignitary, being a Canon, and to reside in the College, had a vicarage or a parish annexed to his seat, in which he employed a Vicar, and had the Tythes to himself, to add to his more sumptuous living. Thus Nairn was annexed to Aldern, &c.

3dly, That

3dly, That the Seat of the Chancellor was afterwards changed and fixed at Inveravon. Fortherves, Lythenes, Lunyn and Duldavie first assigned to the Chancellor, I incline to think were, Fernes in Ardclach, Lethin, Tulidivie in Edinkylie, in all which places there were chapels or churches, and Lunyn, *i. e.* Lundichtie, now called Dunlichtie. This I think the more probable, because the church and parish of Ardclach is but a late erection, not mentioned in any antient writing that I have seen; and Fernes and Lethin were the places of worship there. Likewise Logyn-Fythenach, (*i. e.* the Woody-Logie, so called to distinguish it from Logyn-Dyke which was not Woody,) annexed to the Archdeaconry was, Logie, where Mr Tulloch of Tanachie had his seat, and where there are vestiges of a church. While that church stood, there was no church at Edinkylie, except Duldavie or Tullidivie. And when the wood in Edinkylie was destroyed, land cultivated, and a church and parish erected, depending on the Archdeacon, then Logyn-Fythenach was annexed to Forres.

Transplanted.

Bishop Andrew Moray translated, with the Cathedral, the College of Canons to Elgin; and to the former eight, added fourteen more, making in all twenty-two, which number they never exceeded. To every Canon he gave a toft of land for building a manse upon it, and a croft; and to each of the Dignitaries he gave four acres of land, and two acres to each other Canon. (*M. S. Catalogue of the Bishops, pen. Mr King of Newmiln*) I find, in some Writings, the following twenty-two Canons, viz. The Ministers of Aldern, Forres, Alves, Inveravon, Kenedar, Dallas, Raffort, Kingusie, Duthel, Advie, Aberlaur, Dyple, Botarie, Inverkethnie, Kinnore, Pettie, Duffus, Spynie, Rynie, Moy, Croy, and the Vicar of Elgin. All these had manses and gardens within the precinct of the College, and severals of them had crofts of land near

The Canons.

Sect. 3. THE ROMISH OR POPISH CHURCH.

near to it, as yet called the Deans-Crook, Dyple-Croft, Moy-Croft, &c. Every Canonry had a Vicarage annexed to it, for the better subsistence of the Canon, who had the Great Tythes of both parishes, and generally was Patron of the annexed Vicarage. Thus, Aldern had annexed to it, Nairn; Forres, Edinkylie; Alves, Langbryde; Inneravon, Urquhart; Kenedar, Essil; Dyple, Rathven; Kinnore, Dunbenen; Rynie, Essie; Botarie, Elchies; Advie, Cromdale; Kingusie, Insh; Duthel, Rothemurchus; Pettie, Bracklie; Croy, Moy in Strathern; Moy, Dyke; Raffart, Ardclach; Aberlaure, Skirdustan. I find not that Duffus, Spynie, or Elgin had any Vicarage.

The Precinct of the College was walled round with a strong stone-Wall, about 4 yards high and 900 yards in circuit, a great part of which remains yet entire. It had four Gates. The East-Gate, called the Water-Gate, or the Pan's Port, appears to have had an Iron-Grate, a Port-Cullis, and a Porter's-Lodge; and probably the other gates, now fallen, had the like fences. Within this Precinct stood the Houses of all the Canons, and likewise the Cathedral, and a spacious Church-Yard, inclosed with a stone-wall, and a paved street round it, leading to the several gates. Without the Precinct Westward towards the Town of Elgin (which was not then built so far to the East, as now it is, Vid. Pag. 66.) there was a small Burrough depending on the Bishop and the College. " On July 3d, 1402, Alexander Mac-
" Donald, third Son of the Lord of the Isles, entered the College
" of Elgin, and wholly spoiled and plundered it, and burnt a
" great part of the Town (*App.* N°. XXXII.). For this he was
" excommunicated, but was after absolved, and he offered a
" sum of Gold, and so did his captains, according to their a-
" bility; all which was applied for erecting a Cross and a Bell,
" in that part of the Chanonry which is next to the Bridge of
" Elgin *(Mr King's M. S.)*" Probably that Cross stood, where

The Precinct.

The Burrough.

now stands the Little Cross; and the Bridge, which was no doubt of wood, stood near to the land now called Burrough-Bridge Lands. Having described the Cathedral and College, I shall next give some account of

The BISHOP's PALACE.

Bishop's Palace.

The proud Prelate, vying with Temporal Princes, must have his habitation called, not a House but, a Palace. It is probable, that, as in Mortlich, so in Moray, the Revenues were at first inconsiderable, and such as did not admit of Grand and Sumptuous Palaces. Although Bishop Bricius informs us, that his predecessors resided at Birnie, Spynie or Kenedar, as they fancied, and that he got the Cathedral fixed at Spynie; and tho' in Bishop Andrew Moray's time, the Cathedral was translated to Elgin anno 1224, we have no account of a House or Palace **At Kenedar** before Bishop Archibald, who built a House at Kenedar about the year 1280. The vestiges are visible, and some part of the walls remain. It was a large double House, pretty near the Church, which likewise was spacious, and in the form of a Cross. The distance of four miles from the Cathedral, and from the market at Elgin, the coldness of the situation so near the Sea, and the total want of fuel, would induce them to build in a more convenient place. They could not have chosen a more commodious situation and **At Spynie.** pleasant, than where the Palace of Spynie stands. It is situated on a rising ground, upon the South bank of the Loch of Spynie, in a pure air, a dry and warm Soil, commanding the view of the Loch, and of the fertile plains of Kenedar and Duffus to the North and North-West, and of the plains of Innes and the winding of the River Lossie to the East and

South-

Spynie Palace Moray-shire, from the South

South-East, within a mile of the Cathedral, in view of and but two miles from the Sea.

 This Palace, when it stood entire, was incomparably the most stately and magnificent I have seen in any Diocess in Scotland. The Area of the buildings was near a square of sixty yards: In the South-West corner stood a strong Tower, called "Davy's "Tower" 20 yards long, 13 broad, and about 20 high. It consisted of vaulted rooms in the ground story, and above these, four apartments of rooms of state and bed rooms, with vaulted closets or cabinets in the wall, which is 9 feet thick, with a broad and easy stair winding to the top. The whole Tower is vaulted at top, over which is a Cape-House, with a battlement round it. This Tower was built by Bishop David Stewart, who died anno 1475. Having some debates with the Earl of Huntley, he laid him under Ecclesiastic Censure, which provoked the Gordons so much, that they threatened to pull the Bishop out of his pigeon-holes, meaning the old little rooms. The Bishop is said to have replied, That he should soon build a House, out of which the Earl and his Clan should not be able to pull him.

 In the other three corners, stood small Towers with narrow rooms. In the South side of the area, betwixt the Towers, there was a spacious Tennis Court, and parallel to it on the inside a Chapel. The East side betwixt the Turrets, was planted with stables and other offices; and the North and West sides were filled up with Bed-rooms, Cellars, and Store-rooms. The Gate or Entry, was in the middle of the East wall, secured by an Iron Grate or Port Cullis. Over the gate stand the Arms of Bishop John Innes, who was consecrated anno 1406. viz. "Three Stars and the initial letters of his name." This affords a conjecture, but no certainty, that he was the first who built any part of that Court. In the South wall of Davy's Tower,

The Palace of Spynie Described.

are placed the Arms of Bishops David and Andrew Stewart, and Patrick Hepburn. The Precinct round this Palace was well fenced with a high and strong stone wall; and within it were gardens, plots of grass, and pleasant green walks. (See more concerning this Palace in the next Section). A Palace so large and stately required a good rent to uphold it, which leads me to speak of

The REVENUES of this BISHOPRIC.

REVENUES. It is probable, that, for some time after the erection, the Revenues were small. I find not any donations of King David I. or Malcolm IV. to this Church; but King William was a liberal benefactor; for besides a small toft or plot of ground in many Burroughs, he gave " Decimam meam de reditibus " meis de Moravia, et de placitis meis per totum Episcopatum " Moravienfem." And because the people were backward to pay these Teinds, it is added " Firmiter præcipio Balivis meis " de Moravia, ut ipsi, sine disturbatione, faciant Ricardo Epis- " copo, et suis successoribus, singulis annis, plenarie, et integre " habere prædictam decimam de reditibus meis." (*Chart. Morav.*) Severals of our Kings and great men afterwards granted Lands, Forrests, Fishings, &c. to this Church, and the Revenues of it became very rich. I cannot pretend to ascertain all the Church Lands within this Diocess, or the lands that belonged to it in Ross, Strathnaver, &c. The rental *(Appendix,* No. XXI.) shews, that the Church had lands in almost all the parishes within the Diocess, besides some parishes, as Birnie, Kenedar, Ogston, St Andrews, Laggan, that wholly belonged to it. The said Rental, is only the Annuity or Feu-duty, now paid out of these lands, of which the Bishop was formerly the proprietor, and received the whole real rent. But these rich

Revenues

Sect. 3.   THE ROMISH OR POPISH CHURCH.   287

Revenues were so dilapidated and sold, particularly by Bishop Patrick Hepburn, that, in the year 1563, when an account of all Ecclesiastic Benefices was taken, the rent of the Bishopric of Moray, as then given up, and recorded in the Book of Assumption, was as under:

Money	Wheat	Barley.	Oats.	Salmon.	Poultry
L. s. d.	Ch. B. F. P.	Ch. B. F. P.	Ch. B. F. P.	Lasts. Barrels.	No.
1649 7 7	0 10 0 0	77 6 2 2	7 8 0 0	8 0	223

The Lands, which in 1563 paid this rent, no doubt pay at this time more than L. 3000 Sterling. Besides, it was found, and complained of at that time, that full rents were not given up; and scarce one half of the lands of this Diocess remained unsold. To the Rental ought likewise to be added, the Revenue arising from the Regality of Spynie, and from the Commissariots of Moray and Inverness, which, before the Reformation, was very considerable. To shew the converted prices of Victual and other commodities, about the year 1563, I add the following Diagram, in Scots Money.

Wheat per boll.	Bear per boll.	Meal per boll.	Malt per boll.	Oats per boll.	Mutton No. 1.	Goose No. 1.	Capons per doz.	Poultry per doz.	Cheese pr. stone.	A Pork.	A Kid.	Salmon per bar.
L. s. d.	L. s. d.	L. s. d.	L. s. d.	L. s. d.	L. s. d.	L. s. d.	L. s. d.	L. s. d.	L. s. d.	L. s. d.	L. s. d.	L. s. d.
2 0 0	1 13 4	1 13 4	2 0 0	0 10 0	0 9 0	0 1 0	0 12 0	0 4 0	0 6 8	1 0 0	0 1 0	4 0 0

This view, though imperfect, of the Revenues of the Diocess of Moray, shews, that the Bishops might live as little Princes. And indeed, in imitation of the Princes of this world, as they had their Thrones and Palaces, so likewise their Ministers and Officers of State.

DIGNI-

DIGNIFIED CLERGY:

Dignified Clergy. The DIGNITARIES, or Dignified Clergy, who were honoured with a higher station than the Inferior Clergy, were the following five:

Dean. The DEAN, *Decanus*, who anciently presided over ten Cannons. In the Bishop's absence, he presided in the Chapter, in Synods, &c. The Minister of Aldern, was Dean of Moray.

Arch-Deacon. The ARCH-DEACON (with us the Minister of Forres) was *Alter Episcopi Oculus*; visited the Diocess, examined Candidates for Orders, gave Collation, &c. and was the Bishop's Vicar.

Chantor. The CHANTOR or PRIMICERIUS, (the Minister of Alves) regulated the Music, and, when present, presided in the Choir.

Chancellor. The CHANCELLOR, (the Minister of Inveravon) was the Judge of the Bishop's Court, the Secretary of the Chapter, and Keeper of their Seal.

Treasurer. The TREASURER (the Minister of Kenedar) had the charge of the Treasure or Common Revenues of the Diocess.

All these had rich livings, and Deputies to officiate for them; and, with some Canons, constituted the Bishop's Privy Council, or

Chapter. CHAPTER CAPITOLUM, or Little Head of the Diocess, the Bishop being the Head. Bishops of old had their Clergy residing with them, to assist them in their work; and after Parishes were erected, a Dean, with some Canons or Prebendaries, made the Chapter or Council. They advised and assisted the Bishop; signed with him all public acts and deeds: And in a vacancy elected, for Bishop, whom the King recommended by his *Conge de Elire*. The Chapter consisted of the Bishop, the Dignified Clergy, and Canons or Prebendaries chosen by the Bishop; and, in the Bishop's absence, the Dean presided.

Sect. 3.   THE ROMISH OR POPISH CHURCH.   289

INFERIOR CLERGY.

The INFERIOR CLERGY were, Parsons, Vicars, Ministers of Mensal Churches and Common Churches, and Chaplains. *Inferior Clegy.*

PARSONS were they who, *in propria persona*, had the right to the Tythes, and were the Ministers and Rectors of Parishes. What Parishes were Parsonages within this Diocess I cannot precisely determine, nor is it of importance to know. *Parsons.*

VICARS *fungebant vice Persone seu Rectoris.* To augment the revenues of the Bishop, the Dignified Clergy, and Canons, Parish Churches were annexed to the Churches in which these served, and they were the Rectors or Parsons of such Annexed Churches, *e. g.* The Minister of Aldern, as Dean, had Nairn and Calder annexed to his Parish; He was Parson of these Churches, had a right to the Tythes, and he sent Vicars to serve the Cure, to whom he allowed what portion of the Tythes he thought fit, as a Stipend; and hence they were called *Stipendiarii.* At first Vicars were employed only during pleasure, and were called "Simple Vicars." But the avarice of the Parson made the Cure to be much neglected in this way: Wherefore Vicars were afterwards settled for life, and called "Perpetual Vicars." They generally had the Small Tythes allowed them. The Parsons, who had Vicarages depending on them, claimed the Patronage of them; and hence it is, that after the Reformation, the Patron of the Parsonage acted as Patron of the Vicarage. *Vicars.*

MENSAL CHURCHES, were such as were *de mensa Episcopi,* for furnishing his table. He was Parson and Titular, and employed a Vicar or *Stipendiary* to serve the cure. Such Churches were, St Andrew's, Ogston, and Laggan, besides Mensal Tythes that the Bishop had in other parishes. (*Appendix,* No. XXXIII.) *Mensal Churches*

O o   The

The Bishop was Patron of all Mensal Churches, and planted them *jure proprio et absoluto*.

Common Churches. COMMON CHURCHES were so called, because the Tythes of them were the common good, or for the public and common exigencies of the Diocess. The Bishop and Chapter were Patrons, and concurred in planting them. We see (*Appendix*, No. XXXIII.) that Fernua, Laggan, Kinchardin, Abernethie, Altyre, Calder, and Arntullie, probably were Common Churches, and so was Daviot. Tho' the Tythes of these Churches were appointed for the public charges of the Diocess, yet it cannot be doubted that the Bishop and Chapter shared in them. This benefit at least they had, that they themselves laid out no part of their benefices in the common affairs of the Diocess.

Chapels of Ease. CHAPLAINS were those Clergy who officiated in Chapels; and these Chapels were of different kinds. In Parishes of great extent, Chapels of Ease were erected in distant corners, for the conveniency of the aged and infirm, and the Rector of the Parish maintained a Curate there to read prayers, and sing Masses. Vestiges of such Chapels are to be seen in many Parishes.

Free Chapels. Some Chapels were called FREE CHAPELS, which were not dependent on any Parish, but had proper endowments for their own Ministers, whose charge was called "A Chaplainry," and the Minister "A Parochial Chaplain." * Generally such Chapels as had Churches, Church-yards, and Glebes, were, I think, either Chapels of Ease, or Free Chapels.

Domestic Chapels Besides these, there were Domestic Chapels, or Oratories, built near the residence of great men, in which the Domestic Chaplain or Priest officiated. Such Chapels were at Calder, Kilravock, Boharm, &c. And almost in every parish there were

Private Chapels. PRIVATE CHAPELS, one or more, built by private persons, that Masses might be said or sung there for their own souls, and that

---

* Such, I think was the Chapel of Unthank in Duffus, of Langmorn (*Lhan-Morgan*) in Elgin, Dalefs in Calder parish.

Sect. 3.   THE ROMISH o POPISH CHURCH.   291

that of the Souls of their friends. Some small salary was mortified for that end, and usually granted to the Priest of the Parish. In the College of Elgin, I find the Private Chapels of St John, St Thomas, St Culen, and the Holy Cross.

The office of saying Mass in such Chapels, " was called Chantery, or Chanting Masses." The Salary for the Priest's officiating, or saying Mass at an Altar, was called ALTARAGE. The Service performed for the dead, how soon they expired, was the OBIT, and the Register of the Dead was called Obituary. In the first Antiphone of the Office of Obit, are the words *Dirige nos Domine*; and hence came the DIRGE. These, and the like, were shifts to increase the Revenue of the Clergy.

Altarage.

Obit.

Dirge.

GOVERNMENT of the DIOCESS.

Let us now take a view of the Government of the Diocess, both Clergy and Laity. The Bishop was properly the only Prince, Governor and Ruler, in whom alone the power of Jurisdiction was lodged; and for his conveniency he had Officers and Courts, Ecclesiastic, Civil, and Criminal. Of these Courts,

Government of the Diocess.

The CHAPTER was the principal one, in which, or rather in the Bishop, the Legislative power was lodged. The Bishop, with the advice of the Chapter, made Laws, Canons, and Regulations for the Diocess; erected, annexed or disjoined Parishes; purchased, sold, or sett in lease or tack Church Lands and Tythes, &c.

Chapter.

Diocesian Synods were sometimes called at the Bishop's pleasure. In these the Bishop presided, when present; and in his absence the Dean. Cases of Discipline, and appeals from Deanries, were cognosced in these Synodical meetings; and from them the Protestant Church took the plan of Provincial Synods.

Synod.

The Diocess was divided into Deanries. It appears (*Appendix*, No XXX.) that these Deanries were only four, viz. Of Elgin, of Inverness, of Strathbogoie, and of Strathipey. These seem to have

Deanries.

have been in some respects, what Presbyteries are now, and to have been the model on which Presbyteries have been formed.

Consistory. The Consistorial Court, to which the Commissariot succeeded, was held in the Bishop's name by his Official. This Court judged in all matters of Tythes, Marriages, Divorces, Widows, Orphans, Minors, Testaments, Mortifications, &c. I shall give an instance or two of the frauds that were countenanced in these Courts. The one is, That persons within the seventh degree of Consanguinity, or fourth of affinity, might not marry without a dispensation: But by a dispensation a man might marry the two sisters, or a woman the two brothers. It is incredible what money these Dispensations, whether Papal or Episcopal, brought in! No less shameful was it, that if one died intestate, all his moveable goods were given to the Bishop, *per aversionem*, and his wife, children and relations, yea, and creditors were excluded! The pretence for this vile practice was, that such effects ought to be laid out, for promoting the good of the Soul of the deceased. In this Diocess there were two Consistorial Courts, one at Elgin, the other at Inverness, which brought a rich branch of Revenue to the Bishop.

Regality. The Courts of Regality likewise added to the Bishop's Revenue. In 1452, King James II. erected the Village of Spynie in a free Barony, and all the Church Lands of the Diocess, into one Regality. The Bishop, as Lord of the Regality, had his Bailives and Deputes, in Aberdeen, Banff, Inverness, Ross and Sutherland counties, for in all these he had lands. In a word, such was the power and riches of the Clergy that Bishops, Abbots, and Priors made fifty-three votes in Parliament; and in all public impositions, paid one half of the taxation.

Arms of the See of Moray. The Arms of the See of Moray were, The Image of a Saint, bearing a Cross, and standing in the Porch of a Church.

Sect.

Sect. IV. *The Protestant Church.*

THE gross corruption of Doctrine, extreme indolence, most open and scandulous dissolution of manners, and barbarous cruelty of the ROMISH CLERGY in this Kingdom, concurred to bring about the Reformation of Religion, which was established by Parliament anno 1560. From that time, as the REGULAR CLERGY were suppressed, so the SECULAR had no legal establishment, though much connived at by the Royal House of STEWART.

PROTESTANT CHURCH.

The PROTESTANT Religion was gradually propagated, and the number of its Ministers being at first very small, some years must have passed before the Northern Counties could be planted. I shall not here treat of the Doctrine and Worship of the Reformed Church in this Kingdom, any further, than briefly to consider the Changes that happened, as PRESBYTERY or PRELACY alternately prevailed in the Government of the Church. And let me glance at.

1st, The Several PERIODS since the REFORMATION.

I. PERIOD.

The first Period reaches from anno 1560 to 1572, during which PRESBYTERY was the Government of the Church. It is true, the few Protestant Ministers at the Reformation were distributed among the Royal Burghs, and made it more their concern, to establish and propagate the pure Doctrines of Religion, than to determine and fix any one model or form of Church Government. And until the Government should be deliberately

I. Period, 1560—1672.

deliberately settled, a few SUPERINTENDANTS were appointed. But these could, in no propriety, be called BISHOPS, such as were under Popery, or in some after-Periods of the Reformation; for they had no Episcopal Consecration; They were Solemnly set apart to their Office by mere Presbyters; They neither claimed, nor exercised a sole power of Ordination or Jurisdiction; They never pretended to be an Order superior to Presbyters; They were accountable to, and censured by the General Assembly; And, what shews they were but a temporary expedient, there were but five named, of which number, when one died, there was no successor to him appointed. And when Presbyteries were erected, the Superintendant's office ceased.

SUPERINTEN-DANTS.

Where there were no Superintendants, COMMISSIONERS were appointed; and Mr Robert Pont, a Senator of the College of Justice, was named Commissioner of Moray, anno 1570 (*Appendix*, No. XLVI.) But I know not if he acted as such.

COMMISSIONERS.

GENERAL ASSEMBLIES began to be kept in 1560, and were continued annually. But how soon PROVINCIAL ASSEMBLIES were kept, I find not. It could not have been early, for want of Ministers to make such a meeting in some Provinces; and yet the ASSEMBLY 1568 appointed, "That the Members of "ASSEMBLY should be elected at the meetings of SYNOD," which makes it probable, that SYNODS were generally erected at that time. The oldest Register of a SYNOD in Moray, of which I can find any account, began in 1606. How long before that time they had Synods, I know not.

ASSEMBLIES.

SYNODS.

There were no PRESBYTERIES, such as they are now, within this Period. But there were meetings for Exercise very early; and the ASSEMBLY, 1579, expressly says, "That the Exercise "may be accounted a PRESBYTERY."

PRESBYTERIES.

As to CONGREGATIONAL SESSIONS, they were held from the beginning of the Reformation, and exercised Government

SESSIONS.

and

and Discipline. It is no marvel, if, in this infant state of the Church, the Government was not fully established; yet the constitution of it was plainly PRESBYTERIAN, and inconsistent with PRELACY.

II. PERIOD.

The second Period runneth from anno 1572 to 1592, during which a sort of EPISCOPACY obtained in the Church. During the Regency of the Earl of Moray, no alteration in the Ecclesiastic Government was attempted. But how soon the Earl of Morton (a man of insatiable avarice) became Regent, he brought about a change. The Popish Bishops, who were allowed two thirds of their Revenues during life, were generally dead. Morton obtained a grant of the Temporalities of the Archbishopric of St Andrews: Other Noblemen procured, or hoped to procure, the like Grants. But they could not enjoy these Revenues directly, with any colour in Law; wherefore Morton got it agreed, in a meeting of some ambitious men of the Clergy, and a Committee of the Privy Council, "That the " name and office of ARCHBISHOP and BISHOP should be " continued during the King's minority, but subject to the " ASSEMBLY as to their Spiritual Jurisdiction." These Bishops, introduced anno 1572, were, by way of ridicule, but justly called, "Tulchan Bishops." A *Tulchan* was, the Skin of a Dead Calf, stretched on a frame of wood, and laid under a Cow, to make her give milk: And these Bishops had the name, that by a private agreement, and allowing them a small benefice, the Dioceses might yield their milk or Revenues to the Noblemen.

This Regent further gratified his avarice at the expence of the Clergy. In the year 1561, a part of the Thirds of Ecclesiastic

II. Period, 1572—1592.

Tulchan Bishops

tic Benefices was allowed to the Protestant Clergy for their subsistence; but this came to be very ill paid. Morton got the Clergy to resign the Thirds in his favour, and he promised duely to pay their Stipendiary allowance. But he assigned three or four Churches to one Minister, with the stipend of only one Church, and applied the rest to his own uses.

These *Tulchan* or Nominal Bishops, had possession of the Episcopal Palaces; had their Chapters, and both Consistorial and Regality Jurisdictions. But they were in no proper sense BISHOPS; They were admitted or consecrated by Presbyters, and were subject to, and deposed by the Assemblies. The Government of the Church was really Presbyterian, by General Assemblies, and Provincial Synods. And in 1581, the Assembly declared the office of BISHOP, as then exercised within the Realm, to have no foundation or warrant in the Word of GOD; and Presbyteries were erected throughout the Kingdom, whereof there were three in Moray, viz. The Presbyteries of Elgin, of Forres, and of Inverness. Notwithstanding this, the Titular Bishops continued till the year 1592.

PRESBYTERIES Erected.

III. PERIOD.

III. Period, 1592—1610. PRESBYTERIAN GOVERNMENT established.

The third Period from anno 1592 to 1610, was strictly Presbyterian. The *Tulchan* Bishops having titles of honour, a seat in Parliament, with Revenues or Stipends somewhat greater than other Ministers, had neglected their spiritual employments, were despised by the Gentry, and considered as profane by the Populace. Yet King James VI. would gladly have continued them, as a set of men slavishly devoted to him, and to whom they owed their promotion. The King himself, by his partial favour to Papists, and his shameful conduct in the affair of MORAY's murder, had sunk greatly in his character,

and

Sect. 4.   THE PROTESTANT CHURCH.   297

and the Chancellor (SEATON) was become odious, as to him was imputed the King's Conduct. For thefe reafons the King favoured the Clergy, and eftablifhed the Prefbyterian Government in the moft ample manner, by an Act of Parliament Anno 1592.

A new divifion was now made of the Church, into SYNODS and PRESBYTERIES: and, in Moray four Prefbyteries were appointed, viz. Invernefs, Forres, Elgin, and Ruthven. By this laft, I think, is meant the Prefbytery of Strathboggie, which might be appointed to meet at Ruthven or Cairnie.

The Church did not long enjoy the peaceable exercife of this Government. The King wanted much to have Bifhops reftored to their full power, as fome fort of a ballance to the Nobles in Parliament; But they were become fo odious, that he was afraid to revive the Order. Yet, by flattery, promifes or threats, he got a Majority of the Clergy to agree, Anno 1597 and 1598, that fome Minifters fhould reprefent the Church in Parliament. After that he obtained to have conftant Moderators in Prefbyteries. And upon his acceffion to the Throne of England, defirous to eftablifh a Hierarchy in Scotland, He, by an Act of Parliament 9th July 1606, reftored the Temporalities of Bifhops, and granted them a feat in Parliament. In confequence of this Act, thofe whom the King named, acted as Bifhops; but it was not before the year 1610, that a packt General Affembly allowed the office of a Bifhop: I fay, " a packt General Affembly ;" for Sir James Balfour, in his M. S. Annals, Vol. I. relates, " That, in the Ge-
" neral Affembly held at Linlithgow, anno 1606, the Earl
" of Dunbar diftributed, among the moft needy and clamo-
" rous of the Minifters, 40,000 Merks, to facilitate the work,
" and obtain their Suffrages. And, anno 1610, after the
" Affembly was up, the Earl of Dunbar paid L. 5000 Scots to

Overturned.

P p   " the

"the Moderators of Presbyteries for bygone service." Thus, by bribing, banishing, intimidating, and imprisoning Ministers, the Presbyterian Government of the Church was overturned.

IV. PERIOD.

IV. Period. 1610—1638. Episcopacy re-established

The Fourth Period, from anno 1610 to 1638. The General Assembly at Glasgow, anno 1610, having enacted, that Episcopacy shall be the Government of the Church, Spottiswood, Lamb, and Hamilton, Ministers, were brought up to London to be consecrated. They objected, That this might be construed, a subjecting the Church of Scotland to that of England. No, replied the King; for the Archbishops shall have no hand in it. A poor reason, yet it satisfied them. Then Bishop Andrews moved, That they should be first ordained Presbyters, because they had not Episcopal Ordination. Although such Re-Ordination would be a declaring all their former Ministrations null, yet, so forward were they to obtain the Dignity of Bishops, that they made no objection. But the Archbishop of Canterbury answered, That there was no necessity, because Ordination by Presbyters is Lawful, where Bishops cannot be had; else it might be doubted, if there was a Lawful Mission in most of the Reformed Churches. Upon this they were consecrated by the Bishops of London, Ely, and Bath; and upon their return to Scotland, they consecrated others. Here let me observe, That according to the Laudean and Bodwelian Zealots, these Bishops were made *per Saltum*, and so their Ministrations were null. Be this as it may, the Civil Sanction was given, anno 1612, to this change of Government. But the new Bishops were charactized in the following Verses:

Vina

Sect. 4. THE PROTESTANT CHURCH 299

* *Vina amat* Andreas, *cum vino* Glasgua *amores,*
 Ross *cætus, ludos* Galva, Brichæus *opes.*
Aulam Orcas, *ollam* Moravus, *parit* Insula *fraudes,*
 Dumblanus *tricas, nomen* Aberdonius.
Fata Caledonius *fraterni ruminat agri,*
 Rarus adis Parochos, O Catanæe, *tuos.*
Solus in Argadiis Presul *meritissimus oris,*
 Vera Ministerii symbola solus habes.

During the life of King James VI. the subordination of Judicatories was regularly kept up, and the Bishops, afraid of General Assemblies, kept within some bounds of moderation and decency. But how soon King Charles mounted the Throne, Synods and Presbyteries were continued, but Assemblies were quite laid aside. Then the young Bishops, having no check or controul, became proud, ambitious, and idle, encouraged Tyranny in the State, and Innovations (both in Doctrine and Worship) in the Church. King James, having in vain tried to introduce the English Liturgy into Scotland, dropt the design. But his Son, governed by fiery Zealots, would rather set the three Kingdoms in a flame, than fail in bringing the Church of Scotland into a full conformity with that of England. The Bishops became so hateful, that all ranks concurred in throwing them out; and the King finding it necessary to call a General Assembly, anno 1638, that meeting condemned Episcopacy, deposed six of the Bishops, and both deposed and excommunicated the other eight.

Condemned.

With

---

* "The Bishop of St. ANDREWS was fond of Wine; GLASGOW of Wine and Amours;
"Ross delighted in Company; GALLOWAY in Diversions; and BRECHIN in Riches;
"ORKNEY haunted the Court; and MORAY the Kitchen; the BISHOP of the ISLES con-
"trived Frauds; DUNBLANE loved Trifles, and ABERDEEN a Name; DUNKELD coveted
"his neighbours Land; CAITHNESS was seldom with his Flock.——The Bishop of
"ARGYLE was the only worthy Clergyman, and had alone the true Symbols of the Mi-
"nisterial office."

With respect to the Province of MORAY, I find no alteration in this Period, but what was the Consequence of the change of Government, from Presbytery to Prelacy; except that two new Presbyteries, viz. Aberlaure and Abernethie, were erected.

V. PERIOD.

**V Period.
1638—1662.
PRESBYTE-
RY rivived.**

The fifth Period, from anno 1638 to 1662. The General Assembly 1638 having condemned Episcopacy, at least in this Church, and having revived the exercise of Presbyterian Government in its full vigour; the bad circumstances of the King's affairs, and not his own inclination, made him, in Parliament 1641, ratify this Change. Then the Clergy discovered how difficult it was for them, when vested with power, to behave with moderation. What they loudly complained of under the foregoing Period, they themselves now violently run into. They complained, that the King and Bishops would impose upon the Church of Scotland the Liturgy of the Church of England, or worse; and now, by the Solemn League and Covenant, they would impose the Government and Worship of the Church of Scotland, upon the Churches of England and Ireland. During this Period, General Assemblies were annually kept, till anno 1653: When the Assembly was constituted on July 16th that year, a troop of Horse and some companies of Foot surrounded the house, and Colonel Lilburn entered with a File of Musketeers, and bid them be-gone; which they obeyed. From this time, till anno 1690, there was not a meeting of the General Assembly.

The Division of the Clergy into *Resolutioners* and *Protesters*, proved fatal to them. Their Commissioners, particularly Mr James Sharp, whom they employed at London, to take care of the interest of the Church, treacherously betrayed them; and King Charles II. who was no more to be trusted than his fa-

ther

ther or grand father had been, wrote, by Mr Sharp, to Mr Robert Douglas the letter following:

"Whitehall, August 10th, 1660.

"CHARLES REX, Trusty and well beloved: We "graciously accepted your Address, and we are well satisfied "with your carriages, and with the generality of the Ministers "of Scotland, in this time of trial. We by this assure you, that "we resolve to discountenance profanity, and all Contemners "of Gospel Ordinances; and to protect, and preserve the Go"vernment of the Church of Scotland, as it is settled by Law, "without violation. This you shall make known to all "Presbyteries in the Church."

This letter was Mr Sharp's contrivance; and the Jesuitical equivocation in the words, "As Settled by Law," was unworthy of a Prince; for next year, by the Act Rescissory, all was rescinded and annulled, that had been transacted in Parliament since the year 1633; and so the Government Settled by Law, was EPISCOPACY, as practised before 1633.

Overturned

VI. PERIOD.

The sixth Period, from anno 1662 to 1690. The Government of the Church by Bishops was now restored, not by the Church or the State, the Clergy or Laity, but by the King's Prerogative Royal, and was ratified in Parliament anno 1662. The four Gentlemen now consecrated Bishops at London, were first ordained Deacons and Presbyters; a tacite confession, that former Bishops were properly no Bishops. No General Assembly was called during this Period; but Synods and Presbyteries were allowed to meet; yet not by these Presbyterian names, for now they were called "Diocesian Assemblies and Exercises." A Popish King and a Profane Ministry warmly resented the severities under the late Usurpation; and the new Bishops, formerly

VI Period. 1662—1690

Prelacy Restored.

merly Presbyterians and Covenanters, would tolerate no man, that would not thoroughly conform to both Church and State.

Ministers Ejected.

This brought on a Persecution that lasted during this Period. In the year 1663, about 400 hundred Ministers were ejected out of their parishes and livings, because they would not swear to Despotism in the State, and Prelacy in the Church. Such as have curiously enquired into the number of sufferers for non-conformity to Church and State during this Period, have calculated, that by hanging, drowning, tumults, intercommuning, imprisoning, and banishing, at least 18,000 were cut off. In England, the Persecution for non-conformity was, for a time, very hot. But when James laid aside the mask, and shewed his design of introducing Popery, the Bishops and Doctors made a faithful and firm stand for the Protestant Religion, and heartily joined in maintaining it.

Conduct of Bishops.

But in Scotland, the Bishops became abject Flatterers of that Popish King, and seemed to wish for Popery and Slavery; for when they heard of the Prince of Orange's expedition, for preserving Religion and Liberty in Britain, they wrote a letter to their King, dated November 3d 1688, in which they did not once mention the Protestant Religion, but prayed, " That " God might give him the necks of his enemies, and clothe " with shame all who should invade his rights, and that Hea- " ven might preserve his son, to sway the Royal Sceptre after " him." This letter was signed by all the Bishops, except Argyle and Caithness. (*Appendix*, No. L.)

Upon the Prince of Orange's landing, and King James's abdicating the Throne, and flying to France, the people in the West, who had been rendered mad by oppression and persecution, became unruly, and violently drove away many of the Episcopal Ministers, who had been too much the authors of their sufferings. And upon the 11th April 1689, the Convention

Sect. 4. THE PROTESTANT CHURCH.

tion of Estates (consisting of two Dukes, two Marquises, twenty-eight Earls, six Viscounts, twenty-one Lords, and fifty Commissioners of Counties and Burroughs, and some Bishops) "declared Prelacy a great and insupportable grievance to the nation, and that it ought to be abolished." This declaration was carried by so great a majority, that there were only eleven against it, whereof seven were Bishops.

Prelacy a Grievance.

In this Period, there was nothing peculiar to the Province of Moray, but what shall be taken notice of in some General Remarks, after I have spoken a little concerning

VII. PERIOD.

The seventh Period, which runneth from the year 1690 to the present time. In the year 1690, the Presbyterian Government was restored, and established by Parliament, and that year the General Assembly met, after it had been discontinued ever since the year 1652. The Episcopal Ministers now conformed generally to the Civil Government, and were indulged to keep their Churches and Benefices during life. By this means the number of Presbyterian Ministers in the Diocess of Moray was so small, that they made but one Presbytery, called "The Presbytery of Moray," till the year 1702. Before this year they had no meeting of Synod; but in March 1702, the Commission of the Assembly recommended to them to meet in Synod. In pursuance of which, in a meeting at Forres 23d June 1702, they erected themselves into three Presbyteries, viz. the united Presbytery of Inverness and Forres; the united Presbytery of Elgin, Aberlaure, and Abernethie; and the Presbytery of Strathboggie. In October the same year, they met in Synod for the first time. The number of Ministers soon increasing, by the demise of the Episcopal Incumbents,

VII. Period. 1690 — to the present Time.

Presbytery established.

Presbytery of Moray.

Synod.

Aber-

Aberlaure and Abernethie were disjoined from Elgin anno 1707, and made a distinct Presbytery. In 1708, Inverness and Forres became two Presbyteries; and in 1709, Aberlaure and Abernethie were disjoined, and made two Presbyteries. In 1706, the Assembly annexed Mortlich to the Synod of Moray. And in the year 1724, the Assembly having erected a new Synod, called " The Synod of Glenelg," the parishes of Laggan, Bolesken, and Urquhart, were disjoined from the Synod of Moray, and included in that new Synod. I shall now close this Section with a few REMARKS.

Glenelg Synod.

I. REMARK. Upon perusing the ECCLESIASTIC Records, it is apparent, that True, Rational, Christian Knowledge, which was almost quite lost under Popery, made very slow progress after the Reformation. It was long before Ministers could be had to plant the several corners, and particularly the Highlands. In the year 1650, the Country of Lochaber was totally desolate, and no Protestant Ministers had before that time been planted there. And when the number of Ministers increased, very few of them understood the Irish Language, and Teachers were settled in the Highlands, who were mere Barbarians to the People: Thro' want of Schools, few had any Literary Education; and they who had, would not dedicate themselves to the Ministry, when the Livings were so poor as not to afford Bread.

Slow Progress of Knowledge.

Hence Ignorance prevailed in every corner. To which, besides the want of Public Teachers, many things contributed. The number of Papists was great: They who professed the Protestant Religion retained strong prejudices in favour of the Religion of their Ancestors: Popish profaneness and irreligion, too grateful to flesh and blood, could not soon be abolished. So little was the Lord's-Day regarded, that in the town of Elgin, in the year 1591, their annual Fairs were held on that day;

Ignorance prevailing.

Sect. 4.   THE PROTESTANT CHURCH.   305

day; and many years after, the shops were open on that day for buying and selling.

The unsettled state of the nation increased this Ignorance. During the Reign of King James VI. Tumults, Insurrections, Violence, Murder and Blood-shed, filled the Land. The Civil Wars, in the Reign of his Son, turned Church and State into the utmost confusion; and under the Reign of the two Royal Brothers, the high ambition was, to root out the Northern Heresy, and to re-establish Popery in our land.   *Unsettled State of the Nation.*

The Changes in the Doctrines and Government of the Church, likewise nourished ignorance and vice. Our Reformers taught the Calvinistic Doctrine, and settled Presbyterian Government. But King James VI. overturned that Government; and sought to abolish that Doctrine. His Son made further advances in these changes. Arminianism became the favourite scheme of Doctrine; and Episcopacy, absolutely necessary to Salvation, the plan of Government. During the Usurpation, Enthusiasm and Anarchy prevailed: And with the Restoration, Deism, and a general dissolution of manners, like a flood, came in; the transition from one extreme to another being easy and common.   *Changes in the CHURCH.*

The Reign of Charles II. is well described by Mr POPE in the following lines.

> In the fat age of Pleasure, Wealth and Ease,
> Sprung the rank weed, and thriv'd with large increase;
> When Love was all an easy Monarch's Care,
> Seldom at Council, never in a War.
> Tilts ruled the State, and Statesmen farces writ,
> Nay Wits had Pensions, and Young Lords had Wit:
> The Fair sat panting at a Courtier's Play,
> And not a Mask went unimprov'd away:
> The modest Fan was lifted up no more,
> And Virgins smil'd at what they blush'd before.

Q q   The

Conduct of the Clergy. The conduct of the Clergy had a bad influence. When the Presbyterians ruled, they exercised too little prudence, charity or discretion: And when the Bishops governed, they encouraged Persecution and Bloodshed. These having no Superiors (no General Assemblies to restrain them) but the King, whose creatures they were, became proud and insolent, little regarded any concernments of the Church except their own power and revenues, and quite neglected the means of diffusing and propagating the Knowledge of Religion and Virtue; in so much, that there were scarce any Schools of Learning in this Province, except in Royal Burghs, till after the Revolution. I well remember, when from Spey-mouth (through Strath-Spey, Badenoch and Lochaber) to Lorn, there was but one School, viz. at Ruthven in Badenoch; and it was much to find, in a parish, three persons that could read or write.

Superstition. Such prevailing Ignorance was attended with much Superstition and Credulity. Heathenish and Romish customs were much practised. Pilgrimages to Wells and Chapels were frequent. **Apparitions.** Apparitions were every where talked of and believed. Particular Families were said to be haunted by certain Demons, the good or bad Genius's of these Families: Such as; on Spey-side, the Family of Rothemurchus, by *Bodach an Dun, i. e.* "The "Ghost of the Dune." The Baron of Kinchardine's Family, by *Red Hand,* or "A Ghost one of whose hands was blood-red." Gartinbeg by *Bodach-Gartin.* Glenlochie, by *Brownie.* Tullochgorm, by *Maag Moulach, i. e.* "One with the left hand all over hairy." I find in the Synod Records of Moray, frequent orders to the Presbyteries of Aberlaure and Abernethie, to enquire into the truth of *Maag Moulach's* appearing: But they could make no discovery, only that one or two men declared, they once saw, in the evening, a Young Girl, whose left hand was all hairy, and who instantly disappeared.

Almost

Sect. 4.   THE PROTESTANT CHURCH.   307

Almost every large Common was said to have a Circle of FAIRIES. Fairies belonging to it. Separate Hillocks upon plains, were called *Sigh an*, *i. e.* "Fairy Hills." Scarce a Shepherd but had seen Apparitions and Ghosts. Charms, casting nativities, cur- CHARMS. ing diseases by inchantments, Fortune-telling, were commonly practised, and firmly believed: As Dr GARTH well describes the Goddess Fortune,

> *In this still Labyrinth around her lye,*
> *Spells, philters, globes, and schemes of Palmistry;*
> *A Sigil, in this hand, the Gipsy bears,*
> *In t'other a prophetic Sieve and Shears.*

Witches were said to hold their nocturnal meetings in WITCHES. Churches, Church-Yards, or in lonely places; and to be often transformed into Hares, Mares, Cats; to ride through the Regions of the Air, and to travel into distant Countries; to inflict Diseases, raise storms and tempests: And for such incredible feats, many were tried, tortured and burnt. If any one was afflicted with Hysterics, Hypochondria, Rheumatisms, or the like acute Diseases, it was called Witch-craft: And it was sufficient to suspect a Woman for Witch-craft, if she was poor, old, ignorant and ugly. These effects of ignorance were so frequent within my memory, that I have often seen all persons above twelve years of age solemnly sworn four times in the year, that they would practise no Witch-craft, Charms, Spells, &c.

It was likewise believed, that Ghosts or departed souls, of- GHOSTS. ten returned to this world, to warn their friends of approaching danger, to discover murders, to find lost goods, &c. That Children dying unbaptized (called TARANS) wandered in TARANS. woods and solitudes, lamenting their hard fate, and were often seen. It cannot be doubted, that many of these stories concerning Apparitions, Tarans, &c. came out of the Cloysters of Monks and Friars, or were the Invention of designing Priests.

Priests, who deluded the World with their stories of *Purgatory* and *Limbus Infantum*. But after the Revolution, the most distant Corners being planted with Ministers, Schools erected in almost every Parish, Charity-Shools set up for instructing the Poor; Christian Knowledge propagated, and Natural Philosophy much improved; Ignorance was gradually removed, and Superstition lost Credit. Apparitions, Fairies, Witches, Tarans, have disappeared; and few regard the stories concerning them, except stupid old people who cannot shake off their Prejudices, and begotted Papists who give implicite faith to their Priests.

II. REMARK.

Church Government.

It appears all along since the Reformation, that the Clergy either looked on Church Government as alterable or ambulatory, or made little account of the difference betwixt Presbytery and Episcopacy, notwithstanding their wrangling about the *Jus Divinum*. The zealous Prelatists, before 1638, fully complied with Presbytery and the Covenant: And the bigotted Covenanters as readily complied with Prelacy in 1662. And if, at the Revolution, few conformed to Presbytery, it was, because they were allowed their Benefices for Life, upon qualifying to the Civil Government, and their not conforming to the Ecclesiastic Government eased them of considerable expences, in attending upon Judicatories, paying *Centesimas*, &c.

III. REMARK.

Ambition of the Clergy.

One cannot but observe, that the Clergy of both Denominations are too ambitious of power, and ready to abuse it into severity and persecution. In time of Presbytery, after the year 1638, Ministers who would not subscribe the Covenant, or who conversed with the Marquis of Huntly, or the Marquis of Montrose, or who took a protection from them, were suspended, deprived or deposed: And Gentlemen, who took part with

Huntley

Huntly or Montrose, were tossed from one Judicatory to another, made to undergo a mock-penance in Sack-Cloth, and to swear to the Covenant. Under Prelacy, on the other hand, after the Restoration, the Presbyterians, and all who opposed Court Measures, had no enemies more virulent than the Clergy. They informed against them, made the Court raise a cruel persecution, and make insidious and sanguinary Laws for Fineing, Imprisoning, Intercommuning, Hanging, &c. It is never better with Religion, than when the Clergy are entrusted with little power, and have no share in the Civil Administrations.

IV. REMARK. Excommunication.

Under both Presbytery and Prelacy, they brought the high Censure of Excommunication into Contempt, by the frequency of it, and applying it to improper objects. Ladies of Quality were excommunicated, purely because they were Papists or Quakers, though otherwise regular and moral. And yet such Time-Servers were they, that the most zealous against Popery before the Restoration, after it, became cold and faint, knowing the Disposition of the Court.

V. REMARK. Sacrament.

In the year 1600, by Act of Parliament, all Persons were required to partake of the Sacrament of the Supper once in the year, under these Penalties: An Earl, L. 1000. A Lord, 1000 Merks. A Baron, 300 Merks. A Yeoman, L. 40. A Burgess, as the Council shall modify. I am not surprized, that such an Act was made by that King, especially, as it was made upon pretence of obliging Papists (a strange way of converting them) to become Protestants. But it is shameful to find the Clergy zealous in executing this Profane Law, and prostituting an Ordinance so Sacred. Yet this they did, both under Prelacy and Presbytery.

Always,

VI. Remark. Always, upon the Eſtabliſhing of Epiſcopacy, Miniſters were ſtrictly prohibited by the Biſhops, to marry any Widower or Widow, till the Teſtament of the former Huſband or Wife was confirmed: And they were required to remit quarterly to the Commiſſioners, Liſts of all dying within their Pariſhes. It was pretended, that this was done for the Benefit of the Children and near Relations: But it was, in truth, for the Benefit of the Biſhop: And the Parliament 1690 aboliſhed this avaricious, cruel, Popiſh practice, of robbing poor Widows and Children; and now no one needs confirm, unleſs he inclines.

VII. Remark. The moderation and lenity of the Civil Government ſince the Revolution, compared with former Reigns, is very obſervable. In former Periods, whatever was the Church Government eſtabliſhed by Law, no diſſenting from it, or non-conformity to it, was connived at; far leſs was it tolerated. Diſſenters, I mean Proteſtants, were oppreſſed and perſecuted. But now Papiſts are connived at, Prelatiſts have a legal toleration in their favour; and they, who on account of their Jacobite principles, will not accept of it, are connived at, and ſuffered to keep their private meetings for Worſhip. And tho' the Eſtabliſhed Church is rent by Seceders, Cameronians, MacMillanites, Glaſſites, &c. yet no Sect is diſturbed or oppreſſed. I ſhall cloſe this Section with one Remark more, viz.

VIII. Remark. The conduct of the Epiſcopal Clergy, at and ſince the Revolution. In June 1690, the Parliament eſtabliſhed Preſbytery as the Government of the Church, and required all the Epiſcopal Miniſters, who would remain in their Charges, not only to ſwear the Alledgeance, but to ſubſcribe the Aſſurance, " Own-
" ing King William and Queen Mary as the only lawful King
" and Queen of this Realm, as well *de jure* as *de facto*, and
" promiſing

"promising to maintain, and defend their Title and Govern-
"ment against the late King James, &c." This they brought
upon themselves, by their Jesuitical distinction of *de jure* and
de facto. The Parliament likewise considered, That the Episcopal Clergy who qualified to the Government, and so continued in office, were more numerous than the Presbyterian
Ministers, and, if admitted to a share in the Government,
would over-ballance these: Therefore the Parliament committed the Government to those Ministers, now alive, who had
been ejected since January 1661, and to such as they did or
should admit. Of these consisted the Assembly which met in
October 1690. Few more were yet ordained: In the North,
the Episcopal Clergy generally qualified to the Government,
and kept their Churches. In the Diocess of Moray upwards of
forty did so.

These Episcopal Ministers, though qualified to the Government, joined the Jacobite Laity, in endeavouring to restore
their King and Episcopacy. In order to this last, it was con-
trived, that a Body of Episcopal Ministers, more numerous
than the Presbyterians, should apply to the next General
Assembly, to be received into a Coalition, upon such terms,
as they thought, could not be refused. If received, they hoped soon to overturn Presbytery. If rejected, they would represent the Presbyterians to the King and Parliament, as of an
unpeaceable, seditious, and persecuting spirit, and hoped in
this way to succeed. And if Prelacy was once restored, they
would work up the Nation to a new Revolution. This scheme
seems to have been formed by the Viscount of Tarbet *(vid.
Birch's Life of Archbishop Tillotson,* 1752) a Nobleman of some
learning, but of less integrity, who insinuated himself into
King William's favour, and yet lived and died a keen Jacobite. The Scots Bishops communicated a part of this design

to

to the English Bishops. They, together with Lord Tarbet, prevailed with the King, who was a stranger, to defer calling an Assembly in 1691, for the sake of peace, as they pretended; but in fact that their scheme might be ripened.

All things being now ready, an Assembly was called to meet in January 1692, and the King in his Letter recommended to receive, into a share in the Government, all who should desire to be thus comprehended. Then Dr Canaries, at the head of 180 Episcopal Ministers, and in the name of many more, appeared and desired to be received, and they would subscribe the following Formula: " I, A. B. do sincerely promise, and declare, that I will submit to the Presbyterian Government of the Church, as it is now established in this Kingdom, and that I will subscribe the Confession of Faith, and the Larger and Shorter Catechisms ratified by act of Parliament in the year 1690, as containing the Doctrine of the Protestant Religion professed in this Kingdom."

The Assembly knew Dr Canarie's character; they saw the design of these men was no more, than what a Jesuit, or a Mahometan, might offer. These men did not promise to believe the Doctrine, and not to overturn the Government of the Church. In short, such equivocation was condemned, and their offer was rejected. Upon this Canaries appealed to the King for redress; and the Earl of Lothian Commissioner dissolved the meeting *sine die*. But the Assembly asserted unanimously the right of the Church, and appointed the time of their next meeting.

The Jacobites now hoped to triumph, but were disappointed. Their designs were seen into: The King was undeceived; and the Parliament having met in April 1693 ordained, " That no one be admitted or continued a Minister or Preacher, till he first subscribe the Alledgeance and Assurance; also
" subscribe

Sect. 4. THE PROTESTANT CHURCH.

"subscribe the Confession of Faith as the Confession of his "Faith, and own the Doctrine therein contained to be the "true Doctrine, to which he will constantly adhere; and like- "wise own Presbyterian Church Government, submit thereto, "and never endeavour, directly or indirectly, the prejudice or "subversion thereof, and observe the Worship as at present "performed; and that they apply in an orderly way, each man "for himself, to be admitted." The Parliament likewise addressed his Majesty to call an Assembly, which he did, and they met in March 1694, and drew up a Formula, agreeable to the Act of Parliament, offering to receive all who would subscribe it.

Few complied with the Act of Parliament. Many qualified to the Civil Government, and kept their Churches without molestation. But the zealous Jacobites would not conform to Church or State. Some of them continued in their Churches by the favour of Jacobite Patrons or Heritors. Some intruded into vacant Churches; and some set up Private Meetings. The Union of the two Kingdoms, anno 1707, secured the legal establishment of the Church; yet an almost unlimited toleration was granted, anno 1712, to the Episcopal Clergy. But as it required them to abjure the Popish Pretender, very few took the Benefit of it. They kept up their Unqualified Meetings, and looked for some Revolution that would dissolve the Union. This was nearly effected in the end of Queen Ann's Reign; and being disappointed by her death, they heartily joined in the Rebellion anno 1715, and thereafter in the year 1745.

These being crushed, they seemed to despond, and published and dispersed the following elegant, but virulent, Threnodia, in the style of a Monumental Inscription, which exhibites a lively picture of High Church.

The Notes at the foot of the page will serve as a Key to it.

(1.) 𝔐. 𝔐. ℭ. 𝔖. ℭ. 𝔖.

Sifte Viator, lege et luge,
Miraculum nequitiæ.
Sub hoc marmore conduntur Reliquiæ
(2.) Matris admodum venerabilis,
(Secreto Jaceat, ne admodum proftituatur!)
Quæ mortua fuit dum viva,
Et viva dum mortua.
O facinus impium et incredibile!
(3.) Defenfore nequiffime orbata,
(4.) Tyrannis miferrime oppreffa,
(5.) Proceribus vicini regni Infulatis
(referens tremifco) nefarie obruta;
(6.) Aulicis impie afflicta,
(7.) Filiis nonnullis perfide deferta,
(8.) Spuriis omnibus peffime calcata, trucidata, ludibrio habita:
Sacrificium fuffragiis τῶν πολλῶν,
(Ne dicam τῶν παντῶν,)
Votivum, et Phanaticorum furore!
Rogas,
Quanam in terra hoc?
In Infula,
Ubi Monarcha contra Monarchiam,

Ecclefiaftici

(1.) Memoriæ Martris Chariffimæ Scoticanæ Ecclefiæ Sacrum.
(2) High Church.   (3) The Popifh King James VII.
(4.) Kings William, George I. and George II.
(5) The Bifhops of England.   (6) The Miniftry.
(7.) The Oppofers of the Ufages.   (8.) The Church of Scotland.

Sect. 4. THE PROTESTANT CHURCH.

Ecclesiastici contra Ecclesiam,
Legislatores contra Legem,
Judices contra Justitiam,
Concionatores, Atheistice, contra veritatem,
Milites audaciter, impudenter, (9) Wilhelmo Neroniano Duce,
Contra honorem, contra humanitatem
Agunt.
Pudet hæc opprobria nobis!
Nam propter exsecrationem, perjurium, luget hæc Terra!
In cujus testimonium multi equidem sunt Testes vivi et recentiores.
Apage! Apage!
Ægrotavit, proh dolor! Mater charissima, beatæ memoriæ,
(10.) Anno MDCLXXXVIII.
Tum manibus, tum pedibus, væ mihi, clauda fiebat
(11.) Anno MDCCVII.
Tandem per multis flagellis, ærumnis, miserere mei Deus! exhausta,
(12.) Obiit Anno MDCCXLVIII.
Vos omnes Seniores, Filii Filiæque
(13) Orate pro ea, ut quiescat in pace, et tandem beatam obtineat
Resurrectionem.   Amen.

Cum temerata fides, pietasque inculta jaceret,
Desereretque suum Patria nostra (14.) Patrem;
Illa Deum, patriamque suam, patriæque (15.) Parentem,
Sincera coluit religione, fide:
Tramite nam recto gradiens, (16.) Nova dogmata spernens,
Servavit (17.) Fines quos posuere Patres.

(9.) The DUKE of CUMBERLAND.
(10.) At the Revolution.   (11.) By the Act of Security.
(12.) By the Act against Unqualified Meetings.
(13.) In Testimony of the Doctrine of Praying for the Dead.
(14.) King James VII.   (15) The Popish Pretender.
(16.) Reformation Doctrines.   (17.) The Unscriptural Popish Usages.

Sacred to the Memory of our Dearest Mother, the CHURCH of SCOTLAND.

> Stop Traveller, Read and Lament,
> A Miracle of Iniquity.
> Under this Marble lye the Remains
> Of a very venerable Mother.
> (Let her lye concealed, that she may not be too much exposed!)
> Who was dead while alive,
> And alive while dead.
> O Impious and Incredible Wickedness!
> Iniquously deprived of her Defender,
> Miserably oppressed by Tyrants,
> By the mitred Clergy of the neighbouring Kingdom
> (I tremble at relating it) wickedly abused;
> Impiously afflicted by Courtiers,
> By certain Sons treacherously deserted,
> Trampled on by all spurious, maltreated, held in derision:
> A votive Sacrifice by the Suffrages of Many,
> (I need not say of ALL,)
> And " likewise" by the Fury of the Fanatics.
> Do you ask,
> In what Land is this?
> In an Island,
> Where the Monarch acts against the Monarchy,
> The Churchmen against the Church,
> The Legislators against the Law,
> The Judges against Justice,
> The Preachers atheistically against the Truth,
> The Soldiery boldly, impudently, William (cruel as Nero) their General,
> Against Honour, against Humanity.
> This, an opprobrious, and shameful conduct in us.
> For this Land mourns for wickedness, perjury!
> As a proof of this we have many living and late witnesses.
> Away! Away! with it.
> Alas! our dearest Mother, of happy memory, became sick,
> In the year 1638.
> Woes me, She became lame both in the hands and feet,
> In the year 1707.
> At length, have mercy on me, O God! worn out by many strokes, griefs,
> She died in the year 1748.
> All ye Seniors, Sons and Daughters,
> Pray for her that she may rest in peace, and at length obtain
> A happy resurrection. AMEN. &c.

Sect. 4.   THE PROTESTANT CHURCH   317

2*d*, The BISHOPS of MORAY since the REFORMATION; the CATHEDRAL, PALACE, CHAPTER, and REVENUES.

PATRICK HEPBURN, the last Popish BISHOP of Moray, died June 20th, 1573, and

Protestant Bishops of Moray.

1. GEORGE DOUGLAS was the first Protestant Bishop. He was bastard son of Archibald Earl of Angus, and was admitted Bishop 5th February 1573—4. For in that Period there was no Consecration, except what was performed by mere Presbyters, yet he soon elected a Chapter; for I find him and the Chapter consenting and subscribing to a tack of Teinds, July 18th 1574 (*Appendix*, No. XLV.) He died at Edinburgh December 28th 1589 (*Keith's Catal.*) He was the only *Tulchan* Bishop in this See. The next Bishop was,

2. ALEXANDER DOUGLAS, probably son of the former. This Gentleman was ordained Minister of Elgin about the year 1582, (*Sess. Records of Elgin.*) and served as a Presbyterian Minister till the year 1606. In that year, he, with others, grasped at the Erastian Prelacy established by Parliament, and in 1610, received a sort of Consecration (See III. and IV. Periods). He died May 11th 1623, and was buried in the Isle of St Giles Church in Elgin, where his wife, a daughter of the Laird of Innes, erected a stately monument. He was succeeded by

3. JOHN GUTHRIE, Minister of Edinburgh, who was consecrated anno 1623, and was deposed by the General Assembly which met anno 1638. He did not, as other Bishops, fly into England, but kept possession of the Castle of Spynie; and when the Covenanters took arms anno 1640, he garrisoned it. But in July that year, Major General Munro marched with

with 300 men to reduce it. Mr Joseph Brodie Minister at Keith, and son-in-law to the Bishop, prevailed with him to surrender on July 16th, and only the arms and riding horses were carried off. The Bishop retired to his paternal inheritance of Guthrie in Angus (*Spald. M. S.*). From that time there was no Bishop, till after the Restoration, when

4. MURDAC MACKENZIE was preferred. He was, for some time chaplain to a regiment in the army of Gustavus Adolphus King of Sweden; after which he was settled minister of Contane in Ross; from thence translated to Inverness anno 1640, and thence to Elgin anno 1645. Upon the Restoration he was consecrated Bishop, May 7th 1662. He had been accounted a superstitiously zealous Presbyterian and Covenanter, and so much an enemy to the keeping of Holy-days, that it is commonly said at Elgin, that at Christmass 1659, he searched the houses in that town, that they might not have a Christmas Goose. But a Bishoprick cured him of these blemishes, and he soon deposed some of his Clergy for non-conformity. In the end of the year 1676, he was translated to the See of Orkney, and died in February 1688.

5. JAMES AITKINS, Rector of Wimphrey in the County of Bristol, was, upon the King's recommendation, elected January 10th 1677, and soon after consecrated. He was accounted a pious man, and maintained strict order and discipline among his Clergy, without any severity against Dissenters: But warmly maintained the rights of his See, particularly a fishing on the river Spey. The Marquis of Huntley, and Earls of Moray and Dunfermline, proprietors of a Fishing on that river, prevailed to have him translated to Galloway anno 1680, and he died 1687. He was succeded by

6. COLIN

6. COLIN FALCONER, son of William of Dunduff, who was son of Alexander Falconer of Hawkerton, was ordained Minister of Essil anno 1651, transported to Forres in 1658, and in 1679 elected to the See of Argyle: But not having the Irish language, he was not fond of that Charge, and in 1680 was consecrated Bishop of Moray. He died November 11th 1686, and was buried in the Isle of St Giles Church in Elgin.

7. ALEXANDER ROSE (of the family of Inch in Garrioch, a branch of the family of Kilravock, and whose father was Prior of Monemusk) was successively Minister at Perth, Professor of Divinity at Glasgow, and Principal of St Mary's College in St Andrews; and was consecrated Bishop of Moray in March 1687, and before the end of that year was translated to Edinburgh, where he died March 20th 1720.

8. WILLIAM HAY, D. D. (of the family of Park in Moray) was Minister at Perth, and was consecrated Bishop of Moray March 11th 1688, at St Andrews. After his deprivation in 1689, he retired to the house of his son-in-law, John Cuthbert of Castlehill near Inverness, where he died March 17th 1707.

These were the Reformed Bishops in the See of Moray; and in their time the Diocess, in its extent, was much the same as under Popery. I have above taken notice of the division of it, into PRESBYTERIES.

The CATHEDRAL or COLLEGE CHURCH had gone to ruin, CATHEDRAL. as above observed; and these Bishops used St Giles Church in the town of Elgin, as their CATHEDRAL, the Bishop being the Parson or Rector of the Parish of Elgin, and the other Minister his Vicar.

PALACE. The PALACE of SPYNIE was kept in repair, and there the Bishops resided. But at the Revolution, though the Palace and Precinct were annexed to the Crown, and not sold, but pays annually twelve pounds Sterling of rent; yet the house not being inhabited, the Lesees or Tacksmen of the Precinct either carried off, or suffered others to carry off, the iron gate, the iron chair of the port-cullis, the oaken joists or roof, the doors, flooring, &c. In a word, all the iron work and timber was carried away, and only the stone walls remain.

CHAPTER. The DIGNIFIED CLERGY, and their Seats, were the same as under Popery. In an agreement, in June 1666, betwixt the Bishop and Chapter, and Sir Ludowick Gordon of Gordonstoun, compared with tacks of teinds, with consent of the Bishop and Chapter, I find the following Members of the Chapter, viz. The Minister of Aldern, Dean; of Forres, Arch-Deacon; of Alves, Chantor; of Inveravon, Chancellor; of Kenedar, Treasurer; Dallas, Sub-dean; Rafford, Sub-chantor; Moy, Pettie, Duffus, Dunlichty, Spynie, Kinore, Botarie, Kingusie, Birnie, Vicar of Elgin, and Prebendary of Unthank. But I know not, if these Ministers were always of the Chapter, or at any time made up the whole of it.

JURISDICTION. The CONSISTORIAL JURISDICTION, by Commissaries in Elgin and in Inverness, brought a considerable Revenue to the Bishop. " After the Reformation (says the Author of Essays
" on Brit. Antiq.) the Bishops took a great care to preserve
" their right. They had spies in all corners; and no sooner
" was a man laid in his grave, than they thundered out all their
" artillery of the law, to force his relations to apply for Letters
" of Administration."

I

Sect. 4.   THE PROTESTANT CHURCH.   321

I find in the Synod Register of Moray, that how soon Prelacy was re-established at the Restoration, the Bishop, anno 1663, caused intimate from all the Pulpits in the Diocess " That no " Widower, Man or Woman, shall be married, until they re" port a certificate of the Confirmation of the former Husband " or Wife's Testament." As long as Prelacy was established, this grievance was not redressed. But immediately after the Revolution (Parliament 1690. Act 26.) it was enacted, " That " no person shall be bound to give up inventory of a Defunct's " goods; and that there shall be no Confirmation, unless at the " instance of the relict, children, nearest of kin, or creditors."

The Bishop's power and perquisites, as Lord of the extensive Regality of Spynie, were not to be dispensed with; and therefore that Jurisdiction was kept up.

With respect to the REVENUES. The Papal Heirarchy having been abolished at the Reformation, what of the Church lands had not been sold and disponed by the Popish Bishops, was, by Queen Mary and her Son, lavished away among their courtiers and favourites. When King James re-erected a Hierarchy anno 1610, he had but very poor livings for his Bishops. And although both he and his Son pressed the surrender of Church lands so warmly and imprudently, that the discontent of the Nobility and Gentry, who possessed these lands, issued in a civil war fatal to Monarchy and Prelacy; yet little of the lands that had belonged to the Church was recovered. However competent Revenues were obtained for the Bishops, by Gentlemen paying an annual Feu-duty for the Church lands they held off the Crown; and this was called " The Bishop's Rents or Feu-duties." I have not seen a full and exact account of the Church lands belonging to the Diocess of Moray; but the following Rental of the Feu-duties (taken from

REVENUES

S f   the

the Collector's Books) points out the Gentlemen who now possess these lands, and shews that the Revenue was great, when the Bishops had the full real rent of those lands.

Feu-Duties of the Bishopric.

RENTAL of the FEU-DUTIES of the BISHOPRIC of MORAY.

SCOTS MONEY	£	sh.	d.	SCOTS MONEY	£	sh.	d.
				Brought over L.	795	4	8
Paid by the Laird of Grant	114	0	0	Hillhead there	6	17	4
By Easter Elchies	11	5	0	Dykeside in Birnie	13	17	8
Grant of Carron	9	3	4	Laird of Brodie for Kenedar,			
Grant of Bellindalach	51	6	8	with a Sow, or L. 8	129	12	0
Grant of Dalvey	36	0	0	Spynie	26	6	8
Grant of Achoinanie	7	0	0	Dipple	24	11	4
By Kilmiles	40	0	0	Gordonstoun for his lands	228	12	0
Hugh Baillie	20	0	0	Moraystoun	2	16	8
Fraser of Kinerries,	18	0	0	Bishopmiln	66	13	4
Cuthbert of Drakies	1	0	0	Sheriffmiln	2	0	0
Fraser of Fohir	8	14	8	Inshbroke	15	16	10
Alexander Chisholm	1	0	0	Findrossie	36	7	0
Laird of MacIntosh	20	15	0	Essil	10	12	0
Laird of Calder	27	0	0	Kirkhill of St Andrews	4	9	8
Bose of Holm	9	11	0	Teind Fishing of Spey	200	0	0
Laird of Kilravock	56	0	0	Killes	71	0	0
Laird of Lethin	26	8	8	Catboll in Ross	16	0	0
Dallas of Cintray	10	2	0	Kirktown of Dallas	5	12	2
Rose of Clava	10	14	4	Myreside	20	0	0
Loggie Ardrie	14	0	0	Lovat's tack duty	40	0	0
Laird of Altyre	24	0	0	Tywick's tack duty	1	10	0
Alterlies	1	6	8	The Precinct of Spynie	150	0	0
Kempcairn	11	8	0	Teind Bolls at L. 5			
Achoinachie	23	6	8	Pitgavenie 32 Bolls; inde,	160	0	0
Birkenburn	5	6	8	Barefiathills 12 Bolls 2 Firlots	62	10	0
School master of Keith	5	6	8	Inch 3 Bolls	15	0	0
Pitlurg	22	6	8	Linkwood 20 Bolls	100	0	0
Ogilvie of Mill-town	4	2	0	Maison Dieu 8 Bolls	40	0	0
Biervie	81	7	2	Peats at 4sh per Load	0	0	0
Moy	1	4	0	Kenedar 80 Loads	16	0	0
Drumriach	2	0	0	Aikenhead 20 Loads	4	0	0
Pherp	10	5	0	Whitefield 20 Loads	4	0	0
Inverlochtie	52	2	6	Milntown 20 Loads	4	0	0
Middletoun	18	0	0	Inverlochtie 50 Loads	10	0	0
Rothes Kirktoun	4	14	0	The 12 Ploughs of Birnie, at 10			
Stank house in Birnie	25	9	0	Loads per Plough; inde 120			
James Stewart's lands in Birnie	10	19	0	Loads	24	0	0
Carry over L.	795	4	8	Total L.	2307	9	4

Sect. 4. THE PROTESTANT CHURCH.

This is the Revenue as it now stands in the Collector's Books; but it is not one-half of the Revenues, as they stood at the Revolution. Several parts of these Rents have been gifted to Gentlemen. The profits of the Regality, and especially of the Commissariot, were very considerable. The Bishop was Parson of the Parish of Elgin, and drew all the Great Teinds. The Churches of St Andrews, Ugston, and Laggan were Mensal, and the Bishop had the whole Teinds. In a word, the Revenues of the See of Moray, at the Revolution, by a moderate Estimation, amounted to 'L. 6000 Scots, or L. 500 Sterl.

The Rental given up by Bishop Hay in 1689, agrees with the above, except in a few articles of small account. And Bishop Hay adds:

" There is payable, out of the Bishopric to the Minister of " St Andrews yearly, the sum of (Scots money) L. 58 6 8.

Let me here give the Articles of Discharge and Credit now allowed to the Collector out of the Bishop's Rents: viz.

To the third Minister of Inverness, by a Royal Grant	881	1	6
To the Minister of Birnie, by Decreet	32	12	2
To the Ministers of Elgin, by Decreet 8 Bolls Barley, at L. 5, is	40	0	0
Deducted for Pitgavenie 20 Bolls; inde	100	0	0
For the Precinct, 12 Bolls	60	0	0
To Surcharge on Lovat's Lands	20	0	0
Total, in Scots money,	L. 1133	13	8
Thus the whole Rental being	L. 2307	9	4
And the Discharge or Credit amounting to	1133	13	8
The Ballance paid by the Collector, is	L. 1173	15	8

3d, THE MINISTERS OF PARISHES SINCE THE REFORMATION.

IN this account, I shall follow the present Division of the Province into Presbyteries, and shall take notice of the Patron Saint, the Civil Patron, the Stipend, the Schools, the Mortifications, the Chapels, the Number of Examinable Persons above Seven Years of Age, and the Protestant Ministers since the Reformation

My Vouchers for these things are, Our Ecclesiastic Histories, the Registers of Inverness, Forres, Elgin, and Strathboggie; Registers of Kirk-Sessions, Original Writs, particularly those in the Appendix, No. XLVII.

In speaking of the Patrons of Churches, I cannot but observe, That by the Act, 10*mo Annæ* or 1712, restoring Patronages, " The Patronage of Churches, which belonged to Arch-" Bishops, Bishops, or other Dignified Persons in the year " 1689, shall belong to the Crown." And since no Prescription can run against the Crown, I leave it to those concerned, to consider how far the Crown has a right to severals in this Province.

PRESBYTERY of STRATHBOGGIE.

There are, within the Province of Moray, but two Parishes of this Presbytery, viz. MORTLICH and BELLIE. Before the year 1706, Mortlich was in the Diocess of Aberdeen.

MORTLICH, dedicated to St BEAN the first Bishop of it. The King presented the present Incumbent; but the Earl of Fife claims the Patronage. The Stipend is not modified, for

Sect. 4.   THE PROTESTANT CHURCH.   325

the *ipsa corpora* of the Small Teinds are paid. But the Stipend, including Element-money, amounts to about L. 1000 Scots. The Salary of the Shool is Legal. William Duff of Dipple mortified 500 Merks to the School, and L. 1000 Scots to the Poor; and there are L. 675 Scots more mortified for the use of the Poor. The Catechisable Persons are 1800, of which about 60 are Roman Catholicks. The Proteftant Ministers are,

 Mr John Maxwell, anno 1615.
  William Forbes, 1640.
  Alexander Seton, 1650.
  Arthur Strachan, 1688.
  Hugh Innes, Ordained about 1700, Died in March 1733.
  Walter Syme, from Glafs, Admitted 22d April 1734, Died 6th Jan. 1763.
  John Touch, from Aberlaure, Admitted 26th October 1763.

BELLIE dedicated to St PETER. The Patronage did belong to the Prior of Urquhart; and with the Lordship of Urquhart came to the Earl of Dunfermline. It now belongs to the Duke of Gordon, by the purchase of Urquhart. The Stipend, by Decreet, is 1200 merks, and 100 merks for Communion Elements. The School is legal. Mortifications for the poor are L. 650 Scots. Catechisable persons 1600. On the Grave-Stone of Mr William Sanders is inscribed, " That he " lived 108 years, and was Minister of Bellie 77 years." The Ministers are,

BELLIE Parish, page ii.

Mr William Sanders, Minifter before 1600. Demitted in 1663.
 James Horn Affiftant, Ordained 28 February 1656, Transported to Elgin 1659.
 William Anand Affiftant, Ordained 19. May 1663, Lived after the Revolution.
 Charles Primrose, Ordained 25 February 1702, Transported to Forres 1708.
 Thomas MacCulloch, from Birnie, Adm 4. May 1709, Died 26. Nov. 1750.
 Patrick Gordon, from Rynie, Adm 3. Oct 1751, Died at London Feb. 1719.
 James Gordon Admitted the 14 March 1770.

PRESBY-

Presbytery of ABERLAUR

Presbytery of Aberlaur

Dundurcos Parish.
page. 15.

Dundurcos was a Vicarage, depending, it is said, upon the Parson of Rathven in the Enzie. Hay of Rannes claims the Patronage; But the Crown is in possession, by presenting Messrs Thomas Gordon, and John Grant. In the North end of the Parish stood the Chapel of Grace, and near to it the Well of that name, to which multitudes, even from the Western Isles, do still resort, and nothing short of violence can restrain their superstition. I have spoken of St Nicholas's Hospital page 263. The Stipend is 64 bolls of Oat Meal, and 400 merks, with 40 merks for Communion Elements. The School is not legal. The Mortifications for the Poor are, L. 240, and three Gardens, and three Ridges of Land, mortified by several persons. The Catechisable persons are about 1000. The Protestant Ministers are,

Mr William Peterkin, Exhorter in Dundurcos and Dipple, 1569. (*Book of Assign.*)
John Marishal, Minister before 1624. Died 1651.
John Ray, from Kirk-Michael, Admitted 1651, Died 1679.
Thomas Ray, Ordained 1666 Assistant. Died after the Revolution.
David Dalrymple, Ordained 8. May 1698, Died 23. February 1747.
Thomas Gordon, Ordained 16. September 1747. Transported to Spey-Mouth 1758.
John Grant, Ordained 28. September 1758.

Rothes Parish.
Page 17.

Rothes was a Parsonage. The Earl of Rothes Patron; but now the Earl of Findlater. The Stipend is 40 bolls of Oat-Meal, and 370 merks, without allowance for Communion Elements, and without a Decreet of Modification. The Salary of the School is not legal. The Catechisable persons are 500. No Mortifications. The Inscription on the Grave-Stone of Mr James Lesly runneth thus, " Here lies ane Nobleman Mr James
" Lesly Parson of Rothes, Brother-German to George Umquhile
" Earl

"Earl of the fame, who departed in the Lord, 13. October 1576." To him succeeded Mr Alexander Lefly, whose successor was Mr Leanord Lefly. In a discharge granted by the Earl of Rothes to one Margaret Anderson, dated at the Castle of Rothes anno 1620, Mr Leanord Lefly Parson is a witness. The Ministers are,

Mr James Lefly, Exhorter and Parson 1570, Died 13. October 1576.
   Alexander Lefly, Died about 1610.
   Leanord Lefly, Parson in 1620.
   John Weems, brother to Lord Weems, Ord. 1 June 1622, Died 25. Feb. 1640.
   Robert Tod, Ordained 5. May 1642, Transported to Urquhart 1662.
   John Lefly, Ordained 4. November 1663, Died about 1692.
   James Allan, Ordained 23. September 1696, Deposed for Burroignionism 29. May 1706.
   George Lindsay, Ordained 22. August 1710, Transported to Aberlaure 1714.
   Alexander Tod, Ordained 11. November 1714, Died 11. April 1716.
   Thomas Fairbairn, Ordained in 1717, Transported to Gartlie 1719.
   John Paul, Ordained 10. November 1720, Died 16. March 1747.
   James Gray, Ordained 14. April 1748, Transported to Lanark 1755.
   Alexander Patterson, Ordained 9. September 1756, Died 28 October 1759.
   Robert Grant, Ordained in 1759, Admitted 17. July 1760, Transported to Cullen 1762.
   James Ogilvie, from Ordequhill, Admitted March 24. 1763.

KNOCKANDO comprehends the united Parishes of KNOCKANDO and *Ma Calen, (i. e. Saint Colin.)* now called ELCHIES. The former was a Vicarage depending on the Parson of Inveravon, and the other depended on the Parson of Botarie. In 1640, the Synod of Moray required the Ministers of Inveravon and Botarie to provide Knockando, and Elchies *(Ma Calen) quam primum,* with Ministers. *(Syn. Records.)* From 1646, these two Parishes remained united till 1683; in which year in October, Mr Alexander Ruddach was settled Minister of Elchies: But after the Revolution they were again united. The Laird of Grant, as Patron of Inveravon, claims the Patronage of Knockando.

KNOCKANDO Parish.
Page 18.

Knockando. The Stipend, including Element money, was 830 merks; but, by decreet in 1767, it was augmented to 1012 merks, (including Communion Elements,) and two Chalders of Meal. The School Salary is not legal. Archibald Grant of Balintome mortified 1000 merks, which, with 100 merks raised from the Interest of that sum, is to make a Salary for teaching poor children. That sum is now become near 1200 merks. There is mortified for the poor about 230 merks. Catechisable Persons are about 1000. The Protestant Ministers are,

 Mr William Watson, Minister before 1624, Transported to Duthel about 1626.
 Gilbert Marshall, Ordained about 1630, Transported to Cromdale 1646.
 William Chalmer, Ordained in 1640. Died in 1668.
 James Gordon, Ordained in 1670, Transported to Urquhart in 1682.
 Thomas Grant, Ordained in 1684, Died about 1700.
 Alexander Ruddach, Ordained at Elchies in 1683.
 Daniel MacKenzie, Ord. 12th February 1706, Transport. to Kingusie 1709.
 James Gordon, Ordained in May 1712. Died in Winter 1725.
 Hugh Grant, Ordained in September 1727, Died 18th September 1763.
 John Dunbar, Ordained May 3d 1764.

BOHARM Parish, Page 23. BOHARM, a Parsonage whereof the Earl Fife is Patron. Ardintullie (called *Artendol*, Appendix N° V.) was the Original Parish, and Boharm (properly *Bocharn*) was only the Chapel of Moray Laird of Boharn. At Galival are the Vestiges of a Domestic Chapel; and probably there was a Chapel of Ease where the Church now stands. There is a Glebe at Ardintullie, and another at Boharm. The Stipend is 32 Bolls Meal, and 600 Merks, with 20 Merks for Communion Elements. The School Salary is not Legal. The Catechisable Persons 600. The Protestant Ministers are,

 Mr William Rothie, Reader in Ardintullie 1569.
  George Frazer was Minister before 1624. Died about 1628.
  Alexander Anderson, Ordained about 1629, Transported in 1633.
  Thomas Law, Ordained in 1634, Transported to Elgin in 1645.

             George

Sect. 4. THE PROTESTANT CHURCH

George Dunbar, Ordained in 1647, Died in 1650.
William Harper, Ordained in 1655, Died in 1685.
Adam Harper, Ordained in 1686, Demitted in 1716.
George Gordon, Ordained 13th May 1717, Transported to Alves in 1728.
John Gilchrift, Ordained in 1729, Transported to Urquhart in 1734.
George Grant, Ordained in 1734. Transported to Rathven in 1752.
Thomas Johnston, from Glenbucket, Admitted 31st May 1753.

ABERLAURE and SKIRDROSTAN (the laft dedicated to St **ABERLAURE** Durstan) were diftinct Charges; but how early they were **Parish,** united, I find not. In 1646, Walter Innes of Auchluncart, **Page 29.** Adam Duff of Drummuir, and James Sutherland Tutor of Duffus, prefented feverally to this Church; and Duffus's Right being examined by the Commiffaries of Moray and Invernefs, and fome Minifters, was found good *(Syn. Rec.)*. Now the Earl of Fife acteth as Patron; probably as coming in the place of Lord Balvanie. I have already taken notice of the Religious Houfe of Kinermonie *(Vid. Pag 264.)*. The Stipend is 850 Merks, with 50 Merks for Communion-Elements. The School is not Legal. The Mortifications:

By Alexander Grant of Alachie	L. 100	0	0
William Innes of Kinermonie, For which the Earl of Fife pays annually 3½ Bolls Oat-Meal.	350	0	0
John Proctor	66	13	4
Patrick Clark in Boharm	30	0	0
Alexander Green	66	13	4
And John MacKeran in Glenrinnes	66	13	4
Total (in Scots Money)	£. 680	0	0

The Catechifable Perfons are 840. The Proteftant Minifters are,

T t Mr John

Mr John Stuart, Settled before 1624, Died 1st April 1639.
George Speed, Ordained in June 1640, Died 22d August 1668.
Robert Stephen, Ordained in Summer 1669, Died December 1705.
Robert Stephen, Ordained 18th September 1707, Transported to Craig of Mucrofs 1714.
George Lindsey, from Rothes, admitted in Winter 1714, Died in 1715.
Daniel MacKenzie, from Kingusie, Admitted December 1715, Transported to Inveravon 1718.
Robert Duff, Ordained in March 1719, Died in July 1738.
John Touch, Ordained 31st May 1739, Transported to Mortlich in 1763.
James Thomson, Ordained in 17 , Admitted 20th February 1706.

N. B. *Lite pendente*, The Duke of Gordon and Earl of Fife agreed to this last Settlement, *Salvo jure*.

Inveravon Parish, Page 30.

INVERAVON, a Parsonage dedicated to St PETER. It was the Seat of the Chancellor of the Diocefs, and the Vicarages of Knockando and Urquhart, beyond Invernefs, depended on it. The Laird of Grant is Patron. Mr William Cloggie, being transported to Invernefs, retained the Revenues of the Chancellory, till the Synod 1624 obliged him to demit them. There was a Chapel of Eafe in the South-Weft corner, called Kil-Machlie, and two in Glenlivat, viz. At Dafkie, and at Dunan. The Stipend, by a Decreet in 1685, was 830 Merks, with 36 Merks for Element Money ; but, anno 1769, an augmentation was obtained of L. 16 Scots, and three Chalders of Meal valued at L. 6 Scots *per* Boll. Mortifications for the Poor are 700 Merks. The School is Legal. Catechifeable Perfons 1660, whereof about 500 are Roman Catholics. The Proteftant Minifters are,

Mr William Cloggie, Settled before 1610. Transported to Invernefs, about 1620.
Alexander Innes, Ord. about 1622, Transported to Rothemay about 1630.
John Chalmers, Ordained about 1631, Transported to Gartlie in 1649.
Alexander Gordon, Ordained in 1650, Depofed for Immorality in 1657.
George Harnay (vid. Alves), Admitt. in 1658, Transp. to Aldern 1664.
Alexander Dunbar, Ordained in 1665, Transported in 1668.

James

Sect. 4. THE PROTESTANT CHURCH. 331

James Stuart, Ordained 22d September 1669, Demitted in 1681, on account of the Test.
John Stuart, Ordained in Summer 1682, Died in 1697.
James Bannerman, Ordained 15th April 1703, Transp. to Forglen 1717.
Daniel MacKenzie, from Aberlaure, Admitt. 1718, Transp. to Pettie 1719.
Alexander Fraser, from Alvie, Admitted 21st September 1721, Died 13th February 1752.
James Grant, Ordained 1751, Admitted 23d November 1752.

PRESBYTERY of ABERNETHIE.

Presbytery of Abernethie.

KIRK-MICHAEL, a Parsonage dedicated to MICHAEL the Archangel. The Laird of Grant is Patron. At Camdale, in the upper end of the Parish, was a Chapel of Ease, dedicated to St Brigida or Bryde. The Stipend is 850 merks, and 50 merks for Communion Elements. There is no legal School. Examinable persons are about 1000, whereof 200 are Roman Catholicks. The Protestant Ministers are,

Kirk Michael Parish.
Page 38.

Mr Peter Grant, was Minister at Kirk-Michael and Cromdale about 1600.
John Ray, Succeeded, and was Transported to Dundurcos in 1651.
Alexander Gordon, Ordained in 1651, Died in 1684.
Colin Nicholson, from Abernethie, Admitted 1685. Died 25. September 1709.
Duncan MacLea, Ordained September 1712, Transported to Doul in 1717.
David Muschet, Ordained in 1718, Died in 1724.
George Grant, Ordained 21. September 1725, Died 27. April 1772.
Robert Farquharson, Ordained 4. October 1772.

CROMDALE, INVERALEN, and ADVIE, are now united in one parish; how early they were so united, I find not: There is a Glebe at Cromdale, and another at Advie. Cromdale is a Parsonage dedicated to St Ma-Luac. The Laird of Grant is Patron. The stipend was 800 merks, and 60 merks for Communion Elements; but about the year 1767, it was augmented to L. 75 Sterling, or 1350 merks Scots. The School is legal.

Cromdale Parish
Page 34.

T t 2 Catechiseable

Catechifeable perfons are at leaft 2200. The Proteftant Minifters are,

> Mr Peter Grant, Minifter of Cromdale, and Kirk Michael, about 1600.
> David Deck was fettled before 1624, Died 1638.
> Gilbert Marfhal, from Knockando, Admitted 1640, Died about 1666.
> Gilbert Marfhal Junior, Ordained 1667, Tranfported to Invernefs 1674.
> John Stewart, Ordained 26. January 1676, Ejected in 1690.
> William MacKay, from Dornoch, Admitted 1694, Did in 1700.
> James Chapman, from Calder, Admitted 25. November 1701, Died in December 1737.
> Francis Grant, from Duthil, Admitted in 1740, Died in July 1746.
> Patrick Grant, Ordained 19. September 1751.

Abernethie Parifh. Page 36.

ABERNETHIE and KINCHARDINE united in one parifh, but diftinct places of Worfhip. The Minifter has a Glebe in each. Abernethie was dedicated to St George. The Laird of Grant is Patron. There was a Chapel in Conigefs in the Eaft end of the Parifh; and another two miles above the Church, on the bank of Nethie. The ftipend was 800 merks, with 50 merks for Communion Service; but about the year 1767, it was augmented to L. 64 Sterling, or 1152 merks Scots. The School is not legal. Catechifeable perfons are about 1200. The Proteftant Minifters are,

> Mr John Glafs Exhorter, in Abernethy and Kingufie 1567.
> Patrick Grant, Minifter in 1624, Died about 1630.
> Colin MacKenzie, Ordained about 1634, Tranfported to Contane in 1646.
> John Sanderfon, Ordained in 1656, Died about 1677.
> Colin Nicholfon, Ordained Affiftant 11. Auguft 1670. Tranfported to Kirk-Michael, 1685.
> James Grant, from Urquhart, Admitted 1686, Ejected in 1690.
> William Grant, (after a vacancy of 19 Years,) Ordained 19. May 1709, Died 27. June 1764.
> John Grant, from Arochar, Admitted 25. September 1765.

Duthel Parifh. Page 38.

DUTHEL and ROTHEMURCHUS united: The former dedicated to St Peter, and the other to St Tuchaldus. The Laird of Grant

Sect. 4. THE PROTESTANT CHURCH.

Grant is Patron. Attempts were made in 1624, and afterwards, to unite Kinchardine and Rothemurchus, but failed for want of stipend; But 1630 Duthil and Rothemurchus have been united, but distinct places of Worship, and a Glebe in each Parish. There was in Achnahatnich in Rothemurchus, a Chapel dedicated to St Eata. The stipend was 800 merks, with 55 merks for Communion Elements; but about the year 1767, it was augmented to L. 64 Sterling, or 1152 merks. Catechiseable persons are 1400. The Protestant Ministers are,

Mr Andrew Henderson, Ordained at Rothemurchus 1625, Transported to Balwhidder 1630.
    William Watson, from Elchies, Admitted at Duthil 1626, Died about 1655.
    James Watson, Ordained about 1657, Died 1659.
    William Fraser, Ordained 1664, Died, or was Transported in 1666.
    William Smith, Ordained in 1667, Deposed in 1672 for immoralities.
    Sueton Grant. Ordained in 1653, Ejected in 1690.
    Donald MacIntosh from Farr, Admitted 1695. Demitted in 1708.
    Francis Grant, after a vacancy of 11 years, Ordained September 1719, Transported to Cromdale 1740.
    Patrick Grant, Ordained 3. December 1740, Transported to Nuig, 1756.
    Robert Grant, Ordained 19. April 1758, Died 12. March 1759.
    Lewis Grant, Ordained 20. September 1759.

ALVIE, a Parsonage dedicated to St Drostan. The Duke of Gordon is Patron. This Parish was sometime united with Laggan (*vid. Laggan.*) There were several Chapels in this Parish: One at Kinrara, on the West side of the River, dedicated to St Eata: A Chapel of Ease at Dunachtin, dedicated to St Drostan; and Ma Luac Chapel in Rates. I have before me a Seasine on the land of Croft Ma-Luac, in favour of James MacIntosh, *Alias* MacDonald Glas, Ancestor to MacIntosh of Strone, by George Bishop of Moray, anno 1575. The Stipend, by Decreet in 1720, is 800 merks, with 90 merks for Communion Elements. There is no School. The Catechiseable persons are 700. The Protestant Ministers are,

ALVIE Parish.
Page 53.

Mr James Spense, Exhorter in 1572.
    James Lyle, was Minister in, and before 1624. (*Vid. Laggan.*)
    Roderick MacKenzie, Ordained 1637, Deposed for Immorality.
    Thomas MacPherson, Ordained 1662, Died about 1707.
    Alexander Fraser, Ordained 13. September 1713, Transp. to Inveravon 1721.
    Ludowick Chapman, Ordained in September 1728. Transported to Pettie 1738.
    William Gordon, from Urquhart, Admitted 16. September 1739.

Kingusie and Insh Parish.
Pgae 54.

KINGUSIE, a Parsonage dedicated to St Coluim; and INCH a Vicarage dedicated to St Ewan. The Duke of Gordon is Patron. How early these parishes were united I find not. Inch (q. *Inis*, an *Island*) is so called, because the river Spey sometimes floweth around the hill on which the Church standeth. The Church of Kingusie was built in 1624, where the Priory stood. There were Chapels at Invertromie, and Noid, and Brigida's Chapel at Benchar: The Minister preaches at both places, and has a Glebe at each. The stipend, by agreement and decreet in 1758, including Communion Elements, is 1000 merks. The School is legal, erected about 1650, by 2000 merks vacant stipend, mortified and lately secured upon some of MacPherson of Clunie's lands. The Examinable persons are 1400. The Protestant Ministers are,

    Mr John Glass, Exhorter in Kingusie and Abernethie anno 1567.
    Archibald Henderson, Parson, 1574.
    Angus MacIntosh, Ordained about 1600, Died in Winter 1643.
    Lauchlan Grant, from Moy, Admitted 1649, Died in 1668.
    Hector MacKenzie, Ordained 30. November 1670, Transported to Inverness 1688.
    Donald Taylor, Officiated till 1701, but not legally settled.
    John MacKenzie, Admitted in 1701. Transported to Laggan 1709.
    Daniel MacKenzie, from Knockando, Admitted 1709, Transported to Aberlaure 1715.
    Lauchlan Shaw, Ordained 20. September 1716, Transported to Calder 1719.
    William Blair, Ordained an itinerant 1721, Admitted 16. September 1724.

Sect. 4.   THE PROTESTANT CHURCH.   335

PRESBYTERY of ELGIN.

DIPPLE, proceeding from East to West, I begin with the parish of Spey-mouth, which comprises the old parishes Dipple and Essil, of which I shall first treat. DIPPLE, a Parsonage dedicated to the HOLY GHOST, whereof the Earl of Moray is Patron. At the Church Yard Style, there stood a small house, commonly called "The House of the Holy Ghost;" around which, Sun-way, the people made a tour with the Corpse at Burials, and could not be restrained from this superstition, till the walls were quite razed of late. The Parson of Dipple was Titular of Rathven in Strathboggie (*Appendix*, No. XLV.) The Protestant Ministers of Dipple were,

Mr William Peterkin, Exhorter in Dipple and Dundurcos, anno 1570.
   Adam Hepburn Parson, anno 1574.
   Alexander Hay Parson, 1591, Died 1624.
   Walter Smith, Ordained 1625, Died 1655.
   Thomas Urquhart, Ordained 13. August 1656, Transported to Essil, 1658.
   George Innes, Ordained 14th October 1658, Demitted for Nonconformity, anno 1663.
   Alexander Marshal, Ordained 24. August 1664, Demitted in 1682, on account of the Test.
   John Scot, Ordained in May 1682, Died in June 1726.
   John Paterson, Ordained 22. March 1727, Transported to St Andrews 1731.

ESSIL, dedicated to St Peter, was the seat of the Sub-Treasurer; and in 1670, Mr David Colless Minister of Kenedar, presented (with consent of Sir Ludowick Gordon of Gordonstoun) Mr Alexander Lindsay. Likewise in 1676, the Minister of Kenedar, with consent foresaid, presented Mr George Cummine. The Protestant Ministers were,

Mr Robert Keith, Minister at Urchard, Langbryde, and Essil anno 1567.
   John Blinshall, Reader in these Parishes, 1567.
   John Peters,   I find not the precise time of his serving.

Presbytery of ELGIN.

Dipple Parish. Page 57.

Essil Parish. Page 57.

William

William Roch, from Ogston, Admitted 1601, Died 2. February 1651.
Colin Falconer, Ordained 2 October 1651. Transported to Forres 1658.
Thomas Urquhart, from Dipple, Admitted 30. June 1658, Deposed 1663, for Non-conformity.
Alexander Dunbar, from Birnie, Admitted 8. July 1663, Transported in 1667.
Alexander Lindsay, Ordained 13. Dec. 1670, Transported to Urquhart 1676.
George Cumming, Ordained 21. September 1676, Died 20 September 1723.
James Gilchrist, Ordained 2. March 1725. Transported to Foveran 1727.
Robert Milne, Ordained 19. Nov. 1728, became Minister of Spey-mouth 1731.

Speymouth Parish.
Page 57.

Speymouth is made up of the parishes of Dipple and Essil, and the Barony of Germach united, and erected into one parish, by a decree of the Court of Session, of date 14th July 1731, to take effect at the death or removal of one of the then incumbent Ministers, which happened that same year, by transporting Mr John Patterson from Dipple to St Andrews. The old kirks were suffered to go into decay, and a new kirk was built in the centre of the united parish in 1732, and called "Speymouth Kirk." But the old Church Yards continue to be the places for burying. No grave is allowed to be digged at the new Church. The Glebes of Dipple and Essil were disponed to Braco (now Earl of Fife), who granted a Glebe and built a Manse at some little distance from the Kirk. By annexing the Barony of Germach to this parish, L. 200 Scots of the Teind Fishing of Spey is added to the stipend. The Town and Barony of Germach, though within half a mile of the Kirk of Essil, was a part of the parish of Urquhart, and three miles from that Kirk: The Bishops kept it in this parish, that they might have the said L. 200. In 1649, Germach was annexed to Essil by the Presbytery, with consent of the Heretors, and the Minister of Essil was to enjoy the L. 200. To explain this, observe, That King Charles I. being indebted L. 7000 Sterling, to James Livingston of the Bed Chamber, granted him in 1642, a gift of the rents and profits of the

Bishoprie

Sect. 4. THE PROTESTANT CHURCH. 337

Bishoprick of Moray and others, for payment, with power to sell and dispone the same. Mr Livingston, in 1647, conveyed his right to John Earl of Crawford Treasurer, who, by his disposition of date 9th June 1648, sold the Teind Fishing of Spey to Sir Robert Innes of Innes, for L. 800 Scots, with the burden of L. 200 to the Minister of Essil. The Minister of Essil enjoyed the L. 200 till 1662, and then the Bishop took the money to himself, and re-annexed Germach to Urquhart. After the Revolution, the King's College of Aberdeen got possession of the L. 200 Scots. But Mr Robert Miln Minister of Speymouth recovered this, as a part of his Stipend.

The Earl of Moray, and the Laird of Gordonston, are Patrons *per vices* of the united Parish (Vid. Kenedar). The Stipend, by Decreet in 1730, is, including Communion Elements, L. 341 : 0 : 4 ; and 109 Bolls, 1 Firlot, 3½ Pecks, whereof 32 Bolls 1½ Peck are Oat-meal, at 8½ Stone per Boll. The School is Legal. Mortifications are, L. 666 : 13 : 4 to the Poor of Dipple ; L. 333 : 6 : 8 to the School of Dipple, and two Bolls Meal annually ; L. 333 : 6 : 8 to the Poor of Essil, and as much to the School thereof ; all by William Duff of Dipple. L. 200 to the poor of Dipple, by William Ego in Beathill : And 2000 merks for a School in Germach, by Peter Gordon watch maker in Edinburgh. The Catachiseable are 840. The Ministers, since the union of the Parishes, are,

Mr Robert Milne, Ordained 19. November 1726, Died 5. January 1758.
Thomas Gordon, from Dundurcus, Admitted 6. July, 1758.

URQUHART, a Parsonage dedicated to St Margaret. The Prior of Urquhart was Patron ; and now the Duke of Gordon, coming in the place of the Earl of Dunfermline Lord Urquhart, is Patron. The stipend, by a decreet in 1650, is 5 Chalders, half barley and half oat meal, L. 300 Scots, with 50 merks for Commu-

URQUHART Parish. p. 58.

U u nion

nion Elements. The Salary of the School is 12 Bolls of meal, mortified by Dunfermline, and paid out of the miln of Urquhart. John Innes of Darkland mortified to the poor L. 133 : 6 : 8. Mr James Park mortified L. 2000 Scots, for two Bursars in Philosophy in the King's College of Aberdeen. The Examinable Persons are 870. The Protestant Ministers are,

   Mr Robert Kieth, Minister at Urquhart, Lanbride and Essil, 1567.
   John Blenshal, Reader in 1567.
   James Guthrie, Minister in 1599, Died in June 1647.
   James Park, Ordained 15. July 1747. Deposed in 1660 for diverse crimes.
   Robert Tod, from Rothes, Admitted 31. December 1662, Died in April 1676.
   Alexander Lindsay from Essil, Admitted 22. July 1676, Died in Sept. that year.
   William Geddes, from Wick, Admitted 1. June 1677, Demitted in 1682, for the Test.
   James Gordon, from Knockando, Admitted 4. July 1682.
   John Stewart, served immediately after the Revolution, Died 6. May 1692.
   James and John Urquharts, (vid. Kinloss.) Admitted 1693, James Died 16. April 1701, and John 30. October 1731.
   John Gilchrist, from Boharm, Admitted 11. March 1734, Died 4. Jan. 1739.
   James Spense, Ordained 26. November 1740, Died March 20. 1768.
   William Gordon, Ordained privately 1768, Admitted January 12. 1769.

LANBRIDE Parish.
p. 63

LANBRIDE, a Vicarage dedicated to St Brigida. The Minister of Alves was Patron and Titular, and had 40 Bolls of Teinds annually paid to him. He presented Mr James Cook anno 1682 ; but Alexander Tod was presented in 1669, by the Bishop, *Jure Devoluto*, with the consent of the Earl of Moray (*Presby. Reg.*) " In 1708, the Treasury gifted the vacant " stipends of Lanbride to the town of Lanark : The Earl of " Moray claimed the stipend as Patron of Lanbride, *qua* Pa- " tron of Alves, for *Patronus Patroni mei est Patronus meus*. " The Lords, 5th February 1709, rejected the Earl's claim, " unless he instruct, that he has a particular right of Patronage " of that Church (*Forb. Decis.*)" Yet the Earl continues to
                                       present

present without interruption. The stipend, by a decreet in 1717, is 100 Bolls, 3 Firlots, 2 Pecks, 3¼ Lippies, of Bear and Meal; and L. 18 : 4 s. for Communion Elements. The Salary for the School is 6 Bolls 3 Firlots, and 25 merks annually of a mortification. Dipple mortified 1000 merks, and Innes of Darkland 900 merks for the Poor. The Catechiseable Persons are 348. The Ministers are,

Mr Patrick Balfour, Minister at Alves and Lanbride, 1567.
   Andrew Stronach, Exhorter, 1567.
   John Blenshal, Reader, 1567.
   Bartholomew Robertson, Minister anno 1603.
   William Fraser, Minister in 1623, Died in 1626.
   Alexander Anderson, Ordained 1627, Died 1667.
   Alexander Tod, Ordained 31. March 1669, Transported to Elgin 1682.
   James Cook, Ordained 21. December 1682, Died 1707.
   Walter Stewart, Ordained 31. January 1710, Died in December 1725.
   John Stewart, Ordained 23 March 1727, Transported to Drumblade 1734.
   Patrick Duncan, Ordained 9. April 1735, Died 25. January 1760.
   James Crombie, Ordained 11. Sept. 1760, Removed to Belfast in Ireland 1770.
   Thomas MacFarlane, Ordained September 5. 1771.

BIRNIE, a Parsonage whereof the Earl of Moray is Patron. The stipend, by decreet in 1774, is 18 Bolls 2 pecks 3¼ Lippies of Bear; 20 Bolls 1 Firlot, 3 Pecks, 1 Lippy oat meal at 8 Stone per Boll; and L. 502 : 2 : 8 Scots. The School is scarcely legal. John Innes of Darkland mortified 200 merks for the Poor. There were likewise given to the Poor of this Parish by a private hand L. 30 Sterling a few years ago. Catechiseable persons are 420. The Ministers are,

Birnie Parish. p. 68.

Mr James Johnston, Exhorter in 1568.
   Alexander Innes, Minister in 1569.
   Colin MacKenzie, Deposed in 1634, for Immorality.
   Alexander Spense, Ordained in 1636 Died 15. April 1658.
   Alexander Dunbar, Ordained 22. June 1659. Transported to Essil 1663.
   William Sanders, Ordained 4. November 1664, Died 13. May 1670.
   John Cummine, Ordained 13. December 1670, Ejected 1690, and became a Papist in Ireland.

Mr John MacEan, Ordained 1696, Died in June 1704.
 Thomas MacCulloch, Ordained 1. July 1708, Tranfported to Bellie in 1709.
 William Dougal, Ordained 1. February 1710, Tranfported to Spynie 1721.
 David Dunlop, Ordained 19. September 1721, Died 29. May 1742.
 Alexander Moray, Ordained 28. April 1743, Died Auguft 13. 1765.
 Jofeph Anderfon, Ordained 18. March 1766.

ELGIN Parifh.
p. 64.

ELGIN, a Parfonage dedicated to St Giles, was the Bifhop's Paftoral Charge. I find not two Minifters in Elgin before the year 1613, after which time the Second Minifter was the Bifhop's Vicar. In 1642, King Charles I. granted the Patronage to the Magiftrates, and Common Council. This was ratified in Parliament 1645; and in that year, Meffrs Murdoch MacKenzie and Thomas Law were prefented by the Town Council: But by the Act Refciffory in 1661, and the re-eftablifhing Prelacy in 1662, the gift in favour of the Town became void, and the King is Patron. The ftipend, by decreet in 1714, is modified to 104 Bolls Bear, and L. 450 Scots to each Minifter, but falleth fhort in the locality near a Boll, and L. 3 to each. The Vicarage of Plufcarden, converted at L. 100, is allowed for Communion Elements. There is but one Glebe, and no Manfe; but there is ground where the Manfe ftood, and a garden adjacent to it. The lands of Eafter Kelles were, in 1657, annexed to Dallas by the Prefbytery, and received the civil fanction: But attempts to disjoin Plufcarden and Blackhills became ineffectual, becaufe not ratified in law. At Langmorn, or *Lhan-Morgan*, i. e. "Morgan's Church," was a Free Chapel, which had its own Minifter, probably till 1613, when a Second Minifter, or a Vicar, was fettled in the Parifh. At Inverlochtie was St John Baptift's Chapel, and another at Bogfide. There is in the Town a Grammar School, endued by the Community, and a School for teaching Englifh and Mufic, endued by King James VI. out of the Revenues of the Preceptory of Maifon Dieu
               (vid.

Sect. 4. THE PROTESTANT CHURCH 341

(vid. page 263). The Church of St Giles, being an old vaulted fabric, fell down in 1679, and was soon rebuilt in the modern way, as it now stands (vid. page 65). The mortifications for the Poor are: By Charles Gordon late Bailie 300 merks: By Alexander Dick late Conveener 1000 merks: By Dykeside 2000 merk: By James Cramond late Bailie, 500 merks: By John Sanders merchant, 150 merks; by Robert Gordon merchant, 100 merks: By William Duff of Dipple, 1500 merks: By Mr James Thomson late Minister, 600 merks to buy Bibles for the poor: By Cummine of Pittulie late Provost, 6037½ merks for four Pensioners; to four Beadmen 16 Bolls annually, of the Revenues of Maison Dieu; besides the rent of the Hospital Croft for gowns to them: By the Kirk Session 350 merks: A considerable growing fund, established by the Guildrie, for decayed Guild brethren: And particular funds by some Incorporations. The Catechiseable persons are above 4000. The Protestant Ministers, besides the Bishops that were not Ministers of Elgin before their consecration, are,

Mr Alexander Winchester Minister in 1568.
 Thomas Robertson, Reader in 1569.
 William Douglass, Vicar in 1579.
 Alexander Douglass, Ordained about 1582, Bishop in 1610, Died 1623.
 David Philp Ordained in March 1613, Died in September 1632.
 John Gordon, from Kenedar, Admitted 31. March, 1633, Deposed for Immoralities 1639.
 Gilbert Ross, Admitted 14. September 1642, Died 14. August 1644.
 Murdoch MacKenzie, from Inverness, Admitted 17. April 1645, Bishop 1662.
 Thomas Law, from Boharm, Admitted 28 Aug. 1645, Died 13. Aug. 1057.
 James Horn, from Bellie, Admitted 28 July 1659, Demitted 1682, for the Test.
 Alexander Tod, from Lawbride, Admitted 11. July 1642, Demitted in 1689.
 Robert Langlands, from Barony of Glasgow, Admitted 21. June 1696, Died 12. August that year.
 James Thomson, from Cullington, Admitted 21. June 1696, Died 1. June 1716.
 Alexander King, from Bonill, Admitted 27. April 701, Died 22 Dec. 1715.
 Charles Primrose, from Forres, Admitted 7. May 1717, Transp. to Crichton 1729.
 Joseph Sanderson, from Alves, Admitted 4. May 1727, Died 15. July 1733.

Mr James

Mr James Winchester, from Aldern, Admitted 5. May 1730, Transported to Jedburgh 1737.

Lauchlan Shaw, from Calder, Adm. 9. May 1734, Resigned 1774, and still alive.
Alexander Irvine from Aldern, Admitted 12. Aug. 1735, Died 22. Dec. 1758.
David Rintoul, from Kirkaldie, Admitted 28. Sept. 1759. } present Ministers.
William Peterkin, Ordained 14th July 1774.

St Andrews Parish.
p. 77.

ST ANDREWS, a Mensal Church, of old called *Kil-ma-Lemnoc*. The King is now Patron. In time of Prelacy this Church, and that of Ogston on the other side of the Loch of Spynie, were committed to one Vicar, that the Bishop might draw the more Teinds. In the North end of the Parish, was the Chapel of Insh; and at Forresters seat, stood the Church of *Kil-ma-Lemnoc*. The stipend, by decreet in 1722, is four Chalders of Bear, and 400 merks, with 50 merks for Communion Elements. The Salary of the School is legal. Mortifications are 200 merks by Innes of Darkland, and 100 merks by George Russel in Linkwood. Catechisable persons are 500. The Protestant Ministers are,

Mr Alexander Lesly Exhorter in 1567.
John Peters, Minister in 1627, Deposed in 1639, for refusing the Covenant.
Robert Tarras, Ordained 3. September 1640, Died in August 1646.
Robert Innes from Spynie, Admitted 29. October 1646, Died in May 1663.
Thomas Craig, Ordained 4. November 1663, Demitted in 1690.
Gavin Wedderspoon, Ordained in 169, Died 26. March 1715.
John Urquhart, from Girtlie, Admitted 12. Nov. 1717, Died 23. June 1725.
Alexander Irvine, Ordained 1. March 1726, Transported to Aldern 1730.
John Patterson, from Dipple, Admitted 23. November 1731.

Kenedar Parish
p. 69.

KENEDAR, a Parsonage, the seat of the Treasurer. In 1753, Sir Robert Gordon of Gordonston purchased the Patronage from John Innes of Leuchars. " June 14th 1666, The Bishop, " and Chapter, with Sir Robert Gordon of Gordonston, and " Alexander Brodie of Brodie, Heretors, ratified and approved " the disjunction of Ogston, made in 1642, from St Andrews,

and,

"and the annexation of it to Kenedar, without prejudice to
"the Bishop as Titular of St Andrews and Ogston; and that
"118 merks be paid annually out of Ogston to the Minister
"of St Andrews; and because this will diminish the stipend of
"Kenedar, therefore Gordonston will make up to him
"these 118 merks (*Presb. Rec.*)." The Church, formerly at
Kenedar, was, about 1666, built in the centre of the united parishes, at Dranie, and the Church is now called " The Church
of Dranie," but the Glebe and Manse are at Kenedar, an
English mile from the Church at Dranie. The stipend, by
decreet in 1774, is L. 600 Scots; 2 Chalders Bear; 40 Bolls
oats; and L. 30 for Communion Elements. The Salary of
the School is 12 Bolls. Catechisable persons are 1000. The
Protestant Ministers are,

Mr William Clark Exhorter in 1572.
   William Wiseman, Reader in 1569.
   William Douglas, Minister in 1596 and 1603.
   Alexander Innes, Minister in 1624.
   John Gordon in 1625, Transported to Elgin 1633.
   David Cullefs, from Ugston, Admitted 1634. Died about 1681.
   Michael Cummine, Ord. with the survivance, 7. March 1666, Died about 1696.
   Hugh Anderson, from Rosemarkie, Admitted 17. August 1698, Resigned 1740, Died 1749.
   William Collie, Ordained 17. March 1741, Died April 29. 1768.
   Lewis Gordon, Ordained 28. September 1768.

UGSTON, a Mensal Church, dedicated to St Peter. It is now
annexed to the parish of Kenedar, as above, and Gordonston
acts as Patron: But how far the King may claim a vice Patronage, I shall not determine. The Ministers were,

Mr James Ker, Exhorter, in 1569.
   William Roch, Minister in 1594, Transported to Essil in 1601.
   David Collefs, Minister in 1625, Transported to Kenedar about 1634.
   Robert Innes, about 1634, Transported to Spynie 1640, and had no successor.

Ugston Parish. p. 69.

Duffus.

Duffus Parish,
p. 73.

DUFFUS, a Parsonage dedicated to St. Peter, the Patronage whereof was once tripartite, betwixt the King, Marshal, and Duffus. The Presentation to Alexander Symer, 10th August 1642, runs thus: "Be it kend, me James Sutherland, Tutor "of Duffus, heretable proprietor of one third of the Baronie "of Duffus, as undoubted Patron of the third Vice of the "Kirk of Duffus, sometime belonging to William Earl of Mar- "shall, and disponed by him to me; to have presented, &c." In 1738, Archibald Dunbar of Newtoun *contra* Duke of Gordon, obtained a Declarator of the whole Patronage, and is now Patron and Titular. There was produced to the Presbytery of Elgin, 14th October 1736, for the Duke of Gordon, an extract of an act of Parliament 1621, ratifying the grant of the Patronage of the Church of Duffus and Chapel of Unthank made to Lord Spynie, anno 1593; Also Charter by King Charles II. as *Ultimus Heres* to Lord Spynie, of the said Patronage, in favour of James Earl of Airly, anno 1674; which right Lord Airly assigned to George Marquis of Huntly, anno 1682: But the said Archibald Dunbar produced in process, a Charter to his Authors anno 1527, and another anno 1588. There was in this parish a Free Chapel called *Unthank*, which had its own Minister and Stipend*, likewise a Chapel of Ease in the Burgh.

---

* I know not whence this Chapel is called UNTHANK, if it be not from the Irish word *Intach*. The Country people, who best retain the ancient Orthography and Pronounciation, always call it *Intach*, i. e. "Lonely or Solitary." The situation of it favours this Etymology; and the Monks, who understood not the Irish, gave it a name of a similar sound. Here, and at Ross-Isle near to it, there was a College of Monks, and probably the Chaplain of Unthank was Provost of the College. Unthank was a Free Chapel, and had lands independant of the Parsonage of Duffus; and when after the Reformation, such Chapels were annexed to the Crown, this probably gave rise to the Tripartite division of Duffus into the King's part, Duffus's part, and Marshall's part, and to the Duke of Gordon's claim, of at least a Vice patronage of Duffus. (*Vid. Append.* No. xiiv.)

Sect. 4. THE PROTESTANT CHURCH. 345

Burgh. The stipend, by decreet, is 8 Chalders of Bear, 350 Merks, and 60 Merks for Com. Elements. The Salary of the School is but 7 Bolls, 2 Firlots, 3 Pecks, 2 Lippies of Bear. The Examinable Persons are 1200. The Protestant Ministers are,

Mr William Clerk, Reader in 1569.
  John Keith, Minister in 1570, 1574, 1579.
  John Gibson, Parson of Unthank, and Prebendary 1570.
  Alex. Keith, Minister in 1586, Died about 1609.
  Patrick Dunbar, Minister in 1612, Died about 1632.
  John Guthrie, Ordained in 1633, Deposed 1640 for refusing the Covenant.
  Alex. Symer, Ordained 19th January 1643, Died in 1686.
  Adam Sutherland, Ordained February 1687, Died about 1698.
  Alex. Anderson, Ordained about 1700, Died in March 1721.
  James Dunbar, Ordained 31. March 1724, Died 26. June 1736.
  John Bower, Ordained 15. September 1737, Died 6. February 1748.
  Alex. Moray, Ordained 28. September 1748.

NEW SPYNIE, a Parsonage dedicated to the HOLY TRINITY. The Laird of Innes claims the Patronage: A Sub-synod in Forres, June 1640, appointed Mr Joseph Brodie, to deal with the Laird of Innes, to present some able man to the Kirk of Spynie, *(Syn. Rec.)*; and in September that year, he presented Mr Robert Innes. Likewise, in 1647, Sir Robert Innes presented Mr William Cloggie, *(Presb. Rec.)* The Church was transplanted from Spynie, the very extremity of the Parish, and built at Quarrywood anno 1735; but the Glebe and the Burying-place are at Spynie. There was a Chapel of Ease at Inchbrok. The Stipend, by Decreet in 1730, is 64 Bolls of Bear, L. 300, and L. 60 for Com. Elements. The School Salary is not legal. Mary Bannerman, Lady Finrossie, mortified 1000 Merks for the poor, and they have a share of Dipple's mortification to Elgin. The Catechiseable persons are 700. The Protestant Ministers are,

New Spynie Parish, Page 70.

Mr James Philp, Exhorter anno 1570.
  Alex. Ralphson, Minister in 1579, and in 1603.

Mr Alex. Watson, Minister in 1614.
    Thomas Craig, Minister in 1614, Died in 1639.
    Robert Innes, from Ugston, Admitted 28. September 1640, Transported to St Andrews 1646.
    William Cloggie, (Vide Inverness) Adm. 21. January 1647, Died Dec. 1659.
    Samuel Tulloch, Ordained 27. June 1660. Died in November 1706.
    Robert Bates, Ordained 6. September 1707, Died in October 1719.
    William Dougal, from Birnie, Adm. 7. March 1721, Died 12. October 1766.
    Robert Patterson, Ordained privately, Admitted June 18. 1767.

N. B. This last had a joint Presentation from the Duke of Gordon, and Sir James Innes, *Salvo Jure.*

Alves Parish. Page 85.

ALVES, a Parsonage, the seat of the Chantor. The Earl of Moray is Patron. (Vid. *Lanbride*, and *Kinloss*.) The Stipend, by Decreet in 1712, is 80 bolls of Bear ; L 300, with 50 merks for Communion Elements. The Salary of the School, is 8 bolls of Bear, and L. 33 : 6 : 8 Scots George Duncan late merchant in Inverness, mortified L. 2000 for educating Boys at this School. Catechiseable persons are 1300. The Protestant Ministers are,

    Mr Patrick Balfour, Minister in 1567.
        Alex. Bid, Exhorter in 1570.
        James Muirton, Minister in 1574.
        Gavin Dunbar, Minister in 1613, Died in June 1640.
        George Harvay, Ord. 12. Nov. 1640, Depos. 1646 for opposing the Covenant.
        William Campbell, from Bower, Admitted 16. August 1649, Transported to Olrick 1660.
        Alex. Stuart, Ordained 16. October 1661, Died in October 1675.
        Berould Innes. Ordained 1. March 1676, Ejected 1690.
        John Gilchrist, from Leith, Admitted 1697, Transported to Keith in 1700.
        Joseph Sanderson, Ordained 2 February 1703, Transported to Elgin in 1727.
        George Gordon, from Boharm, Adm. 21. Novem. 1728, Died 3 March 1752.
        Alex. Watt, Ordained 13. March 1753, Transported to Forres 1774.

Presbytery of Forres.

Kinloss Parish was erected by the joint care of the Presbyteries of Elgin and Forres. The erection was approved by the Synod of Moray, in October 1657, and ratified in Parliament, anno 1661. The new Parish, excepting a small part, being taken out of the Parish of Alves, the Earl of Moray, as Patron of the Mother Church, is Patron of Kinloss. From the Reformation downward, Divine Worship was kept in the Abbey Church of Kinloss, and the Presbytery claimed the Precinct, Church, and Church-Yard. But Alexander Brodie of Lethen, who purchased the Abbey Lands from the Lord Kinloss, had sold the stones of the Abbey to the English, for building the Citadel at Inverness, in 1651 and 1652, and agreed with the Presbytery, that he should pay L. 100 Sterling for building the Church, and give one half of the Glebe, both which he performed; and Sir John M'Kenzie of Tarbet, and Muirton gave George's-Yard, for the other half of the Glebe, (*Presbytery Rec. of Forres.*). The stipend, by a decreet in 1730, is 56 bolls of Bear, and, including Communion Elements, L. 396. The Salary of the School is Legal. Examinable persons are about 1000. Mr James Urquhart was the first Minister, and was deposed 19th May 1663, for not conforming to Prelacy. He was reponed by Act of Parliament 1690, and returned to his charge; but was so ill treated, that he demitted anno 1695, and lived with his son in Urquhart, where he died 16th April 1701. The Protestant Ministers are,

Mr James Urquhart, Ordained 19 August 1659. Deposed in 1663.
   Alex. Dunbar, from Kennay, Admn. 19. Octob. 1665, Died 14 March 1669.
   George Innes, from Premnay, Admitted 16. June 1670, Ejected in 1690.
   James Urquhart, Restored in 1690, Demitted in 1695.
   James Gordon, Ordained 5. September 1699, Died 10. December 1752.
   James Munro, Ordained 14. May 1752.

RAFFORD.

RAFFORD Parish.
Page 90.

RAFFORD, a Parsonage, the Seat of the Sub-Chantor. Alexander Brodie of Lethen is Patron. A small part of this Parish was cast into the New-erected Parish of Kinloss; and the Parish of Altyre, formerly annexed to Dallas, was made a part of Rafford Parish, and the disjunction and annexation was ratified in Parliament, anno 1661. The stipend, by decreet in 1752, is 76 bolls 3 firlots Bear, and L. 349 : 13 : 4, whereof 100 merks for Communion Elements. The Salary of the School is legal. Catechisable persons are about 1200. The Ministers are,

Mr James Rawson, Reader in Rafford and Kinloss anno 1567.
 Alex. Urquhart, Minister in Rafford and Kinloss anno 1568.
 Alex. Dunbar, Minister and Sub-Chantor anno 1582.
 Robert Dunbar, Minister anno 1597 and 1614.
 John Hay, Minister in 1624, Transported to Fraserburgh 1643.
 William Fullerton, Ordained 2. April 1644, Died in February 1668.
 Alex. Fordyce, Ordained 8. July 1668, Died in September 1715.
 James Winchester, Ordained 19. April 1716, Transported to Aldern 1726.
 William Porteous, Ordained 28. December 1727, Died 3. January 1738.
 Robert Logan, Ordained 14. September 1738, Died 16. August 1752.
 Duncan Shaw, Ordained 10. May 1753.

DALLAS Parish.
Page 68.

DALLAS, a Parsonage, dedicated to St. MICHAEL, and the seat of the Sub-dean. Sir Robert Gordon of Gordonston is Patron. Upon the annexation of Altyre to Rafford; Easter Kellefs was annexed to Dallas, anno 1657; and about 1631, 200 merks of the Vicarage of Aldern was made, and continues to be, a part of the stipend of Dallas. The stipend, now by decreet 17 , including Communion Elements, is L. 700 Scots. There is no legal School. The Catechisable persons are about 500. The Protestant Ministers are,

Mr William Thomson, Reader, in Dallas anno 1567.
 John Clark, Reader in Altyre and Dallas anno 1569.
 William Patterson, Minister and Sub-Dean anno 1574.
 Alex. Richardson, Minister in 1611 and 1617.
 George Cumming, Ordained about 1624, Died in Summer 1648.

Mr James

Mr James Strachan, Ordained in Winter 1649, Died in October 1671.
   Alex. Cumming, Ordained 13. June 1672, Demitted in 1681 for the Test.
   George Dunbar, Ordained 13. October 1681, Transported to Nairn in 1687.
   Thomas Urquhart, privately Ordained, was Admitted 11. January 1688, Died about 1706.
   John Crokat, Ordained 9. May 1708, Died 22. April 1748.
   Robert Dalrymple, Ordained 23. February 1749, Deposed in May 1763.
   James Hay, Ordained September 27. 1763.

FORRES, a Parsonage, dedicated to St. LAURENCE, and the seat of the Arch-deacon. The Earl of Moray is Patron. There was a Chapel about a mile above the Town, and another at Loggie, (Vid. Edenkyle.) The stipend, by decreet in 1754, is 98 bolls Bear, 20 bolls Oat-meal, L. 410, and L. 80 Scots for Communion Elements. The Salary of the School is legal. Examinable persons are 1600. The Ministers are,

Forres Parish.

Mr David Rae, Minister in 1563.
   John Patterson, Reader in 1567.
   Andrew Simpson, Minister of Forres and Altyre 1568.
   Gavine Dunbar, Minister in 1574 and 1579.
   John Forrester, Minister in 1590.
   Patrick Tulloch, in 1614, Died in Summer 1646.
   Joseph Brodie, from Keith, Admit. December 1646, Died 27. October 1656.
   Colin Falconer, from Essil, Admitted 24. March 1678, became Bishop 1680.
   William Law, Ordained 16. September 1680, Demitted in 1690.
   Thomas Thomson, Ordained about 1693, Transported to Turriff 1697.
   Charles Primrose, from Bellie, Admitted January 1703, Transf. to Elgin 1717.
   John Squire, Ordained 1713, Admitted 17. June 1718 Died 17. Jan 1758.
   Æneas Shaw, from Pettie, Admitted 14. Dec. 1758, Died 5. July 1773.
   Alex. Watt, from Alves, admitted 23. June 1774.

EDINKYLIE, a Vicarage to the seat of the Archdeacon, and whereof he was Patron and Titular. The Minister of Forres presented Mr John Cumming in 1668, and Mr David Cumming in 1672, and the Earl of Moray never presented before 1754. I do not find, that this parish was erected before the Reformation.

Edinkylie Parish. Page 52.

350 THE ECCLESIASTIC HISTORY. Part VI.

tion; but there was a Chapel at Duldavie: and the Chapel of Logie Fythenach was the Archdeacon's Vicarage *(Appendix,* No. XXVIII.) This and Ardclach were, for many years, one united Parish, and were disjoined about 1638. The Stipend, by Decreet in 1764, including Element-money, is 750 Merks, and three Chalders, half Bear, half Meal. There are three Charity-Schools erected in this Parish. The Examinable Persons are about 1200. The Protestant Ministers are,

Mr Andrew Brown, Minister in 1570.
> Robert Dunbar, Minister of Edinkylie and Ardelach in 1624, Died in 1636.
> David Dunbar, Ordain. 8. June 1637, to both parishes, Transf. to Nairn 1638.
> John Dunbar, Ordained to Edinkylie 1638, Died in Spring 1646.
> Patrick Glass, Ordained 1649, Died 18. March 1666.
> John Cumming, Ordained 2. January 1668, Transported to Aldern 1672.
> David Cumming, Ordained 25. April 1672, Died in Summer 1699.
> Alex. Shaw, Ordained 6. May 1702, Died 24. June 1753.
> Alex. Coul, Ordained 13. March 1754.

Moy Parish Page 98.

Moy and Dyke were distinct Parishes, till the year 1624, when they were united, by a Decreet of the PLAT (*Syn. Rec.*). Moy was a Parsonage, but I do not find that Dyke was so. Mr Campbell of Calder is undoubted Patron of Moy, by a Disposition from Alexander Lord Spynie anno 1636. Mr William Falconer seems to have been settled at Dyke about 1625; yet, upon a debate about Teinds, the Earl of Dunfermline presented him in 1641, against which Mr James Campbell of Moy protested, and the Synod, in 1642, ordered this protestation to be recorded in its proper place, in the Register of the Presbytery of Forres. In 1674, Mr William Falconer, the Bishop's Son, was presented by Dunfermline, and the Earl of Moray wrote to the Bishop, approving his settlement (*Syn. and Presb. Rec.*). Dunfermline, as Commendator of Pluscarden, and thereby Heretor or Superior of Grangehill, might have been Patron of

Dyke

Sect. 4.   THE PROTESTANT CHURCH.   351

Dyke, and forfeited to the Crown; but I know not any right that the Earl of Moray has. The Stipend is 97 Bolls 3 Firlots, and 500 Merks, including Communion Elements. The School is Legal. The Family of Brodie has built a Convenient House, and mortified a Salary, for the Education of Girls. Harry Vause, who had long served Major George Grant of Coulbin, mortified to this Parish L. 130 Sterling, for Cloathing twelve Indigent Boys. He mortified the like sum to the Infirmary at Edinburgh, and the same to that of Aberdeen, anno 1757. The Examinable Persons are about 1400. The Protestant Ministers are,

  Mr William Sutherland, Minister in 1564, 1574, and 1579.
    George Simpson, Reader at Moy in 1570.
    Alex. Duff, Reader at Dyke in 1570.
    Harry Dundass, Minister at Dyke in 1613.
    William Dunbar, Minister at Moy in 1613.
    William Falconer, in 1625, Died 18. June 1674.
    William Falconer, Ord. in England, Admitted 23. Sept. 1674, Ejected 1690.
    Alex. Forbes, Admitted about 1691, Died in 1707.
    James Chalmers, Ordained 14. Sept. 1709, Transp. to Aberdeen in 1726.
    Robert Dunbar, Ordained 23. September 1727.

The GENERAL ASSEMBLY 1773 disjoined from FORRES, the Parishes of Ardclach, Auldern, and Nairn; from INVERNESS, Calder and Croy; and from CHANONRY, Arderfier; and erected these six into the Presbytery of NAIRN.

PRESBYTERY of NAIRN.

Presbytery of NAIRN.

ARDCLACH, a Vicarage whereof the Minister of Rafford was Titular, and probably Patron (*Appendix*, No. XLVII.). Brodie of Lethen, as Patron of Rafford, acted as Patron of Ardclach. I do not find, that Ardclach was called a Parish before the Reformation; the Chapels of Fernes and Lethen, depending

Ardclach Parish. Page 95.

ing on the Dean of Aldern, seem to have been the places of Worship (*App.* No. XXVIII.), and the Church of Ardclach was built in 1626. The Stipend, by agreement, is a Chalder of Meal, and 620 Merks, including Element Money. The Protestant Ministers since the disjunction are as below. There is a Legal School. And the Examinable Persons are about 900.

Mr William Brown, Reader in 1570.
    William Simpson, Vicar in 1588.
    Donald MacPherson, Ordained 1638, Transported to Calder in 1642.
    George Balfour, Ordained in 1642, Died 4. January 1680.
    Patrick Grant, Ordained 12. August 1680, Died in September 1715.
    John Duncanson, Ord. 13. September 1716, Transported to Pettie in 1728.
    William Baron, Admitted 24. April 1729.

ALDERN Parish, page 108.

ALDERN, a Parsonage, and the Seat of the Dean. In 1650, some parts of this large Parish were annexed to Nairn, Calder, and Ardclach. The Patronage was disponed by Lord Spynie to Dunbar of Grange, and by him to Hay of Park, from whom it came to the Family of Brodie. The Stipend, by Decreet in 1755, is 6 Chalders, half Bear, half Meal, 400 Merks, 10 Merks for the Dean's Crook near Elgin, 14 Wedders, and L. 60 for Communion Elements. The School is Legal. Examinable Persons are about 1400. The Protestant Ministers are,

Mr Alexander Dunbar, Dean of Moray, in 1560, 1574, and 1586.
    William Reoch, Exhorter at Aldern and Nairn, in 1570.
    Thomas Dunbar Minister and Dean in 1613.
    John Brodie, Minister and Dean in 1624, Died 7. January 1655.
    Harry Forbes from Wick, Admitted 10. October 1655. Demitted in 1663.
    George Hannay, from Inveravon, Admitted 4. July 1664, Died in 1669.
    John Cumming from Edinkylie, Admitted 14. Feb. 1672, Demitted in 1682.
    Thomas Kay, Ord. in the South, Admitted 17. April 1683, Expelled in 1690.
    Alexander Dunbar, Admitted in 1690, Died in 1708.
    David Henderson, Ordained 13. September 1709, Died in June 1727.
    James Winchester, from Rafford, Adm. 12. May 1726, Transp. to Elgin 1730.
    Alexander Irvine from St Andrews, Admitted 7. January 1731, Transported to Elgin 1735.
    Donald Munro, Ordained 23. September 1736, Transported to Tayne in 1745.
    Thomas Gordon, from Cabrach, Admitted 12. February 1747.

Sect. 4. THE PROTESTANT CHURCH.   353

NAIRN, a Vicarage, antiently *Capella de Invernirin*, depending on the Dean of Moray, who was Patron and Titular. In 1687, Mr George Dunbar was presented by the Dean (*Rec. Presbytery of Forres*); and now the Laird of Brodie, as Patron of Aldern, claims the Right, and did present in 1759. The Virgin's Chapel at Geddes was built anno 1220, and in 1475, Pope SEXTUS IV. granted a Bull, dispensing with a hundred days of Pennance, for every Visit paid to it, on the day of Assumption, Nativity, &c. or for repairing the building (*Pen. Kilravock*). The Stipend, by Decreet, is 80 Bolls of Bear, L. 500, and L. 50 for Communion Elements. The School is Legal. Examinable Persons are about 1300. The Protestant Ministers are,

NAIRN Parish.
Page 110.

 Mr John Young, Exhorter in 1568.
  William Reoch, Exhorter in Aldern and Nairn in 1570.
  Andrew Balfour, Minister in 1598.
  John Sanders, Minister in 1614, Died about 1637.
  David Dunbar from Edinkylie, Admitted 1638, Died 1662.
  Hugh Rose, Ordained 4. January 1660 as Assistant, Died December 1686.
  George Dunbar, from Dallas, Admitted 25. May 1687, Died December 1728.
  Alexander Rose, Ordained 7. July 1730, Died 16. December 1757.
  Patrick Dunbar, Ordained 12. April 1759.

ARDERSIER, a Parsonage in the Presbytery of Chanonrie, and the Seat of the Subdean of Ross. The Laird of Calder is Patron, by a Right from Keith of Ravenscraig, anno 1599. (*Pen. Calder*). This Parish was annexed to the Synod of Moray in 1705, but soon after disjoined. The Stipend is 80 Bolls of Victual, and about L. 50 of Vicarage. The Examinable Persons, without the Precinct of the Fort, are about 400. There is no School. And the Ministers, since the Revolution in 1688, are,

ARDERSIER Parish.
Page 124.

 Mr John Dallas, Sub-Dean in 1688, Died about 1693.
  Lauchlan MacBean, from Calder, Admitted 1695, Deprived in 1706.
  Hugh Campbell, Ordained in 1707, Transported to Kiltearn in 1708.

Mr Donald Beaton, Ordained in 1713, Transported to Rosekene in 1717.
   Alexander Falconer, Ordained in 1718, Transported to Ferntosh in 1728.
   Duncan MacIntosh, Ordained in 1729, Died in 1736.
   James Calder, Ordained in 1737, Transported to Croy 1747.
   Donald Brodie, Ordained 11. May 1749, Transported to Calder 1752.
   Harry Gordon, Ordained 5. April 1757, Died March 15. 1764.
   Walter Morrison, Ordained 1763, Admitted September 27. 1764.

CALDER Parish. Page 112.

CALDER, a Parsonage dedicated to St. EWAN, whereof the Laird of Calder is Patron, by a disposition from the Lord Spynie, anno 1606. The Parish was called *Bar-Ewan*, i. e. " Saint, or Excellent Ewan." The Church stood in the South end till the year 1619. Sir John Campbell, being in danger by water coming from *Yla*, vow'd, if he arrived safe at Calder, he would build a church in the centre of the parish, which he performed that same year. There was at Old Calder a Chapel of Ease. In the Court of the Castle was a Private Chapel; and at Dallas in the Streins, was a Free Chapel, with a Glebe and a proper Stipend. The East end of this Parish was disjoin'd from Aldern, and annexed to Calder, anno 1650. The Stipend, by decreet in 1722, is, 20 Bolls Bear, 20 Bolls Meal, 550 Merks, and L. 50 for Communion Elements. The School is legal. Examinable persons 700. The Ministers are,

Mr Allan MacIntosh, Exhorter in 1568, Parson in 1581 and 1586.
   Andrew Balfour, Minister in 1623, Died about 1625.
   Gilbert Henderson, in 1626, Transported in 1641.
   Donald MacPherson, from Ardclach, Admitted in 1642, Died in Dec. 1686.
   Lauchlan MacBean, Ordained in Sept. 1687, Transported to Arderfier 1695.
   James Chapman, Ordained 1699, Transported to Cromdale in 1702.
   John Calder, Ordained in 1704, Died in March 1717.
   Lauchlan Shaw, from Kingusie, Admitted 19. Nov. 1719. Transf. to Elgin 1734.
   Patrick Grant, Ordained 7. May 1735, Transported to Urray in 1749.
   Donald Brodie, from Arderfier, Admitted 13. May 1752, Died 21. May 1771.
   Kenneth MacAuly, from Ardnamorchoan, Admitted 17. November 1772.

Sect. 4. THE PROTESTANT CHURCH. 355

CROY and DALCROSS were distinct Parishes, and have still a Glebe in each, but I find not how early they were united. Croy was a Parsonage, on which Moy in Strathern depended as a Vicarage. Dalcross was a Vicarage, depending on the Prior of Urquhart; and in 1343, there was an agreement between the Prior of Urquhart, and the Baron of Kilravok, that the Vicar of Dealg-an-Rofs, now Dalcross, should officiate in the Private Chapel of Kilravok, (*Pen. Kilrav.*) The Laird of Calder is Patron of Dalcross, by a disposition from Alexander Earl of Dunfermline and Lord Urquhart in 1610; and he likewise claims the Patronage of Croy, for Kilravok has few acts of Pessession. There was in the South of the Parish, a Chapel of Ease, called *Kil-Doich*, i. e. "Dorothy's Church," another in the North at Chapeltoun; and probably there was at Kilravok, a Chapel dedicated to one of the name Ravok. The Stipend, by decreet, is 5 Chalders Bear, 500 Merks, and 50 Merks for Communion Elements. The School is Legal. Examinable Persons 1800. The Ministers are,

Croy and Dalcross Parish. Page 117.

Mr James Vaufe, Reader at Croy and Moy anno 1567.
    Patrick Lyddel, Minister at Croy in 1585.
    James Vaufe, from Dunlichtie, Admitted in 1618, Died in 1660.
    Hugh Frafer, Ordained in December 1662, died about 1699.
    Alex. Frafer, Ordained in Spring 1703, Transported to Ferntosh in 1715.
    Ferchard Beaton, Ordained in Winter 1718, Died in Feb. 1746.
    James Calder, from Ardersier, Admitted 28. April 1747.

PRESBYTERY of INVERNESS.

MOY and DALARASIE were distinct Parishes, and there is still a Glebe in each: How early they were united, I find not. Kilravok, as Patron of Croy on which Moy depended, claims the Patronage, but I know not by what right. The Stipend is 800 Merks, and 50 Merks for Communion Elements. There is no School. The Examinable persons are 1000. The Ministers are,

Presbytery of INVERNESS. Moy and Dalarassie Parish. Page 97.

Mr Andrew

Mr Andrew Dow Fraser, Transported to Boleskin in 1624.
    Lauchlan Grant, Ordained in 1627, Transported to Kingussie in 1649.
    Roderick MacKenzie, Ordained in 1653. Died in February 1680.
    Alex. Cumming, Ordained in May 1680, Died 27. April 1709.
    James Leslie, Ordained in August 1716, Died 28. October 1766.
    James MacIntosh, Ordained 14. July 1767.

Daviot and Dunlichtie
Page 122.

DAVIOT and DUNLICHTIE were distinct parishes, united about the year 1618, and the Minister has a Glebe in each. Dunlichtie was a parsonage, of which the Laird of Calder is Patron. Daviot was a common Kirk. The Bishop presented Mr Alexander Fraser in 1664, and having presented Mr Michael Fraser in 1673, Calder obliged the Bishop to annul the settlement, to declare the Church vacant, and then Calder presented the same Mr Michael Fraser, *(Rec. Presb. of Invernefs.)* The Stipend, including Communion Elements, is 1000 Merks. The School is Legal. MacPhail of Inverarnie has mortified 400 Merks; and MacIntosh of Farr 300 Merks, for the Poor. Examinable Persons are about 1000. The Ministers are,

    Mr John Dow MacDonachie, Reader anno 1569.
        Hugh Gregory, Parson of Lundichty anno 1579.
        James Vause, Parson in 1613, Transported to Croy in 1618.
        Alex. Thomson, Minister in 1625, Deposed in 1646.
        Alex Rose, Ordained in 1647, Died in 1660.
        Alex. Fraser, Ordained 31. Aug. 1664, Deprived 1672 for Non Conformity.
        Michael Fraser, Ordained 19. February 1673. Died in April 1726.
        James Fraser, Ordained 13. March 1729, Died 18. June 1736.
        John Campbell, Ordained 14. January 1738, Died 4. November 1759.
        Patrick Grant, Ord. 22. April 1761, Transported to Boleskin 10. May 1770.
        Alex. Grant, Admitted 2. April 1771.

Pettie and Brachlie Parish.
Page 125.

PETTIE and BRACHLIE were distinct Charges, and have distinct Glebes. Petty is a Parsonage, dedicated to St. Coluim, and Brachlie a Vicarage depending thereon. The Earl of Moray is Patron. The stipend is 80 bolls Bear, 500 merks, and 50 merks for Communion Elements. The School is legal. The

Sect. 4. THE PROTESTANT CHURCH 357

The Examinable perfons are about 1100. The Proteftant Minifters are,

Mr Andrew Braboner, Exhorter in 1568.
 James Dunbar, Parfon in 1579.
 Donald MacQueen, in 1613, Died about 1630.
 Alex. Frafer, Ordained in 1633, Died in Summer 1683.
 Alex. Denune, Ordained privately, Admitted 20. April 1684, Depofed 1706, Died 1718.
 Daniel MacKenzie, from Inveravon, Admitted 8. October 1719, Tranfported to Invernefs 1727.
 John Duncanfon, from Ardclach, Adm. 18. June 1728, Died 6. May 1737.
 Lewis Chapman, from Alvie, Admitted 1738, Died 19. April 1741.
 Æneas Shaw, from Comrie, Adm. 8. June 1742, Tranfp. to Forres in 1758.
 John Morifon, Ord. an Itinerant, Admitt, 21. Aug. 1759, Died Nov. 1774.

INVERNESS is a Parfonage, dedicated to the Virgin Mary; and in 1618, the Parifh of BONA, likewife a Parfonage, was annexed to it by the PLAT*. Lord Spynie, Patron of Bona, did, in 1623, difpone his right to Frafer of Strichen, who, as Vice-Patron, prefented Mr John Anand in 1640: and the Synod of Moray in 1648, found that the other Vice belonged to the Crown. Yet, after this, the Family of Seafort claimed a Vice, but by what right, I find not; and in 1674, the Lord Kintail prefented Mr Gilbert Marfhal. But in a Sub-Synod at Forres in 1674, the Bifhop produced two letters to him from the Primate, difcharging him to plant the Church of Invernefs upon Seafort's Prefentation: And yet in 1688, Seafort prefented Mr Hector MacKenzie (*Rec. of Syn. and Presb. of Invernefs.*) Now by the forfeiture of Seafort and of Lord Lovate, to whom it is faid Strichen had fold the Patronage with his lands, both *vices* have come to the Crown, and the third Charge is a Royal Gift, the Patronage of which, without doubt, is in the Crown. I have not found two Minifters in Invernefs before 1638. For

INVERNESS Parifh. Page 126.

many

---

* The word PLAT, means fuch Members of Parliament, as were appointed to modify Stipends, annex or disjoin Parifhes.

many years after the Reformation, few Towns had more than one Minister, one Manse, and one Glebe; but a second Glebe and Manse at Inverness were obtained as follows: " Messrs " John Annand and Murdoch MacKenzie, with consent of Stri- " chen the Patron, and James Cuthbert of Drakies Provost, " and James Rose of Markinch one of the Baillies, Commissi- " oners from the Town, and Presbytery of Inverness, in the Ge- " neral Assembly held at Aberdeen, in August 1640, did, " with the approbation of the Assembly, agree, that the whole " Stipend, due to the said Ministers, for the year 1640, with " the sum of 700 Merks advanced by the Magistrates, should " be laid out in purchasing a Manse and Glebe, for the said Mr " Annand, and his Successors' in office, which was accordingly " done." This Deed is, at large, recorded in the Synod Re- gister, *Ad Annum* 1651, page 201, &c. The Stipend of two Ministers, by Decreet in 1755, is to each 84 Bolls, 1 Firlot, 2 Pecks, 2 Lippies of Meal, and L. 491 : 6 : 8, with L. 50 to each for Communion-Elements. In the year 1706, a living for a Third Minister was obtained as follows: Mr Robert Bailie, one of the Ministers, understood not the Irish Language, and Mr Hector Mackenzie, the other Minister, was superannuated, by which means the Irish People were totally neglected; wherefore the Queen, by her Royal gift, dated 4th October 1706, grant- ed out of the Rents of the Bishoprick of Moray, the sum of L. 881 : 1 : 6 Scots annually, as a Maintainance for a Third Mi- nister; but he has no allowance for a Manse, or Glebe, or Com- munion-Elements.

The Three Ministers are Colleagues, keep one General Sessi- on or Consistory, and agree upon a Partition of their Ministe- rial Work.

There are in the Town a Grammar School, and a School for teaching English, Writing, Arithmetic, &c.; and the Charity School

Sect. 4.   THE PROTESTANT CHURCH.   359

School erected by the Donation of Mr John Raining of Norwich merchant, who mortified L. 1200 Sterling, is fixed in this Town.

There is a valuable Library, the Donation mainly of Dr Bray, and Mr James Fraser, Son of Mr Alexander Fraser, some time Minister at Pettie, who not only gave many Books, but likewise a sum of Money to purchase more, and afford a Salary for a Keeper of the Library.

The Principal Stock of the Hospital of Inverness, in Bonds, Lands, Fishing, at Martinmass 1746, was, L. 2303 : 3 : 9¼ Sterling. Item, a separate Rent paid out of the Weigh House and Hospital Garden annually, L. 3 : 6 : 8 Sterling. The Laird of MacIntosh's Mortification in the Trust of the Hospital Treasurer, is of Principal L. 166 : 13 : 4 Sterling. George Duncan's Mortification is L. 200 Scots annually, whereof one-half towards repairing the Church, and the other to maintain Boys at Raining's School.

With respect to the Succession of Ministers, I have not found any Minister in Bona before the junction of the Parishes, except Mr Thomas Innes, who was Parson of Bonaw in 1598. Mr William Cloggie was brought to Inverness in 1620, and served with faithfulness till 1640, when some of the Heretors and Magistrates entered a complaint against him before the Synod of Moray, from which he was honourably assoilzied; but judged himself so ill used, that he would serve no longer in that Town; and therefore demitted his Charge. Of Mr Angus MacBean's conduct I shall speak afterwards. At the Revolution, Mr John MacGilligin preached for some time at Inverness, but was not settled, and died 8th June 1689. Likewise Mr James Fraser of Brae preached there for some time, but was not settled Minister. The number of Examinable Persons in Town and Parish to Landward, is about 6000. The Protestant Ministers are,

Mr Thomas

Mr Thomas Howeson, Minister in 1568 and 1590.
Thomas Innes, Parson of Bona in 1598.
James Bishop, Minister in 1617.
William Cloggie, from Inveravon, Admitted in 1620, Demitted in 1640.
George Munro, Irish Minister, Ordained 1638, Demitted in 1640 for want of maintainance.
Murdoch MacKenzie, from Contane, Adm. 1640, Transp. to Elgin in 1645.
John Annand, from Dunbenan, Admitted 1640, Died in November 1660.
Duncan MacCulloch, Ordained 1642, Transported to Urquhart 1647, for want of maintainance.
William Fraser, Ordained 1648, Died in September 1659.
James Sutherland, Ordained in April 1660, Died in September 1673.
Alexander Clerk, Ordained in April 1663, Died in September 1683.
Gilbert Marshal, from Cromdale, Admitted in Sept. 1674, Died about 1690.
Angus MacBean, privately Ord. Adm. 29th Dec. 1683, Demitted in 1687.
Hector MacKenzie, from Kingusie, Adm. 2d May 1688, Died 14th June 1719.
Robert Bailie, from Lambinton, Admitted in 1701, Died 11th Feb. 1726.
William Stewart, from Kiltearn, Adm. in 1705, Transp. to Kiltearn in 1726.
Alexander MacBean, from Douglas, Adm. Nov. 1720, Died 2d Nov. 1762.
Alex. Fraser, from Ferntosh, Adm. 4th April 1727, Died 6th May 1750.
Daniel MacKenzie, from Pettie, Adm. 10th Oct. 1727, Died 21st March 1730.
William Bailie, Ordained 22d July 1731, Died 14th May 1739.
Murdoch MacKenzie, from Dingwal, Adm. 13th July 1742, Died 7th April 1774.
James Grant, Ordained 14th April 1752, Died 14th Decemb. that same year.
Alexander Fraser, from Avoch, Admitted 13th November 1754.
Robert Rose, Ordained 27th September 1763.
—— Watson, from Kiltearn, Admitted 1775.

Durris Parish. .
Page 130.

DURRIS, a Parsonage in the Gift of the Prior of Urquhart, and now the Laird of Calder is Patron by a Disposition from Alexander Earl of Dunfermline Lord Urquhart in 1610. The Stipend is 48 Bolls of Meal, 650 Merks, with 50 Merks for Communion-Elements. The School is legal. Examinable persons are about 1100. The Protestant Ministers are,

Mr James Dow, Reader in Durris and Boleskin in 1567.
Alexander Thomson. Minister at Durris 1617.
Patrick Dunbar, Minister in 1618, Died in 1658.
William Cummine, Ordained in 1663, Transported in 1664.
James Smith, Ord. in March 1666, Demitted in 1682 on account of the Test.

Mr Thomas

Sect. 4.   THE PROTESTANT CHURCH.   361

Mr Thomas Fraser, Ord. privately, Admitted 11th March 1683, Died in May 1729.
  Archibald Bannantyne, from Ardchattan, Admitted 14th September 1731, Died 20th June 1752.
  John Grant, Ordained 1st May 1753.

KIRKHILL, formerly the Parishes of WARDLAW and FEARNUA, a Parsonage dedicated to the VIRGIN MARY. This Church stood formerly at Dunbalach, a mile up the River, and was dedicated to St MAURICE. I have seen, in the hands of Mr Fraser of Dunbalach, a Papal Bull, dated anno 1210, for translating the Church of Mauritius from Dunbalach to Wardlaw. WARDLAW Parish made the West End of the present Parish. And FEARNUA (in Irish *Eagluis Fearnaic*, so called either from some Legendary Saint, or from Fearn, *i. e.* "The Alder-tree," which abounds there) made the East End; and they were united in 1618. Lord Lovate was, and the King now is, Patron. The Stipend is, including Element Money, 56 Bolls, half Bear and half Meal, 400 Merks, and Vicarage worth 150 Merks. The School is Legal. The number of Examinable Persons is 800. The Protestant Ministers are,

KIRKHILL Parish.
Page 144.

Sir William (an Ecclesiastic Knight) Dow Fraser at Wardlaw, Died about 1588.
Mr Donald Dow Fraser at Wardlaw, from 1589, to 1600.
  Andrew MacPhail at Fernua, anno 1589, Died about 1606.
  Bartholomew Robertson at Wardlaw, from 1601, to 1610.
  John Houston, Ordained in 1611, Died in December 1659.
  James Fraser, Ordained in 1661, Died in October 1709.
  Robert Thomson, from Clyne, Admitted 2. April 1717, Died 30. April 1770. aged 85.
  Alexander Fraser, Ordained May 5. 1773.

KILTARLATY and CONVETH, seem to have been distinct Parishes, but how early united, I find not. CONVETH was a Vicarage depending on the Priory of Beaulie. KILTARLATY, a Parsonage dedicated to St THALARGUS. Lord Lovate was, and the King now is, Patron. The Stipend, by Decreet in 1635, is

KILTARLATY Parish.
Page 145.

Z z   48 Bolls

48 Bolls Meal, 300 Merks, 400 Merks Vicarage, and 30 Merks for Communion Elements. The Salary of the School is Legal. Examinable Persons are 1600. The Protestant Ministers are,

Mr William Fraser, in 1624, Died in Winter 1665.
 Hugh Fraser, Ordained in 1667, Died about 1708.
 Patrick Niccolson, Ordained 16th July 1716, Died 7th March 1761.
 Malcolm Niccolson, Ordained September 24th 1761.

Presbytery of ABERTARF.

Presbytery of Abertarf

Urquhart and Glenmoriston Parish.
Page 142.

URQUHART and GLENMORISTON. The former is a Parsonage dedicated to St MARY; and in the other was a Chapel dedicated to St RICHARD. Urquhart was always dependent on, and in the Gift of the Chancellor of Moray, and now the Laird of Grant, as Patron of Inveravon, the seat of the Chancellor, acts as Patron of Urquhart. Attempts have been made to unite Glenmoriston and Abertarf into one Parish, but have failed for want of a maintainance. The Stipend of Urquhart is 800 Merks, and 50 Merks for Communion-Elements. There is no School. The number of Examinable Persons is about 1600. The Protestant Ministers are,

Mr James Farquharson, Exhorter anno 1568.
 Alexander Grant, Minister in 1624, Died in 1645.
 Duncan MacCulloch, from Inverness, Admitted 1647, Deposed 1658, Reponed 1664, and Demitted 1671.
 James Grant, Ordained 10th April 1673. Transported to Abernethie in 1685.
 Robert Munro, Ordained in 1676, to Glenmoriston and Abertarf, Died about 1688.
 Robert Cummine, privately Ordained, Admitted 24th October 1686, Died in 1729.
 William Gordon, Ordained 24th December 1730, Transported to Alvie in 1739.
 John Grant, Ordained in 1740.

BOLES-

Sect. 4. THE PROTESTANT CHURCH.

BOLESKIN and ABERTARF were distinct parishes. I find (*Append.* No. XXVIII.). Gilibride Parsona de Abertarf, before the year 1216. James Dow Vicar sold the Vicarage of Abertarf to the Tutor of Lovate, about the year 1570, and for want of a living, Abertarf was annexed to Boleskin. In 1676, it was disjoined from Boleskin, and Ecclesiastically united with Glenmoriston; but the Civil Sanction was not obtained, and therefore Abertarf was again annexed to Boleskin about the year 1688. Lord Lovate was, and the Crown now is, Patron. The stipend, about 1764, was augmented to 1300 merks. There is no School. Examinable Persons are 1150. The Protestant Ministers are,

<small>BOLESKIN and ABERTARF Parish. Page 133.</small>

Mr James Dow, Exhorter in Dorris, Boleskin and Abertarf, anno 1569.
   Andrew Dow Fraser, from Moy, Admitted about 1624, Murdered by the Irishes 1646.
   Thomas Houston, Ordained in 1648, Died about 1704.
   John Morrison, from Glenelg, Admitted in 1706, Transported to Urray in 1710.
   Thomas Fraser, Ordained in March 1714, Died 10th February 1766.
   Patrick Grant, from Daviot, Admitted 1770.

LAGGAN a Mensal Church dedicated to St Kenneth: The Bishop was Patron, and settled the parish *jure proprio*. Now the King is properly Patron, and the family of Gordon has no act of possession. This parish was sometimes by the Bishop annexed to Alvie, that he might draw the more Teinds from it. Mr James Lyle served long in both parishes, and, it is said, understood not the Irish language; such penury was there of Ministers having that language. Upon his demitting, the parishes were disjoined; but were again united in 1672, and so continued to the death of Mr Thomas MacPherson. About the year 1767 the stipend was augmented to 1260 merks. There is no School. The number of Examinable Persons is 1100. The Protestant Ministers are,

<small>LAGGAN Parish. Page 55.</small>

Mr

Mr Alexander Clark, Exhorter in 1569.
    James Lyle, Minister of Laggan and Alvie, long before 1624, Demitted for age in 1626.
    Alexander Clark, Ordained in 1638, Deposed in 1647.
    James Dick, Ordained to Laggan and Alvie in 1653, Deposed in 1665.
    Thomas MacPherson, in 1672.
    John MacKenzie, from Kingusie, Admitted in 1709, Died in 1745.
    Duncan MacPherson, Ordained in April 1747, Died 13th August 1757.
    Andrew Gallie, Ordained 6th September 1758.

Number of Inhabitants in this Province.

The Number of Catechisable Persons, of seven or eight years of age and upwards, as contained in the above account, is   57,678

To which, if, for children under that age, we add one fifth more, viz.   11,535

The Number of Souls in this Province is   69,213

I cannot say that this Number is strictly exact; but if there be any error, it must be but small.

State of RELIGION from the Reformation.

4th, The State of RELIGION in the PROVINCE, from the REFORMATION.

I shall now conclude these Collections, with a succinct account of the state of Religion in this Province, from the Reformation anno 1560, to this time.

How early the first Dawning of the Reformation of Religion appeared in Scotland, I will not pretend to determine. It cannot be denied, that the Keledees remained in this Kingdom in the beginning of the fourteenth century; and it may be supposed, that the purity of Doctrine and Worship, and the simplicity of Government maintained by them, were the seeds of the Reformation in this Kingdom.

Be

Sect. 4. THE PROTESTANT CHURCH.

Be this as it will, it is certain, that the scandalous schism in the Church of Rome, of a long continued series of Anti-Popes, and the gross corruption both of the doctrine and manners that every where prevailed, were the more immediate causes of the Down-fall of Popery.

In every age, from the days of the Apostles, there were some who openly maintained the pure Doctrines of Christianity. In the twelfth Century, the Weldenses and Albigenses made an avowed secession from the Romish Church. The barbarous persecution of these faithful witnesses, long continued, verified, " That the Blood of Martyrs is the Seed of the Church." Their Doctrine spread through many Kingdoms of Europe, and in England John Wicklif openly taught it in the fourteenth Century, and his Disciples carried it into Germany and France, and no doubt into Scotland. In England, the Reformation began right early, in the reign of King Henry VIII. anno 1533, by renouncing the Pope's authority. And in 1542, many of the Scots Nobility and Gentry being made, or rather surrendering themselves, prisoners at Solway Moss, and remaining in England for sometime, upon their return to Scotland, openly favoured the Reformation, encouraged the preachers of it, and it soon spread into the several Counties. Before that time, even in 1407, John Roseby, and in 1432 Paul Craw, were publickly burnt for their opposition to the Church of Rome. In 1527, Mr Patrick Hamilton Abbot of Fern in Ross, a man of Noble Birth, was burnt by Bishop Beaton. It cannot be doubted, that this eminent Martyr propagated the Reformed Doctrine in Ross, and in the neighbouring Counties. The cruelty of his death, and of the death of Mr George Wishart son to Pittarow, in 1545, rendered Popery odious, and induced the people every where to favour the Reformation.

Although

Although I have not met with particular instances of Gentlemen, or others, in the Province of Moray, who had embraced the Protestant principles before the year 1560; yet I question not but there were many such. For in the Parliament that year, which abolished Popery, and established the Reformation, William Innes of Innes, John Grant of Grant, William Sutherland of Duffus, and a Commissioner from the Town of Inverness, were members, and concurred in that good work (*Keith's History*). And by the above Catalogue of Protestant Ministers, it appears, that, before the year 1570, almost all the Parishes in the Diocess of Moray had Protestant Teachers (*Appendix*, No. XLVI.), and a Protestant Bishop, with a formal Chapter, was settled in 1573—4.

From the Reformation downward, no County in the North, and few, if any, in the South, adhered more firmly to the Protestant Principles, even in the worst of times, than did the Inhabitants of Moray; insomuch that, except what influence the Family of Gordon had (of which afterwards), Popery has found no Countenance among them. And, although in time of Prelacy, the People behaved with due subjection to Civil authority, yet they never could be brought to a chearful submission to Prelatic power, but joined in throwing off that yoke at different Periods. The Ministers banished by King James VI. to the North, and particularly Mr Robert Bruce, who was banished to Inverness anno 1604, and remained there four years, contributed to confirm the People in Protestant and Presbyterian Principles.

In 1638, the People of Moray heartily concurred in opposing the Liturgy, the Canons, the Ecclesiastic Commission, and the Order of Bishops. Messrs William Falconer at Dyke, John Hay at Rafford, David Dunbar at Edinkylie, John Howeson at Wardlaw, Patrick Dunbar at Durris, Ministers; William

Ross

Sect. 4. THE PROTESTANT CHURCH.

Ross of Clava, John Dunbar Bailiff of Forres, James Fraser of Brae, and Robert Bailie Bailiff of Inverness, Ruling Elders, were Members of that Assembly. And Messrs John Gordon at Elgin, and John Guthrie at Duffus, Ministers, were, October 25. 1638, elected Commissioners from the Presbytery of Elgin, to that Assembly, and Mr Gordon was present in it, though omitted in the Roll *(Reg. Presbytery of Elgin).* That Assembly having deposed and excommunicated, among others, the Bishop of Moray, the Clergy of his Diocess who had vowed canonical obedience, and of whom some were ordained by him, intimated the Sentence from their Pulpits; and the Laity rejoiced in being delivered from Ecclesiastic Domination. In the Subsequent Assemblies of the Church, Innes of Innes, Brodie of Brodie, Brodie of Lethen, Fraser of Brae, &c. are found to have been Members.

All Ranks in the Province signed the National Covenant, and the Solemn League; some with chearfulness; and many, to avoid the direful censures of the Church. In the Civil Commotions, not improperly called, "The Bishops War," the People in general, except the Vassals and Dependents of the Marquis of Huntly, and the Roman Catholics, joined the Covenanters at first. But in 1648, when they thought, that not so much Religion, as Monarchy and the Civil Constitution were in danger, then the Frasers, MacIntoshes, Roses, Inneses, &c. joined in the expedition called "The Duke's Engagement," and after the defeat at Preston, the Churches were filled with Mock Penitents. The King being cut off in 1649, and his Son Charles II. being called home from Breda, and crowned, both Church and State became infatuated. The King raised an army, which was routed at Worcester in September 1651, and many Gentlemen in Moray suffered much in this ill conducted expedition into England. At the same time the Church split into Parties, and made a breach not yet fully healed up.

The

The King had three several times sworn the Covenants; but many very justly questioned his sincerity. The Covenanters being defeated at Dunbar in 1650, Cromwell being at Edinburgh, and having that Castle in his hands, the Courtiers laboured, that all capable of serving their Country might be received into the army, and not be hindered or deterred by Church Censures. Against this a Body of Gentlemen, Military Officers, and Ministers remonstrated, and directed a Subscribed Remonstrance to the Committee of Estates, " Advising them " to adhere to the King, only in defence of Religion and Li- " berty, and if he shall forsake the Counsels of the Church and " State, and be guided by Malignants, that he be removed from " the exercise of Government." The Committee of Estates, in November 1650, condemned that Paper as Scandalous: and at the same time, the Commission of the General Assembly first approved, but afterwards, by Court Influence, condemned the Remonstrance, which made several Ministers enter a Dissent. The King persuaded the same Commission to meet at Perth, *pro re nata*, on December 14. that year, and the Parliament asked them a Solution of this Question, " What Persons shall be ad- " mitted to take arms against the Sectaries, and in what capaci- " ty?" To which they answered: " That all fencible Persons, " except the excommunicated, forfeited, and professed Enemies " to the Covenants, may be employed." The same Commission met on December 26. and then many protested against this resolution, because it encouraged the Enemies of Religion, and put it in the power of the King and his Courtiers to overturn all that had been contended for since the year 1637. Hence came the opposite parties of Resolutioners and Protestors, who, by imprudently meddling with the affairs of the Civil Government, and by their fierce animosities, occasioned the Change of Church Government.

In

Sect. 4. THE PROTESTANT CHURCH.

In the year 1651, the same Commission of the Church met in April, and gave it as their opinion, that the Parliament might admit into public offices, and places of trust, all subjects, provided the Guilty did undergo Church Censures. Upon this mock Penitents crowded into the Church; those called *Malignants* soon got into offices and posts; and the Protesters loudly complained, that a door was opened to infidelity, irreligion, and profaneness. But the Resolutioners would maintain what they had done, and meeting on May 24th in Commission, required all Presbyteries to cite to the ensuing Assembly, all who should oppose the Resolutions.

The General Assembly met on 16th July at St Andrews; but because of the civil tumults, soon removed to Dundee. Twenty-one members protested against the freeness and legality of the meeting, because by the conduct of the Commission in May, there could be no free election, all Protesters being under citation. Yet the Assembly condemned the Remonstrance, approved the Resolutions, condemned the Protesters, deposed three, and suspended one of them, and ordered all Presbyteries to ask the opinion of their members concerning the Remonstrance, the Resolutions, and the lawfulness of this Assembly. This kindled a flame in almost every Synod and Presbytery.

In the Province of Moray, the Synod met *pro re nata*, on November 13th 1651, and approved of the meeting of last Assembly. But Messrs John Brodie at Aldern, Joseph Brodie at Forres, William Frafer at Inverness, James Park at Urquhart, and Patrick Glas at Edinkylie Ministers, with Sir Robert Gordon of Gordonston, Alexander Brodie of Brodie, and Hugh Campbell of Achindune, Elders, protested against this, because that Assembly was not free or regular in the election of its members, and several things done in it were, in their opinion, dishonouring to God, and contrary to the Covenants and the engagement.

ment. Thus was the Province split into parties; but the Synod promised to treat the Protesting members with all brotherly love and benevolence. The Kingdom being now under the feet of Usurpers, General Assemblies being by them discharged, and Synods and Presbyteries often interrupted, a social and friendly intercourse was, at least seemingly, kept up in this Province for some years. But in the Synod of Moray, met in October 1660, a copy of King Charles IId's Jesuitical letter to the Presbytery of Edinburgh was read (*Append.* No XLVIII.) I call this letter *Jesuitical*, because the King promised " To " maintain inviolate the Government of the Church as establish- " ed by law." Although it was resolved to overturn it; and in a few months the Act Recissory was passed in Parliament, rescinding, repealing, and annulling all acts made in Parliament Convention or Assembly, since the year 1633, and so leaving the Government of the Church what it was that year 1633. An equivocation unworthy of a King or a Christian. That letter being read, the Synod observed, that the King promised, to cause the authority of the Assembly 1651 to stand in force. Upon this they instantly, in a mean and base strain of adulation, persecuted their brethren, contrary to their former promise. Mr Patrick Glas, the only Minister now living who had protested in 1651, was sharply rebuked, and made to sign a Recantation, which was recorded. And Sir Ludowick Gordon of Gordonston, Alexander Brodie of Brodie, and Hugh Campbell Protesters, with Alexander Brodie of Lethen, Patrick Campbell of Boath, John Niccolson, James Buchan, William Alves in Forres, and Robert Watson in Rafford, Elders, who had approved of the Protestations were all deposed in absence. This was both unjust and ungenerous, to expose their brethren, as much as they could, to the King's resentment.

But now the design of re-establishing Prelacy, was communicated

cated to some of the Clergy, and the Synod, met 2d July 1661, sent an address to the Earl of Middleton, the King's Commissioner in Parliament, in which they did not once mention the Protestant Religion, or Presbyterian Church Government (*Appendix*, No XLIX.) Nay it is apparent, that they had already privately agreed, to approve of the intended change; for Mr Murdoch MacKenzie Minister at Elgin, who was to be one of the new Bishops, was sent up with the Address, that he might receive the Rochet; and the Synod set up, what in divine Worship was looked on as the Badge of Episcopacy, I mean the *Gloria Patri*, and parents repeating the Apostle's Creed at the Baptism of their Children.

The transition from one extreme to another is easy; but it is difficult to stop in a just medium. This was apparent upon the Restoration in 1660. Under the former period, the Clergy ran into a wild extreme, of meddling with, and managing, all matters, Civil, Ecclesiastic, Criminal, and Military, and the language of their conduct, and of many of the Laity, was, " Bind your King with Chains, and your Nobles with Fetters." Now they ran into the opposite extreme: All power, Civil and Ecclesiastic, was lodged in the King: He was declared absolute: Christ's right, as Head of the Church, was yielded up to him; and all became abject slaves to his will.

Prelacy being restored in 1662, the King proposed to revive General Assemblies, and the Parliament drew up a form of their constitution. But the Bishops could not bear such a check, and the project was dropt. Diocesan Synods and Presbyteries were kept up, and the new Bishops lost no time in prosecuting Non-conformists (See Page 302). Messrs George Innes at Dipple, and Harrie Forbes at Aldern prevented deposition, by demitting their charges in 1663. And Messrs Thomas Urquhart at Essil, James Urquhart at Kinloss, and George Meldrum

Meldrum at Glafs, were that year depofed; as was Mr Alexander Frafer at Daviot in 1672; and all the reft conformed. Some Minifters from Rofs, as Meffrs James Frafer of Brae, Thomas Hogg, Thomas Rofs, John MacGilligin, &c. were often driven into Moray, and joining the Non-conformifts there, performed Gofpel Miniftrations in private, and were much regarded and protected by the Gentry. The Bifhops of Moray were more moderate than other Bifhops; yet thefe Minifters were informed againft; moft of them were intercommuned, apprehended, and kept long prifoners in the Bafs, and in other places.

The Gentlemen of the Country, and the common people by their example and influence, behaved with much prudence, gave no umbrage to the Civil powers; and though they protected the perfecuted Clergy, yet they difcouraged Field Preaching; by which means, both the Minifters, and their hearers in private houfes, were the lefs expofed to troubles. The houfes of the Lairds of Innes, Grant, Kilravock, Brodie, Lethen, the Sheriff of Moray, and Sir Hugh Campbell of Calder, were fo many Sanctuaries to the oppreffed. The laft mentioned Gentleman, was, at one time, bail in L. 1500 Sterling for perfecuted Minifters. In a word, for twenty years after the Reftoration, by the prudence and piety of families of diftinction, Moray enjoyed more peace than other counties, and Religion flourifhed greatly.

The impofing the Teft, in 1681, opened a new fcene of troubles. Thereby they fwore, " To own and adhere to the Con-
" feffion of Faith recorded in Parliament 1567, and to difown
" all principles or practices contrary to the Proteftant Religion,
" and the faid Confeffion : That the King is only the Supreme
" Governor in all caufes, Civil and Ecclefiaftic: That it is un-
" lawful for fubjects, upon any pretence, to enter into Cove-
" nants

"nants and Leagues, or to convene in any Aſſemblies to treat
"of any matter of State, Civil or Eccleſiaſtic, without his
"Majeſty's expreſs licence; Or to take up arms againſt the
"King, or thoſe commiſſioned by him: Not to endeavour any
"change or alteration in the Government, in Church or
"State as now eſtabliſhed: Never to decline his Majeſty's
"Power and Juriſdiction, &c." A ſtrange medlay of Eraſtianiſm, and contradiction! To maintain the Proteſtant Religion; and to bring in a Popiſh ſucceſſor! To ſwear in the Confeſſion, that Chriſt is the only King of the Church; and yet that the King is the only Supreme! To allow any one having the King's commiſſion, to cut all the throats in the Kingdom! Not to convene to Preaching or Praying! &c.

Mr Colin Falconer Biſhop of Moray, and the Clergy of his Dioceſs, met at Elgin in December 1681; and Miniſters, Schoolmaſters, and Students in Divinity, ſwore the Teſt, with the Council's Explication allowed by the King: viz.

1. That they did not ſwear to every propoſition in the Confeſſion of Faith, but only to the true Proteſtant Religion, in oppoſition to Popery and Fanaticiſm.

2. That there is reſerved entire to the Biſhops and Paſtors, all the intrinſic Spiritual power of the Church, and the Preaching of the Word, Ordination of Paſtors, &c. as in the three firſt Centuries.

3. That this Oath is no prejudice to the Epiſcopal Government of the Church now eſtabliſhed by Law. An Explication this ſo poor, that rather than Comply with it, the following Miniſters quitted their Charges, viz.: Meſſrs James Stuart at Inveravon, Alexander Marſhall at Dipple, William Geddes at Urquhart, James Horn at Elgin Alexander Cumming at Dallas, James Smith at Durris, William Speed at Botriſnie, and John Cumming at Aldern. This laſt Gentleman did ſubſcribe the

Teſt;

Test; but, upon reflection, chose to demit in 1682: And being a pious and peaceable Man, he was settled at Cullen; and, by the favour of the Earl of Findlater, lived undisturbed. The conduct of the Clergy, in so readily complying in this point, very much sullied their characters.

Few of the Gentlemen of this Province had posts or offices that obliged them to take this Oath. But it was soon made a Test of Loyalty in all Ranks. And to drive the People into a full conformity to Church and State, or to ruin them if they became Recusants, Justiciary Courts were appointed through the Kingdom, with power to impose the Test, to enquire into Conventicles, and absenting from Church; and to fine, confine, banish, and hang, as they should see cause. In December 1684, a Commission was granted to the Earls of Errol and Kintore, and Sir George Munro of Coulrain, for the bounds between Spey and Ness; and, on 19th January 1685, their power was extended to Inverness, Ross, Cromarty, and Sutherland; and Lord Duffus, with a troop of Militia, was ordered to attend them. A letter was likewise written by the Council to the Bishop of Moray, requiring him to cause all the Clergy to attend the Justices on January 21d, with their Elders, and to bring Lists of all Persons either guilty or suspected.

Such a parade and meeting of Justices, Bishop, Ministers, Elders, Militia, Gentlemen, Ladies, and Common People, was held at Elgin, 22d January, and the subsequent days; and as it was unusual, could not but strike terror: And the more sensible People must have concluded, That a Government, either in Church or State, must have been odious, that needed such support. These Justices made their report to the Council on 2d March, as follows:

" We made up Lists of the Heretors, Wadsetters, and Life-
" renters, who offered three months supply, signed a Bond of
" Peace,

Sect. 4. THE PROTESTANT CHURCH.

"Peace, and took the Test, except a few. We fined some, banished others, and remitted some to the Council. We ordered to imprison Munro of Fowles at Tain, and his Son at Inverness, and sent Mr William MacKay (N. he was afterwards Minister at Cromdale) a Vagrant Preacher in Sutherland to Edinburgh. We banished Messrs James Urquhart, John Stuart, (N. thereafter at Urquhart) Alexander Dunbar, (N. thereafter at Aldern) and George Meldrum Ministers, Alexander and Mark Mavors in Urquhart, Donald and Andrew Munros in Elgin, Alexander Munro of Maine, and Jean Taylor. We fined the Laird of Grant in L. 42,500; The Laird of Brodie in L. 24,000; Alexander Brodie of Lethen in L. 40,000; Francis Brodie of Milnton in L. 10,000; Francis Brodie of Windyhills in L. 3333:6:8; Mr James Brodie (Grand-Father to the present Lethen) of Kinlie in L. 333:6:8; Mr George Meldrum of Crombie in L. 6666:13:4; Thomas Dunbar of Grange, the Laird of Innes, William Brodie of Coltfield, William Brodie of Whitewrae, and Mr Robert Donaldson in Arr, were cited to appear when called."

Besides these, there were imprisoned at Elgin, John Montfod Chamberlain to Park, Jean Brodie Relict of Alexander Thomson merchant in Elgin, Christine Lesly daughter, and Beatrix Brodie relict of Lesly of Aikenway. Although the Justices who met at Elgin were not severe, and Sir George Munro was a friend to the oppressed; yet it is probable, that to please the Court and Bishops, some executions would have been made, if the King's death had not prevented it. For how soon the Justices arrived at Elgin, they ordered a new Gallows to be erected. But the King having died on 6th February 1685, the account of it reached Elgin on the 13th. The Justices left the town next day; the prisoners were released; and many who were

were under citation, were eased of the trouble of appearing because the Commission of the Justices was vacated, and became null.

The gentlemen that were fined, were brought to much trouble: Non-conformity, absence from Church, and attending Conventicles, were their only crimes; and not so much the conduct of the Gentlemen, as of their Ladies. They thought it hard to be punished for their wives faults. The Laird of Brodie had a non-conforming Chaplain, and some Conventicles in Brodie House; and though he went to London to get some composition, yet he was forced to pay 20,000 merks Scots to Collonel Maxwell a Papist. Lethen's fine was gifted to the Scots College of Doway, to be paid to Mr Lewis Innes a member of that College. The estate of Lethen was adjudged in order to secure payment, and upon Lethen's death, the Laird of Grant (married to Lethen's only child) becoming executor to him, paid L. 30,000 to the Earl of Perth. The Laird of Grant petitioned the Privy Council, shewed his own loyalty, and his Lady's inability to travel to Church through want of health; yet the Council ordered him to be prosecuted for the fine; but he spun out his defences, till the Revolution delivered him. Milnton's fine was granted to Gray of Chrichie, as a reward of his decyphering some of Argyle's letters; but the Revolution prevented paying it.

Besides the severitie used by this Court of Justiciary, the Sheriff Courts put many to distress and trouble. The Hereditary Sheriff of Moray, refusing the Test, was divested of his office; and Lord Down was made Sheriff Principal, and Tulloch of Tanachie, Depute, who fined David Brodie of Pitgavenie, Brother to Lethen, in L. 18,000, whereof a great part was paid. The Sheriff of Inverness fined many in that County. And MacKenzie of Suddie, by a special warrand from the Council,

Council, prosecuted many in Ross and Cromarty. These prosecutions were carried on in all Counties, and they who have calculated the fines imposed, and for the most part exacted, make them amount to L. 4,000,000.

As in the Body Natural, so in the Political and Ecclesiastic, too hot a Regimen of Medicines doth but inflame the disease, which it is intended to cure. The severities used at that time, mainly for Non-conformity, increased the number of Non-conformists, although they durst not avow it, and brought the Administration, both of Church and State, into the greater contempt. Upon the accession of King James VII. to the Crown in 1685, he would willingly have compounded matters for a season, and grant a respite to Non-conformists, that he might with the better grace favour the Roman Catholics. To this it was owing, that, failing to get the penal statutes against Popery repealed, he granted an ample toleration, and the Non-conformists had rest. But the Scottish Bishops being infatuated, although they knew of the Prince of Orange's intended expedition, to preserve the Religion and Liberties of Britain, yet in their Address *(Appendix,* No. L.) gave their King such a taste of their Loyalty, and the nation such a specimen of their Religion and temper, that it was no wonder, that next year the Convention of Estates declared Prelacy a grievance to the nation.

The last Sufferer I know, in Moray, for Non-conformity, was Mr Angus MacBean, son to MacBean of Kinchyle, and Minister of Inverness. He was a man of parts and piety, and was admitted Minister of Inverness December 29th 1683. It was with great reluctancy that he entered into the Ministry, under the then establishment; for his dissatisfaction with the Government, and the tyrannical conduct of the Church, made him in June 1687, withdraw from their judicatories, and on 23d October

ber, being the Lord's Day, he preached from *Job, chap.* xxxiv. *ver.* 31. 32. publckly renounced Prelacy, and demitted his charge. In January 1688, he was carried a prisoner to Edinburgh, examined before the Council, and on 27th February was deposed by the Archbishop of St Andrews. He was remanded to prison, and though, on account of the languishing state of his health, Sir Robert Gordon of Gordonstoun, and Duncan Forbes of Culloden, offered a bail of 10,000 merks Scots, to present him when called, yet the Chancellor would not liberate him. He lay in prison, till upon the Chancellor's running away in December 1688, the mob opened the prison doors. After this he continued in a languishing way, and died at Edinburgh in February 1689, in the thirty-third year of his age.

The happy Revolution, in 1688, put an end to tyranny and persecution. I have (pages 303, &c.) given some account of the state of Religion in this Province, at, and since the Revolution, and shall now only observe,

That the Episcopal Clergy being by law indulged, upon their qualifying to the Civil Government, to keep their charges and livings, they saw this so much for their ease and wordly advantage, that they all, very few excepted, complied with it. Thereby they were eased of the trouble and expence of attending upon Presbyteries, Synods, Assemblies, and Commissions, and of bearing a share in frequent contributions of money, for promoting Religion and Piety. No one was disturbed or ejected, except those who refused to acknowledge King William and Queen Mary, and who still looked for the Restoration of their abdicated King. I own, that in Strathspey the Laird of Grant did take advantage of the Ministers of Cromdale, Abernethie, and Duthel, who neglected to qualify to Government within the time limited. And upon this, he, in a manner too summary, caused shut up their Churches. In the town of Elgin, so disaffected were the Magistrates, and influenced by the Lord Duffus, that for eight years they kept the Pastoral Charge vacant. And in Inverness, so great was the disaffection (to which Mr Hector MacKenzie Minister contributed not a little, although he himself had qualified to the Civil Government), that upon the death of Mr Marshal in 1691, the Magistrates would not suffer the charge to be declared vacant. Upon 21st June that year, all avenues to the Church were beset with armed men, and double centries placed at the doors, that no Minister might enter; and when Duncan Forbes of Culloden sought to open the doors, he was thrust back and struck violently. This made Culloden and others represent the case to the Council; and in August 1691, Leven's regiment was sent North to protect the well-affected in obeying the law. They made patent doors; but for ten years, no Minister could be got settled in that town *(Min. Presb. of Moray.)*

It remains now, that I give some account of the state of Popery in this Province. The favour showed by our Kings to Roman Catholics, ever since the Reformation, is well known. King James VI. did not dissemble, that he would meet them half way; His Son, though called a zealous Protestant, protected, employed, and encouraged Papists, during his unfortunate reign. King Charles II. was known to be, and died, a Roman Catholic; and his Brother openly professed that Religion. Notwithstanding the influence and example of those Princes, very few in this Province, except the dependents on the Family of Gordon, and the MacDonalds and Chisholms, have been seduced into Popish errors. Among the Highland Clans, the Frasers, MacIntoshes, Grants, MacPhersons, MacGilliwrays, scarce any Papists are to be found. Even in the country of Badenoch, though all are either Vassals or Tenants

State of Popery in Moray.

of the Duke of Gordon, there are few, if any, of that Religion. This has been owing in a great measure to the Gentry and Chiefs of Clans, who early embraced the Reformation, and both encouraged and promoted it in their lands.

The MacDonalds of Glengary, never that I know, were reformed. The Gentlemen of that name have their sons educated in the Scots Colleges abroad, especially at Doway; and they return home, either avowed or concealed Papists. In the year 1726, in all Glengary and Achadrom, which may consist of 800 souls, I could find very few Protestants. Since that time they have not become much better; but have diffused their errors into the neighbouring Countries of Abertarf, Glenmoriston, and Strathglass.

The most Noble Family of Gordon, till of late, were Roman Catholics; and altho' now they are Protestants, yet Popery still prevails in their lands, within this Province: particularly in Glenrinnis, Glenlivat, and Strathavon. I remember, when a Seminary, or Academy of Priests, was openly kept in Glenlivat, where the Languages, Philosophy, and Divinity were regularly taught; and a draught of the most promising boys was sent to France, who returned home Priests and Jesuits. I am not certain, if such a Seminary is now kept up there; but a Popish meeting-house continues; and at High Mass, 600 people or more convene to it. To conclude this account, in Glenrinnis, Glenlivate, and Strathavon; in Abertarf, Glengary, and Achadrom, and in Strathglass, there are, in my opinion, at least 3000 Roman Catholics.

Society for propagating Christian Knowledge.

It may not be improper here to observe, the happy increase of Christian Knowledge since the Revolution, by means of the early education of youth. All the parishes in this Province, excepting

excepting three or four, have now Schools erected in them according to law: And some Society Schools are settled, where Popery prevails, or the extent of parishes requires. This valuable Society had its rise from the piety and benevolence of some private Christians in Edinburgh, about the year 1700, who, pitying the lamentable condition of the Highlands and Islands, through ignorance, idolatry, superstition, and profanness, did themselves cheerfully contribute, and prevailed with others to concur with them, for erecting Schools. Their first School was in the country of Stratherick, within this Province; but not meeting with the success expected, they applied to the General Assembly, who laid the design before her Majesty Queen Anne, and obtained letters patent, of date 25th May 1709, Eerecting the Contributers into a Society, by the name of "The Society in Scotland for Propagating Christian Knowledge." The stock of the Society, in the year 1774, is, for Scotland L. 28,901 Sterling, and for America L. 4,032 Sterling. They have now established 121 Schools, (besides some lately suppressed), at which above 6000 Boys and Girls are educated; and they have Missionaries in Georgia, North Carolina, and other parts of America. The happy effects of this truely pious Institution are visible in this Province. Christian Knowledge is increased, Heathenish Customs are abandoned, the number of Papists is diminished, disaffection to the Government is lessened, and the English language is so diffused, that in the remotest glens it is spoken by the young people; and in the low Country, in Inveravon, Glenlivat, Knockando, Edinkylie, Nairn, and Arderfier, where, till of late, public worship was performed in Irish, there is now no occasion for Ministers having that language.

APPENDIX.

APPENDIX.

Nº I. King ROBERT's Charter to RANULF Earl of MORAY: Nº I.
from ESSAYS *on* BRITISH ANTIQUITIES.

ROBERTUS, Dei gratia, Rex Scotorum, omnibus probis ho-   Carta
minibus totius terræ suæ, salutem. Sciatis, Nos dedisse, Thomæ
Ranulfi.
concessisse, et hac presenti carta nostra confirmasse, Thomæ
Ranulpho, Militi, dilecto nepoti nostro, pro homagio et servitio suo, omnes terras nostras in Moravia, sicut fuerunt in manu
Domini Alexandri Regis Scotiæ prædecessoris nostri ultimo
defuncti, una cum omnibus aliis terris adjacentibus, infra
metas et divisas subscriptas contentis; Incipiendo, videlicet, ad
aquam de Spee sicut cadit in mare; et sic ascendendo per eandem aquam, includendo terras de Fouchabre Rothenayks,
Rothays et Bocharine, per suas rectas metas et divisas, cum
suis pertinentiis; et sic ascendendo per dictam aquam de
Spee usque ad marchias de Badenach; et sic includendo omnes
terras de Badenach et Kyncardyn, et de Glencarn, cum pertinentiis, per suas rectas metas et divisas; et sic sequendo marchias de Badenach usque ad marchiam de Louchabre; et sic includendo terras de Louchabre, de Maymez, de Lezharketh, de
Glengarech, et de Glenelg, cum pertinentiis, per suas rectas metas
et divisas; et sic sequendo marchiam de Glenelg usque ad mare
versus occidentem; et sic per mare usque ad marchias boreales
Ergadiæ, quæ est Comitis de Ros; et sic per marchias illas usque ad marchias Rossiæ; et sic per marchias Rossiæ quousque
perveniatur ad aquam de Forne; et sic per aquam de Forne
quousque

quousque perveniatur ad mare orientale: Tenendas et habendas dicto Thomæ, et heredibus suis masculis de corpore suo legitimè procreatis seu procreandis, de nobis, et heredibus nostris, in feodo et hereditate, in LIBERO COMITATU, ac in libera regalitate, cum quatuor querelis ad coronam nostram regiam spectantibus; et cum omnibus placitis et querelis, tam in communibus indictamentis, quam in brevibus placitabilibus; et cum omnibus aliis loquelis quibuscunque ad liberam regalitatem pertinentibus, vel aliquo modo pertinere valentibus, adeo liberè, quietè, plenariè, et honorificè, sicut aliqua terra infra regnum nostrum, in regalitate, liberius, plenius, quietius, aut honorificentius, dari poterit aut teneri; unà cum magna custuma nostra burgi de Invernis, et coketo ejusdem, et libertatibus suis in omnibus, exceptâ tantummodo parvâ custumâ dicti burgi; cum plenaria potestate attachiandi, accusandi, et in omnibus ministrandi ac judicandi omnes illas dicti vicecomitatis injurias, dampna seu præjudicia facientes indebitè custumæ prædictæ, adeo liberè in omnibus, sicut nos vel aliquis ministrorum nostrorum ipsos attachiare, accusare, ministrare seu judicare potuimus, seu poterit, in præmissis; et quod dictus Comes, et hæredes sui, amerciamenta, excaetas seu forisfacturas inde contingentes, adeo liberè et quietè habeant et possideant in futurum, sicut nos, seu aliquis prædecessorum nostrorum, dicta amerciamenta, excaetas seu forisfacturas, aliquo tempore habuimus. Quare vicecomiti nostro de Invernis, et balivis suis, ac præpositis et balivis dicti burgi qui pro tempore fuerint, ac ceteris quorum interest, firmiter præcipimus et mandamus, quatenus præfato Comiti, et heredibus suis prædictis, ac suis ministris, sint intendentes et respondentes, consulentes et auxiliantes, super his, si necesè fuerit, nostra regali potentiâ invocatâ, sine aliquo alio mandato nostro speciali interveniente. Volumusque et concedimus, quod dictus Thomas, et heredes su

prædicti

prædicti, habeant, teneant, et possideant dictum comitatum, cum manerio de Elgyn, quod pro capitali mansione comitatus Moraviæ de cetero teneri volumus et vocari, et cum aliis omnibus maneriis, burgis, villis, thanagiis, et omnibus terris nostris dominicis, firmis, et exitibus infra prædictas metas contentis, cum advocationibus ecclesiarum, cum feodis et forisfacturis, cum silvis et forestis, moris et maresiis, cum viis et semitis, cum aquis, stagnis, lacubus, vivariis, et molendinis, cum piscationibus tam maris quam aquæ dulcis, cum venationibus, aucupationibus, et avium aëriis, cum omnibus aliis libertatibus, commoditatibus, aysiamentis, et justis pertinentiis suis, in omnibus, et per omnia, tam non nominatis quam nominatis: quibus heredibus dicti Thomæ masculis deficientibus, quod absit, volumus, qud dictus comitatus ad nos, et heredes nostros, liberè et integrè, ac sine aliqua contradictione, revertatur. Volumus etiam et concedimus, pro nobis et heredibus nostris, quòd omnes barones et libere-tenentes dicti comitatûs, qui de nobis et prædecessoribus nostris in capite tenuerunt, et eorum heredes, dicto Thomæ, et heredibus suis prædictis, homagia, fidelitates, sectas curiæ, et omnia alia servitia faciant, et baronias et tenementa sua, de ipso, et heredibus suis prædictis, de cetero teneant: salvis tamen baronibus et liberè-tenentibus prædictis, ac eorum heredibus, juribus et libertatibus curiarum suarum hactenus justè usitatis. Volumus insuper et concedimus, quòd burgi et burgenses sui de Elgyn, de Fores, et de Invirnarne, easdem libertates habeant et exerceant quas tempore Domini Alexandri regis Scotiæ prædicti et nostro habuerunt; hoc solùm salvo, quòd de nobis tenebant sine medio, et nunc de eodem Comite teneant, cum eisdem libertatibus. Salvo etiam nobis, et heredibus nostris, in hac donatione nostra, burgo nostro de Invirnefs, cum loco castelli et terris ad dictum burgum pertinentibus, cum piscatione aquæ de Nifs, et cum molendinis

aquæ

aquæ ejufdem, cum fequela dicti burgi, et terrarum ad ipfum burgum tantummodo pertinentium: et falvis nobis et heredibus noftris fidelitatibus epifcoporum, abbatum, priorum, et aliorum prælatorum ecclefiæ Moravienfis, et advocatione feu jure patronatûs ecclefiarum earundem, et eorum ftatu, in omnibus quem habuerunt tempore Regis Alexandri prædicti, et aliorum prædeceflorum noftrorum Regum Scotiæ: excepto quod homines eorundem citati per nos ad defenfionem regni noftri intendant vexillo, et fequi teneantur vexillum dicti Thomæ Comitis, et heredum fuorum prædictorum, unà cum aliis qui vexillum Moraviæ fequi folebant antiquitùs: faciendo nobis, et heredibus noftris, dictus Thomas, et heredes fui prædicti pro dicto comitatu, fervitium octo militum in exercitu noftro, et Scoticanum fervitium, et auxilium de fingulis *davacis* debitum et confuetum, tantummodo, fine fecta curiæ ad quamcunque curiam noftram facienda. In cujus rei teftimonium, praefenti cartæ noftræ figillum noftrum praecepimus apponi. Teftibus, Venerabilibus Patribus Willelmo Sancti Andreæ, Willelmo Dunkeldenfi, Henrico Aberdinenfi, Dei gratia, Epifcopis; Bernardo Abbate de Aberbrothock Cancellario noftro, Malcolmo Comite Levenox, Gilberto de Haya, Roberto de Keth Marefcallo Scotiæ, Alexandro Margus et Henrico de Sancto Claro, Militibus.

N° II.   N° II. St Nicolas's Hospital at Spey: from *Chart Morav.*

St Nicolas's Hospital at Spey.

MURIEL de Poloc omnibus: Sciant, Me dedifle Deo et Beatæ Mariæ, et Sancto Nicolao, Totam terram meam de Inverorkil per rectas divifas, in puram Eleemofynam, ad habendum in ea Domum ad receptionem pauperum tranfeuntium. Teftibus, Andrea Moravienfi Epifcopo, Nicolao Vicario de Rothys, Symone Vicario de Dundurkus, &c.

N° III.

APPENDIX.

Nº III. Collatio ad Capellam Sancti NICOLAI: *Ibid.*   Nº III.

ALEXANDER, D. G. Rex Scotorum, omnibus: Sciant, Me dedisse, et hac Carta confirmasse, Deo et Ecclesiæ Beatæ Mariæ, et Capellæ Sancti Nicolai juxta pontem de Spe, ad sustentationem Capellani in dicta capella, quatuor marcas annuatim percipiendas de firma Molendinorum nostrorum de Invernarin. Testibus, Willelmo de Bond Cancellario, W. filio Alani Senescalli Justiciario Scotiæ, M. Comite de Angus et Katanea. Apud Invercullan 7mo die Octobris, anno regni 18vo; A. D. 1232.

Collatio ad Capellam Sancti Nicolai

Nº IV. Carta super Ecclesia de ROTHAIS: *Ibid.*   Nº IV.

OMNIBUS Sanctæ matris Ecclesiæ filiis, Andreas Episcopus Moraviensis. Noveritis, Me dedisse, et hac Carta confirmasse, Deo et Beato Nicolao, et Hospitali ejusdem sito juxta pontem de Spe, ad sustentationem pauperum, in puram Eleemosynam, Ecclesiam de Rothais, cum omnibus justis pertinentiis. In horum testimonium, huic scripto appensum est sigillum nostrum, cum subscriptione Fratrum.

Carta super Ecclesia de ROTHAIS.

Nº V. Collatio Ecclesiæ de ARTENDOL: *Ibid.*   Nº V.

WILLELMUS fiilius Willelmi Freskyni, Salutem. Noverit universitas vestra, Me dedisse Ecclesiæ Sanctæ Trinitatis de Spyny, Ecclesiam de Artendol, cum omnibus ad eandem juste pertinentibus; Exceptis decimis bladi, et duabus Davach quæ sunt juxta castellum meum de Bucharm, viz. Bucharm et Athelnathorch, quarum omnes decimæ de blado, authoritate Bricii Episcopi Moraviensis, assignatæ sunt Capellæ meæ; de Castello meo de Bucharm, ad sustentationem Capellani ejusdem Capellæ. Testibus, D. B. Morav. Episcopo, Hugone fratre meo, &c.

Collatio Ecclesiæ de ARTENDOL.

Nº VI.

Nº VI. Nº VI. Concessio de Ecclesia de INVERAVEN: *Ibid.*

Concessio de Ecclesia de INVERAVEN.

OMNIBUS, &c. Ricardus D. G. Moraviensis Episcopus, Noverit Universitas vestra, Me dedisse Andreæ Presbytero de Brechyn, Ecclesiam de Inverhoven in puram Eleemosynam, cum omnibus justis pertinentiis, salvis in omnibus Episcopalibus rectitudinibus et consuetudinibus. Testibus, Gilchryst Com. de Mar, Magistro Roberto Archidiacono, &c.

Nº VII. Nº VII. Collatio de Ecclesia de INVERHOVEN: *Ibid.*

Collatio de Ecclesia de Inverhoven.

UNIVERSIS Sanctæ matris filiis, Malcolmus Comes de Fyfe Salutem. Sciant, praesentes &c. Me dedisse, et hac Carta confirmasse, Deo et Episcopo Moraviensi, Ecclesiam Beati Petri de Inverhoven, cum una Davach terræ ad eam justè pertinente in Inverhoven, quam Bricius tenuit, et cum omni Parochia totius Strathoven, cum decimis et oblationibus, in perpetuam Eleemosynam. Testibus, Duncano et Davide fratribus meis, Willielmo filio Duncani, &c.

Nº VIII. Nº VIII. INDENTURE, ROBERT STUART and ISABEL MacDUFF: *Sybbald's Hist. of Fife.*

Indenture, ROBERT STUART and ISABEL MACDUFF.

INDENTURE betwixt Robert Senescall Earl of Menteith and Isabel Countess of Fife, of the date the penult day of March 1371; By which the said Countess acknowledges the said Earl to be her lawful heir apparent, as well by the Tailzie made by Umquhile Duncan Earl of Fife her Father, to Allan Earl of Menteith, the Grand Father of the Lady Margaret, the Spouse of the said Robert, now Earl, as by the Tailzie made by the Lady Isabel herself, and her Umquhile Husband Walter Senescall, the Brother of the said Robert Earl of Menteith, to the foresaid Earl, whereby upon the Earl's asisting her in the recovery of her

her Earldom, which she by force and fear had resigned, when it is recovered, she shall presently resign it in the King's hands, to infeft the Earl in it, who shall receive Sasine of the Feud of the Earldom, with the leading of the men of it, their wards, reliefs, marriages, and escheats. The Courts of the Earldom shall be holden by him. And the said Countess is to have, all the days of her life, the free tenement of the lands of the Earldom, except the third part allotted to Mary Countess of Fife, the Mother of the said Lady Isabel, all the time of her life in assedation; and upon the death of the said Mary the Countess, the said Earl shall have her whole third part. And it is agreed, the said Earl shall have, in his keeping, the Castle of Falkland, with the Forest of it. To the performance of all which, they on both sides bound themselves by their oath corporally, and put to it their seals, &c.

Nº IX. DONATIO Super ECCLESIAM de CROMDALE. *Chart. Morav.*   Nº IX. DONATIO Super Ecclesiam de CROMDALE

OMNIBUS, &c. MALCOLMUS Comes de Fife, Salutem: Sciant, Me dedisse, et praesenti carta confirmasse, Episcopis Moraviensibus, in perpetuam Eleemosynam, Jus Patronatus Ecclesiae de Cromdale. Testibus, Thoma Priore de Urchard, Davide Comitis filio, Waltero de Moravia, Alexandro Vicecomite de Elgyn, Thoma Rectore Ecclesiae de Lannabryde.

Nº X. CHARTA de FYNLARG. *Ibid.*   Nº X. CHARTA de FYNLARG.

ALEXANDER Rex Scottorum, &c. Sciant, Me dedisse et confirmasse Andreae Episcopo Moraviensi, et Successoribus ejus, Tres Davach de Fynlarg in Strathspe, in excambio nemoris quod appellatur Kawood, et in excambium Logynsythenach,

thenach, de qua, fciz. Logynfythenach, idem Epifcopus fatisfaciet pro nobis, et plenarium grantum faciet Willelmo Archidiacono Moravienfi et fuccefforibus ejus. Teftibus, P. Comite de Dunbar, M. Comite de Fyfe, W. filio Alani Senefcalli Jufticiario Scotiæ, &c. Apud Difchington in Northumbria, undecimo die Septembris, anno D. Regis 22do.

N° XI. N° XI. COLLATIO ECCLESIÆ de INVERALYEN. *Ibid.*

Collatio Ecclefiæ de INVERALYEN.
WALTERUS de Moravia Miles, &c. Sciant univerfi, Me dediffe Deo et Ecclefiæ Sanctæ Trinitatis de Elgyn, in perpetuam Eleemofynam, ad fuftentationem fabricæ ejufdem, Ecclefiam de Inveralyen, cum omnibus jufte pertinentiis. Teftibus, Andrea Epifcopo Moravienfi, Comite de Rofs, Symone Vicario de Dundurkus, &c.

N° XII. N° XII. DE ROTEMORCHUS. *Ibid.*

De ROTEMORCHUS.
ALEXANDER D. G. Rex Scottorum, &c. Sciant, Me dediffe, et confirmaffe, Deo et Ecclefiæ Moravienfi, et Andreæ Epifcopo Moraviæ, et fuccefforibus ejus, terram de Rotemorchus, per fuas rectas divifas, in efcambium terrarum quas prædictus Epifcopus petiit in Foreftis noftris, viz. unam Davach terræ et dimidium in forefta de Inverlailan apud Galrunclon et Belothin, et dimidium Davach * in landis Morgund, et quartam partem unius Davach in Plufcarden, et Dimidium Davach in Tarnua, et in eadem Forefta dimidium Davach ex altera parte aquæ de Findaren ex oppofito Ecclefiæ de Logyn, et triginta acras in Whytefield apud Rath, et quindecim acras apud Duldavy. Salvis eidem Epifcopo, et fuccefforibus ejus,

aliis

---

* " A Davioch or Davach of land is Four Ploughs of land."

aliis terris et pasturis per rectas divisas, quas ipse, et prædecessores sui, juste habuerunt in forestis nostris ante istam donationem; tenendas prædicto Episcopo et successoribus ejus, ita libere et quiete, sicut alii Episcopi Scoti terras suas quietius et liberius tenent et possident, Faciendo forinsecum servitium, quod ad terram illam pertinet. Concessimus igitur prædicto Andreæ, et successoribus ejus, prædictam terram de Rotemorchus in forestam: Quare prohibemus firmiter, ne quid in eadem terra, sine eorum licentia, siccetur aut venetur, super nostram plenariam forisfacturam decem librarum. Testibus, Comite Patricio, Comite Malcolmo de Fyfe, Alano filio Rolandi Cancellario, &c. apud Stryvelyn, 31mo Martii, anno regni 12mo.

N° XIII. Concessio super Ecclesiam de ROTEMORCHUS: *Ibid.*

OMNIBUS, &c. *Andreas* Moraviensis Episcopus salutem. Noveritis universi, Me dedisse, et hac Carta Confirmasse, et consensu et voluntate capituli, Deo et Beatæ Mariæ in ecclesia Sanctæ Trinitatis de Elgyn, ad lumenare ejusdem ecclesiæ, ecclesiam de Rotemorchus in Strathspe in perpetuam eleemosinam. Et hanc paginam, manu propria scriptam, sigilli nostri appositione duximus corroborandum. Testibus, Freskyno Decano, Magistro Ricardo Cantore, Magistro Henrico Thesaurario, &c.

N° XIV. Carta de INNES: *pen. Dom. de Innes.*

MALCOLMUS Rex Scottorum, omnibus probis hominibus totius terræ suæ, salutem. Sciatis, Me in feodo et hereditate dedisse Berowaldo Flandrensi in Provincia de Elgyn Incess et Ester-Urecard per rectas eorum divisas, tenendum sibi
et

et heredibus suis, de me et heredibus meis, hereditarie, libere quiete in bosco, in plano, in campis, pratis, pascuis, in moris et aquis; Faciendo mihi inde servitium unius militis in castro meo de Elgyne. Præterea ei dono in burgo meo de Elgyne unum toftum plenarium. Tenendum simul cum prædicto feodo suo, ita libere et quiete sicut aliquis ex paribus suis liberius et quietius tenet toftum suum aut feodum suum. Testibus, Willielmo Moraviensi Episcopo Sedis Apostolicæ Legato, Marlesuano filio Colbani, Willielmo filio Fresgyn. Apud Perth, in Natali Domini proximo post concordiam Regis et Sumerledi.

N° XV. N° XV. *MUNIMENTA Domus Dei (MAISON DIEU) juxta ELGYN: *Chart. Mor.*

Munimenta Domus (Maison Dieu) juxta ELGYN.

UNIVERSIS, &c. Johannes ecclesiæ Moraviensis Minister, Salutem: Noverit universitas vestra, Nos inspexisse quandam Cartam excellentissimi Principis Domini David D. G. Regis Scottorum, sigillo suo authentico signatam, Cujus Cartæ tenor talis est, viz. " David D. G. Rex Scotorum. Sciant, Nos inspexisse Car-
" tam bonæ memoriæ Alexandri Regis prædecessoris nostri,
" Cujus Cartæ tenor, de verbo in verbum, est talis, viz. Alex-
" ander D. G. Rex Scotorum, Sciant, Nos dedisse Deo et
" Sancto Johanni Evangelistæ, et Domui Dei juxta Elgyn in
" perpetuam eleemosynam, Terras de Monben et de Kelles,
" per rectas divisas suas, ad receptionem pauperum, et susten-
" tationem eorundem in eadem domo. Testibus, Willielmo
" Episcopo Glasguensi Cancellario, W. filio Alani Senescalli
" Justiciario Scotiæ, Alano Hostiario Comite Atholiæ, David de
" Hastyngys, apud Aberdeen, 23° Februarii, anno Regni 21°
" (1235.)"

N° XVI

* MUNIMENTA, in Law, were such authentic deeds and writings, by which a man was enabled to defend his title to his estate.

APPENDIX.

Nº XVI. Collatio de DALDELEYTH: *Ibid.*   Nº XVI.

OMNIBUS, &c. Hugo Herock burgenſis de Elgyn. Noveritis, Me, pro ſalute animae meae, dediſſe Deo et Sanctae Mariae, necnon et Eccleſiae Sanctae Trinitatis de Elgyn, et Archibaldo Epiſcopo Movarienſi, Totam terram meam de Daldeleyth, cum omnibus pertinentiis, ad ſuſtentationem duorum Capellanorum: Ita, viz. ut unus teneatur divina celebrare ad altare Sancti Nicolai in Eccleſia Sanctae Trinitatis de Elgyn, et alter ad altare Sanctae Crucis in Eccleſia parochiali de Elgyn. Teſtibus, D. Andrea Abbate de Kynlos, Simone Priore de Pluſcarden, W. Priore de Urechard, D. Willelmo de Doleys milite: Apud Elgyn, die Dominico in feſto Nativitatis Beatae Virginis, A. D. 1286.

Collatio de DALDE-LEYTH.

Nº XVII. Carta DUNECANI Regis: *Dalr. Collect.*   Nº XVII.

EGO Dunecanus filius Regis Malcolumb. conſtans heredetarie Rex Scotiae, dedi in Eleemoſina Sancto Cuthberto et ſervitoribus, Tinengeham, Aldeham, Scuchale, Cnolle, Hatheruuich et de Broccefmuthe, omne ſervitium quod inde habuit Fodanus Epiſcopus; et haec dedi in tali quietantia, cum facca et focco, qualem nunquam meliorem habuit Sanctus Cuthbertus, ab illis de quibus tenet ſuas Eleemoſinas: Et hoc dedi pro meipſo, et pro anima patris mei, et pro fratribus meis, et pro uxore mea, et pro infantibus meis, et quoniam volui quod iſtud donum ſtabile eſſet Sancto Cuthberto, feci quod fratres mei conceſſere. Qui autem iſtud voluerit deſtruere, vel miniſtris Sancti Cuthberti aliquid auferre, maledictionem Dei et Sancti Cuthberti, et meam habeat; Amen.

Carta Dune-CANI Regis.

D d d   Nº XVIII.

Nº XVIII. Estimation of Geddes and Kilravock: *Pen. Kilravock.*

Eſtimation of Geddes and Kilravock.

EXTENTUS terrarum de Kilravok et Eſter Geddis, quæ ſunt Hugonis de Roſe et Mariotæ ſponſæ ſuæ, factus apud Innernarin, die Mercurii in feſto Sancti Laurentii, anno Gratiæ milleſimo ducenteſimo nonageſimo quinto, per bonos probos et fideles homines patriæ non ſuſpectos, viz. per tales, per Robertum Falconarium, Wilhelmum Thanum de Moyithes, Donevaldum Thanum de Kaledor, Thomam Venatorem, Ferguſium Judicem, Alexandrum Huſband, Johannem filium Duncani, Duncanum de Urchnie, Walterum filium Thomæ, Ricardum Muil, Wilhelmum Wod, Johannem Orlet, Hugonem filium Wilhelmi, Henricum de Kildrumie, Eliam Siſter, juratos magno ſacramento interveniente, et diligenter examinatos: Qui omnes unanimo conſenſu dixerunt, quod terra de Kilravok, cum omnibus pertinentiis ſuis, ſciz. cum molendino, braſinis, quarellis, et boſto, valet per annum XXIIII libras. Item dixerunt, quod terra de Eſter Geddis, cum molendino et brandiniis, valet per annum XII libras. Summa utriuſque XXXVI Libræ.

Nº XIX. Carta de URCHANBEG. *Chart. Morav.*

Carta de Urchanbeg.

UNIVERSIS, &c. Henricus Epiſcopus Movarienſis. Noveritis, Nos dediſſe, et ad feodum firmum donuiſſe, nobili viro Donaldo de Kaledore Thayno ejuſdem, pro ſuis beneficiis, auxiliis, &c. nobis et dilectæ eccleſiæ noſtræ, totam terram noſtram de Urchanbeg, cum pertinentiis, jacentem infra dominium de Fortherves: Reddendo inde inſuper annuatim dictus Donaldus, et heredes, nobis et ſucceſſoribus, tredecim ſolidos et quatuor

quatuor Denarios usualis monetæ Scotiæ, ad duos anni terminos consuetos, viz. Pentecostis et Sancti Martini, per equales portiones. Apud Canoniam Moraviensem, 1º die Martii, A. D. 1421.

No XX.   Homagium Domini de LOVETH.   *Ibid.*

ANNO Domini millesimo trecentesimo sexagesimo septimo, 12º die Septembris, in capitulo Ecclesiae Moraviensis, Hugo Fraser Dominus de Loveth, portionarius terrarum de Ard, fecit homagium pro parte sua dimidiae Davachae terrae de Kilcalargy et de Esser, Domino Alexandro Episcopo Moraviensi, Praesentibus D. Wilhelmo de Keith milite Mariscallo Scotiae, Johanne de Dolais Thano de Cromdale, &c.

No. XXI.

Nº XXI.   Nº XXI.

The VALUED RENT of the Shire of MORAY, as it was fixed and subscribed by the Commissioners, May 30th 1667.

Valued Rent of the Shire of MORAT.

	Scots Money	£.	sh.	d.
Parish of BELLY.				
The Marquis of Huntley	L.	240	8	0
Parish of ESSIL.				
Archibald Geddes		216	12	6
Corskie		95	6	0
Stynie		88	15	5
John Hamilton		218	6	7
Redhall		77	19	8
Crofts		72	2	11
Milton and Bethil		145	4	5
Miln of Craig		26	13	1
Belnacoul		34	2	5
DIPPLE.				
Laird of Innes for all Urquhart		877	7	9
URQUHART.				
Laird of Innes for Innes and Germach		2887	14	7
The Fishing		391	4	10
Forefalds		88	12	5
Callender's land rent		1454	14	0
His Fishing		880	2	0
Ladies Fishing		440	1	6
Earl of Moray's Fishing		585	15	2
James Dunbar's Fishing		244	13	4
Leuchars		437	3	3
Over Meft		191	1	3
Alexander Maver		136	9	3
Nether Meft		218	6	3
Loch		218	6	3
Threpland		20	9	5
Finfan		102	6	8
William Gadderer		34	17	1
James Brander		47	15	5
John Duncan		35	1	3
Michael Maver		46	10	1
Robert Chalmers		27	10	8
John Russel		8	10	3
Archibald Dunbar		112	18	4
Maverston		75	1	5
Matthew Miln		96	6	0
Carry over	L.	10874	9	5

	Scots Money	£.	sh.	d.
Brought over	L.	10874	9	5
Robert Innes		62	3	0
James Sclater		53	17	0
LANBRIDE.				
Pitnascir		68	5	0
Cockston		515	19	4
Hattoun		313	16	4
Cotts		146	4	0
St ANDREWS.				
Linkwoods		471	5	6
Barmukatie Milns		462	5	0
Kirkton and Kirkhill		316	15	6
Dunkintie and Gilmorside		214	8	8
Easter Caldcotts		109	13	1
Wester Caldcotts		109	13	1
Scotstoun-hill		88	14	4
Shearistoun		219	3	4
Bishop of Ross's heirs		203	0	0
James Tarve's land		48	10	2
Archibald Geddes		24	5	1
Isabel Innes		24	5	1
Cald-hame		244	10	8
Forresters seat		238	16	2
Pitgavenie		341	2	8
Inch		61	8	6
SPYNIE.				
Sheriff miln		163	15	4
Myreside		192	16	2
Burroughbridge		82	7	10
Finrosie		347	5	2
Spynie		28	17	8
Inchbrook		51	3	10
Moraystoun		97	9	4
Kintrae		473	4	6
Quarrywood		582	7	10
Westfield		437	12	4
Bishop-miln		265	4	8
Aldrouchtie		87	15	0
BIRNIE.				
Laird of Grant		72	2	2
Mr John Dunbar		115	3	4
Carry over	L.	18194	16	1

APPENDIX.

Scots Money	L.	fh.	d.
Brought over	L. 18194	16	1
Alexander Dunbar's relict	69	9	4
David Stewart	136	0	0
Middleton	193	15	0
Mr Alexander Spence's heirs	102	0	0
George Leflie	32	10	8
Patrick Gow's heirs	6	16	6
James Donaldson	6	16	6

DUNDURCOS.

The Earl of Rothes	177	18	2
James Gordon	41	17	6
Mulben	567	9	0
Ordewhifh	41	17	6
Freefield and Collie	103	13	2
Cairntie	90	15	6
Inchberrie and Ellie	134	0	8
Achrofk	41	17	6
Mulderies	737	7	2
Gerbatie	192	2	4
Archibald Geddes	235	8	0
Ortoun	148	18	0
Miln of Ortoun	27	6	0

ROTHES.

The Earl of Rothes	1298	6	0
Andrew Leflie	109	15	0

ELGIN.

Laird of Grant	1512	4	4
Francis Brodie	807	1	4
Pittenriech	1134	1	0
Eafter Kelles	116	19	4
Over Monbein	29	5	2
Inverlochtie	95	11	0
Colin MacKenzie	199	3	4
John Watfon	71	3	4
Rydevie	72	6	0
Mr Angus MacKenzie	157	18	8
George Gibfon	75	11	4
Teinds of Monbein	111	0	0
Dean's Crook	20	9	6
Langmorn	191	2	4
Wefter Whitewry	194	18	8
Maine	407	13	4
Blackhills	208	2	2
Cockftoun's lands	377	0	0
James Chalmers	251	9	8
Bishop of Rofs	252	9	2
Mr Robert Martine	66	15	8
David Seaton	20	9	6
Moy Croft	14	12	6
Carry over	L. 28990	2	11

Scots Money	L.	fh.	d.
Brought over	L. 28990	2	11
Sub-dean's Croft	13	13	0
Dipple Croft	8	15	6
Sub-chanter's Croft	6	16	6
Friar-haugh	82	6	0
Teinds of Whitefield and Moftowrie	83	0	0

DUFFUS.

Lord Duffus	2308	5	8
Sir Ludowic Gordon	412	4	2
Robert Sutherland	80	0	0

KENEDAR.

Lord Brodie	831	12	8
Sir Ludowic Gordon	2213	4	8

DALLAS and ALTYRE.

Sir Ludowic Gordon for Dallas	692	17	6
Laird of Altyre	726	13	0
Edinvele	39	2	0
	35	2	0
Rymichie	9	8	0
Craigmiln	64	10	4
Little Phorp	41	18	6
Wefter Kelles	154	15	0
Meikle Branchils	172	18	0
Bellachragan	34	6	2
Little Branchils	64	4	2

ALVES.

Eafter Alves	739	17	0
Ardgaoith	625	15	0
Monachtie	867	14	0
Wefter Alves	529	5	2
Miln of Monachtie	61	8	6
Laird of Muirtoun	1786	12	2
Ditto for Langeouts	73	2	6
Laird of Lethen	764	13	4
Kilbuyack	380	7	0
Ernfide	254	13	4
Aflifk	238	16	2
Windyhills	272	18	8
Kirkoun	171	16	4
William Brodie	354	1	6
Inchtellie	67	0	8
John Watfon	177	0	8
James Giizean	87	15	6
William Gilzean	44	5	0
Archibald Watfon	44	5	0
Hempriggs	545	10	8
Carry over	L. 45152	19	11

398   APPENDIX.

	Scots Money £. sh. d.		Scots Money £. sh. d.
Brought over	L. 45152 19 11	Brought over	L. 57237 0 8
RAFFORD.		Grant of Newtoun	39 0 0
		Easter Tulliglens	73 2 6
Woodhead	53 17 0	Commissary Stewart	45 0 4
Burgie's lands	877 13 8	Knock of Brae-Moray	181 7 4
Lentoun	188 13 8	Dallas Brachtie	73 2 0
Struthers and Winderlaw	286 11 8	Ernside's lands	134 18 2
Blairie	214 9 0	Sluie	73 2 6
John Falconer	238 6 0	Presley	73 2 6
East Grange	326 8 0	Loggy	138 18 2
Tarves	446 13 4	Wester Tulliglens	40 19 0
Half of West Grange	244 0 7	Rylucas	194 9 8
Clunie	95 1 6	Dunduff	94 6 8
Braco	54 2 4	Earl of Moray	327 8 0
		Harie Stewart's heirs	37 6 0
		Muirs and Drummine	100 17 8
FORRES.			
		KNOCKANDO and ELCHIES	
Laird of Grange	213 8 8		
Bogs	109 3 4		
Chapeltoun	54 12 0	Laird of Grant	628 3 10
Belliferie	100 0 0	George Grant of Kirdels	426 10 0
Milns of Forres	200 0 0	Bellintome	195 12 4
Sheriff's mother	255 17 6	Wester Elchies	423 11 2
Belnageith	225 3 4	Easter Elchies	314 1 6
Dunphail	126 9 6		
Tanachie	379 6 2	DUTHEL.	
Thornhill	127 18 10		
Lord Brodie	432 15 4	Laird of Grant	861 17 8
Burdsyards	538 13 0	ABERNETHIE.	
Earl of Moray	127 18 10		
Sluie	63 0 0	Earl of Moray	28 0 0
		Laird of Grant	712 4 4
MOY and DYKE.			
		INVERALLON.	
Easter Binns	390 17 2		
Mr John Campbell	218 10 6	Laird of Grant	182 10 10
Kincorth	371 18 6	INVERAVON.	
White mire	109 13 0		
Grangehill	1602 15 8	Laird of Bellindalach	292 0 8
Earl of Moray, Tarnua, Fenties, &c.	322 10 8	ADVIE.	
Earl-miln, &c.	391 4 2	Laird of Bellindalach	486 17 8
Lord Brodie	1263 0 6	Dalvey	317 5 4
Coulbin	913 18 4	Patrick Grant of Dellay	58 10 0
Meikle Ferry	51 4 0	CHURCH-MEN.	
Baraley	39 0 0		
		Bishop of Moray	1400 0 0
EDINKYLIE.		Parson of Duffus	200 0 0
		Minister of Urquhart	50 0 0
Dunphail	314 7 0	Minister of Dyke	50 0 0
Carry over	L. 57237 0 8	Total	L. 65501 6 6

The Legal Valuation of the County of Moray, in the year 1667, was as above; but now amounts to L. 65,603 Scots Money.

APPENDIX.

Nº XXII. Concessio de Inverlochtie: *Chart. Morav.*   Nº XXII.

OMNIBUS Christi fidelibus, Eva Morthac Domina de Rothais, salutem: Noveritis, Me, pro salute animæ meae, dedisse Sanctae Trinitati et Ecclesiae Moraviae, et Archibaldo Episcopo et successoribus, totam terram meam de Inverlochtie, cum omnibus pertinentiis, in puram Eleemosynam. Testibus, D. W. de Dune Decano Moraviensi, Henrico Precentore, D. W. Priore de Urchard, D. Gilberto de Roule milite, tunc Vicecomite de Elgyn. Datum anno 1263.

Concessio de Inverlochtie.

Nº. XXIII. Charter to the Burrough of Inverness, by King James VI.   Nº XXIII.

JAMES, by the grace, &c. Know, That We, considering the ancient erection of Inverness, by our famous progenitors, into a free Burrough of this Kingdom, have ratified, and by this present Charter, do ratify, and perpetually confirm, all and sundry the Charters, Confirmations, Rights, Liberties and Privileges granted and confirmed by our Progenitors, William, Alexander, David, and James the first of that name, Kings of Scotland, to our said Burrough: Likewise the Charter and Confirmation lately granted by our grand-father James V. of that name; also the Charter granted in favour of Divine Service, and of the Ministers of God's word, and of the Hospital, by our mother Mary Queen of Scots; and the Lands, Houses, Churches, Chapels, Crofts, Milns, Fishings, and all others mentioned in that Charter, of date 21st of April 1567 years: Moreover, We of new grant, and in perpetual feu set and confirm, to the Provost, Bailies, &c. of our said Burrough, the Lands, Territories and Commonty thereof, with all parts and privileges: As also all the Lands of Drakies, and the Forest thereof; the Lands of Merkinsh,

Charter to the Burrough of Inverness.

kinſh, with the paſturage thereof, with the Parks and Woods; likewiſe the Lands called the Barn-hills, Claypots, Miln and Fields, the Carſe, and the Carn-laws, with the common Muir of the ſaid Burrough; Likewiſe the water of Neſs on both ſides, from Clachnagaick to the ſea, with all Fiſhings, Ports, Havens, Creeks, the Still-fiſhing, the Red-pool, with power to begin to fiſh on the ſaid water with boats and nets on the 10th of November yearly, and to uſe Crives and Water-kiſts; With the Ferry of Keſſack, and right of Ferrying on both ſides: Further, all the Milns called the King's Milns, the Suckin and Multures thereof, with the aſtricted and dry Multures of the Caſtle Lands, and all Corns which have, or ſhall receive fire or water, within the liberty, territory and Pariſh of Inverneſs, as well out-Suckin as in-Suckin, to pay Multure and Knaveſhip at the ſaid Milns: With power and liberty of Paſture, Peats, Foggage, Turf, &c. in all places uſed and wont; and particularly in Craig-phadrick, Capulach-muir, Daviemont, and Bogbayne, with power of Ferrying on Lochneſs: With Mercats weekly on Wedneſday and Saturday, and eight free Fairs in the year, viz. on Palm Sunday, on July 7. St Andrew's fair, on Auguſt 15. Mary maſs, in September Roodmaſs, on November 10. Martinmaſs, in December St Thomas' Fair, on February 1. Peter Fair, and on April 25. St Mark's Fair; every Fair to hold for eight days: With the Petty cuſtoms of all Cities, Towns, and Villages within the ſhire, and particularly of the Colleges of Tain in Roſs, Merkinſh, Chanonrie, Dornoch, Thurſo, and Wick in Caithneſs, to be applied to the publick good of Inverneſs: That no ſhip break bulk betwixt Tarbetneſs and Inverneſs: And our ſaid Burrough ſhall have Coroners and Sheriffs within themſelves; and a Guildry with a Dean of Guild: That there be but one Tavern: That no one in the ſhire make Cloth but Burgeſſes. With power to make Statutes and Rules for the Burrough, &c.

N° XXIII,

No XXIV. CHARTERS to the BURROUGH of ELGIN. No XXIV.

Charters to the Burrough of ELGIN.

KING JAMES II. by his Charter dated at Aberdeen 5. November 1457, confirms to the Burrough of Elgin all the Grants and Concessions made by Alexander, Robert, and others his predecessors Kings of Scotland, and particularly the Lands of Mostowie, Douallygreen, Greeship, and Strathcant. *Archiv. de Elgin.*

King JAMES VI. grants to the Burrough of Elgin the Hospital of Maison Dieu, with the Patronage thereof, and the lands of Maison Dieu, Over and Nether Monbens, Haugh thereof, Over and Nether Cardels, Over and Nether Pitnafeir, refuming his charter dated 22d March 1594, for sustaining the poor in the said hospital, and maintaining a Master of Music for instructing the youth in Music, and performing the ordinary services in the church, dated the last day of February 1641. *Ibid.*

King CHARLES I. by his charter, with a signature, dated 15. November 1641, and ratified in Parliament 8. March 1645, grants to the Burrough of Elgin the lands of Glasgreen, and the right of Patronage of two Ministers for the parish, and one Reader. *Ibid.*

King CHARLES I. by his Charter, dated 8th October 1633, grants, and confirms to the Provost Bailies and Community of Elgin, the town of Elgin, with all the lands and others pertaining thereto. And particularly the greeship lands of Elgin, the lands of Doually-green, Glass-green, Mostowie, with the mosses thereof, and the moss of Strathcant; all the ports, stations, bays, and creeks of Lossie and Spey, and betwixt Spey and Findhorn, where any ship or boat can be received; the town and lands of Over Bareflathills, and the haugh thereof; the Hospital and Preceptory of Maison Dieu, with the Patronage thereof; the areable lands of Maifon Dieu; the lands of Over and Nether Monben, with the haugh thereof called Broomtoun; the lands of Bogfide, with the miln thereof, miln lands, adftricted multures and fequels; the lands of Cardels Over and Nether, alias Pitcroy, Delnapot, and Smiddy Croft, with the miln, miln lands, multures, and fequels, with the falmon fifhing on the river Spey; the lands of Over and Nether Pitnafier; the Black Friar eroft; the lands and gardens belonging to the predicant brethren lying in the North fide of the Burrough: With power of holding annual fairs and weekly mercats, and that none elfe fhall hold fairs or mercats within four miles of the town: With power of creating Officers, holding Courts, enjoying all Privileges and Immunities belonging to Royal Burroughs: Uniting and erecting the Burrough, Hofpital, and all lands belonging to them, into one free Burrough, and one faifine to be taken for the whole. (*Ibid.*)

N° XXV.

Charter to the Burrough of Forres.

N° XXV. CHARTER to the BURROUGH of FORRES.

JAMES, Underftanding, that the ancient Charters granted to the town of Forres have been deftroyed in time of war, or by the violence of fire, We have of new granted and confirmed to the Community of the faid Burrough of Forres, in free Burgage, with the lands and others formerly thereto belonging; particularly the lands called Grivefhip, Bailie-lands, Meikle Bog, with the King's Meadow, Lobbranftoun, with Crealties and Ramflat, and common pafturage in the Foreft of Drummonfide and Tulloch, with moffes, muirs; the water and Fifhing of Findhorn, from Dunduff to the Bank of Findhorn, both in frefh and in falt water, with mufcles, mufcle-fcalps, with power to fet the fame in tack, to fifh with boats and nets, and to have ports and harbours for fhips upon the faid water:

ter: With power annually to elect and appoint a Provost, Bailies, and other Magistrates and Officers necessary: And to constitute the Provost, and Bailies, Sheriffs within the Burrough and its liberties; and discharge the Sheriff of the Shire of Elgin and Forres to exercise his office within the said Burrough or its liberties: With power to the Burrough to have a Cross, a weekly Mercat on Monday, and an annual fair beginning on the Vigils of St Laurence, and to continue for eight days. With power also to hold Burrough and Sheriff Courts, and of packing, peeling: And with all and sundry other privileges and immunities of a free Burrough: Paying yearly to the Abbot of the Convent of Kinloss twenty merks current money, out of the farm of the said water and the fishing. At Edinburgh, June 23d, 1496 years, and of our Reign the ninth year.

N° XXVI. A PAPAL BULL to KINLOS: *From the Original M. S. penes the* AUTHOR.

ALEXANDER Episcopus, servus servorum Dei, dilectis filiis Rainerio Abbati Sanctæ Matris de Kinloss, ejusque fratribus, tam praesentibus quam futuris, regularem vitam professis. In P. P. M. ad hoc universalis Ecclesiæ cura nobis a provisore omnium bonorum Deo commissa est, ut religiosas diligamus personas, et bene placentes Deo religiones Studeamus, modis omnibus propagare. Quapropter, dilecti in Domino filii, vestris justis postulationibus clementer annuimus, et præfatum monasterium in quo divino mancipati estis obsequio sub Beati Patri et nostra protectione suscipimus, et praesentis scripti privilegio communimus. Inprimis statuentes, ut ordo monasticus, qui, secundum Deum, et Beati benedicti regulam, atque institutionem Cisterciensium fratrum in eodem loco institutus esse

esse dignoscitur, perpetuis ibidem temporibus inviolabiliter observetur. Praeterea, quascunque possessiones, quaecunque bona idem monasterium in praesentiarum juste et canonice possidet, aut in futurum justis modis poterit adipisci, firma vobis vestrisque successoribus et illibata permaneant. In quibus haec propriis duximus exprimenda vocabulis. Locum ipsum in quo praefatum monasterium situm est, cum terris, aquis, pratis, pascuis, piscaturis, Sylvis, molendinis, grangiis; asiamenta, forestae materiam, pasnagium, corticem, et ad ignem necessaria, et fodinas. Sane, laborum vestrorum quos propriis manibus aut sumptibus colitis, sive de nutrimentis vestrorum animalium, nullus omnino decimas a vobis praesumat exigere. Addicimus etiam, ut sive in mari, sive in fluminibus, fratres vel famuli ipsius monasterii piscationes suas exercuerint, ubicunque applicuerint, nullus a vobis decimas exigat. Prohibemus insuper auctoritate Apostolica, ne quis, fratres vestros, Clericos viz. sive Laicos, post factam in Monasterio vestro professionem, absque vestra licentia, suscipere audeat vel detinere. Sancimus etiam, ne quis Archi-Episcopus vel Episcopus, sive cujuslibet ordinis persona, locum vestrum a divinis interdicat officiis, nisi Abbatis, vel fratrum ipsius loci, evidens ac manifesta culpa extiterit. Licet autem vobis, cum commune interdictum terrae fuerit, clausis januis, et exclusis excommunicatis, et interdictis, non pulsatis campanis, suppressâ voce divina officia celebrare. Paci quoque et tranquillitati vestrae paterna sollicitudine providentes, auctoritate Apostolicâ inhibemus, ut nullus infra ambitum Ecclesiae vestrae, sive Grangias vestras, violentiam, vel rapinam, seu furtum facere, aut ignem imponere, vel hominem capere seu interficere audeat. Praeterea omnes libertates, seu etiam immunitates ac regias consuetudines, a bonae memoriae David quondam rege Scotorum, vobis et Ecclesiae vestrae rationabiliter indultas, et Scripti

sui

sui pagina roboratas, auctoritate Apostolica confirmamus, et illibatas statuimus perpetuo permanere. Prohibentes, ne quisquam hominum vos aut Ecclesiam vestram de omnibus auxiliis, et geldis, et hydageis, et danegeldis, et assisis, et murdris, placitis, querelis, veteragiis, chalarrio, passagiis, pontagio, et de omni tala, et omnibus occasionibus, et omnibus consuetudinibus, omnique terreno servitio et seculari exactione audeat infestare; sed liberi ac quieti ab hujusmodi exactionibus maneatis, quemadmodum praedictus Rex David Scriptis suis vobis confirmavit. Praesenti quoque scripto sancimus, ne Episcopus, vel aliquis secularis persona, aut quaelibet persona alterius ordinis, in quorum Episcopatibus vel potestatibus Monasteria vestra consistunt, regularem vel canonicam electionem Abbatis vestri unquam impediant; nec de removendo ac deponendo eo, qui pro tempore fuerit, contra statuta Cisterciensis ordinis, et authoritatem privilegiorum suorum, se ullatenus intromittant. Liceat etiam vobis Clericos vel Laicos, et absolutos è seculo fugientes, ad conversionem vestram recipere, et eos absque ullius contradictione in vestro Collegio retinere. Decernimus ergo, ut nulli omnino hominum liceat prefatum Monasterium temerè perturbare, aut ejus possessiones auferre, vel ablatas retinere, minuere, seu quibuslibet vexationibus fatigare; sed illibata omnia et integra conserventur eorum, pro quorum gubernatione et sustentatione concessa sunt, usibus omnimodis profutura, salva sedis Apostolica auctoritate. Si qua igitur in futurum Ecclesiastica secularisve persona, hanc nostrae constitutionis paginam sciens, contra eam temere venire tentaverit, secundò tertiove commonita, nisi presumptionem suam dignâ satisfactione correxerit, potestate honorisque sui dignitate careat, reamque se divino Judice existere, de perpetrata iniquitate cognoscat, et a sacratissimo corpore et sanguine Dei et Domini Redemptoris nostri Jesu Christi aliena fiat, atque in extremo

examine

examine districtè ultione subjaceat; Cunctis autem eidem loco sua Jura servantibus, sit pax Domini nostri Jesu Christi, quatenus et hic fructum bonae actionis percipiant, et apud destrictum Judicem praemia eterne pacis inveniant. AMEN ac AMEN.

Nº XXVII. Charter of STRATHYLA in STRATHBOGGIE to KINLOSS.

WILLIELMUS D. G. Rex Scotorum. &c. Sciant praesentes et futuri, Me, pro salute animae meae, et animarum omnium predecessorum et successorum, Dedisse Deo et Beatae Mariae et omnibus Sanctis, et Abbati et Monachis de Kinloch, totam terram de Strathylese cum pertinentiis, per rectas suas metas, quas eisdem fecimus per meliores et antiquiores patriae perambulari, viz. a loco ubi Lagyn descendit in Hylef, ascendendo per album ficum in rubeo musso usque ad summitatem orientalis Belach, et per summitatem utriusque Belach, usque eque ultra fontem qui vocatur Leskyngowin; Et ab eodem fonte sicut rivulus ipsius fontis descendit per Grodok in Hylef, Et sic ascendendo per Hylef usque Geth, et usque ubi Forgyn descendit in Hylef, Et inde ascendendo per Forgyn usque Algarg, et sic usque Aldrochyn, Et ab inde usque Algargadyn, Et ita usque Ferthekinir, et usque Telinire, et Badnagir, Et sic per ascensum aquae usque Hachindaling, Et ita usque Polenterf, Et inde usque Elangyrloy, Et sic usque Tubernamin, Et sic usque Clochindush, Et ab inde descendendo per Logyn in Hylef. Tenendam—in puram Eleemosynam. Testibus, R. Episcopo Moraviensi, J. Episcopo Catanensi, R. Episcopo Rossensi, H. Cancellario, Willelmo filio Freskyn, Hugone filio Freskyn. Apud Elgyn, ultimo die Julii.

Nº XXVIII.

Nº XXVIII. The CATHEDRAL and CHANONS at SPYNIE: Nº XXVIII.
Chart. Morav.

BRICIUS Moraviensis Episcopus, universis Sanctae matris Ecclesiae filiis. Cum praedecessores nostri nullam certam et stabilem in Ecclesia tenuere sedem, sed pro libitu in una tantum Ecclesiarum, viz. Brenuth, aut de Speny, aut de Kenedar, sedem adoptaverunt; Domino nostro Papae INNOCENTIO humiliter supplicavimus, ut in Eclesia Sanctae Trinitatis de Speny pro futuris temporibus sedem tenerent. Qui mandavit Episcopis Sancti Andreae, et de Brechyn, et Abbati de Lundoris, ut praefatam Ecclesiam Cathedralem honoris titulo decorarent. Quapropter venerabiles illi viri, auctoritate Apostolica, praefatam Ecclesiam Sanctae Trinitatis Cathedralem decorarunt, eam in futuris temporibus Moraviae Episcopis statuentes et confirmantes Cathedralem. In honorem et reverentiam dictae Ecclesiae, et in amplificationem divini cultus, octo Canonias, cum omnibus justis pertinentiis assignavimus, viz. 1ma Canonia Decanatui assignata, Ecclesia de Erin cum capella de Innernarin. 2da Canonia Cantariae assignata, Ecclesia de Lamnabryde, et Ecclesia de Alvais, et Ecclesia de Raffus. 3tia Canonia Thesaurariae assignata, Ecclesia de Kinedar, et Ecclesia de Eskyles. 4ta Canonia Cancellariae assignata Fortherves, Lythenes, et Lunyn, et Duldavy; salva tenura Willelmi filii Willelmi filli Freskini in praedictis terris, viz. Lunyn et Duldavy, item terra de Logyn juxta Duffus. 5ta Canonia Ecclesia Sancti Petri de Strathoven, et Ecclesia de Urchard ultra Innernys. 6ta Canonia Forais et de Logyn Fythenach. Hanc autem Canoniam Archidiaconatui nostro in perpetuum assignamus. 7ma Canonia Ecclesia de Speny. 8va Canonia Ecclesia de Ruthvon et de Dupol. Ego Bricius Moraviensis

Moravienſis Epiſcopus Subſcribo. Ego Radulfus Abbas de Kin loſs. Ego Ricardus Prior de Urchard. Ego Gilbertus Abbas de Aberbroth. Willielmus Perſona de Edindum. Johannes Perſona de Artyndole. Gregorius Vicarius de Altyre. Andreas Vicarius de Duffus. Gilbried Perſona de Abertarf. Alexander Perſona de Elgyn. Walterus Sanctae Columbae de Petyn. Stephanus Perſona de Glas.

N° XXIX.   No XXIX. Concessio ſuper Præbendis de Kingusy, &c. *Ibid.*

Conceſſio ſuper Præbendis de Kinguſy, &c.

IN nomine Patris, &c. Amen. Ego Andreas Moravienſis Epiſcopus, ad amplificandum cultum divinum in Eccleſia noſtra Cathedrali, conſtituo duas Prebendas, et eas eidem Eccleſiae aſſigno. Unam, ſciz. de Eccleſiis de Kinguſy, vel de Inſhe, cum manſis ſuis: Et aliam de Eccleſiis de Croyn et Lunyn, cum manſis ſuis. Quare volo, ut ille habeat, qui pro tempore in Eccleſia Cathedrali Vicarius meus fuerit, et Canonicus ſit ejuſdem eccleſiae, cultum facturus in eadem tanquam Vicarius meus. Actum anno Gratiae 1226.

Nota. Andrew Biſhop of Moray confirmed the gift of Biſhop Bricius for eight Canonries; and to them he added the Kirks of Rynie, Dunbenan, Kynor, Inverkethny, Elethin, (now Elchies) and Buchary, (now Botary) Cromdale and Advyn, Kinguſy and Inſh, Croyn and Lunyn, (probably now Croy and Lundichty or Dunlichtie.)

No XXX.

APPENDIX.

Nº XXX.   *Procurationes Decanatuum.   *Ibid.*   Nº XXX.

Decanatus de Elgyn.	Sol.	De De Devoth De De Croyn Summa 25 Lib.	Procurationes Decanatuum.
Ecclesia de Aldheryn	40		
Dyke, Moy, et Altyre conjuncti	40		
Rothac	40	**Decanatus de Strathbolgie.**	
Dolas Michel	40		Sol. Drs.
Alvays	40	Ecclesia de Glas	40
Duffus	40	De Rynie et Essie	40
Elgyn, Spynie et Broneth	40	De Ruthven	40
Urchard	40	De Kinore et Dunbenan	40
Essyl	40	De Aberkerdir	40
Dundurkus	40	De Rothemay	40
Rothus	40	De Garntully et Drumdalgy	53 4
Kinedar	40	De Keith	43
Summa 25 lib. praeter Monasteria de Urchard et de Pluscarden.		Summa L. 21 13 4.	

Decanatus de Strathspe.

	Sol.
Logy Kenny	40
Kingusy et Inshe	40
Alveth	40
Rotemorcus	20
Kyncardyn	20
Dochal	40
Inveraleyn	20
Aberneth	20
Cromdal et Advey	40
Summa 14. Lib.	

Decanatus de Inverness.

	Sol.
Eccesia de Invernyss	40
De	
De Lundichty	40
De	
De	
De	
De Fernua	
De	

* Procurations were, a composition paid by the Parish Priest to his Ecclesiastical Judge, to commute for the Entertainment, which was otherways to be provided for him at his Visitation.

N° XXXI. Nº XXXI. SUPER TRANSMUTATIONE SEDIS. *Ibid.*

SuperTransmutatione Sedis.

HONORIUS Episcopus servus servorum Dei, venerabili fratri Episcopo Cathanensi, et dilectis filiis Abbati de Kinlos, Moraviensis Diocesis, et Decano de Rosmark, salutem et Apostolicam benedictionem. Veniens ad presentiam nostram, venerabilis frater noster Moraviensis Episcopus saepe nobis exposuit, et nostris frequenter auribus inculcavit, quod ipsius sedes, praeter id quod est in loco minus tuto, in tam solitario loco subsistit, ut nulla ibi contingat venalia reperire, unde plerumque sit, ut clericis, pro emendis sibi necessariis longinquius accedentibus, divinorum cultus officiorum non modicum impeditur. Quare idem Episcopus cum multa precum instantia postulavit a nobis, ut sedem eandem ad locum transferri habiliorem, viz. Sancti Trinitatis juxta Elgyn (carissimo filio nostro illustri Rege Scotorum, et Moraviensi Capitulo hoc ipsum, ut dictus Episcopus asserit, affectantibus) mandaremus. Nos igitur, discretioni et prudentiae vestrae in Domino confidentes, per Apostolica vobis scripta mandamus, quatenus vocatis quos videtis evocandos, proviso etiam, quod necessitas vel utilitas fieri hoc exposcat, pensatis insuper circumstantiis universis, super translatione hujusmodi, auctoritate Apostolica faciatis, quod sedem Domini, et utilitatem, et honestatem Moraviensis Ecclesiae cognoveritis expedire. Quod si non omnibus his exsequendis potueritis interesse, tu, frater Episcope, cum eorum altero ea nihilominus exsequare. Datum Laterani, 4° Idus Aprilis, Pontificatus nostri A° 8° (i. e. A. D. 1224.)

CONFIRMATIO.

APPENDIX.

CONFIRMATIO.

OMNIBUS Christi fidelibus hoc scriptum visuris vel audituris, Gilbertus Dei Gratia Katanensis Episcopus, et H. Decanus de Ross, salutem. Mandatum Domini Papae in haec verba accepimus. Honorius Episcopus, &c. Venerabili fratri, &c. (as above) Hujus Auctoritate mandati, una cum tertio conjudice, vocavimus quos vidimus evocandos, certum locum et diem vocatis praefigentes; constitutis igitur in presentia nostra, propter hoc evocatis, praedicto conjudice nostro, mandato Apostolico exsequendo interesse non valente, et per literas suas patentes se ad totum negotium excusante, Reverendo Domino nostro Alexandro illustri Regi Scotiae, translationem dictae sedis quamplurimum affectante, et super hoc per literas nobis instantius supplicante, de desiderio et voluntate Moraviensis Capituli hoc ipsum affectantis, et cum summa instantia praefatam translationem postulantis, diligentius inquirendo certiores effecti sumus. Constante igitur nobis plené et evidenter, de his quæ per Episcopum Moraviensem Apostolicæ sanctitati tam veraciter quam fideliter fuerunt suggesta, translationem dictæ sedis non solum necessitatem sed utilitatem evidentem exponere manifeste perpendimus. Ideoque auctoritate Apostolica praedictam sedem usque ad dictam Ecclesiam Sanctæ Trinitatis de Elgyn, duximus transferendam, Eamque Cathedralis honoris titulo decoravimus, Ipsamque in posterum omnibus futuris Episcopis Moraviensibus Statuentes Cathedralem. Quod ut universitati vestrae innotescat, praesentis scripti paginam, Sigillorum nostrorum appositione signavimus. Datum in ipsa Ecclesia Sanctae Trinitatis de Elgyn, anno Gratiae 1224, Regnante illustrissimo Rege Alexandro Praesidente venerabili in Christo, Patre Andrea Moraviensi Episcopo 14°, Kalend. Augusti. In nomine Domini Amen. Valete in Domino.

Nº XXXII. The Burning of the CATHEDRAL: (*Ibid*)

POST obitum Roberti Senefcalli Regis, et ante coronationem filii ejus Comitis de Carryke, gentes domini Alexandri Senefcalli filii Regis defuncti, in fine menfis Maii, anno 1390, combufferunt vilam de Foryfs, et Chorum Ecclefiae Sancti Laurentii et manerium Archidiaconi fubditus villam. Et menfe Junii fequentis, in festo beati Botulphi abbatis, praefente eodem Domino Alexandro, combufferunt totam villam de Elgyn, et Ecclefiam Sancti Egidii in ipfa, domum Dei juxta Elgyn, decem nobiles et octo manfiones nobilas et pulchras Canonicorum et Capellanorum. Et quod amarius et dolendum, nobilem et decoram Ecclefiam Moravienfem, fpeculum patriae et decus Regni, cum omnibus libris et bonis aliifque patriae in ea reconditis. Alexander de infulis, filius tertio genitus Domini de Infulis, cum fuis capitaneis intravit violenter in Canoniam de Elgin tertio die menfis Julii anno 1402, et ipfam depredavit totaliter de omnibus bonis repertis in ea, et villam de Elgyn pro magna parte combuffit.

Nº XXXIII. CONCESSIO de Ecclefia de FERNUA, &c. (*Ibid*)

OMNIBUS, &c. Andreas Epifcopus Moravienfis. Noveritis, Nos, pro cultus divini amplificatione, dediffe Ecclefiae Sanctae Trinitatis de Elgin, ad communam canonicorum, Ecclefiam de Fernua cum pertinentiis, excepta una dimidia Davach pertinente ad menfam noftram, Ecclefiam de Logyn-kenny, excepta una Davach ad menfam noftram, Ecclefiam de Kynchardyn in Strathfpe, falva una dimidia Davach terrae ad menfam Epifcopalem; Ecclefiam de Aberneth, de Altyre, de Euan in Brenach, de Artendol, in perpetuum, predictis canonicis habendas

bendas cum fructibus earum, ad communem fratrum residentiam tantum. Actum anno Gratiae 1239, mensis Decembris penultimo die.

N° XXXIV. Confirmatio de Ecclesia de DEVETH: (Ibid.)

BRICIUS D. G. Episcopus Moraviensis. Noverit universitas vestra, Nos, ad instantiam et petitionem Freskyni de Kerdal avunculi nostri, dedisse Ecclesiam de Deveth, cum pertinentiis, Ecclesiae Sanctae Trinitatis de Spynie Fabricae ejusdem Ecclesiae. Testibus, Hugone de Duglas, Alexandro et Henrico fratribus nostris, &c.

N° XXXV. Concessio de Ecclesia de DALERGUSIE: (Ibid)

OMNIBUS, &c. Andreas Moraviensis Episcopus. Noveritis, Nos hac Carta confirmasse Deo et Beatae Mariae et Ecclesiae Sanctae Trinitatis de Elgyn, ad luminare ejusdem, Ecclesiam de Dalergusie in Strathern in perpetuam Eleemosynam.

N° XXXVI. Carta de Forrays et de DYKE: (Ibid.)

WILLIELMUS D. G. Rex Scottorum. Sciant, Me dedisse et confirmasse Ricardo Episcopo Moraviensi in perpetuum, Ecclesiam de Forrays, et Ecclesiam de Dyke cum pertinentiis, in puram eleemosynam. Testibus, Comite David Fratre meo, Hugone Chancellario meo, Comite Duncano, W. filio Freskyn, Hugone filio suo. Apud Elgin.

N° XXXVII.

Nº XXXVII. Carta Ecclesiæ CATHEDRALI: *Ibid.*

Charta Ecclesiæ Cathedrali.

ALEXANDER D. G. &c. Sciant. Nos, pro salute animae nostrae, dedisse ad sustentationem unius capellani pro anima Regis Dunecani, et animabus fidelium in Ecclesia Cathedrali de Elgyn, tres marcas singulis annis percipiendas de firma burgi nostri de Elgyn, medeitatem ad Pentecosten, et aliam ad festum Sancti Martini. Testibus, W. Episcopo Glasguensi Cancellario, W. Cummyn Com. de Mynteith, apud castrum puellarum, 21 die Aprilis, anno Regni Domini Regis vicesimo primo.

Nº XXXVIII. Donatio Regis WILLIELMI: *Ibid.*

Donatio Regis WILLIELMI.

WILLIELMUS Rex Scottorum concessit Ricardo Moraviensi Episcopo, et successoribus ejus, unum toftum in Burgo de Banef, unum in Inverculan, unum in Elgyn, unum in Forrays, unum in Eren, unum in Invernyss, et unum in Kynthor. Apud Elgyn.

Nº XXXIX. Concessio de Logynanadel: *Ibid.*

Concessio de Logynanadel.

RICARDUS D. G. &c. Episcopus Moraviensis. Sciant, Me dedisse Willelmo filio Freskyn, et heredibus suis, Logynanadel et Logyndykes. Reddendo annuatim unam petram cerae ad festum Sancti Patricii. Etiam concessimus Deo et Ecclesiae Sancti Petri de Duffus plenarias decimas ejusdem terrae. Testibus, Willielmo filio Wysman, Augustino de Elgyn. Datum Anno Gratiae 1190.

Nº XL.

APPENDIX. 415

Nº XL. De situ MOLENDINI de AUCHTERSPYNIE: *Ibid.* Nº XL.

ANDREAS Episcopus Moraviensis. Noverint universi, Nos, consensu Capituli nostri, dedisse Waltero de Moravia, et heredibus suis, unum situm Molendini super Lossy, in terra nostra de Auchterspynie. Et Volumus, ut possideat jure perpetuo ad molendum Bladum suum et hominum suorum. Reddendo singulis annis unam petram piperis, et aliam libram cumini. Actum anno 1231, Sextus Idus Octobris. Testibus, David de Strathbolgyn, Willielmo Agno. + Ego Andreas Episcopus Moraviensis Subscribo.

De situ Molendini de AUCHTERSPYNIE.

N. B. The Members of the Chapter subscribe, with Crosses before their Names.

Nº XLI. COLLATIO ECCLESIÆ de KYLCALARGY: *Ibid.* Nº XLI.

JOHANNES Byseth omnibus, &c. Significo, Me, pro anima Willielmi Regis Scotiae, dedisse Deo et Ecclesiae Sancti Petri de Rothsan, ad Sustentationem Leprosorum ibi Deo servientium, Jus Patronatus, et quicquid habui in donatione Ecclesiae de Kylcalargy, sibi et Successoribus suis. Testibus, D. Andrea Episcopo, F. Decano, &c.

Collatio Ecclesiæ de Kylcalargy.

Nº XLII. COLLATIO de ROSS: *Ibid.* Nº XLII.

OMNIBUS, &c. Fergus de Androssan miles. Noveritis, Me dedisse Deo, et Archibaldo Episcopo Moraviensi et Successoribus, totam terram de Ross, viz. Duas davachas de Clon, quam tenui de Freskyno de Moravia, ad Sustentationem Capella-

Collatio de Ross.

norum in Ecclesia Cathedrali de Elgyn. Datum Apud Perth, 7º. Kal. Aprilis, anno Gratiae 1262.

N° XLIII. Nº XLIII. Collatio Annuitatis Ecclesiæ Cathedrali: *Ibid.*

Collatio Annuitatis Ecclesiæ Cathedrali.

ALEXANDER Rex Scotorum. Sciant, Me dedisse ad Sustentationem unius Capellani, in Ecclesia Cathedrali Tres marcas singulis annis percipiendas de firma Burgi nostri de Elgin, ad Penticostem et Festum Sancti Martini. Testibus, W. Episcopo Glasguensi Cancellario, W. Byseth, &c. apud Castrum puellarum, anno regni 21°, i. e. 1235.

N° XLIV. Nº XLIV. Concessio Advocationis de DUFFUS: *Ibid.*

Concessio Advocationis de Duffus.

OMNIBUS, &c. Willelmus de Fedreth, et Christiana de Moravia uxor sua, Noveritis, Nos pro salute animarum nostrarum, et parentum, et Successorum, Concessisse Deo et Sanctae Trinitati de Elgyn, et D. Archibaldo Moraviensi Episcopo, omne jus advocationis seu Patronatus quod nos habemus in Ecclesiam Sancti Petri de Duffhus, seu in vicaria vel Capellis ejusdem. Datum apud Kinedar in Moravia, die Martis proximo ante festum Apostolorum Symonis et Judae, anno Gratiae 1294.

N° XLV. N° XLV. Tack of the Teinds of Ruthven in Strathboggie.

Tack of the Teinds of Ruthven in Strathboggie.

MR Adam Hepburn Parson of Dipple granted to John Gordon of Craigullie, a Tack or Lease of the Teynds of Ruthven in Strathboggie, of date July 18th 1574, to which did consent and subscribe George Bishop of Moray, Alexander Dunbar Dean, James Muirton Chantor, Dunbar Arch-deacon,
John

APPENDIX. 417

John Kneycht Parson of Duffus, William Sutherland Parson of Moy, Robert Keith Parson of Kinore, Alexander Lesly Parson of Botarie, William Patterson Subdean, and Archibald Henderson Parson of Kingusie. *(N.)* The original was in the hands of Mr Milne late of Speymouth.

N° XLVI. From the Book of ASSIGNATIONS anno 1570, *in* N° XVI. *the Lawyers Library.*

MINISTERS of MORAY.

MR Robert Pont, Commissioner to plant Kirks from Ness to Spey, CCCC merks. *From the Book of Assignations, anno 1570.*

Elgin, Alexander Winsaster Minister, C libs. and L merks sen Beltyn 1568.

Forres and Altyre, Mr Andrew Sympson Minister, C merks.

Inverness, Mr Thomas Huison Minister, C lib.

Raffart and Kinloss, Alexander Urchard Minister, LXXX merks, and XX merks mair sen Beltyn 1568, providing he await upon his office, and use himself without selander.

Duffus and Kinedour, Mr John Keith Minister, VIXX lib. without ony third.

Edinkylzie, Mr Andro Brown Minister, IIIIXX marks.

Urchard, Lambryde, and Essil, Robert Keith Minister, IIIIXX marks, November 1567.

Alves and Lambryde, Mr Patrick Balfoure Minister, XL lib. November 1567, now to have the heal thyrd of the Chantory, with the thyrds of the saids Kirks.

EXHORTERS.

Dundurcus and Dupil, William Peterkin Exhorter, XL lib.

Birnay, James Johnston, XL marks, and XX marks mair sen Lambas

Lambmass 1568, because he is scribe to the Assemblis in Moray.

Spynie, James Philp, L marks.

Pettie and Brathollie, Andro Braboner, XL lib. and XX marks sen Beltyn 1568.

Urchard and Glenmoriston, Mr James Farquharson, XL lib.

Nairn, John Zoung, XL lib.

Rothes, Mr James Lesly Exhorter and Person, the thyrd of his benefice.

Lambryde, Andro Stronach, XX lib. Candlmass 1567.

Sanct Androis Kirk, Mr Alexander Lesly, XL marks Candlmass 1567.

Brayevia and Braichlie, Alan MacIntosh Exhorter and Reider in the Irish tongue, XL lib. Candlmass 1567.

Abernethie and Kingusie, John Glas Reider and Exhorter in Irish, L. 33 : 6 : 8.

Durris, Boleskin, and Abertarf, James Dubh, XX lib. and XX lib. mair sen November 1569.

Ugstoun, James Ker, XL marks November 1569.

Alves and Kinloss, Alexander Bad, XL marks sen Beltyn 1570.

Laggan, Alexander Clark, XL marks November 1569.

Aldern and Nairn, William Reech, L. 26 : 13 : 4, November 1570.

Alvie, James Spens, XL marks Beltyn 1572.

N. on the margin. Mr John Keith Commissioner, admitted the

Kynedward, William Clark, XL lib. Beltyn 1572, in Mr William Wiseman's room.

REIDERS.

Dolas, William Thomson, X lib. November 1567.

Croy

APPENDIX.

Croy and Moy, James Vaus, XX lib. Candlmafs 1567.
Forres, John Patterson, XX lib.
Moy, George Symson, XX lib.
Dyck, Alexander Duff, XX lib.
Ugstoun, James Ker, XX lib. now Exhorter sen November 1569, has VI lib. mair.
Duffus, William Clark, XX lib. Candlmass.
Urchard, Lambryde, and Effil, John Blendshel, XX lib. November 1567.
Bonach, William Symson, XX lib. Candlmafs 1567.
Durris and Boleskyn, James Dubh, XX lib. Candlmass.
Laggan and Alvie, Alexander Clark, XX lib. luck amang the Exhorters.
Raffort and Kinlofs, James Rawson, XX lib.
Keith, Andro Guthrie, XX lib.
Ardintullie, William Rethie, XX lib.
Innerkythnie, James Abernethie, XX lib.
Rothimay, Lorence Donaldson, XX lib.
Altire and Dolas, John Clark, XX lib. Lambas 1569.
Ardclach, William Brown, the thyrd of the Vicarage extending to L. 3:6:8, the Dean of Moray to pay the rest of his Stipend, Lambas 1570.
Kynedward, Mr William Wyseman, X lib. Lambas 1569 and X lib. mair sen Candlmas 1570.
Elgyne, Thomas Robertson, X lib. Lambas 1569.
Alves, Alexander Bad, XX lib. Lambas 1569, now Exhorter sen Beltyne 1570, has mair L. 6:13:4 Beltyne 1570.
Lundichtie and Dawick, John Dow-MacCondoquhy, XX lib. November 1569.

N° XLVII.

Nº XLVII. Nº XLVII. ORIGINAL WRITS belonging to CAMPBELL of CALDER.

Original Writs belonging to CAMPBELL of CALDER

TACK of Teinds, by Mr Alan MacIntoſh Parſon of Evan, to Sir John Campbell of Calder, dated 16th May 1586, and ſubſcribed by George Biſhop of Moray, Alan MacIntoſh, Alexander Dunbar Dean, and John Keith Parſon of Duffus.

Tack of the Teynds of Ardclach, by Mr Robert Dunbar Subchantor of Moray, to John Grant of Freuchie, dated anno 1614, narrating a former Tack granted by the ſame Mr Robert Dunbar, anno 1597.

Tack of the Teinds of Ardclach, by Mr Alexander Dunbar Subchanter of Moray, to John Roſe of Bellivat, anno 1582.

Tack of the Vicarage of Ardclach, by William Simſon Vicar thereof, to Hugh Roſe of Kilravock, dated July 22. 1588, with conſent of George Biſhop of Moray.

Acquittance of Stipend by Mr Alan MacIntoſh Parſon of Evan, dated anno 1581.

Tack of the Teinds of Croy to David Roſe of Holm, by Mr Patrick Lyddle Parſon of Croy and Moy, with conſent of the Biſhop and Chapter, dated at Elgin Auguſt 9. 1579, and ſubſcribed by George Biſhop of Moray, Patrick Lyddale, Alexander Dunbar Dean, Gavin Dunbar Archdeacon, John Kneycht Parſon of Duffus, John Gibſon Prebendary of Unthank, William Sutherland Parſon of Moy, Hugh Gregory Parſon of Lundichty, Alexander Ralphſon Parſon of Spynie, James Dunbar Parſon of Petty, and William Douglas Vicar of Elgin.

Tack of the Teinds of Croy to David Roſe of Holm, by Mr Patrick Lyddale Miniſter at Croy, dated anno 1585.

Tack

APPENDIX. 421

Tack of the Teinds of Lundichty, to Mr William Campbell of Brachly, by Mr James Vaufe Parfon of Lundichty, with confent of Sir John Campbell of Calder Patron, and of the Bifhop and Chapter, dated at Elgin, July 26. 1613, and fubfcribed by Alexander Bifhop of Moray, Thomas Dunbar Dean, Patrick Tulloch Archdeacon, Gavin Dunbar Chanter, William Dunbar Parfon of Moy, Donald MacQueen Parfon of Pettie, and Patrick Dunbar Parfon of Duffus.

Acquittance of Stipend by Mr James Vaufe Minifter at Croy, bearing that he was fettled Minifter there, and that Mr Patrick Dunbar was Minifter at Durris anno 1618.

Bond, Alexander Thomfon Minifter at Durris, to Sir John Campbell of Calder, concerning a hundred Merks of Penfion granted to him, dated at Invernefs, May 30. 1617, Witnefs Mr James Bifhop at Invernefs.

Renunciation of the Lands of Benchar by Alexander and Janet Rofe, in favour of John Campbell of Calder, dated June 3. 1598, Andrew Balfour Minifter at Nairn, Witnefs.

No. XLVIII. An ABSTRACT of K. CHARLES IId's LETTER to the Prefbytery of Edinburgh.

N° XLVIII

CHARLES IId's Letter to the Prefbytery of Edinburgh.

CHARLES R. Trufty and well beloved, We let you know by this Bearer, Mr James Sharp, how well we are fatisfied with the generality of the Minifters, whilft fome, under fpecious pretences, fwerved from the allegiance they owed to Us. We affure you, that, by the grace of God, we refolve to difcountenance profanity, and all contemners and oppofers of the Ordinances of the Gofpel. We do alfo refolve, to protect and preferve the Government of the Church of Scotland, as it is fettled by Law without violation. We will alfo take care, that

that the Authority and Act of the General Assembly at St Andrews and Dundee 1651, be owned and stand in force until we shall call another Assembly, which we purpose to do as soon as our affairs will permit. This you shall make known to the several Presbyteries within that our kingdom. Given at Whitehall, August 10. 1660.

No XLIX. SYNOD of MORAY'S ADDRESS to the Earl of MIDDLETON, July 2. 1661.

MAY it please your Grace. The Assembly of Moray being conveened occasionally here at Elgin, have had a gracious Proclamation from his Majesty anent Church affairs, by Providence brought into their hands. For which we hold ourselves deeply engaged to bless the King of Heaven and Earth, who hath both restored and established our gracious Sovereign over these Kingdoms, and has put it in his Majesty's Royal heart, not only to look to the Settlement of the Civil State, but likewise to own the Interest of Jesus Christ, in the preservation of his precious Truths, in their purity and power. And as we are very sensible of his Majesty's care, and gracious goodness in this, so we do promise, in an humble acknowledgement of our addebted allegiance, not only to disclaim former acts of disloyalty, whereby a Yoke of Slavery has been wreathed upon our necks by Usurping Oppressors, in these years lately bypast ; but also we shall still, in our Ecclesiastic station, practise and preach up Loyalty and Obedience to his Majesty's Authority and Royal Government. And we cannot but be confident, that so pious, so wise, and gracious a King will still improve his Royal power, entrusted to him by God, for the welfare of the Civil State, and happy Government of the Church of Christ in this his antient Kingdom, as it is expressed in his Majesty's jesty's gracious Proclamation to that effect; and seeing we conceive ourselves, and all within this Nation, inhibited by his Majesty to meddle in matters belonging to Church-Government, we shall only seriously pray for the Spirit of Wisdom, and right discerning to his Majesty, that he may carry as the Lord's Vicegerent set over us for a signal mercy, after our long bondage under much misery. We will not presume to give your Grace, who is taken up with the weighty affairs of the public, any further trouble, but to present our humble submission to his Majesty's gracious proclamation, and humbly beseeches you, in the name of our Lord and master Jesus Christ, that your Grace will improve the power and favour wherewith God has blessed you in the sight of the King, for the good of his Church in this Nation: And we subscribe ourselves, &c.

N° L. The BISHOPS Address to King JAMES VII. November 3d. 1688.

MAY it please your Sacred Majesty. We prostrate ourselves to pay our most devout thanks and adoration to the Sovereign Majesty of Heaven and Earth, for preserving your sacred Life and Person so frequently exposed to the greatest hazards, and as often delivered, and you miraculously prospered with Glory and Victory, in defence of the rights and honour of your Majesty's August Brother, and of these Kingdoms: and that, by his merciful goodness, the raging of the sea, and the madness of unreasonable men, have been stilled and calmed, and your Majesty, as the Darling of Heaven, peaceably settled on the Throne of your Royal Ancestors, whose long, illustrious, and unparallelled line, is the greatest glory of this your ancient Kingdom. We pay our most humble gratitude to your Majesty, for the repeated assurances of your Royal protection to our

National

National Church and Religion, as the Laws have established them. We magnify the Divine Mercy in blessing your Majesty with a son, and us with a Prince, whom, we pray Heaven may bless and preserve to sway your Royal Sceptre after you; and that he may inherit, with your Dominions, the illustrious and Heroic virtues of his August and most Serene Parents. We are amazed to hear of the danger of an Invasion from Holland, which excites our prayers, for an universal repentance, from all orders of men, that God may yet spare his people, preserve your Royal person, and prevent the effusion of Christian blood, and to give such success to your Majesty's arms, that all, who invade your Majesty's just and undoubted rights, may be disappointed and clothed with shame, and on your Royal head the Crown may still flourish. We shall preserve in ourselves, and promote in your subjects, an unshaken loyalty; not doubting, but God will give you, the hearts of your subjects, and the necks of your Enemies.

N. B. This was signed by all our Bishops, except Munro of Argyle, and Wood of Caithness.

Nº LI.   No LI.

THE General Assembly in 1773, upon the petition of some Ministers in the Presbyteries of Inverness and Forres, did disjoin the Parishes of Nairn, Aldern, and Ardclach from the Presbytery of Forres; the Parishes of Calder and Croy from Inverness; and the Parish of Arderseir from Chanonry Presbytery; and erected these six Parishes in a Presbytery called " The Presbytery of Nairn." This adds a seventh Presbytery to the Diocess of Moray.

Nº LII.

No LII. Oath of Trust.

EVERY Freeholder, who shall claim to vote at an Election, or in adjusting the Rolls of Freeholders, instead of the Oath appointed by 12th ANNE, shall, upon request of any Freeholder formerly enrolled, take and subscribe the Oath following: viz.

"I A. B. in the presence of God, declare and swear, that the lands and estate of   for which I claim a right to vote in the Election of a Member to serve in Parliament for this County [or Stewarty] is actually in my possession, and do really and truly belong to me, and is my own proper estate, and is not conveyed to me in trust, or for, or on behalf of, any other person whatsoever; and that neither I, nor any person to my knowledge, in my name, or on my account, or by my allowance, hath given, or intends to give, any Promise, obligation, Bond, Backbond, or other security whatsoever, other than appears from the tenor and contents of the title upon which I now claim a right to vote, directly or indirectly, for redisponing, or reconveying, the said lands and estate in any manner of way whatsoever, or for making the rents or profits thereof forthcoming to the use or benefit of the person from whom I have acquired the said estate, or any other person whatsoever; and that my title to the said lands and estate is not nominal or fictitious, created or reserved in me, in order to enable me to vote for a member to serve in Parliament, but that the same is a true and real estate in me for my own use and benefit, and for the use of no other person whatsoever. And that is the truth, as I shall answer to God."

Nº LIII. CHARTER to Sir ROBERT GORDON of Gordonston, of Lands in NOVA SCOTIA; containing a Patent creating him a KNIGHT BARONET of the ORDER of NOVA SCOTIA; by King CHARLES I. anno 1626.

CAROLUS, Dei gratia, Magnæ Britanniæ, Franciæ, et Hiberniæ rex, fideique Defensor, OMNIBUS probis hominibus totius terræ suæ, clericis et laicis, salutem. SCIATIS, Nos, cum consilio et consensu praedilecti nostri consanguinei et consiliarii Johannis Marriæ comitis domini Erskine et Garioch, &c. magni regni nostri Scotiæ thesaurarii, computorum rotulatoris, collectoris, ac thesaurarii novarum nostrarum augmentationum, ac dilecti et familiaris nostri consiliarii, domini Archibaldi Napier de Merchingstoun, militis, nostri in eisdem officiis deputati, ac etiam dominorum nostri secreti concilii ejusdem regni nostri Scotiæ, nostrorum commissionariorum, pro propagatione religionis Christianæ infra bondas regni et dominii nostri Novæ Scotiæ, jacen. infra terminos Americæ, limitibus Novæ Angliæ confinis, per dilectum nostrum dominum Willielmum Alexander de *Menstrie*, militem, pro magnis suis sumptibus et impensis tam mari et navigationibus, quam terra, non ita pridem inventi, et supervisi, nunc haereditarium proprietarium ejusdem regni, et dominii, et nostrum locum tenentem, et deputatum, infra easdem bondas, pro promptiori opere et auxilio in plantatione et policia ejusdem, et ad reducendum dictum regnum ad nostram obedientiam, proque bono et gratuito servitio nobis per dilectum nostrum DOMINUM ROBERTUM GORDON, militem, filium quondam Alexandri Sutherlandiæ comitis, et pro diversis aliis magnis et gravibus considerationibus, nos moven. Dedisse, concessisse, et disposuisse, tenoreque praesentis cartæ nostræ, cum consilio antedict. dare, concedere, et disponere, praefato praedilecto nostro DOMINO ROBERTO GORDON, militi, filio quondam Alexandri Sutherlandiæ comitis, *hæredibus suis masculis, et assignatis quibuscunque, hæreditarie*, TOTAM ET INTEGRAM illam partem et portionem dict. bondarum et terrarum regni et dominii Novæ Scotiæ, ut subsequitur, vulgari nostro sermone particulariter bondat. et limitat. To WITT, Beginnand on the sea-cost at the south-west part of land, upon the east-most side of that bay callit Port de Montoun, and from thence going eastward thrie myllis alongst the cost, and from thence passing northward from the said sea-cost unto the mayn land, anent these thrie myllis, till the quantitie thairof extend to sexteen thousand acres of land, keeping alwayis thrie myllis in bried; cum castris, turribus, fortaliciis, maneriarum locis, domibus, aedificiis extructis vel extruendis, hortis, pomariis

plantatis

plantatis vel plantandis, toftis, croftis, parcis, campis, pratis, molendinis, multuris, terris molendinariis, et fequelis, filvis, pifcationibus, tam rubrorum quam alborum pifcium, falmonum, aliorumque magnorum et parvorum pifcium, tam in falfis quam aquis dulcibus, advocatione, donatione beneficiorum ecclefiarum et capellaniarum, et juribus patronatuum earund. annexis, connexis, dependentiis, tenentibus, tenandriis, libere tenentium fervitiis, una cum omnibus et fingulis fodinis, mineralibus, venis, faxis latoniis, tam metallorum et mineralium, regalium vel regiorum, auri et argenti, infra dictas bondas et terras, quam aliarum fodinarum ferri, chalybis, ftanni, electri, cupri, plumbi, aeris, aurichalci, et aliorum mineralium quorumcunque; Una etiam cum omnibus et fingulis pretiofis lapillis, gemmis, margaritis, unionibus, chryftallis, aluminibus, lie curell, et aliis; et cum plenaria poteftate, privilegio, et jurifdictione liberæ regalitatis infra totas et integras praedictas bondas et terras, omnium et fingularum partium, pendiculorum, pertinentium, privilegiorum, et commoditatum earund. terrarum, aliorumque fupra mentionat. CUM plenaria poteftate et privilegio praefato domino Roberto Gordon, fuis haeredibus mafculis, et affignatis, venandi, tentandi, fodiendi, eruendi, ac fcrutandi fundum dictarum terrarum pro dictis fodinis, mineralibus, pretiofis lapillis, gemmis, margaritis, unionibus, aliifque fupra fcript. et utendi omni legitima et ordinaria induftria pro inventione et recuperatione eorundem, et lucrandi, extrahendi, evelandi, purgandi, examinandi, re-examinandi, et purificandi eadem, tam dict. aurum et argentum, quam alia metalla, pretiofos lapillos, margaritas, uniones, et alia fupra mentionat. et eadem ad fuos proprios ufus convertendi et applicandi, fimiliter et tam libere quam praefatus dominus Willielmus Alexander, fui haeredes, et affignati, virtute originalis infeofamenti, ipfis defuper fact. et conceff. de data apud Windfor, decimo die menfis Septembris anno Domini millefimo fexcentefimo vigefimo primo, facere potuerunt. RESERVATA tamen nobis, noftris haeredibus et fucceforibus, decima parte regalium metallorum, communiter vocat. lie ore auri, et argenti, lucrandorum, et obtinendorum, omnibus temporibus a futuris, infra dictas bondas et terras, et reliquis metallis mineralibus, pretiofis lapillis, gemmis, margaritis, unionibus, aliifque quibufcunque, in ufum et proprietatem praefati domini Roberti, haeredum fuorum mafculorum, et affignatorum, in perpetuum integre cefluris, per ipfos intromittendis, cum omnibus proficuis, divoriis, et commoditatibus earund. Cum poteftate etiam praefato domino Roberto Gordon, fuis haeredibus mafculis, et affignatis, aedificandi, extruendi, et erigendi infra bondas ejufdem et fundi terrarum, fuper quacunque parte earund. civitates, urbes, oppida, villas, burgos baroniae, liberos

portus,

portus, sinus, navium habitationes et stationes, infra eosdem, castra, turres, fortalicia, munimenta, exstructiones, valles, aggeres, propugnacula, infra easdem bondas, terras, civitates, burgos, stationes, portus, aliaque loca quaecunque, tam per mare et littora, quam per terras, munita, supportata, et inhabitata, mœnibus, et praesidiis militum et armatorum, pro fortificatione, roboratione, tutela, et defensione earund. Et similiter erigendi, et constituendi nundinas, mercaturas, et mercimoniorum loca, infra dictas civitates, burgos, urbes, villas, et baroniae burgos, et infra aliquam aliam partem omnium et singularum dictarum bondarum et terrarum, vel in burgis, vel villis custodiend. observand. et manutenen. quibus temporibus, particularibus diebus, anni temporibus, locis, et occasionibus, prout praefato domino Roberto, suis haeredibus masculis, et assignatis, expediens videbitur; et imponendi, exigendi, tollendi, et recipiendi, omnes et quascunque tolonias, custumas, anchoragia, primitias, lie vrymguilts, carmarum salaria, lie doksilver, et alias divorias earundem civitatum, burgorum, oppidorum, villarum, portuum, stationum, nundinarum, et fororum, prout praefato domino Roberto, suis haeredibus masculis, et assignatis, magis videbitur expedien. cum omnibus et singulis privilegiis, libertatibus, et commoditatibus eisdem spectan. Et similiter faciendi, et constituendi capitanos, imperatores, ductores, et gubernatores, majores officiarios, praepositos, et balivos dict. civitatum, burgorum, urbium, villarum et burgorum baroniae et regalitatis, portuum, stationum, castrorum, et munimentorum, una cum justiciariis pacis, constabulariis, aliis officiariis, tam in causis criminalibus, quam civilibus, pro regimine, vera et legitima administratione justiciæ infra easdem, et reliquas bondas praescript. terrarum, bondarum, et littorum; et si ipsis videbitur eosdem magistratus et officiarios, pro promptiori et meliori praefatarum bondarum regimine, alterand. et mutand. et ordinem ineundi pro ipsorum regimine, prout ipsis expediens videbitur, necnon faciendi, constituendi, et ordinandi hujusmodi particulares leges, ordinationes, et constitutiones, infra totas et integras præfatas terras et bondas, tam in burgis quam in villis, prout ipsis expediens videbitur, omni tempore a futuro observandos, praevaricatores et contravenientes eisdem castigandi, corrigendi, et conformiter puniendi. Ac etiam, aedificandi et extruendi naves, navigia, et vasa, tam magna quam parva, tam bello quam mercimoniis apta; vel infra dictum dominium Novæ Scotiæ, et partes dictarum terrarum, praefato domino Roberto, suis haeredibus masculis, et assignatis, specialiter supra designat. cum omni genere munitionum, bombardarum magnarum seu parvarum, pulveris sulphurei, globuli armorum, et omnium armorum, invasioni vel defensioni convenien. et omnibus aliis ingenii et belli

exerci-

exercitationibus. Et fimiliter, tranfportandi eifdem, ut quibufcunque aliis navibus ad dictum regnum Novæ Scotiæ, et fpeciales bondas fupra defignatas, tormenta, femitormenta, lie cannonis, femicannonis, fufilia, et alias munitiones, magnas feu parvas, pro defenfione, falute, et tuitione dicti regni. Et fimiliter, cum expreffa poteftate, privilegio, et licentia, praefato domino Roberto, fuis haeredibus mafculis, affignatis et deputatis, vel aliis ipforum nominibus, tranfportandi de dicto regno Scotiæ, vel aliis noftris dominiis, vel alio pro ipforum arbitrio, omnes et quafcunque perfonas, milites, bellicofos colonos, artifices, mercatores, vel alios ftrategos cujufcunque qualitatis, ftatus, feu graduum, cum fuis bonis, fupellectilibus, equis, catellis, bovibus, ovibus, munitionibus, magnis feu parvis armis, provifionibus, et commeatu ad dict. fundum et terras, pro meliori armatu et propagatione dictae plantationis. Et fimiliter, utendi et exercendi omni legitimo genere mercimoniorum, pro meliori policia earundem bondarum et terrarum, et excludendi, prohibendi, inhibendi, refiftendi, repellendi, et invadendi vi et armis, omnes et quafcunque perfonas intendentes plantationem, occupationem, vel poffeffionem dictarum bondarum et terrarum, vel ad exercendum, utendum, mercandum, aut negotiandum infra eafdem, abfque expreffo avifamento, licentia, et confenfu dicti domini Roberti Gordon, fuorum haeredum mafculorum, affignatorum, vel deputatorum, ad id effectum habito et obtento, et confifcandi, intromittendi, detinendi, et authorendi omnes et fingulas naves, bona, catella, et fupellectilia, vel pel mare vel terras ufurpantium in contrarium, et eadem ad proprios ufus, utilitatem, et commodum dicti domini Roberti, fuorumque praedict. applicandi, cum expreffis warranto et mandato omnibus noftris vicecomitibus, fenefcallis, et balivis regalitatum, jufticiariis pacis, majoribus, fenioribus, praepofitis, balivis, et ferjandis, conftabulariis, et jufticiæ miniftris quibufcunque, concurrendi, fortificandi, et affiftendi praefato domino Roberto, fuifque praefcript. in eifdem, et in debita et legitima executione omnium et fingulorum punctorum, claufularum, et articulorum, dictæ cartæ et infeofamenti; Et quod paratam habeant navigationem ad omnes occafiones, pro fuis hominibus, copiis, bonis, catellis, munitionibus, armis, loricis, commeatu, et praeparationibus, ad et a dictis bondis et regni Novæ Scotiæ, cum ipfis, fi videbitur fuis, rationabilibus fumptibus et impenfis, ut congruit. Cum poteftate etiam praefato domino Roberto, fuis haeredibus mafculis, affignatis et deputatis, in cafu rebellionis, tumultus, vel feditionis infra dictas bondas, fundum, et terras, vel in curfu itinerum, vel navigationum, ad vel ab iifdem, ut fi contigerit aliquam perfonam, vel perfonas, infra eafdem bondas et terras, et qui erunt fub imperio et mandato eorum in dictis itineribus,

neribus, et navigationibus, praevaricare et contraire ipsorum mandatis; In hoc casu, vel aliquo eorum casuum, utendi, et exercendi potestatem et privilegium omnium jurium militarium contra delinquentes, et reos puniendi, et corrigendi eosdem hujus legibus, prout ipsis videbitur expediens. Excludendo per praesentis cartae nostrae tenorem, nostrum locum tenentem, et omnes alias personas quascunque, ab usu et exercitatione quarumcunque legum militarium contra dictas personas, vel earum aliquam infra dictas bondas, in dictis itineribus et cursibus, in et abs eisdem; exceptis dicto domino Roberto, suis haeredibus masculis, assignatis, vel suis deputatis tantum. Ac Etiam, Nos, pro nobis et successoribus nostris, cum consilio et consensu antedicto, tenore praesentis cartae eximimus, quiete clamamus, et liberamus praefatum dominum Robertum, suos haeredes masculos, et assignatos ab omni poena, arrestatione, tortura, et executione jurium vel legum militarium, quae contra ipsos, vel ipsorum aliquem per nostrum locum tenentem, vel aliquam aliam personam, vel personas quascunque, infligi, intendi, vel exerceri, poterint. Et si contigerit etiam praedictas personas, vel aliquam ipsarum, sub imperio, manutenentia, vel dependentia dicti domini Roberti, suorumque praescript. abstrahere vel subducere seipsos ab obedientia dicti domini Roberti, suorumque praescript. vel suis servitiis in dicta plantatione, et defensione ejusdem, vel per mare, vel per terras, vel in ipsorum cursu et itinere ad et a dicto regno Novae Scotiae, vel subducere et abstrahere se ipsos, sua bona, vel catella, a ministerio et obedientia dicti domini Roberti, vel removere seipsos, vel bona, vel catella, a bondis et fundo earundem terrarum, vel ab hujusmodi partibus et portionibus earundem; tunc, in iis casibus, vel aliquibus eorum foris facien. perdent et amittent ipso facto omnes et singulas possessiones, terras, bona, et catella infra dict. terras existentia. Et licitum erit praefato domino Roberto, suis haeredibus masculis, assignatis et deputatis, confiscare, recognoscere, et possidere easdem terras, bondas, possessiones, bona, et catella, et applicare eadem suis propriis usibus, libere, absque periculo juris, vel aliqua ulteriore declaratura de eisdem. Et Similiter, si aliquae venditiones, alienationes, vel conditiones fiant inter praefatum dominum Robertum, suos haeredes masculos, assignatos, vel deputatos, cum quacunque alia persona seu personis, sive nativis dicti regni, sive extraneis, alienis, vel aliis personis quibuscunque, pro transportatione quorumcunque bonorum, catellorum, mercemoniorum, mercium, ammunitionum, armorum, commeatuum, praeparationum, vel aliorum quorumcunque, vel pro implemento cujuscunque facti vel factorum, praefato domino Roberto, vel suis praescript. vel infra dictum regnum Novae Scotiae, vel per

mare

mare curfum, vel tranfitum, in vel ab eodem regno, fub quibufcunque
pœnis vel pecuniarum fummis; Et fi fregerint aut violaverint eadem
pacta, contractus, fœdera, vel conditiones, vel defecerint in perficien-
do et implemendo earundem, in damnum et detrimentum dicti domini Roberti, fuorumque praefcript. et impediant, et moram faciant
dict. laudabili intentioni in faepefata plantatione, et policia ejufdem;
tunc, et in iis cafibus, vel in aliquo eorundem, licitum erit praefato
domino Roberto, et fuis praefcript. intromittere, uti, et poffidere eadem bona, catella, mercantia, pecuniarum fummas, et alia, ad fuos
proprios ufus, abfque ulteriori proceffu aut declaratione juris. NEC
NON cum expreffa poteftate et privilegio praefatis domino Roberto,
fuis haeredibus mafculis, affignatis, et deputatis, fuis hominibus, tenentibus, et fervis, infra dictas terras et bondas frequentandi, utendi,
et exercendi, mercandi, negotiandi cum nativis et filveftribus dicti
regni, et faciendi, capiendi, ob contrahendi pacem, et fidelitatem,
affinitatem, et fœdera cum ipfis, et familiaritatem et amicitiam cum
eifdem frequentandi, et cum ipforum ductoribus, gubernatoribus, et
praecipientibus; et, in cafu offenfionis, violationis officii, promiffo-
rum, vel amicitiae fuis partibus, capiendi et utendi armis adverfus eos
omni hoftili modo, tam per mare quam per terras; Cum poteftate et
privilegio etiam praefato domino Roberto Gordon, et fuis praefcript.
omni tempore a futuro, exportandi de dictis bondis et regno Novæ
Scotiæ, omnia mercimonia, mercantias, et commoditates quafcunque,
et importandi et inducendi eadem in dictum regnum Scotiae vel ad
quafcunque alias partes, pro ipforum arbitrio; nec non exportandi de
dicto regno Scotiæ et aliis locis quibufcunque, omnes mercantias,
mercimonia, et commoditates quafcunque, et inducendi et inferendi
eafdem dicto regno Novæ Scotiæ, pro folutione fummæ quinque librarum monetæ Scotiæ, cuftumæ pro quibuslibet centum libris tantum,
abfque folutione alterius cujuslibet acuftumæ, impofitionis vel divoriæcu-
jufcunque, tollendi, capiendi, vel inde exigendi per nos, haeredes, vel
fucceffores noftros, vel noftros publicanos, feu cuftumerias deputatos, vel officiarios, ver per aliam aliquam perfonam quamcunque, vel
infra dictum regnum Scotiæ, vel regnum Novæ Scotiæ. Inhibendo,
tenore praefentis cartæ noftræ, noftros cuftumarios et officiarios, ne
exigant ulteriorem impofitionem vel cuftumam ex eifdem, et de ipforum officiis in hac parte; cum poteftate etiam faepefato domino Roberto, fuifque praefcript. per feipfos, fuos deputatos, officiarios, et
alios fuis nominibus levandi, exigendi, et recipiendi ab omnibus
noftris, et fuccefforum noftrorum fubditis, quos contigerit negotiari
feu mercari infra dictas bondas, fundum, et terras fupra defignatas,
portus, et ftationes earund. quinque libras monetae ante dict. cuftumae

pro

pro quibuslibet centum libris omnium bonorum, mercimoniorum, vel commoditatum, vel importandorum eidem per ipsos, vel ipsorum aliquem, vel exeundi reportandorum; et summam decem librarum ab omnibus extraneis, pro quolibet centum omnium bonorum, mercium, et mercimoniorum exportandorum et importandorum per ipsos, vel ipsorum aliquem, et id praeter et ultra dictam summam quinque librarum, nobis, et nostris successoribus, ut praemittitur, debitam. Et Praeterea nos pro nobis, nostris haeredibus, et successoribus, cum avisamento et consensu ante dict. tenore praesentis cartae nostrae volumus, concedimus, ordinamus et declaramus, quod dicta summa quinque librarum monetae ante dict. custumae designatae, ut praemittitur, solvend. nobis, haeredibus et successoribus nostris, custumariis nostris, et deputatis, pro omnibus bonis, mercimoniis, mercantiis et commoditatibus, vel exportandis de dicto regno Novae Scotiae, vel eidem importandis, serventur et reddantur praefato domino Willielmo Alexander, suis haeredibus, et assignatis, nostri dicti regni locum tenentibus, et non aliis, pro spatio sex decem annorum diem datae praesentis cartae nostrae immediate subsequend. Et in hunc finem, quod licebit praefato domino Willielmo Alexander, et suis praescript. tollere, exigere, petere, et recipere easdem acquittantias, et exonerationes desuper dare et concedere, quas nos, tenore praesentis cartae nostrae pro nobis, haeredibus et successoribus nostris, volumus et declaramus sufficientes fore recipientibus dictarum acquittantiarum, et persolventibus, dictam summam quinque librarum custumae. Et Cum potestate praefato domino Willielmo Alexander, et suis praescript. durante dicto tempore, utendi et convertendi dictam summam quinque librarum pro quolibet centum, sic ut praemittitur, levandi, suis propriis usibus et utilitati, prout ipsis videbitur expediens pro suo meliori auxilio, ope, et manu tenenti suorum onerum et expensarum in regimine dicti regni, et propagatione dict. plantationis. Et quamquam nullo modo licitum sit alieno nobili vel generoso, terras habenti infra regnum Scotiae, transire de eodem absque licentia nostra, nos pro nobis, haeredibus, et successoribus nostris, volumus, concedimus, ac tenore praesentis cartae nostrae declaramus, praesentem hanc nostram cartam esse et fore sufficientem licentiam et warrantum, omni tempore a futuro, praefato domino Roberto Gordon, et suis praescript. et omnibus aliis personis laesae majestatis non reis, vel alioquin specialiter non inhibitis, cum ipsis vel eorum aliquo proficisci cupientibus dictis terris et bondis, libere eundi de dicto regno Scotiae et proficiscendi, et reparandi ad dictas terras et regnum Novae Scotiae, absque aliquo periculo, inconvenientia ipsis, in suis corporibus, terris, bonis, seu catellis penes quam nos, cum avisamento ante. dict. pro nobis, et

nostris

APPENDIX.

noſtris ſucceſſoribus, diſpenſavimus, ac per praeſentis cartæ noſtræ tenorem diſpenſamus in perpetuum. Et Praeterea, dedimus, conceſſimus, et declaravimus, tenoreque praeſentis cartæ noſtræ pro nobis, haeredibus et ſucceſſoribus noſtris, cum aviſamento et conſenſu ſupra-ſcript. damus, concedimus, volumus, declaramus, et ordinamus, quod omnes noſtri ſubditi, et aliæ perſonæ quaecunque, quibus ſubjicere ſeſe noſtrorumque haeredum, et ſucceſſorum obedientiæ placebit, qui quocunque tempore impoſterum profecturi ſunt ad dictas bondas et terras, praefato domino Roberto Gordon per praeſentes diſpoſitas, ad inhabitandum eaſdem, vel aliquam earundem partem, cum licentia, conſenſu, et permiſſu dicti domini Roberti, ſuorum haeredum maſculorum, et deputatorum, quod omnes et ſingulae dictae perſonae, cum ſuis liberis et poſteris reſpective habebunt, tenebunt, fruentur, gaudebunt, et poſſidebunt omnes et quaſcunque libertates, privilegia, et immunitates liberorum, et naturalium ſubditorum dicti regni noſtri Scotiæ, aliorumque noſtrorum dominiorum, ac ſi nati et procreati fuiſſent infra eadem regna et dominia. Et pro conſtitutione majoris auctoritatis, imperii, poteſtatis, et juriſdictionis omni tempore a futuro, in perſona dicti domini Roberti Gordon, haeredum ſuorum maſculorum, aſſignatorum, et deputatorum, infra dictas terras, nos pro nobis, haeredibus, et ſucceſſoribus noſtris, cum aviſamento et conſenſu ante dict. dedimus et conceſſimus, tenoreque praeſentis cartae noſtrae, damus et concedimus haereditarie praefato domino Roberto Gordon, haeredibus ſuis maſculis, et aſſignatis quibuſcunque, juſticiariam et vicecomitatum dictarum omnium particularium bondarum et terrarum ſupra ſpecificat. Et fecimus et conſtituimus, tenoreque praeſentis cartae noſtrae facimus et conſtituimus praefatum dominum Robertum Gordon, ſuos haeredes maſculos et aſſignatos, noſtros haereditarios vicecomites, quaeſitores, juſticiarios, haereditarie in perpetuum, infra omnes et ſingulas dictas particulares terras et bondas ſupra ſpecificatas, et ſpecialiter deſignatas, cum omnibus et ſingulis libertatibus, privilegiis, franchiſis, immunitatibus, et commoditatibus dict. vicecomitatui et juſticiariæ ſpectan. cum poteſtate dicto domino Roberto Gordon, ſuis haeredibus maſculis, aſſignatis, vel deputatis, ſedendi in judicio, cognoſcendi, et decernendi, in omnibus et quibuſcunque cauſis, tam civilibus quam criminalibus, infra dictas bondas et juriſdictionem earundem terrarum, ſimiliter, et tam libere omnibus modis, tanquam aliquis alius juſticiarius, quaeſitor, vel vicecomes quicunque poteſt, vel poterit facere aliquo tempore praeterito vel futuro. Et ne aliqua quaeſtio occurrat de tempore infra quod praefatus dominus Robertus, ſuique praeſcript. tanquam vicecomites vel juſticiarii ſedeant, cognoſcant, et

† Iii *decernant*

decernant in causis criminalibus post commissa crimina, nos pro nobis, haeredibus et successoribus nostris, cum avisamento et consilio antedict. tenore praesentis cartae nostrae volumus, concedimus, et declaramus, quod licitum et legitimum erit iisdem accusare quoscunque reos criminaliter offendentes infra dictas bondas et terras, pro quibuscunque criminibus per ipsos commiss. et sedendi, cognoscendi, judicandi, et decernendi de iisdem, quocunque tempore infra spatium sex mensium, diem commiss. criminis immediate subsequen. durante quoquidem spatio, licebit tantum praefato domino Roberto, et suis praescript. et non aliis, examinare, cognoscere, judicare, et procedere de eisdem, excludendo, durante dicto spatio, nostro locum-tenente, et omnibus aliis personis quibuscunque, ab exercitatione cujuscunque judicii vel jurisdictionis de eisdem, et ab attachiamento, arrestatione, adjuramento, vocatione, vel conventione dictorum criminaliter offendentium, et crimina committentium, quocunque modo vel ratione. Proviso tamen quod si, post dictum spatium sex mensium excurrentium, dicta crimina et criminaliter offendentes non fuerint judicati nec examinati, vel discussi per dictum dominum Robertum, et suos praescript. in eo casu licebit deinceps nostrum locum-tenenti, suis haeredibus et assignatis, nostrum locum-tenentibus, et suis deputatis, accusare, attachiare, arrestare, citare, et convenire dictas personas reas, et judicare et cognoscere de criminibus per ipsos commiss. prout ipsis expediens videbitur, cum potestate etiam dicto domino Roberto, et suis praescript. non obstante provisione supra script. post expirationem dict. sex mensium, omnibus temporibus, in absentia dicti domini Willielmi Alexander, suorum haeredum et assignatorum, nostrum locum-tenentium, et eorum deputatorum, judicandi, cognoscendi, et decidendi in omnibus causis criminalibus, et puniendi omnes criminaliter offendentes infra dictas bondas, pro ipsorum arbitrio; et simili modo, in ipsorum absentia extra dictum regnum, vel infra spatium sex mensium, vel postea quocunque tempore, remittendi, et condonandi dict. crimina et criminaliter offendentes infra dictas terras et bondas, pro hujusmodi rationalibus causis et considerationibus, prout ipsis videbitur expediens. ET PRÆTEREA, cum potestate dicto domino Roberto, et suis praescript. sedendi, judicandi, et cognoscendi de omnibus criminibus et criminaliter offendentibus infra dictas bondas, et vel puniendi, remittendi, vel condonandi dicta crimina et criminaliter reos, prout ipsis videbitur expediens, omnibus temporibus dicto spatio sex mensium elapso, antequam praefatus dominus Willielmus, sui haeredes et assignati, nostrum locum-tenentes, et sui deputati provocaverint, citaverint, vel indictaverint dictos criminaliter offendentes, ad comparendum coram ipsis in judicio, quamquam in regno Novæ
Scotiæ

APPENDIX.

Scotiæ pro tempore fuerint, absque præjudicio tamen praefato domino Willielmo, suis haeredibus, et assignatis nostrum locum-tenentibus, et suis deputatis, si primi fuerint citatores, post elapsos sex menses, sedendi, judicandi, cognoscendi, puniendi, vel remittendi dicta crimina et criminaliter offendentes, pro eorum arbitrio, ut præmittitur. Et similiter, tenore præsentis cartæ nostræ ordinamus, quod si contingat praefatum dominum Robertum, vel suos præscript, condonare et remittere aliqua ex dictis criminibus, vel criminaliter, ut præmittitur, offendentes, quod tunc et in eo casu, eorum remissio et indulgentia sic conceden. publicabitur et proclamabitur infra dictas bondas, die et data concessionis ejusdem, per aliquem ex dict. particularibus officiariis per ipsos ad id effectum designandis; et post publicationem ejusdem, quod eadem remissio insumabitur in regiftro dicti domini Willielmi, suorum hæredum et assignatorum, nostrum locum tenentium ejusdem regni, infra spatium sexaginta dierum, publicationem ejusdem proxime subsequentem, ad minimum, quod eadem offeretur et praesentabitur, coram duobus fide dignis testibus, dicti regiftri custodi, si dicti regiftri clericus, vel custos ejusdem, in dicto regno Novæ Scotiæ pro tempore fuerit, cum plenaria potestate et privilegio similiter praefato domino Roberto Gordon, suis hæredibus masculis, assignatis et deputatis, in sempiternum sedendi, affigendi, et tenendi, vel tenere causandi, suis nominibus curias justiciariæ, vicecomitum curias, liberæ regalitatis curias, et baronis et baroniæ curias, infra et super totis et integris prædictis bondis, et terris ipsi, ut præmittitur, designatis, vel super aliqua parte earundem, omnibus temporibus et occasionibus prout ipsis visum fuerit, clericos, officiarios, serjandos, adjudicatores, et alia curiæ membra quaecunque faciendi et creandi, aeschetas et amerciamenta curiarum ordinandi, exigendi, levandi, recipiendi, et ad ipsorum proprios usus, prout ipsis expediens visum fuerit, applicandi, cum omnibus aliis et singulis privilegiis, libertatibus, commoditatibus, et casualitatibus ad dicta officia et jurisdictiones justiciariæ liberæ regalitatis, et vicecomitatus, aliaque supra expressa spectan. vel juste cadere aut spectare poterint; Cum libera potestate, et privilegio etiam praefato domino Roberto, suis haeredibus masculis, et assignatis, vendendi, alienandi et disponendi haereditarie vel aliter, totas et integras praedictas bondas et terras supra designatas, pro ipsorum arbitrio; cum omnibus et singulis libertatibus, licentiis, immunitatibus, et commoditatibus supra et infra expressis, tenore praesentis cartæ nostræ ipsis concess. vel cum tot ex dictis libertatibus, commoditatibus, et aliis, quot ipsis et suis praescript. expediens videbitur, cuicunque alteri personæ vel personis, suis haeredibus, et assignatis sub nostra obedientia existentibus, tenen. de nobis, nostris haeredibus, et successoribus, vel de praefato domino Roberto, suis haeredibus masculis, et assignatis, pro arbitrio dicti domini Roberti, suorumque antedict. Quae quidem terrae, bondae, privilegia, aliaquae supra expressa, vel aliqua pars earundem sic disposita per praefatum dominum Robertum, vel suos praescript. cuicunque alteri personae, seu personis, tenen. de nobis, nostris haeredibus, et successoribus, nos, nostri haeredes et successores recipimus, et admittimus ipsos, et eorum unumquemque tanquam nostros liberos vassallos et immediatos tenentes earundem; et concedimus ipsis et eorum unicuique talia sufficientia infeofamenta earundem, et cum eodem modo tenendi, qualia nunc concessimus praefato domino Roberto, suis haeredibus masculis, et assignatis, quandocunque eadem ipsi requisiverint, cum potestate etiam praefato domino Roberto, et suis antedict. et singulis alteri personae vel personis, sub nostra obedientia existentibus, quibus ipsos alienare et disponere aliquam partem seu portionem dictarum terrarum contigerit, insignire et vocare easdem, vel aliquam partem seu portionem earundem, per aliquod nomen seu titulum temporibus futuris, prout ipsis expediens videbitur; nec non licebit haeredibus masculis, vel successoribus dicti domini Roberti quibuscunque, et suis assignatis, intrare seipsos, tanquam haeredes suis predecessoribus, dictis terris et bondis aliisque quibuscunque praefato domino Roberto concess. et disposit. vel ad aliquam partem earundem, virtute hujus praesentis cartae nostrae; et id vel per ordinem cancellariae dicti regni nostri Scotiae, per servitium brevium, retornatuum, et praeceptorum ex eadem directorum, et modis in similibus casibus in hujusmodi materia usitatis et consuetis, vel alioqui per ordinem capellae et cancellariae dicti regni Novae Scotiae, pro arbitrio et optione haeredum masculorum, et successorum dicti domini Roberti, et suorum assignatorum quorumcunque. CUM POTESTATE etiam praefato domino Roberto, et suis praescript. et eorum deputatis, omni tempore futuro, convocandi omnes et singulos homines tenentes, servos, et incolas suos quoscunque dictarum omnium bondarum et terrarum supro designatarum, omnibus temporibus et occasionibus, prout ipsis visum fuerit pro bono, defensione, et propagatione ipsorum, vel dictarum bondarum et terrarum, ad resistendum exteris hostibus, ad reprimendum insolentias, et crimina turbulentorum, seditiosorum, et populi rebellantis, ad reducendum silvestres et aborigines ad conformitatem et debitam obedientiam, et ob alias legitimas urgentes et necessarias causas quascunque. ET PRAETEREA, dedimus et concessimus, tenoreque praesentis cartae nostrae, pro nobis, nostris haeredibus et successoribus, cum avisamento et consensu antedict. damus, concedimus, volumus, ordinamus, et declaramus, quod praefatus dominus Robertus, suique praescript. omni tempore a futuro habebunt suffragium

APPENDIX.

suffragium et vocem in condendis omnibus et singulis legibus, imposterum faciendis de publico statu, bono, et regimine dicti regni Novæ Scotiæ, et in omnibus comitiis, parliamentis, synodis, conciliis, et conventionibus convocandis, conveniendis, vel in eum finem tenendis; et quod debite et legitime ad id effectum promovebunt, quod nullæ leges de eisdem fient, statuent, aut validæ erunt absque avisamento et consensu dicti domini Roberti, suorumque praescript. et absque consensu reliquorum baronettorum, parem et similem quantitatem et proportionem terrarum infra dictum regnum habentium, ad ipsos suosque haeredes haereditarie spectan. qualem tenore praesentis cartæ nostræ, praefato domino Roberto disposuimus, viz. singuli eorum sexdecem milium acrarum terræ ad minimum, absque avisamento et consensu majoris partis totidem eorum, qui convenient simul ad ferendum voces et suffragia, super debita et legitima praemonitione ipsis desuper faciendo, concludendo, et proponendo prima conventione et synodo, per ipsos et nostrum locum-tenentes, vel eorum haeredes aut assignatos, tenenda, nostrum locum-tenentes pro condendis legibus et statutis dicti regni; et quod nulla persona, seu personæ quaecunque, quæ non fuerint haeredes quaelibet ipsarum sexdecem millium acrarum terrarum infra dictum regnum, habebunt vocem vel suffragium in condendis quibuslibet legibus dictum regnum concernen. absque avisamento, consilio, et consensu dicti nostri locum-tenentis, haeredum suorum et assignatorum, nostrorum successorum locum-tenentium, et dicti domini Roberti, suorumque praescript. et reliquorum baronettorum. INSUPER, si praefatus dominus Robertus, suique haeredes masculi, et assignati praescript. non fuerint personaliter praesentes in dictis parliamentis, comitiis, consiliis, conventionibus, et synodis, quæ tenebuntur, vocabuntur, et convenientur, ad effectum supra script. infra dictum regnum Novæ Scotiæ, tunc et in eo casu, deputati seu actornati, seu habentes potestatem et auctoritatem suam, ac habentes quantitatem mille acrarum terrarum ipsis infra dictum regnum haereditarie spectan. habebunt similem vocem et suffragium, ac si ipsi personaliter interessent; sed si aliquæ conventiones vel synodi tenebuntur ad id effectum, infra dictum regnum Scotiæ, si personaliter interfuerent pro tempore infra dictum regnum, habebunt vocem et suffragium, tantum per seipsos, et non per delegatos, vel actornatos; sed casu absentiæ extra dictum regnum, hujusmodi temporibus, in eo casu, sui deputati et actornati, haben. suam potestatem et warrantum, habebunt similem vocem et suffragium, ac si personaliter interessent. ET QUOD praefatus dominus Robertus, et reliqui nostri subditi et incolæ illius regni Novæ Scotiæ, omni tempore futuro, judicabuntur, regentur, et gubernabuntur, in omnibus causis civilibus et criminalibus,

bus, legibus dicti regni tantum, et non aliis; absque praejudicio tamen praefato domino Roberto, et suis praescript. per seipsos et deputatos, faciendi tales particulares leges, constitutiones, et statuta, infra proprias suas bondas particulariter supra designat. quae sibi usui sint pro meliori policia, bono, et regimine earundem et inhabitantium ibid. et pro conservatione boni ordinis, et administratione juris et justitiae ibidem. Et absque praejudicio dicto domino Roberto, et suis praescript. alterius cujusquam particularis libertatis, privilegii, immunitatis, clausulae seu conditionis qualiscunque supra vel infra expreff. in favorem ipsius concept. Proviso omnimodo, quod quaecunque leges generales faciendae et constituendae modo praescript. publicum statum, bonum, et regimen dicti regni concernen. vel per praefatum dominum Robertum, et suos antedict. in ipsorum particularibus bondis, ut praemittitur, fiant conformes, et aequales legibus dicti regni Scotiae quoad convenienter poterint, respectu habito ad circumstantias temporis, loci, et situationis ejusdem regni, et inhabitantium, et conditionum et qualitatis earund. Et Praeterea, tametsi per expressam conditionem dict. originalis infeofamenti nostrum locum-tenenti conceff. constitutum est, quod ipsi, et haeredes ac assignati sui, ut convocent omnes et singulos inhabitantes regni Novae Scotiae proclamationibus, vel aliter, modo et forma inibi specificat, nihilominus concessimus, voluimus, et ordinavimus, tenoreque praesentis cartae nostrae, pro nobis, haeredibus et successoribus nostris, cum avisamento et consensu antedict. volumus, concedimus, declaramus, et ordinamus, quod nullo modo licitum erit nostrum locum-tenenti, suis haeredibus, successoribus, vel assignatis, aut quibuscunque aliis nostri, seu nostrorum successorum, officiariis quibuscunque, vocare, convocare, cogere per proclamationem, vel aliter, dictum dominum Robertum, suos haeredes et assignatos, successores, deputatos, homines tenentes, servos, vel incolas dictarum particularium bondarum, praefato domino Roberto sic ut praemittitur, dispositarum, nisi pro rationalibus, necessariis, et legitimis causis, quae invenientur utiles et expedientes reipublicae dicti regni, per legitimum nostrum locum-tenentem, suosque praedict. cum avisamento et consensu dicti domini Roberti, suorumque antedict. et reliquarum personarum supra mentionat. designatarum, ut habeant vocem et suffragium in condendis legibus, ut praemissum est. Quaequaedam personae, et quilibet ipsorum, sui haeredes, successores, assignati, deputati, homines tenentes, servi, vel incolae dict. separatarum bondarum, simili conditioni subjicientur; et similiter, non erit licitum nec legitimum dicto nostrum locum-tenenti, vel suis praescript. vel quibuscunque aliis, nostris, haeredum vel successorum nostrorum officiariis, exigere, imponere, vel levare aliquam taxationem, vel

impositionem

impofitionem a vel fuper dictum dominum Robertum, fuos haeredes maf-
culos, affignatos, deputatos, homines tenentes, fervos, vel inhabitantes
dictarum terrarum et bondarum particulariter fupra difpofitarum, vel
fuper dictis fuis terris, redditibus, bonis, feu catellis, abfque fpeciali confenfu dicti domini Roberti, vel fuorum praefcript. non obftante aliqua
poteftate noftro locum-tenenti et fuis antedict. per dictum originale infeofamentum conceff. vel virtute cujufcunque alterius tituli vel juris
fact. et conceff. vel per nos, noftros haeredes, vel fucceffores, praefato locum-tenenti noftro, vel alicui alteri perfonae cujufcunque faciendi
vel concedendi, abfque praejudicio tamen praefato domino Roberto,
et fuis praefcript. infra bondas particulariter fupra defignat. et per
praefentes fibi difpofit. vocandi, cogendi, et conveniendi fuos homines
et incolas, omnibus temporibus et occafionibus, modo et propter cau-
fas fupra expreffas, ut praemittitur, ipfas tangen. NEC NON dedimus,
conceffimus, et difpofuimus, tenoreque praefentis cartae noftrae, pro nobis et fuccefforibus noftris, cum avifamento et confenfu antedict. damus, concedimus, et haereditarie in perpetuum difponimus, dicto domino Roberto, et fuis praefcript. omnia et quaecunque alia privilegia,
libertates, licentias, commoditates, et immunitates, proficua, praerogativa, dignitates, et cafualitates, generaliter et particulariter in dicto
originali infoefamento, praefato domino Willielmo Alexander, et fuis
antedict. conceff. fpecificat. et expreff. et id tam plenario, libero, et
amplo modo et forma, ac fi eadem privilegia, praerogativa, immunitates, libertates, licentiae, dignitates, commoditates, et alia, cum omnibus
claufulis et conditionibus, in hac praefenti carta noftra ad longum
fpecialiter infinuatae et contentae effent, quatenus extendi et concerni
poterint particulares bondas et terras fupra defignatas, virtute hujus
cartae noftrae praefato domino Roberto, et fuis antedict. tanquam haeredibus earund. difpofit. Excepto omnimodo et refervato praefato
domino Willielmo Alexander, fuis haeredibus et affignatis, officio
noftri locum-tenentis dicti totius regni et dominii Novae Scotiae, poteftate et privilegio cudendae pecuniae, officio principalis jufticiarii ge-
neralis ejufd. regni, in caufis criminalibus, officio admiralitatis, faciendi officiarios ftatus, conferendi titulos honorum, cum plena poteftate et
jurifdictione liberae regalitatis, capellae, et cancellariae dicti regni, et privilegio condendi leges publicam ftatum, bonum, et regimen dicti regni concernentes, illi per fuum originale infoefamentum praedict. conceff. PROVISO tamen quod eadem refervatio et exceptio, in favorem
dicti domini Willielmi, fuorumque praefcript. nunc concepta, nullate-
nus praejudicabit vel prejudicatio erit praefato domino Roberto, et
fuis antedict. penes omnes, vel aliquod ex particularibus privilegiis,
licentiis, libertatibus, immunitatibus, commoditatibus, aliifque fupra

et

et subtus mentionat. praefato Domino Roberto, et suis antedict. tenore praesentis cartae nostrae concess. modo generaliter et particulariter supra et subtus specificat. QUAEQUIDEM terræ, bondæ, advocatio et donatio beneficiorum, ecclesiarum, et capellaniarum, fodinae, mineralia, metalla, margaritæ, silvæ, piscationes, molendina, multuræ, officia, privilegia, et jurisdictio liberæ regalitatis, justiciæ et justiciariæ, vicecomitis, vicecomitatuum, et omnes aliæ libertates, immunitates, privilegia, commoditates, licentiæ, custumæ, casualitates, aliaque universa generaliter et particulariter supra mention. debite et legitime resignatæ, sursum redditæ, et extradonatæ fuerunt per dict. dominum Willielmum Alexander, et legitimum procuratorem suum, ipsius nominibus, in manibus nostris tanquam immediati sui superioris, earundem per fustem, et baculum, ut moris est, resignatione earundem facta, apud Quhythall, vigesimo sexto die mensis Maii, anno domini millesimo sexcentesimo vigesimo quinto; una cum omni jure, titulo, interesse, et jurisclameo quæ seu quas in et ad easdem, aliquam earundem partem, habuit, habet, seu quovis modo in futurum habere vel clamare potuerat, IN ET AD FAVOREM dicti Domini Roberti Gordon, suorum haeredum masculorum, et assignatorum quorumcunque, sub modo, provisionibus, limitationibus, exceptionibus, et reservationibus respective quibus supra, ET ID pro novo hoc nostro haereditario infeofamento, per nos praefato domino Roberto Gordon, suis haeredibus masculis, et assignatis quibuscunque, desuper dando et concedendo, simul universum erigendis, uniendis, annexandis et incorporandis in unam plenam, integram et liberam baroniam et regalitatem, in perpetuum, BARONIAM DE GORDON omni tempore a futuro nuncupandam TENEN. DE NOBIS, haeredibus, et successoribus nostris, coronæ regni nostri Scotiæ successuris, in libera alba firma, pro solutione annuatim unius denarii usualis monetæ dicti regni nostri, super fundo dict. terrarum et bondarum, vel alicujus partis earundem, ad festum nativitatis Domini, nomine albae firmae, si petatur tantum; Cum dispensatione, etiam non introitus earundem omnium terrarum, bondarum, et baroniae, censuum, firmarum, proficuorum, et divoriarum earund. duran. eodem non introitu. ET INSUPER DE NOVO dedimus, concessimus, et disposuimus tenoreque praesentis cartae nostrae, pro nobis et successoribus nostris, ex nostra certa scientia, et proprio motu, cum avisamento et consensu praedicto, pro diversis bonis et gratuitis servitiis, per praefatum Dominum Robertum nobis praestitis et impensis, proque aliis gravibus causis, et bonis considerationibus, nos moventibus, DE NOVO damus, concedimus, et disponimus praefato Domino Roberto, haeredibus suis masculis, et assignatis haereditarie in perpetuum, TOTAS ET INTEGRAS praedict. terras, bondas, molendina, silvas, piscationes,

APPENDIX.

cationes, advocationem, donationem beneficiorum et capellaniarum, ac ecclefiarum, necnon jura patronatus earund. fodinas, mineralia, metalla, pretiofos lapillos, cum poteftate, privilegio, et jurifdictione jufticiariae et vicecomitatus, in omnibus caufis civilibus et criminalibus, curias, efchetas, amerciamenta, curiarum exitus, lie out-lawis, et omnes et fingulas alias libertates, immunitates, licentias, cuftumas, cafualitates, proficua, divorias, aliaque quaecunque particulariter feu generaliter fupra fpecificat. quæ nos pro nobis haeredibus et fuccefforibus noftris, cum avifamento et confenfu antedict. tenore praefentis cartæ noftræ volumus, et reputamus tanquam in hac praefenti carta noftra fpecialiter et particulariter infinuata, repetita, inferta, et expreffa, cum particularibus exceptionibus, limitationibus, et refervationibus refpective et fpecialiter fupra fcript. ET DE NOVO erigimus, unimus, annexamus, et incorporamus, omnes et fingulas praenominatas terras, bondas, molendina, filvas, pifcationes, advocationem, et donationem beneficiorum ecclefiarum, et capellaniarum, et jura patronatuum earund. fodinas, metalla, mineralia, margaritas, gemmas, officia, regalitatem jufticiariam, vicecomitatum, libertates, licentias, privilegia, immunitates, cuftumas, emolumenta, cafualitates, dignitates, poteftatem, jurifdictionem, et alia quaecunque generaliter et particulariter fupra expreffa, quæ nos pro nobis, et fuccefforibus noftris, tanquam in hac praefenti carta noftra repetita, et particulariter inferta, tenemus, cum fpecialibus exceptionibus, et refervationibus particulariter fupra mentionat. cum generalitate in perpetuum difpenfando, IN UNAM, INTEGRAM plenariam, et liberam baroniam et regalitatem de GORDON, TENEN. ET HABEN. praefato domino Roberto Gordon, fuis haeredibus mafculis et affignatis, DE NOBIS, et noftris coronæ et regni noftri Scotiæ fuccefforibus in libera haereditate, unius baroniæ et regalitatis in perpetuum, per omnes rectas metas fuas antiquas, novas, et divifas, prout jacent in longitudine et latitudine, in domibus, ædificiis, bofcis, planis, moris, marefiis, viis, femitis, aquis, ftagnis, rivulis, pratis, pafcuis, et pafturis, molendinis, multuris et eorum fequelis, aucupationibus, venationibus, pifcationibus, petariis, turbariis, carbonibus, carbonariis, cuniculis, cuniculariis, columbis, columbariis, fabrilibus, brafinis, braferiis, et geniftis, fylvis, nemoribus et virgultis, lignis, tignis, lapidiis, lapide et calce, cum curiis, et earum exitibus, herezeldis, bludwitis et mulierum merchetis, cum communi paftura, libero introitu et exitu, et cum furca, foffa, fek fak, thole themm, vert, wrak, wair, venyfoun, waiff, pit et galous, infangthief, et outfangthief earund. Et cum omnibus aliis et fingulis libertatibus, commoditatibus, proficuis, afiamentis, privilegiis, praerogativis, dignitatibus, et cafualitatibus, per nos vel noftros praedeceffores cuicunque baroni majori vel minori infra dictum regnum Scotiæantehac concessis, aliisque omnibus in dicto originali infeofamento defuper contentis, et quæ nos, per nofinetipfos vel quemcunque alium ex regiis noftris progenitoribus et anteceſſoribus, dedimus, conceſſimus, et difpofuimus, vel virtute quarumcunque cartarum, infeofamentorum, literarum patentium, donationum et conceſſionum quibufcunque ex noftris fubditis cujufcunque qualitatis, ftatus, vel gradus, conceſſ. extiterint, vel quibufcunque focietatibus, caetibus, vel aliis particularibus earundem membris, petentibus, ducentibus, impetrantibus, acquirentibus, conquirentibus, aut protegentibus, quafcunque extraneas terras vel colonias, dare, concedere, vel difponere poſſimus, SUB exceptionibus, refervationibus, et provifionibus fpecialit. fupra mentionatis; et tam plena, libera, et ampla forma, et modo, quam eadem privilegia, libertates, commoditates, et immunitates, cum omnibus et fingulis claufulis, conditionibus, et provifionibus eafdem concernen. ad longum fpecialiter in hac praefenti carta noftra infinuata, inferta et comprehenfa forent, una cum omni jure, titulo, intereſſe, jurifclameo, tam petitorio quam poſſeſſorio, quæ nos, noftri praedeceſſores vel fucceſſores, habuimus, habemus, feu quovis modo habere, clamare, vel praetendere poterimus, ad eafdem terras, vel ad cenfus, firmas, proficua, et divorias earundem terrarum, baroniæ, aliorumque fpecialiter et generaliter fupra mentionat. de quibufcunque annis et terminis praeteritis, pro quacunque caufa feu occafione praeterita. Renunciando et quiete clamando eifdem, cum omni actione et inftantia nobis inde competen. IN ET AD favorem praefati domini Roberti Gordon, fuorum haeredum mafculorum et aſſignatorum in perpetuum, tam pro non folutione divoriarum in dicto originali infeofamento content. quam quod non fecerunt debitum homagium juxta tenorem ejufd. vel ob non puram plectionem cujufcunque articuli ejufdem originalis infeofamenti, vel quod commiferunt aliquod factum, actum, omiſſum vel commiſſum, eidem praejudiciale vel unde originale infeofamentum infringi, impugnari, vel in quaeftionem legitime trahi quocunque modo poterit; acquietando, et extradonando eafdem fimpliciter, cum omni actione quæ nobis, noftris haeredibus vel fucceſſoribus, quomodocunque inde competit, vel competere poterit; et renunciando eifdem jure lite et caufa, cum pacto de non petendo, ac cum fupplemento omnium defectuum et imperfectionum tam non nominat. quam nominat. quæ tanquam pro re-expreſſ. in hac praefenti carta noftra habere volumus. REDDENDO inde annuatim praefatus dominus Robertus Gordon, fui haeredes mafculi, et aſſignati, nobis, noftris haeredibus, et dictæ coronæ et regni noftri Scotiæ fucceſſoribus, praefatam albæ firmæ divoriam unius denarii ufualis monetæ dicti regni,

fuper

super fundo dict. terrarum et baroniæ ad dictum festum nativitatis Domini nostri, nomine albæ firmæ, si petatur tantum, pro omnibus aliis divoriis, servitiis, quaestione, seu demanda quæ inde exigi, vel supra dictis terris et baronia imponi poterint: ET QUIA dictæ bondæ et regnum Novæ Scotiæ tanto intervallo distant, et separantur ab antiquo regno nostro Scotiæ, et quia idem regnum Novæ Scotiæ adhuc omnino detestituitur notariis et tabellionibus publicis, pro auctoritate danda sasinis et instrumentis conferendis de possessione ejusdem, necnon respectum habentes ad diversa et multifaria incommoda quæ inde accedere poterint, in defectu debitæ et tempestivæ sasinæ, vel sasinarum, super dicta carta, et similibus cartis et infeofamentis capiendarum de dict. terris et baronia praefato domino Roberto Gordon, suis haeredibus masculis et assignatis, dandis et concedendis, et quia dictum regnum Novæ Scotiæ et originale infeofamentum ejusd. de dicto antiquo regno Scotiæ tenetur in capite, nuperque inventum, supervisum, extentum, et acquisitum sit, per praefatum dominum Willielmum Alexander, nostrum locum-tenentem, ejusd. suis propriis impensis, nativum dicti regni nostri Scotiæ, et jam partim plantatum et plantandum cum colonis et nativis dicti regni nostri, et ob id appellatum, et nomen, stilum, et titulum Novæ Scotiæ, juste promeren. unde fit ut idem regnum partem dicti regni nostri Scotiæ jam reputari et existimari oporteat; idcirco, cum avisamento antedict. tenore praesentis cartæ nostræ, decernimus, declaramus, et ordinamus, quod unica sasina, capienda apud *castrum Edinburgenum* tanquam locum dicti regni nostri Scotiæ maxime conspicuum et principalem, vel in arbitrio et optione dicti domini Roberti, suorumque praescript. capienda super fundo et baronia de GORDON, vel aliqua parte ejusdem, stabit, et sufficiens erit sasina omni tempore a futuro, pro totis et integris eisdem terris et baronia, vel aliqua earundem vel cujusdem parte seu portione; et pro omnibus et singulis privilegiis, et aliis specialiter et generaliter supra mentionatis; penes quam dispensavimus, tenoreque praesentis cartæ nostræ dispensamus in perpetuum; ET QUUM dict. terræ et baroniæ tenentur in libera alba firma, ut praemissum est, et cum in defectu tempestivi et legitimi introitus haeredis, seu haeredum masculorum, praefati domini Roberti Gordon, suorumque assignatorum, hujusmodi baroniæ et aliis succeden. qui difficulter, debite, et debito tempore per ipsos fieri poterit, propter magnam distantiam earund. a dicto regno nostro Scotiæ; unde fieri possit, quod eadem baronia et bondæ, ratione non introitus in nostras et successorum nostrorum manus cadant et deveniant, usque donec legitimus haeres, vel haeredes masculi et assignati dicti domini Roberti, legitime intraverint ad easdem, nos nullo modo volentes vel cogitantes quod dict. baronia et terræ aliquo

tempore

tempore cadant in non introitum, nec etiam quod dictus dominus Robertus suique praescript. beneficio et commodis earund. interea frustrabuntur; IDCIRCO, cum avisamento antedict. pro nobis et successoribus nostris, dispensavimus, tenoreque praesentis cartæ nostræ dispensamus cum dicto non introitu; omnino renunciando eidem, nec non exonerando, quiete clamando, et liberando praefatum dominum Robertum, suosque praescript. simpliciter ab eodem non introitu, qandocunque dict. terræ et baronia in nostras, vel nostrorum haeredum et successorum manus ratione non introitus cadere vel devenire contigerint, cum censibus, firmis, proficuis, vel divoriis earund. et omni actione et instantia exinde competen. jure, lite, et causa simpliciter, quæ desuper sequi poterint. PROVISO nihilominus, quod haeredes masculi praefati domini Roberti et sui assignati, infra spatium septem annorum post decessum suorum praedecessorum, vel introitum eorum ad possessionem earund. terrarum et baroniæ, facient homagium pro eisd. per seipsos, vel suos legitimos procuratores, in eum finem constitutos, habentes sufficientem potestatem ad id effectum, nobis et dictæ coronæ et regni Scotiæ nostris successoribus, et intrentur et recipientur per nos, nostrosque successores, ad easdem terras, baroniam, aliaque supra mentionat. modo praescript. quo casu haeres, vel haeredes masculi, dicti domini Roberti, suique assignati, habebunt, possidebunt, gaudebunt, et fruentur omnibus et singulis beneficiis et privilegiis earundem. una cum totis et integris eisdem terris et baronia, censibus, firmis, proficuis, et divoriis earundem, aliisque quibuscunque specialiter et generaliter supra mentionat. similiter et tam libere quam dictus non-introitus nunquam extitisset, vel in manus nostras revenisset. ET SIMILITER, quod si contigerit praefatum dominum Robertum, suosque praescript. in fata decedere ante sasinam, virtute praesentis cartæ nostræ, vel suorum infeofamentorum desuper sequi captam, nos, cum consensu antedicto, pro nobis et successoribus nostris, tenore praesentis cartæ nostræ, volumus, declaramus, et ordinamus, quod, non obstante dicto decessu similia praecepta de novo ex nostra cancellaria dicti regni Scotiæ dirigentur, si visum fuerit, pro infeofamento et sasina praefato domino Roberto, suis haeredibus masculis, et assignatis, danda juxta priora warranta et praecepta primo directa, vel in eum finem dirigenda, de totis et integris praedictis terris, baronia, et aliis inibi content. eadem vi, forma, et modo quibus infeodari et investiri in eisdem antea debuerant et poterant. Ac ETIAM, si contigerit, (quod Deus prohibeat,) nos, vel nostros successores, morte praevenire ante eandem sasinam vel sasinas, per praefatum dominum Robertum et suos praescript. capiendas; eo casu, cum avisamento antedict. pro nobis, et nostris successoribus, volumus, et

declaramus,

APPENDIX.

declaramus, quod, non obstante, praecepta de dicta cancellaria dicti regni nostri dirigentur pro infeofamento et sasina praefato domino Roberto Gordon, suisque haeredibus masculis et assignatis, de eisdem terris, baronia, aliisque praedict. danda, eadem forma, vi et modo quo praescripta et warranta sasinarum nunc diriguntur, vel dirigentur antea ad id effectum, eodem et simili modo, ac si infeofamenta et sasina earundem terrarum, baroniæ, et aliorum supra script. vel alicujus partis earund. rite, debite, legitime, et via ordinaria et tempore expedita, perfecta, et desuper capta fuissent. ET PRÆTEREA, considerantes virtutem et industriam honoribus et præeminentiis in primis promovendam, et exinde generosos spiritus ad aggrediendum et prosequendum nobiles actiones et intentiones, animari et excitari, et quod omnis honoris et dignitatis splendor, originem et incrementum habeat a rege, tanquam a primo fonte ejusdem, ad cujus altitudinem et praeeminentiam erigere et instituere novos honorum et dignitatum titulos proprie spectat, tanquam ab eo unde primatim honores, originaliter promanarunt ; et ex eo volentes nobilissimos nostros progenitores, et antecessores, æternæ memori dignos imitari, qui habuerunt, et in usum redegerunt potestatem creandi, et erigendi novas dignitates et gradus inter subditos hujusmodi honoribus dignos ; NOS ex nostra regia potestate, et auctoritate, ereximus, creavimus, locavimus, constituimus et ordinavimus, tenoreque praesentis cartæ nostræ pro nobis, haeredibus et successoribus nostris, de speciali gratia, favore, certa scientia, proprio motu, et deliberato animo, cum avisamento et consensu antedict. facimus, erigimus, constituimus, creamus, et ordinamus quendam haereditarium statum, gradum, nomen, ordinem, dignitatem, et stilum BARONETTI, nunc et omni tempore a futuro, infra dictum regnum nostrum Scotiæ et regionem Novæ Scotiæ, habendum, et gaudendum hujusmodi personis quas nos, nostri haeredes vel successores, in incrementum et propagationem dict. plantationis, et aliter, pro dignitate et merito, facturi sumus baronettos et praelaturi hujusmodi gradibus et stylis : ET IDCIRCO, pro auxilio, ope, et assistentia per praefatum Robertum dominum Gordon praefata, et propagatione dict. plantationis hactenus exhibita, proque diversis aliis bonis et gratuitis servitiis, nobis per ipsum praestitis, et diversis aliis justis et gravibus causis et considerationibus nos moven. EREXIMUS, tenoreque praesentis cartæ, pro nobis, haeredibus et successoribus nostris, ex speciali gratia, favore, certa scientia, mero motu, et deliberato animo, cum avisamento et consilio antedict. erigimus, praeserimus, praeponimus, et creamus praefatum DOMINUM ROBERTUM GORDON, SUOSQUE HAEREDES MASCULOS QUOSCUNQUE, de tempore in tempus omni tempore a futuro

futuro, IN ET AD praefatum haereditarium statum, gradum, ordinem, nomen, dignitatem et stilum BARONETTI, cum omnibus et singulis praerogativis, privilegiis, praecedentiis, conditionibus, et aliis specialiter et generaliter subscript. NEC NON fecimus, constituimus, et creavimus, tenoreque praesentis cartae nostrae facimus, constituimus, et creamus memoratum dominum Robertum Gordon, et suos haeredes, masculos, haereditarie BARONETTOS in perpetuum, et ut habeant et gaudeant omnibus et singulis praerogativis, privilegiis et titulis et aliis particulariter et generaliter subscript. in eorum favorem conceptis; et dedimus, concessimus, voluimus, ordinavimus, et declaravimus, tenoreque praesentis cartae nostrae, pro nobis, haeredibus et successoribus nostris, ex speciali gratia, favore, certa scientia, mero motu, et deliberato animo, cum avisamento et consensu antedict. Damus, concedimus, volumus, declaramus, et ordinamus quod dictus dominus Robertus Gordon, et sui haeredes masculi quicunque, de tempore in tempus, virtute praesentis cartae nostrae dicti status, gradus, ordinis, dignitatis, et stili Baronetti sibi per praesentis cartae nostrae tenorem concess. habebunt, tenebunt, capient, et gaudebunt omni tempore a futuro, diem datae praesentis cartae nostrae sequen. et infra dictum regnum nostrum Scotiae, et regionem Novae Scotiae, et alibi, *locum, prioritatem, praeeminentiam, et praecedentiam in omnibus et quibuscunque commissionibus, brevibus, literis patentibus, appellationibus, nominationibus, et scriptis quibuscunque*; et in omnibus et universis sessionibus, conventionibus, comitiis, synodis, et omnibus temporibus et occasionibus quibuscunque, ante omnes milites auratos hactenus factos et creatos, aut quocunque tempore a futuro faciendos et creandos, et prae omnibus baronibus, lie Lairdis, armigeris, lie Esquyris, et generosis quibuscunque, lie Gentilmen, excepto nostrum locum-tenente, suisque haeredibus nostrum locumtenentibus dicti regni Novae Scotiae, et non aliter; quorum uxores et liberi habebunt, et juxta gaudebunt simili loco et praecedentia, et exceptis similiter talibus Equitibus Bannerettis, vulgo Knichts Banneretts appellat. quos contigerit fieri et designari per nos, nostros haeredes, vel successores, sub nostro vexillo, et erecto signo lie standart, et displayit banner, in omnibus exercitibus regiis, in aperto bello, lie oppen warre, nobismet ipsis personaliter praesentibus, et non aliter, neque alio modo, et hoc durante tempore vitae dictorum equitum bannerettorum tantum, et non diutius; *et ante omnes baronettos quoscunque* aliquo tempore a futuro per nos, nostros haeredes et successores, faciendos, et ante suos haeredes et successores, tametsi contigerit alios baronettum vel baronettos in posterum per nos faciendos, et literas suas patentes dicti gradus, dignitatis, status, nominis, ordinis, tituli, et stili Baronetti

sub

sub nostro magno sigillo dicti regni nostri Scotiæ, perficere et expedire, antequam præfatus dominus Robertus, suique haeredes masculi, absolvent et expedient hanc nostram cartam, nostro sub magno sigillo, non obstante aliqua lege, consuetudine, vel constitutione quacunque in contrarium. ET SIMILITER voluimus, concessimus, declaravimus, et ordinavimus, tenoreque præsentis cartæ nostræ, pro nobis, haeredibus et successoribus nostris, cum avisamento et consensu antedict. de specialibus nostris gratia, favore, certa scientia, mero motu, et deliberato animo, volumus, concedimus, declaramus, constituimus, et ordinamus, quod uxor et uxores dicti domini Roberti Gordon suorumque haeredum masculorum praescript. de tempore in tempus in perpetuum, virtute præsentis cartæ nostræ, et dicti gradus, status, et dignitatis suorum maritorum, habebunt, tenebunt, capient, et gaudebunt omni tempore a futuro, *loco, præcedentia, prioritate, et præeminentia*, tam durante vita suorum maritorum quam ex inde durante sua vita, si contigerit ipsas diutius superstites, ante uxores omnium personarum quarumcunque pro quibus præfatus dominus Robertus, vel dicti sui haeredes masculi, debent vel poterint, virtute præsentis cartæ nostræ, vel dicti gradus, status, dignitatis, nominis, ordinis, tituli, vel stili baronetti, tenore præsentium concess. habere, tenere, capere, et gaudere loco, prioritate, praecedentia, et praeminentia, et ante uxores dict. militum Bannerettorum prius except. propterea quod dictus gradus baronetti est haereditarius gradus sanguinis; NEC NON quod filii et filiæ respective dicti domini Roberti, et suorum haeredum masculorum, in perpetuum, virtute præsentis cartæ nostræ, et dict. dignitatis baronetti præsentibus concess. præfato domino Roberto, suisque haeredibus masculis, habebunt, tenebunt, capient, et gaudebunt loco, prioritate, praecedentia, et praeeminentia præ filiis et filiabus respective omnium personarum præ quibus præfatus dominus Robertus, vel sui haeredes masculi, locum capere et praecedentiam poterint, vel debent, vel virtute præsentis cartæ nostræ, vel dicti gradus, et stili baronetti ipsis præsentibus concess. præ filiis militum bannerettorum prius except. ET SIMILITER, quod uxores filiorum dicti domini Roberti, suorumque haeredum masculorum, omni tempore a futuro respective habebunt, tenebunt, capient, et gaudebunt loco, prioritate, et praecedentia ante uxores omnium personarum quarumcunque, præ quibus ipsarum mariti locum capere poterint, vel debent; idque tam durante vita ipsorum maritorum quam postea. INSUPER, ex specialibus nostris gratia, favore, certa scientia, mero motu, et animo deliberato, tenore præsentis cartæ nostræ pro nobis, hæredibus, et successoribus nostris, cum avisamento antedict. volumus, concedimus, ordinamus, declaramus, et promittimus quod quocunque tempore

tempore, et quam primum filius natu maximus, et apparens haeres masculus dicti domini Roberti, vel filius natu proximus, aut haeres apparens masculus quorumcunque haeredum masculorum ipsi succeden. venerint ad aetatem viginti unius annorum, quod ipse, et unusquisque eorum respective, per nos, haeredes et successores nostros, milites lie KNIGHTS inaugurabuntur, quandocunque ipsi, vel eorum aliquis, hujusmodi ordinem requisiverint, absque solutione mercedum et expensarum quarumcunque, et quod dictus dominus Robertus, et sui haeredes masculi praescript. habebunt, et habere et gerere in perpetuum dehinc poterint, vel in paludamentis, vulgo lie canton in thair coit of armis, vel in scutis, vulgo lie scutcheons, pro eorum arbitrio, arma regni Novae Scotiae, quae sunt.

Et quod dictus dominus Robertus, hae redesque sui masculi praescript. ex tempore in tempus in perpetuum habebunt locum, omni tempore a futuro, in omnibus exercitibus nostris, haeredum et successorum nostrorum, in media acie, prope et juxta vexillum nostrum regium, vulgo neir about our royal standart, nostrorum haeredum et successorum, pro defensione ejusdem; et quod dictus dominus Robertus, suique haeredes masculi praescript. in perpetuum habeant et habebunt, omni tempore a futuro, duos assistentes seu asseclas sui corporis, vulgo twa assistants of his body, ad supportandum volamen, lie paill, et unum principalem lugentem, et sibi quatuor assistentes, in suis funeribus. Et quod dictus dominus Robertus, suique haeredes masculi respective, in perpetuum omni tempore a futuro, nominabuntur, vocabuntur, et designabuntur nomine BARONETTI, et quod in omni vulgari sermone Scotiae et scriptis haec additio (SIR) et in omnibus aliis linguis, sermonibus, et scriptis similia signativa verba nominibus respective dicti domini Roberti, et suorum haeredum masculorum respective in perpetuum praemittentur. Et quod dictus stilus, et titulus Baronetti fini ipsorum cognominum apponetur et subjicietur in omnibus et singulis nostris, et successorum nostrorum literis patentibus et in omnibus et singulis aliis literis, scriptis, et cartis quibuscunque, tamquam vera legitima, et necessaria dignitatis additio. Et Quod inde praefatus dominus Robertus nunc, et omnibus temporibus futuris, nominabitur, vocabitur, et intitulabitur, DOMINUS ROBERTUS GORDON BARONETTUS; Ac etiam quod uxor et uxores dicti domini Roberti, suorumque haeredum masculorum respective, in perpetuum habebunt, tenebunt, fruentur, et possidebunt, omni tempore a futuro, stilum, titulum, et appellationem dominae, vulgo Ladie Madame et Dame respective, juxta usum et phrasim in sermonibus et scriptis; Et praeterea, ex nostra speciali gratia, favore, certa scientia, mero motu, animoque deliberato; or dinavimus,

mus, et promisimus, tenoreque praesentis cartae nostrae pro nobis, haeredibus et successoribus nostris, cum avisamento et consensu antedict. damus, concedimus, ordinamus, declaramus, et promittimus praefato domino Roberto, et suis haeredibus masculis respective in perpetuum, quod numerus baronettorum, tam infra regnum nostrum Scotiae quam regionem Novae Scotiae, nunquam pro praesenti, vel aliquo tempore a futuro, excedet, vel augebitur in totum ultra numerum centum et quinquaginta baronettorum: NEC NON EX speciali nostra gratia, favore, certa scientia, mero motu, animoque deliberato, dedimus, concessimus, declaravimus, ordinavimus et promisimus, tenoreque praesentis cartae nostrae pro nobis, haeredibus et successoribus nostris, cum avisamento et consensu antedict. damus, concedimus, ordinamus, declaramus, et promittimus praefato domino Roberto, haeredibus suis masculis respective in perpetuum, quod neque nos, haeredes vel successores nostri, erigimus, vel nunc, aut aliquo tempore a futuro, erecturi, facturi, creaturi, vel constituturi sumus aliquas alias dignitates, gradus, status, ordines, titulos, vel stilos; nec dabimus, concedemus, permittemus, ordinabimus, vel constituemus locum, prioritatem, vel praecedentiam aliquibus personis quibuscunque, sub vel infra stilum et gradum domini parliamenti dicti regni nostri Scotiae, altiorem, priorem, vel parem dicto gradui, ordini, titulo, vel stilo baronetti per nos praefato domino Roberto, suis haeredibus masculis respective, tenore praesentis cartae, dat. concess. et ordinat. et quod dictus dominus Robertus, suique haeredes masculi respective habebunt, et omni tempore a futuro libere et quiete habere, tenere et possidere poterint, omnes et singulas praedictas suas dignitates, loca, praecedentias, praerogativa, privilegia, ante et prae omnibus aliis personis quibuscunque factis, vel faciendis, creandis, vel constituendis, in aliquo tali gradu, gradibus, statibus, ordinibus, titulis, vel stilis, vel cui aliquis hujusmodi locus vel praecedentia datur, dabitur, aut concedetur. ET QUOD uxores, filii, filiae, filiorumque uxores dicti domini Roberti, et sui haeredes masculi, respective omni tempore a futuro dicta sua loca, prioritates, et praerogativa juxta et convenienter exinde habebunt, tenebunt, et possidebunt. Et praeterea, si quae dubitatio vel quaestio, praesentibus non enodata, oriatur de aliquo loco, praecedentia, vel praerogativa praefato domino Roberto suisque haeredibus masculis, uxoribus, filiis, filiabus, vel filiorum uxoribus respective, vel alicui eorum quocunque tempore a futuro debita, quod hujusmodi dubitationes et quaestiones determinabuntur et decidentur usu et praxi consuetudinis et legis, prout aliae graduum haereditariae dignitates ordinantur et diriguntur de loco, praerogativa, et praecedentia. ET ULTERIUS, quod nulla persona, seu personae quaecunque, aliquo tempore a futuro fient Baronetti Scotiae, vel regni Novae Scotiae, vel praeferentur dicto gradui, statui, dignitati, nomini, ordini, titulo, vel stilo Baronetti, per nos, haeredes vel successores nostros, nisi qui primo perficient et perimplebunt conditiones, per nos pro bono et propagatione plantationis Novæ Scotiæ constitut. et manifestabunt easdem nobis, et commissionariis per dictum nostrum locum-tenentem constituendis. ET PRAETEREA, quod praesentes sunt et erunt validæ, sufficientes, et efficientes omni tempore a futuro, omnibus suis punctis, ut praemissum est, praefato domino Roberto, et suis haeredibus masculis respective, in omne aevum, et suis uxoribus, filiis, filiabus, et filiorum uxoribus respective, et eorum singulis de jure, contra nos, haeredes et successores nostros, et contra omnes alias personas quascunque in omnibus nostris, haeredum, et successorum nostrorum curiis, et omnibus aliis locis quibuscunque, omnibus temporibus et occasionibus, non obstante quocunque jure, consuetudine, praescriptione, praxi, ordinatione, seu constitutione hactenus fact. ordinat. vel publicat. vel in posterum quocunque tempore faciend. ordinand. et publicand. ordinand. vel providend. et non obstante aliqua alia materia, causa, vel occasione quacunque. INSUPER, pro munificis et amplis auxiliis, et impensis nobis hactenus praestitis per praefatum dominum Robertum Gordon, pro auxilio et propagatione dictæ plantationis Novæ Scotiæ, ordinavimus hanc cartam nostram, absque aliquo fine vel compositione nobis, vel nostro thesaurario vel deputato solvenda, perficiendam et expediendam. ET PROPTEREA, tenore praesentis cartæ nostræ ordinamus, et declaramus, quod nec nunc, nec aliquo tempore praeterito, diem datæ praesentis cartæ nostræ praeceden. fecimus, nec creavimus aliquos barones vel baronettos, nec praetulimus aliquam personam, vel personas, dicto statui, gradui, dignitati, nomini, ordini, titulo, vel stilo Baronetti, exceptis praefato domino Roberto Gordon, et domino Alexandro Strachan de Thornetoun milite. Et quod dedimus locum, prioritatem, praecedentiam, praeeminentiam inter ipsos duos, praefato domino Roberto Gordon militi. ET PRAETEREA, per praesentis cartæ nostræ tenorem, declaramus, quod nec fecimus, nec creavimus aliquem baronettum, vel baronettos quoscunque, nec praetulimus aliquam personam vel personas quascunque dicto statui, gradui, nomini, ordini, titulo, seu stilo Baronetti, præ vel ante praefatum dominum Robertum Gordon, infra dictum regnum nostrum Scotiæ. POSTREMO, nos, pro nobis, et successoribus nostris, cum avisamento et consensu antedict. volumus, decernimus, declaramus, et ordinamus praesentem hanc nostram cartam, cum omnibus et singulis privilegiis, libertatibus, clausulis, articulis, et conditionibus antedict. in proximo nostro parliamento dicti regni nostræ Scotiæ, vel aliquo alio parliamento ejusdem deinceps celebrand. pro arbitrio dicti domini Roberti Gordon, suorumque

rumque haeredum masculorum ratificandam, approbandam, et confirmandam; et ut habeat robur, vim et effectum decreti et sententiæ illius supremi et præeminentis judicii, penes quam nos pro nobis, et successoribus nostris, volumus et declaramus hanc nostram cartam et clausulas inibi content. ad hunc effectum, sufficiens fore warrantum; promittend. in verbo Principis idem fore perficiendum. INSUPER dilectis nostris, &c. et vestrum cuilibet, conjunctim et divisim,. vicecomitibus nostris in hac parte specialiter constitutis, salutem. VOBIS præcipimus et mandamus, quatenus præfato domino Roberto Gordon, vel suo certo actornato, latori præsentium, sasinam totarum et integrarum prædict. terrarum et baroniæ de GORDOUN, cum omnibus et singulis partibus, pendiculis, privilegiis, libertatibus, commoditatibus, licentiis, et immunitatibus iisdem spectan. seu spectare valen. et aliorum quorumcunque specialiter et generaliter supramentionat. quamquidem sasinam, cum avisamento et consensu antedict. pro nobis, haeredibus et successoribus nostris, tenore præsentis cartæ nostræ volumus, declaramus, et ordinamus tam fore legitimam et sufficientem quam si præcepta sasinæ separatim et ordinarie ex nostra cancellaria ad id effectum super dicta carta fuissent directa; penes quam, cum avisamento antedict. pro nobis, nostris haeredibus et successoribus dispensavimus tenoreque præsentis cartæ nostræ dispensamus in perpetuum. IN CUJUS REI TESTIMONIUM huic præsenti cartæ magnum sigillum nostrum apponi præcipimus, TESTIBUS prædilectis nostris consanguineis et consiliariis, Jacobo marchiono, de Hamilton comite Araniæ et Cambridge, domino Aven et Innerdail, Gulielmo Marishall comite domino Keyth regni nostri marescalla prædilecto nostro conciliario, domino Georgio Hay de Kinfauns milite nostro cancellario, et prædilecto nostro consanguineo et consiliario Thoma comite de Melrose nostro secretario, dilectis nostris familiaribus consiliariis dominis Ricardo Cockburn de Clerkingtoun nostri secreti sigilli custodi, Johanne Hamilton de Magdalenis nostrorum rotulorum registro ac consilii clerico, Georgio Elphingston de Blythiswood nostræ justiciariæ clerico, et Johanne Scot de Scottistarvet nostræ cancellariæ directore, militibus. APUD QUHYTHALL, vigesimo octavo die mensis Maii, Anno Domini millesimo sexcentesimo vigesimo quinto, regnique nostri anno primo.

ROYAL

ROYAL WARRANT by KING CHARLES I. to the KNIGHTS BARONETS of NOVA SCOTIA, anno 1629.

CHARLES R.

RIGHT trusty and right well beloved Cousin and Councellor, right trusty and well beloved Cousins and Councellors, and right trusty and well beloved Councellors, WE greet you well: WHEREAS, upon good consideration, and for the better advancement of the Plantation of NEW-SCOTLAND, which may much import the good of our Service, and the honour and benefit of that our Antient Kingdom, our Royal Father did intend, and WE have since erected the Order and Title of BARONET in our said Antient Kingdom, which we have since established, and conferred the same on divers Gentlemen of good quality; And seeing our trusty and well beloved Councellor Sir WILLIAM ALEXANDER Knight, our principal Secretary of that our Antient Kingdom of SCOTLAND, and our Lieutenant in NEW-SCOTLAND, who, these many years bygone, has been at great charges for the discovery thereof, hath established a Colony there, where his Son Sir WILLIAM is now resident: And We being most willing to afford all the possible means of Encouragement that conveniently We can to the BARONETS of that our Antient Kingdom, for the furtherance of so good a Work, and to this effect they may be honoured, and have place in all respects, according to their Patents from us: WE have been pleased to Authorise and Allow, as by these presents, for Us and our Successors, WE Authorise and Allow the said LIEUTENANT and BARONETS, and every one of them, and their Heirs-male, to wear and carry about their necks, in all time coming, an Orange Tannie Silk Ribbon, whereon shall hang pendent in a Scutcheon Argent a Saltyre Azure thereon, in an Escutcheon of the Arms of Scotland, with an Imperial Crown above the 'Scutcheon, and encircled with this Motto, FAX MENTIS HONESTÆ GLORIA: Which cognizeance our said present LIEUTENANT shall deliver now to them from Us, that they may be the better known and distinguished from other Persons: And that none pretend ignorance of the respect due unto them, Our pleasure therefore is, That by open Proclamation at the Market-Cross of Edinburgh, and of all other head Burghs of our Kingdom, and such other places as you shall think necessary, you cause intimate our Royal pleasure and intention herein to all our Subjects; And if any Person, out of Neglect or Contempt, shall presume

fume to take place or precedency of the said BARONETS, their Wives or Children, which is due to them by their Patents, or to wear their Cognizeance, We will, that upon notice thereof given to you, you cause punish such Offenders, by fining or imprisoning them as you shall think fitting, that others may be terrified from attempting the like: And WE Ordain, that from time to time, as occasion of Granting or Renewing their Patents, or their Heirs Succeeding to the Dignity, shall offer, that the said Power to them to Carry the said Ribbon and Cognizeance shall be therein particularly Granted and Inserted: And We likewise Ordain thir Presents to be Inserted and Registrated in the Books of our Council and Exchequer, and that you cause Registrate the same in the Books of the LYON KING of ARMS and the Heralds, there to remain *ad Futuram rei Memoriam*, and that all Parties having Interest may have Authentic Copies and Extracts thereof; And for so doing, these our Letters shall be unto you, and every one of you, from time to time, your sufficient Warrant and Discharge in that behalf; Given at Our Court at Whitehall, the 17th day of November, 1629 years.

INDEX.

INDEX.

A

	Page		Page
Abbey	254	Chapter	278, 288, 320
—— of Kinloss	255	Christianity planted in Scotland	251
Aberlaure P.	29, 326, 329	Clergy,	254, 265, 288, 289
Abernethie P.	36, 331, 332	College	280, 281
Abertarf P.	361, 363	Convents	261
Address, Synod of Moray	422	Common Churches	290
Address, the Bishop's	423	Counties	182
Advie P.	34, 331	Count or Earl	178
Aldern P.	108, 352	Courach	164
Altyre F.	92	Gry to War	231
Alves P.	85, 346	Croy, P.	117, 355
Alvie P.	53, 333	Cromdale, P.	34, 331
Ardclach P.	95, 351	Cummine, F.	91, 93
Arderfier P.	124, 207, 353	Customs, Military	229
Avon R.	5		

D

		Dalaraffic P.	97, 355

B

Badenach	43	Dallas, P.	68, 348
Bards	230, 244	Dalcross,	117, 355
Baronies	186, 199	Daviot, P.	122, 356
Barons	190	Deasoil	238, 248
Battles	209	Diocess	272, 291
Belly P.	11, 325	Dyple P.	57, 335
Bigla	39	Druids	234
Birnie P.	68, 339	Dukes	181
Bishops	267, 268, 295, 317	Duff F.	26
Black-Cock	164	Dunbar F.	81, 82
Boharm P.	23, 328	Dundurcos P.	15, 326
Boleskin P.	133, 363	Dunlichty P.	122, 356
Borlum	46, 131	Durris P.	130, 360
Boroughs	191	Duffus P.	73, 344
Brodie, F.	105	Duffus F.	74
Brachlie, P.	126, 356	Duthel P.	38, 332
Burgh-Sea, or Burgus	210	Dyke P.	98, 350

C

			E
Carns, Druid	239	Edinkylie P.	92, 349
Calder, P.	112, 354	Elchies	327
Calder, F.	113	Elgin P. 64, 193, 203, 217, 276, 340, 401
Canons	281, 282	Episcopacy	295, 298, 301
Caperkylie	161	Ern R.	87
Carmile	153	Essil P.	57, 335
Carngorm	163		
Cascade	ib.	F
Cathedral	274, 319	Familiar spirits	306
Chaplanries	290	Farar R.	5

INDEX

Regalities	185
Farquharson, F.	43
Fearnua P.	144, 361
Fiery Cross	231
Fines imposed	375
Fishings	58, 70
Forbes, F.	128
Forres P.	88, 197, 203, 209, 347, 349, 402
Forts	203
Fortalices	207
Fraser F.	133

G

Glengarie	141
Glenlivet	31
Glenmoriston P.	143, 362
Gordon F.	12
Gordonstoun, F.	70
Grant F.	18, 40

H

Hospitals	263

I

Innes F.	59
Insh P.	54, 334
Inveralen P.	34, 331
Inveravon P.	30, 330
Inverness P.	126, 182, 191, 204, 266, 227, 355, 357, 399
Johannites	265
Jurisdictions	187, 320
Justice Courts	188

K

Keledees	251
Kilmalemnoc P.	77, 342
Kilmanivac P.	140
Kilravok F.	118
Kiltarlatie P.	145, 361
Kinchardin P.	36, 332
Kenedar P.	69, 284, 342
Kingussie P.	55, 261, 334
Kinloss P.	67, 255, 347
Kirkhill P.	144, 361
Kirkmichael P.	32, 331
Knights Baronets	72, 426, 452
Knockando P.	18, 327

L

Laggan P.	56, 363
Laggan Fythenach	92, 350, 389
Lanbryde P.	63, 338
Letter, King Charles II.	421

Locust	165
Lossie, R.	58, 78
Lovat, F.	133

M

MacBean Mr Angus	377
Ma-Calen P.	327
MacDonald, F.	141
MacDuff Earl	26
MacIntosh F.	44
MacPherson F.	48
Maison-Dieu	263
Mensal Churches	289
Military Roads	228
——— Customs	229
Moray County	185
Moray, Earl of	100
Moray, F.	74
Moray, Bishops &c.	268, 317
Moy, P.	79, 98, 350, 355
Mortlich, P.	24, 265, 324

N

Nairn P.	110, 184, 196, 204, 351, 353
Nairn County	184
Natural History	147
Ness R.	127, 129, 130
New Spynie	345
Number of People	364

O

Obelisk at Forres	209
Oath of Trust	425

P

Palace, the Bishop's	284, 320
Parsons	289
Patrons	324
People, Number of	364
Pettie, P.	125, 356
Power, abused by the Clergy	306
Popery	253, 379
Prebendaries	281
Presbytery	293, 296, 300, 303
Priories	257
——— of Urquhart	258
——— of Pluscarden	259
——— of Kingussie	261
Protesters	368

R

Rafford P.	90, 348
Rarities	162
Reformation	365

INDEX

	Page
Remonstrance	368
Rental	322
Resolutioners	369
Revenues, the Bishop's	286, 321
Rose F.	118
Rothes P.	17, 326
Rothemorchus P.	39, 332

S

	Page
Sacrament	309
St. Andrews P.	77, 342
Shaw F.	41
Spey R.	10
Spemouth P.	57, 336
Spynie	78, 285, 345
Skirdrostan P.	29, 329
Strathspey	11
Superintendants	294
Superstition	306

T

	Page
Test, imposed	370
Templars, Knights	264
Thanes	180
Threnodia	314
Tulchan Bishops	295

U

	Page
Ugston P.	69, 343
Unthank	344
Urquhart	58, 142, 205, 213, 258, 337, 362
Urquhart, Priory of	258

V

	Page
Vicars	289

W

	Page
Wardlaw P.	144, 361
Ways, Military	228
Witches	307

FINIS.

ERRATA ET ADDENDA.

Page 2 Line 8 for *Atacold* read *Altacoti*
         9 for *Decaledones* read *Dicalidones*
        14 for *Septimus* read *Septimius*
   9 Line 22 for *N. W.* read *N. E.*
  14 Line 14 for *Kinglaffie* read *Kingufie*
  15 Line 23 for *Dundurcrofs* read *Dundurcofs*
  17 Line 8 for *Dundurcrofs* read *Dundurcofs*
  25 Line 7 for *Pilvaich* read *Pitvaich*
  27 Line laſt, for *Ellachie* read *Allachie*
  28 Line 21 for *Remnay* read *Kemnay*
  30 Line 18 for *Cairngormbeg* read *Cairngormlos*
  30 Line 24 for *Drummuir* read *Drumin*
  33 Line 28 for *Cromdale* read *Camdale*
  34 Line 18 for *Delly* read *Dallay*
  35 Line 4 for *Fayer* read *Toyer*
  57 Line 3 for *Spey* read *Spean*
        15 for *Dundurcrofs* read *Dundurcofs*
  60 Line 4 for *This* read *His*
  61 Line 12 for *Drence* read *Drainie*
  62 Line 6 for *Lochnet* read *Lichnet*
  67 Line penult, for *Braco* read *Bruce*
  70 Line 28 for *Manie* read *Monie*
  70 Line laſt, for *of Kinloſs* read *of Moy*
  76 Line 4 for *This* read *Thus*
  79 Line laſt, for *whoſe daughter and only child Janet* read *whoſe ſiſter Janet*

Page 21 In the Armorial Bearing of the Family of Grant: Motto, above the Creſt, CRAIGELACHIE: Below the Shield, STAND FAST.

Page 63 Motto of the Family of Innes: BE TRAIST.

Page 121 Kilravock's Arm's are: Or, a Boar's Head cooped Gul. betwixt three Water Budgets, ſab. Creſt, an Harp Az. Motto, CONSTANT AND TRUE.

Page 141 MacDonald of Glengary's Arms are: Or, a Double Eagle diſplayed, Gul. ſurmounted of a Lymphad ſab. And in the Dexter chief point a right hand cooped Gul. Supporters, two Boars with Arrows ſticking in their Bodies proper. Creſt, a Raven ſtanding on a Rock, Az.

N. B. Where *Money* is ſpoken of in this WORK, it is always *Scots*, if *Sterling* is not mentioned. And where *Miles* are mentioned, they are *Scots Miles*.

BOOKS publiſhed and ſold by WILLIAM AULD.

I. Inquiry into the Genealogy and Preſent State of SCOTTISH SURNAMES: With the Origin and Deſcent of the HIGHLAND CLANS, and FAMILY of BUCHANAN. By William Buchanan of Auchmar, price 5s.

II. An Account of the CHAPEL of ROSLIN, with an elegant View of the Chapel from the South, price 6d.

III. Sir DONALD MONROE's Deſcription of the WESTERN ISLES; with his Genealogies of the CHIEF CLANS of the ISLES; an Account of HIRTA and RONA.—Account of ST KILDA, &c. price 3s.

IV. The RUDIMENTS of ARCHITECTURE; or YOUNG WORKMAN's INSTRUCTOR: Adorned with twenty-three elegant Deſigns of Buildings, moſtly executed in North Britain, price 7s. 6d. in boards, 4to.

V. The SCOTS FARMER; being a collection of Eſſays upon Agriculture and Rural Affairs, adapted to the Soil and Climate of Scotland, 2 vols large 8vo, price 15s.

In the Preſs, and ſoon will be Publiſhed,

An Hiſtorical and Genealogical Hiſtory of the CLANS and FAMILIES of

MACALPIN and MACGREGOR:

With Their Origin, and Deſcent, from the earlieſt periods down to the preſent time. In which is given,

A faithful Account of their Sufferings and Perſecutions, from the influence of ſome great Families; and their Reſtoration to their Name and Privileges, by the late Act of his preſent MAJESTY.

www.ingramcontent.com/pod-product-compliance
Lightning Source LLC
Chambersburg PA
CBHW051858300426
44117CB00006B/450